The World of the Roosevelts

Published in cooperation with the Franklin and Eleanor Roosevelt Institute
Hyde Park, New York

General Editors:
Arthur M. Schlesinger, Jr., William vanden Heuvel, and Douglas Brinkley

FDR AND HIS CONTEMPORARIES
FOREIGN PERCEPTIONS OF
AN AMERICAN PRESIDENT
Edited by Cornelis A. van Minnen and
John F. Sears

NATO: THE FOUNDING OF THE
ATLANTIC ALLIANCE AND THE
INTEGRATION OF EUROPE
Edited by Francis H. Heller and
John R. Gillingham

AMERICA UNBOUND
WORLD WAR II AND THE MAKING
OF A SUPERPOWER
Edited by Warren F. Kimball

THE ORIGINS OF U.S. NUCLEAR
STRATEGY, 1945–1953
Samuel R. Williamson, Jr. and
Steven L. Rearden

AMERICAN DIPLOMATS IN
THE NETHERLANDS, 1815–50
Cornelis A. van Minnen

EISENHOWER, KENNEDY,
AND THE UNITED STATES
OF EUROPE
Pascaline Winand

ALLIES AT WAR
THE SOVIET, AMERICAN,
AND BRITISH EXPERIENCE, 1939–1945
Edited by David Reynolds,
Warren F. Kimball, and A. O. Chubarian

THE ATLANTIC CHARTER
Edited by Douglas Brinkley and
David R. Facey-Crowther

PEARL HARBOR REVISITED
Edited by Robert W. Love, Jr.

FDR AND THE HOLOCAUST
Edited by Verne W. Newton

THE UNITED STATES AND
THE INTEGRATION OF EUROPE
LEGACIES OF THE POSTWAR ERA
Edited by Francis H. Heller and
John R. Gillingham

ADENAUER AND KENNEDY
A STUDY IN GERMAN-AMERICAN RELATIONS
Frank A. Mayer

THEODORE ROOSEVELT AND
THE BRITISH EMPIRE
A STUDY IN PRESIDENTIAL STATECRAFT
William N. Tilchin

TARIFFS, TRADE AND EUROPEAN
INTEGRATION, 1947–1957
FROM STUDY GROUP TO COMMON MARKET
Wendy Asbeek Brusse

SUMNER WELLES
FDR's GLOBAL STRATEGIST
A Biography by Benjamin Welles

THE NEW DEAL AND PUBLIC POLICY
Edited by Byron W. Daynes, William D.
Pederson, and Michael P. Riccards

WORLD WAR II IN EUROPE
Edited by Charles F. Brower

FDR AND THE U.S. NAVY
Edward J. Marolda

THE SECOND QUEBEC
CONFERENCE REVISITED
Edited by David B. Woolner

THEODORE ROOSEVELT,
THE U.S. NAVY, AND
THE SPANISH-AMERICAN WAR
Edited by Edward J. Marolda

Franklin Roosevelt's Foreign Policy and the Welles Mission

J. Simon Rofe

E
806
.R7255
2007

FRANKLIN ROOSEVELT'S FOREIGN POLICY AND THE WELLES MISSION
© J. Simon Rofe, 2007.

First published in 2007 by
PALGRAVE MACMILLAN™
175 Fifth Avenue, New York, N.Y. 10010 and
Houndmills, Basingstoke, Hampshire, England RG21 6XS
Companies and representatives throughout the world.

PALGRAVE MACMILLAN is the global academic imprint of the Palgrave Macmillan division of St. Martin's Press, LLC and of Palgrave Macmillan Ltd. Macmillan® is a registered trademark in the United States, United Kingdom and other countries. Palgrave is a registered trademark in the European Union and other countries.

ISBN-13: 978–1–4039–8073–1
ISBN-10: 1–4039–8073–X

Library of Congress Cataloging-in-Publication Data

Rofe, J. Simon
    Franklin Roosevelt's foreign policy and the Welles mission / by
J. Simon Rofe.
        p. cm.
    Includes bibliographical references and index.
    ISBN 1–4039–8073–X (alk. paper)
        1. United States—Foreign relations—1933–1945. 2. Roosevelt,
Franklin D. (Franklin Delano), 1882–1945. 3. Welles, Sumner, 1892–1961.
4. Hull, Cordell, 1871–1955. 5. World War, 1939–1945—Diplomatic
history. 6. United States—Foreign Relations—Great Britain. 7. Great
Britain—Foreign Relations—United States. I. Title.

E806.R7255 2007
327.730409'044—dc22   2007052780

A catalogue record for this book is available from the British Library.

Design by Newgen Imaging Systems (P) Ltd., Chennai, India.

First edition: June 2007

10 9 8 7 6 5 4 3 2 1

Printed in the United States of America.

CONTENTS

ABSTRACT

THIS WORK PRESENTS A NEW ANALYSIS of the mission undertaken by Under Secretary of State Sumner Welles to Europe on behalf of President Roosevelt in February–March 1940.

The book's central question asks what Roosevelt's motivations were for undertaking the mission, and what he sought to achieve from it. It considers that the Welles mission was an expression of a number of influences upon Roosevelt that date back to late 1937. These influences, or themes, which provide the broader context and run throughout the period up to the beginning of 1940, are as follows: first, the integral role in Rooseveltian foreign policy played by Sumner Welles. The second theme concerns the position of his superior, Secretary of State Cordell Hull, who was to counsel caution in the face of an increasingly serious world situation, while a third influence was the limits upon American foreign policy making itself. The last element to be considered throughout this study is the influence of Anglo-American relations upon the Welles mission. Further, these themes are not always distinct and are interrelated. And all were subject to the influence of an American public that was deeply interested in, but firmly against intervention in, European affairs.

This work concludes that the mission that resulted developed multiple objectives after being born out of a discussion between Roosevelt and Welles on the role the United States could play in achieving a sound and lasting peace in Europe. Such a hope, reckoned by Roosevelt to be "one chance in a thousand," was at the outset incongruous with the situation in Europe. Roosevelt and Welles knew this to be the case and pressed ahead because of the existence of other objectives that such a mission could achieve. These were the gathering of firsthand information by Welles from the four capitals of Europe, the perpetuation of Italian neutrality, and the prolonging of the "phony war." These objectives were never clarified by the protagonists and evolved in themselves through the deployment of the mission, thus requiring the analysis provided here.

ACKNOWLEDGMENTS

THROUGHOUT MY TIME AS HIS STUDENT I would like to thank Alan Dobson for his expertise and professionalism. He has proved an invaluable mentor. Further thanks must go to my secondary supervisor Mike Simpson, whose initial enthusiasm instilled an ambition to work in Swansea. Although I have Alan and Mike to thank for their expert opinions a number of other people who have read my work have provided invaluable suggestions: Mark Evans, Hans Krabbendam, Jacqueline Dix, and Richard Askwith. At various points, unbeknowingly and in no particular order, academic inspiration has been instilled by the following individuals: David Knight, Patricia Clavin, David Adams, and Andrew Williams.

I am grateful to David Woolner, the Executive Director of the Franklin and Eleanor Roosevelt Institute (FERI), for providing generous support to my research at the Franklin D. Roosevelt Presidential Library where I was ably assisted by archivist Bob Clark. Elsewhere in the United States, my research was supported by the staff at the National Archives, Washington DC, and the Bancroft Library, University of California, Berkeley. I would also like thank the Roosevelt Study Center (Middelburg, the Netherlands) for the award of a grant that enabled me to utilize their resources in the spring of 1999. In the United Kingdom special thanks must go to all those who over many trips helped my research at the National Archives. I am also grateful to the staff at Special Collections Division at the University of Birmingham Library, at the Borthwick Institute at the University of York, and the Churchill Archive Centre, Churchill College, Cambridge. My experience of these archives was pleasurable and informative.

For emotional support and perspective, Caroline has always been there. My family and friends who have sought to ask questions and prompt answers must be thanked also. My final words are for my grandparents, my grandfather in particular, without whose trust none of this would have been possible.

"Take life easy. Study hard, the rest will take care of itself."
Summer 1989, Hamsa Mwapachu

Introduction: The Mission of Sumner Welles to Europe (February–March 1940), Rooseveltian Foreign Policy, and Anglo-American Relations, November 1937–May 1940

IN FEBRUARY AND MARCH OF 1940 SUMNER WELLES, the U.S. Under Secretary of State, visited four European capitals to speak with the leaderships of Italy, Germany, France, and Great Britain. He was undertaking a mission that he and President Franklin Roosevelt had conceived at the turn of the year. It took place during the period known as the "phony war," when a lack of actual fighting on the Western Front seemed to provide a moment to take stock before the expected onslaught in the spring.

The motivations behind, and the objectives of, the mission are the focus of this book. Neither Welles nor Roosevelt ever provided a complete account of their thinking about it. Purity of intention with regard to the Welles mission, as with much else in Roosevelt's foreign policy, is illusory. The Welles mission can only be understood if the longer-term themes that made it possible are considered alongside the objectives that both Roosevelt and Welles sought from it. For the first time this work will provide a comprehensive explanation that draws upon archival research and published primary sources, alongside the relevant secondary literature, by looking at the thoughts and actions of the key protagonists and their circumstances.

The mission has previously been characterized as a failed attempt at an outright American "peace" move during the hiatus of the phony war. The most extensive account to date was produced by Stanley Hilton in the *Journal of American History* (1971–1972). He suggests that the mission was designed to "bolster the position of the Allies by weakening the Rome-Berlin Axis and delaying the spring clash."[1] He dismisses too readily the exploration of peace that Roosevelt and Welles considered at the mission's genesis. While providing a worthy analysis it does not go far enough in considering the broader motivations or the other objectives involved in Roosevelt's decision and thus does not create sufficient context for a thorough examination of Welles' mission.

In addressing this gap in the current literature, this work can claim its originality in three areas. The first is in the nature of the approach this volume takes to understanding the Welles mission. The central question of this book is: what were Roosevelt's motivations for undertaking the mission and what did he seek to achieve from it? Posing this question allows for a broader understanding to be reached, which moves beyond the mission merely being considered as Roosevelt naïvely probing for peace. Further, this approach provides a suitable analytical framework for the investigation of the "themes" that this work considers imperative to understanding the context behind the Welles mission in the period 1937–1940.

The second aspect that makes this work distinct is its conclusions. In answering the central question, this work points to four objectives of the Welles mission: the exploration of a peace compatible with American terms; the gathering of firsthand information through a personal envoy; prolonging the phony war; and perpetuating Italian neutrality. Never before has the intricate interplay of these objectives been considered. The key point is that these objectives evolved during the course of the mission, and their interrelationship is therefore vital.

The third aspect of originality is the use of primary resources, especially of the Sumner Welles papers. The Welles papers were unavailable until they were deposited at the Franklin D. Roosevelt Presidential Library in September 1995, before being opened for public consultation in the spring of 1996. This source was therefore inaccessible to previous scholars looking at the Welles mission. A key advance uncovered during the research for this work relates to providing dates and references for two documents, one of which was unaccounted for and the other undated, referred to in *The Foreign Relations of the United States* section on the Welles mission. Copies of these documents, which refer to the British Ambassador's initial communication to London of Roosevelt's intention to embark on the Welles mission, were found in the Papers of Viscount Halifax as Foreign Secretary (FO 800 324, National Archives, London).

This introduction outlines the nuanced arguments that this book will employ concerning the contextual themes and objectives of Welles' mission. In examining this mission it is vital to consider the necessary, but not absolute, distinction between motives and objectives: "the first a push of the past, the second the pull of the future."[2] This analysis allows the events under consideration to be examined in a comprehensive fashion by looking first at the background to the way in which American foreign policy was made between 1937 and 1940 and then at the mission itself.

Naturally, this work makes considerable use of secondary literature, but it has been predominantly based on archival research in the United States and the United Kingdom. Primary research was conducted in the newly accessible Sumner Welles papers and the Papers of Franklin D. Roosevelt, both of which can be found at the Franklin D. Roosevelt Presidential Library, New York. The State Department records in the National Archives, Washington, DC, were consulted, as were the papers of Cordell Hull and the unpublished draft biography of Joseph Kennedy, both at the Library of Congress. In the United Kingdom, the papers of the key protagonists were consulted at institutions such as the Special Collections Department at Birmingham University, the Borthwick Institute (York), the Churchill Archives Centre (Cambridge), and, for the crucial Foreign Office documents, the Public Record Office, now the National Archives (London).

The clear differences in this work to those that have preceded it in discussing the Welles mission and the period under examination are considered. Robert Dallek's seminal text sees the mission in conventional terms as one of "three peace moves" that Roosevelt undertook in early 1940.[3] He places the mission alongside the visit of General Motors' supremo James Mooney to Berlin and the conversations with other neutrals that Cordell Hull announced on the same day that Roosevelt announced the Welles mission. Dallek accepts that Roosevelt was prepared to consider peace with Germany, but only if it would be more than a temporary truce, that is, on terms compatible with American values. William Langer and Everett Gleason go further in suggesting that "a major objective of the mission [was] to explore peace possibilities even with the Nazi government."[4] Although heavily influenced by their State Department past, and considered a semiofficial text, this volume again fails to account for the additional objectives as well as for the motivations that were involved in Roosevelt's decision making in January 1940. Arnold Offner sees Rooseveltian foreign policy as essentially that of appeasement in avoiding confrontation, and the Welles mission as epitomizing the "full ambiguity of American appeasement in the 1930s," where Roosevelt sought to preserve U.S. interests with little concern for the consequences for Europe.[5] The extent of any ambiguity requires the contextual understanding provided here.[6]

The Anglo-American relationship during the period before the Second World War has received extensive scholarly attention, but there has been little consideration of the Welles mission in it.[7] The exception is the work of David Reynolds, who considers the Welles mission to be a genuine attempt at a "compromise peace." This he sees as a result of an antipathy for Britain, within the State Department that included Welles, and tied into an "underlying Wilsonianism" within the Roosevelt Administration.[8] More recently, in a general volume on Roosevelt and the American entry into the Second World War, Reynolds identifies the goals of delaying the spring offensives and Roosevelt's desire to gain information from a single source in the Welles mission. While making an important contribution, Reynolds however underplays the exploration of a possible peace settlement and fails wholeheartedly to address the consideration of Italian neutrality in Roosevelt's thinking.[9]

One aspect of the Anglo-American relationship that requires concise explanation here is the notion of a "special relationship" between the United States and the United Kingdom. Given its contemporary resonance, the idea that Washington and London have exceptional and distinctive relations owes much to the experience of the Second World War. However, the period under consideration here, up to the spring of 1940, is notable for a lack of under-standing of a number of key national interests. Indeed the impact of the Welles mission on Anglo-American relations exhibits both concord and misunderstanding in almost equal measure. Before any contemporary assess-ment could be made, the events of the summer were so overwhelming, as to relegate the Welles mission from view.

The central focus of this work in terms of an individual is Benjamin Sumner Welles.[10] His papers were deposited for public consultation only in 1995 at the Franklin D. Roosevelt Library. His son Benjamin Welles drew heavily on these papers in producing a revealing biography of Sumner that included a candid acknowledgment of the indiscretions that cost Sumner his job. Nevertheless, Benjamin Welles sees his father as Roosevelt's key foreign policy adviser and the mission of 1940 as primarily a fact-finding one. Irwin F. Gellman, in his examination of the triumvirate relationship between Roosevelt, Hull, and Welles, sees the mission as putting forward a "naïve peace plan." The mission can certainly be considered naïve if looked at in a one dimensional sense but this needs to be qualified by the other, more real-istic, objectives that the mission developed. Christopher O'Sullivan's recent work focuses on Welles' importance in American postwar planning where he sees the Under Secretary as crucial in promoting a postwar order that would best serve the interests of the United States. In considering the Welles mission, O'Sullivan points to it as an attempt to promote an American-brokered peace and also as an effort to delay the spring offensives. Again these are important factors, but the gamut of motivations and objectives are not discussed in this source. Importantly, there is of course Sumner Welles' own book titled *The Time for Decision* that reveals the report that Welles presented to Roosevelt, but little else of Welles' opinions bar his appraisal of the mission as "a forlorn hope."[11] This lack of critical analysis is hardly surprising, given that the work was published in 1944, just a year after Welles had resigned, and with the war continuing. Although it is a crucial text, the report given to Roosevelt by Welles was later published in *The Foreign Relations of the United States*, and so this adds relatively little to any explanation of events surrounding the Welles mission. Tellingly, though, in preparing *Time for Decision* Welles sent a copy to Roosevelt for his perusal. The President then passed it on for review to Samuel Rosenman, his longtime aide and speechwriter. Having read the chapter dealing with the mission, Rosenman wrote, "[Y]ou [Roosevelt] asked him to go because it seemed to you that if the war continued and the all-out offensive by Germany on the Western powers should take place, the results would be unpredictable and there would be greater danger that the United States be involved." While clearly written with knowledge of how the war had unfolded up to that point, Rosenman's view in June 1944 was "Personally, I see no objection to it." Given the ongoing problems confronting Roosevelt at the time and the fact that the account replicated so closely the one Roosevelt had seen in the spring of 1940, it is perhaps hardly surprising that there is no more than a typical "FDR OK" in the file. This is despite the multiple factors that were involved in his decision making behind the mission at the turn of 1940, which will be examined herein.[12]

In short, this work differs in scope, analysis, and sources from the existing literature, as it seeks to place the Welles mission within a framework that explains the complex processes at work in the Roosevelt Administration and Roosevelt's desire to do something at the beginning of 1940. This all led to the multiple objectives of the mission in February and March.

It is only by working through the analysis presented that one can arrive at a comprehensive understanding of the Welles mission. This book finds that the longer-term motivations for the mission have precedents in the foreign policy-making practice of the Roosevelt Administration. Four themes will be explored in this analysis of the Welles mission: the critical role played by Sumner Welles, the caution expressed by Cordell Hull, the limitations upon U.S. foreign policy resulting in policy privately acknowledged as likely to be ineffectual, and consideration of Anglo-American relations. These themes will be explored in the first two chapters, and in doing so they provide the contextual framework to the subsequent examination of the Welles mission. They require some elucidation here, especially in relation to the ubiquitous reach of a further factor that has a direct impact upon Rooseveltian policy of the period: American public opinion. The views of the American people were a continual concern for Roosevelt in his policy making. The impact that the American people exerted on Rooseveltian foreign policy was remarkable in the way that it came to influence the events in this study. But it is important to acknowledge that it was the perception of a potential influence as much as a direct impact that conditioned Administration thinking. The pressure was neither constant nor explicit and reflected two interwoven trends within American opinion. A first element was a deep interest among the American people in events overseas, with sympathy for those facing the Dictators but an equally strong disgust with the policies of the Axis powers. A second facet of American opinion was that it would not countenance the possibility of overseas commitments that might lead to political, and possibly military, entanglements. Thus, far from being what is commonly referred to as "isolationist," implying a completely closed-off view of the world, American opinion can be more accurately termed "nonentangling" in indicating its awareness of the challenges posed by world affairs but its belief that it could remain aloof from them. The dual trends were epitomized in the neutrality legislation of the mid-1930s that sought to eradicate U.S. involvement in any war zone. The importance of clarifying this here is that both trends in American opinion conditioned the scope of Rooseveltian foreign policy between October 1937 and January 1940.[13] It is also important to recognize that the policy moves considered by the Administration were formulated in light of these trends. This resulted in policies that were acknowledged by those who were making them, to stand only the smallest chance of influencing the direct recipients in the stated manner. Given the subsequent events of the war, it is easy to say with hindsight that such policy options were destined to fail and antagonize. Instead, the policy options that were developed, the Welles mission included, should be considered as attempts to influence events within the constraints imposed by American public opinion and in doing so illustrate to American opinion the dangers posed to U.S. national interests.

The opening chapter introduces four themes in Rooseveltian foreign policy-making as the Administration considered a plan for a conference of the world's diplomats, to be convened in Washington on Armistice Day 1937. The proposal was orchestrated and prepared by Welles and reveals how important he had already become to Roosevelt's foreign policy making in 1937 and points to the first theme identified in this work. Welles drew up substantial plans and, although the proposal was temporarily mothballed in early November 1937, it was resurrected early in 1938 only to be overlooked permanently by mid-February. Throughout this five-month period and beyond, Hull's input into the process must be understood in terms of the triumvirate relationship between himself, Roosevelt and Welles. Hull's concerns, the second theme of Roosevelt's foreign policymaking, in relation to the conference proposal contributed to its postponement in 1937, and then, when it was being reconsidered in January 1938, an insistence that the Chamberlain government be sounded out. The Secretary of State was concerned that making any move would unsettle both American public opinion and the democracies while antagonizing further the Axis powers. These anxieties are vital to this work, as Hull maintained them consistently throughout the period in question and are therefore evident in early 1940 when the Welles mission was first being considered. The third element to be considered in relation to Welles' plan is how such a policy was prepared in the face of the constraints imposed by the views of the American people. This manifested itself in policy that was considered in the full knowledge that its impact was likely to be minimal while at the same time creating an impression among the American people of having made an effort to address the situation. Without any thought of resorting to the use of force, moves such as the conference plan reveal how Rooseveltian policy was framed with the views of the American people in mind. The first chapter goes on to explore the state of Anglo-American relations at the beginning of 1938 thus addressing the fourth theme under investigation here: relations between London and Washington. It was then that Roosevelt and Welles contemplated redeploying the plan and approached the Chamberlain government. Chamberlain was against the proposal from the outset, as he feared it would interfere with his own plans to deal with Hitler and Mussolini: the policy of appeasement. The distinct lack of enthusiasm for the proposal in London left Anglo-American relations in a poor state and created a legacy that could be felt throughout the period under investigation.

The latter part of chapter 1 explores the evidence for these themes in the events of 1938 and 1939. These events include those central to the outbreak of war, such as the Munich crisis (September 1938) and also events in the relationship between London and Washington, such as the conclusion of the Anglo-American Trade Agreement (November 1938). Of particular note is how Roosevelt's foreign policy was made on the basis of "long odds." In other words, the Roosevelt Administration, given the constraints upon it, was conducting foreign policy at the margins of what was possible in the full knowledge that it was unlikely to succeed in its stated aims. This notion was summed up by Assistant Secretary of State Adolf Berle, in late August 1939. He wrote of messages sent to Europe by the United States calling for restraint:

> . . . these messages will have about the same effect as a Valentine sent to somebody's mother-in-law out of season; and they have all the quality of naïveté which is the prerogative alone of the United States. Nevertheless, they ought to

be sent. The one certain thing in this business is that no one will be blamed for making any attempt, however desperate, at preserving peace.[14]

This expressive quote is used to establish at the outset of this work how far those involved in producing foreign policy in the United States at this time were realistic as to what they could achieve in terms of influencing events in Europe. This attitude is fundamental to understanding the longer-term motivations for Roosevelt's thinking at the beginning of 1940, which would result in the Welles mission.

A final point of note here is that, faced with this pressure, Roosevelt was ready to employ two strategies to fulfill his foreign policy. The first was the use of personal diplomacy, and the second was circumvention of American public opinion, that is, policy that had ulterior motives to those publicly stated. These elements are interrelated, as the former was often used to fulfill the latter. In the instances examined here, of the visit of Captain Royal E. Ingersoll to London in January 1938 and the royal visit of June 1939, Roosevelt hoped to further wider policy goals rather than just discuss naval plans or entertain the Royal couple. The Welles mission was another example of Roosevelt's propensity to use individuals to fulfill key tasks and illustrates that personal diplomacy was a notable part of the way the President conducted foreign policy. That Welles, a trusted colleague, had already operated under personal direction from Roosevelt in Latin America by the time tensions in Europe reached crisis levels meant he was on hand for the President. This is one of the key trends that this chapter establishes in providing a full comprehension of the Welles mission.

The second chapter of this analysis maintains these themes but is augmented by consideration of the changed circumstances brought by the war. As the war began, the United States adopted the policy of neutrality prescribed by the legislation of the same name. This sought to remove American interests from any theater of war, but once Germany and the Soviet Union had divided Poland in the late summer of 1939, the lack of actual fighting led many in the United States to ask how *real* the war was. Senator William Borah of Idaho, coined the phrase "the phony war" to describe the lack of warlike activity, a phrase that has subsequently been generally applied to the period from the declaration of war in September 1939 through to the German drive westward in April 1940. Nevertheless, the onset of war did raise the issue of neutral rights during war, which the American State Department was very keen to protect. This increased tension with Great Britain to the point at which the British Ambassador, Lord Lothian, referred to a "minor crisis" in Anglo-American relations at the end of January 1940.

Crucially, this chapter charts how the phony war period also served to put the issues of peace and American mediation on the agenda of the Roosevelt

Administration. These areas were discussed in the State Department during the last months of 1939, and both were a product of, and contributed to, a notion that Roosevelt should consider doing something to address the situation in Europe. This in turn was heightened by the universally accepted belief that the hiatus of the phony war would come to an end in the spring of 1940. Many in the United States feared that would mean a return to the horrors of the trenches of the Great War, or the prospect, promulgated by some such as Charles Lindbergh, of indiscriminate aerial bombardment of civilians. These prospects, for a generation who had hoped never again to see total war, imposed further pressure on those in the Administration to address the situation in Europe. Allied to an acknowledgment that their influence in Europe was marginal, and desirous of exhausting every possible policy option, the Roosevelt Administration was left to ask what real harm any American move during the "phony war" could do.

Yet on their own, the broader motivations and the pressure of time in the phony war may not have propelled Roosevelt to decide on a diplomatic mission to Europe without the possibility that it could achieve something to further U.S. interests. In assessing the objectives of the Welles mission it is imperative to accept that they existed alongside the motivations, and these were often intertwined. The story of how the objectives for the Welles mission emerged from the motivations prior to Welles' departure is told in chapter 3 and is epitomized most clearly in the drafting of the mission statement that Roosevelt made public on 9 February. Roosevelt's original objective for a mission to Europe in early 1940 was a long shot: exploring the possibilities for peace in Europe on terms compatible with American interests. This purpose was almost immediately broadened by other potential objectives during January and early February 1940. Although their interplay turned out to be crucial, the full range of considerations have never before been analyzed together. Ultimately the entire span of objectives, in addition to exploring possibilities of peace, came to be the following:

- to gather firsthand information from the Axis capitals;
- to perform the same task in the Allied capitals with a secondary aim of allowing Welles to assess Allied allegiance to their war aims;
- to prolong the hiatus in full-scale conflict of the "phony war"; and
- to perpetuate Italian neutrality.

These aims did not maintain a consistent balance or priority throughout the course of the mission, but they did evolve alongside each other, and this evolution is central to the analysis that follows in chapters 4, 5, and 6. At the outset Roosevelt's initial aim was influenced first by Hull, who largely repeated the concerns he had presented with regard to the Armistice Day plan of 1937, and then by the British through Lothian. These views, expressed at the very end of January and beginning of February 1940, did have a material effect on the mission in one important sense, as the public announcement of the mission made no use of the word "peace."

Nevertheless, when Welles was in Europe he did follow a line of questioning that enquired about possible peace terms. In Italy, his first stop, this may have been for the purposes of genuinely exploring peace terms, but by the time he had finished listening to the Nazis in Germany, all chances of a settlement compatible with U.S. interests had disappeared. However, Welles continued to pose the question of a settlement in Paris, London, and back in Rome. This was with a view to using the possibility of achieving a resolution as a way of furthering the mission's other objectives. In seeking to clarify peace terms in his conversations, Welles was at various points trying to gather information, to ascertain the aims and conviction of the Allies, to prolong the "phony war," and to maintain Italian neutrality. The *exploration of peace terms* thus formed something of an umbrella under which at assorted times the other objectives sheltered. This is important in illustrating how the goal of pursuing peace terms was entwined at various points throughout a spectrum of objectives.

The gathering of firsthand information certainly came under this umbrella. While Roosevelt denied to journalists at the 9 February press conference that he needed a "new reporter" in Europe, he did hope that Welles would be able to provide a comprehensive picture of the situation in Europe in January 1940. Roosevelt would thus be able to learn from a single source the state of affairs on the ground and have it communicated to him directly, as Welles had done previously in orchestrating the "Good Neighbor" policy in Latin America. Roosevelt's desire to see one man fulfill the task across Europe further reveals his disposition toward utilizing personal diplomacy.

The interconnectedness of means and ends in the mission's objectives is illustrated by Welles' quest for information in the Allied capitals on the precise nature of their war aims and their commitment to prosecuting them. Welles was seeking confirmation from the Allies that they were fighting for the cause of liberty and democracy and not for what could be seen as "Old World" interests of territorial acquisition. This would serve a dual purpose: providing the Administration with information it could use to illustrate to the American people the differences between the aims of the Allies and of the Axis, and allowing Welles to pass information to Roosevelt on the personalities of those involved in the conflict. Welles would use discussion in the Allied capitals of a possible settlement not for that as an end in itself, but because it drew out succinct statements of what the belligerents were fighting for. Had the mission been solely, or indeed overwhelmingly, dedicated to the pursuit of peace, and had it not had other objectives, then Welles would have followed up the semipositive response he received from Daladier in Paris to the discussion of a settlement of the conflict, or the heavily qualified comments of a similar vein made by Chamberlain in their final meeting in London. That he did not do this indicates not only that he considered the possibility of a resolution to the war to be impossible after his time in Berlin but also the existence of these other objectives.

The last two objectives developed most clearly after Welles' initial conversations in Rome. Prolonging the "phony war" and perpetuating Italian neutrality were both considered with a view to limiting the scale of any conflict that the spring was expected to bring. Their antecedents, and Welles' involvement, can be seen early in 1940, as Italy—a neutral nation—was not in the original itinerary for the mission. As Roosevelt decided in mid- to late January that Welles would be the one undertaking the mission, the Under Secretary sought to include Italy in order to mitigate domestic criticism that the mission was concerned solely with the warring nations. In doing this Welles also broadened the scope for the mission to make a positive contribution: something that would be evident once Welles was in Europe. Once there, he sought privately to use comments made by Mussolini in their first conversation, that peace might be possible on Axis terms, to encourage the Italian leader to think he might have a role to play and therefore to distance himself from Hitler. Although success was highly unlikely, here again Welles was using a line of discussion with regard to a possible settlement to further the mission's other goals, in this case that of perpetuating Italian neutrality. However, Mussolini was himself trying to assess the extent to which the United States was prepared to contemplate peace with Italy and Germany, especially once Welles had returned to Rome in March. Mussolini had his answer on 16 March, after a telephone conversation between Welles and Roosevelt, which the Italians tapped. The two Americans declined the opportunity for Mussolini to take up with Hitler notions of American involvement. Indeed, Welles' tactic may have precipitated the tightening of the Axis, as at the hastily arranged Brenner Pass meeting (18 March) Mussolini agreed to enter the war. Once Welles had listened to the Nazi position in Berlin, he sought to propagate the view that Roosevelt might act after his return to Washington and so prolong the "phony war." While the Nazis were clearly aware that this would not mean a commitment of American forces, a further diplomatic move might just have complicated preparations for the assault westward. This was undoubtedly an outside chance but reflected the margins in which Welles was operating. He was not to know that, the day before he arrived in Berlin Hitler had given a Führer directive to prepare for the attack on Scandinavia (Operation Weserübung, 8–9 April 1940).

Welles' conduct on his mission to Europe reveals that he was attempting to further a number of objectives at the limit of what was possible. This was typical of Rooseveltian foreign policy, as exhibited in other moves of the late 1930s examined here. The intricate interplay of motivations and objectives, both before and during the mission, necessitate a broad contextual understanding of Rooseveltian foreign policy and Anglo-American relations, provided for the first time by this work.

After spending almost three weeks in Europe, including many hours of discussion, Welles returned to Washington with a report for the President. Roosevelt later announced that there was "scant immediate" prospect of peace in Europe. Two weeks after that Hitler's forces attacked and overwhelmed Denmark and Norway, before the German war machine turned West and drove into the Low Countries, just as Winston Churchill replaced Neville Chamberlain as Prime Minister on 10 May 1940. Given these tumultuous changes to the political landscape of Europe the mission of Sumner Welles had barely any chance of fulfilling its original goal or any of the other objectives. Yet this would hardly have surprised Roosevelt, or indeed Welles. In broaching the subject of the Welles mission with Lothian in early February, Roosevelt offered odds of "one chance in a thousand," that the mission would produce anything that could resolve the conflict in Europe. Yet the Roosevelt Administration had become accustomed to working in the margins of diplomacy, developing policies that were extremely unlikely to succeed outright but, critically, might be able to advance other objectives. The experiences of this between the end of 1937 and the beginning of 1940 provide crucial contextual background to the Welles mission and provide the opening to this volume.

CHAPTER 1

ROOSEVELTIAN FOREIGN POLICY MAKING AND ANGLO-AMERICAN RELATIONS IN 1938 AND 1939— RELATIONSHIPS IN THE MAKING

If we get out of this business without a war it will be principally due to Sumner. He is the only one who apparently keeps his head working aside from his emotions.[1]

THIS DESCRIPTION OF SUMNER WELLES came from Assistant Secretary of State Adolf Berle in the immediate aftermath of Roosevelt's Quarantine address in October 1937 (the implications of which will be discussed). Yet it could have been applied at a number of key points, up to and including the Welles mission, during the subsequent 28 months as the Under Secretary made a crucial contribution to Roosevelt's foreign policy. The chances of outright success in many of the policies considered were minimal, but this was not an impediment to enacting policy within the Roosevelt Administration.

It is pertinent to begin analysis of the Welles mission of 1940 by looking at the period between October 1937 and February 1938. This is a crucial one for Rooseveltian foreign policy, as the President sought to give direction to his foreign policy once firmly secure in a second term. It is also a vitally important time in providing contextual background to the motivations and objectives of the Welles mission. This chapter will present key themes illustrative of the links between the Welles mission and Rooseveltian foreign policy between the end of 1937 and the outbreak of war. The themes that are relevant are fourfold: first, the role played by Welles in formulating Rooseveltian foreign policy; second, and flowing from this, the position of Hull and his relationship with both Roosevelt and Welles; third, how U.S. foreign policy was limited in its options and how this meant policy was being conducted in full recognition that it was unlikely to be able to influence the major powers: in other words, on the basis of "long odds"; and, fourthly, the ongoing status of relations between London and Washington. Furthermore, and pervading the motifs mentioned above, was American public opinion. Rather than exerting a consistent and outright direct pressure on the themes and events of 1938–1939, U.S. public opinion was omnipresent in creating an inhibited atmosphere in which American foreign policy was made. Nonetheless, the themes are evident during the five-month from October 1937 to February in the consideration Roosevelt gave to a plan for a major diplomatic conference. This plan was formulated by Welles and was considered on two occasions (November 1937 and January 1938). The study of this proposed conference will form the opening to this chapter, and through its examination the themes will be explored. They are then considered in relation to the vital events of 1938 and 1939 before the outbreak of war. To a greater or lesser extent, as foreign policy was framed, these themes were visible at the time of the Munich crisis, in the negotiations over an Anglo-American trade agreement, in the "appeals" the Roosevelt Administration put together in April and August 1939, and in Roosevelt's efforts throughout the period to circumvent the influence of those who wanted to see the United States remain nonentangled. Of course these events retain their own unique place in the history of the run-up to the outbreak of war, but by examining them in the light of these themes, this book is able to provide further contextual understanding of Roosevelt's decision making in January 1940 with regard to the Welles mission.

The first theme to be considered in understanding the importance of the Roosevelt Administration's proposal for a diplomatic conference is the role played by Benjamin Sumner Welles. The relationship between Welles and Roosevelt was time and again at the nexus of foreign policy making and so, to fully comprehend the part Welles played, some key elements of their background are required.

Sumner Welles was a vital influence upon Roosevelt's foreign policy during his tenure as U.S. Under Secretary of State.[2] This should be of little surprise, given that Roosevelt made sure Welles was promoted to this position on 20 May 1937. In doing so Roosevelt was calling upon a man who had followed in his own educational footsteps to Groton and Harvard and who had over 20 years of experience in the Foreign Service. Indeed, when Welles had applied to join the State Department in 1915 he had called upon the then

Assistant Secretary of the Navy, Franklin Roosevelt, for a reference. Roosevelt said of his younger compatriot that he would be "most glad to see him successful in entering the Diplomatic Corps. He has travelled extensively, speaks several languages . . . and should give a very good account of himself."[3] Although Welles was ten years Roosevelt's junior, the two men had shared a common upbringing typical of the East Coast establishment families into which Franklin and Sumner were born. Alongside matching educational paths, this background instilled a common set of values that manifested itself in a shared view of the place of the United States in the world. It would be especially evident in their attitude to those nations south of the Rio Grande in the 1930s.

After an initial posting to Japan, Welles devoted his career to Latin American affairs. Indeed by 1920, aged just 28, he had become Chief of Division for Latin American Affairs. Although the 1920s saw him twice resign, he was an authority on Latin American affairs when he and Roosevelt met to discuss foreign policy in 1928.[4] That summer, in preparation for the New York gubernatorial race, and to help articulate the foreign policy of Democratic presidential candidate Al Smith, Roosevelt published an article in *Foreign Affairs*. The article focused largely on addressing European criticism of American behavior in "retreating from responsibility" in the aftermath of the First World War, but did contain a section on Latin America. Welles supplied this.[5] When Roosevelt was successful in the New York race, Welles, often through the internationally minded Norman Davis, supplied him with further information on foreign affairs. This dialogue increased in importance after Roosevelt had become the Democratic presidential candidate in the summer of 1932. Welles campaigned for his friend in his home state of Maryland and was delighted when victory was secured in the November election.

Even before the inauguration had taken place, Roosevelt had given Welles a key task: outlining the scope of inter-American relations. Welles' response was to lay the foundation for what would become the "Good Neighbor" policy, and to outline principles that guided U.S. foreign policy more broadly. These principles of mutual respect for international conduct would be evident in the proposed diplomatic conference in 1937, and elsewhere in Rooseveltian foreign policy up to the Welles mission itself. In 1933 Welles stressed that the United States should make relations with Latin America a keystone of its foreign policy. To secure American interests Welles wanted to bring to an end the era of the United States dispatching the Marines and to replace it with a policy based on mutual responsibility for hemispheric issues. Yet this would be a difficult task for Welles and one that called upon the full range of his diplomatic skills. Through first his appointment as Ambassador to Cuba in 1933, and then in mediating in the Chaco War between Paraguay and Bolivia in 1935 as Assistant Secretary of State, Welles' ideas gained acceptance in Latin America. In both instances and throughout the time Welles spent in

Latin America, the manner in which he operated with Roosevelt set important precedents. These would be evident at the time of the Welles mission. As his son Benjamin Welles writes, Sumner left for Havana "with Roosevelt's authorisation to communicate with him directly by cable or telephone."[6] This direct line of communication would become standard practice for the pair when Welles was overseas. Importantly, this also meant that Welles' direct superior, Hull, was bypassed in the chain of command. The problems this posed within the State Department, particularly during the proposal for the diplomatic conference and then the Welles mission, will be discussed in due course in looking at the role played by Hull.

Nevertheless, Welles' credibility in Latin America enabled him to press, in both Washington and Latin America, for a full inter-American conference in December 1936. The rapturous receptions that Roosevelt received in Rio de Janeiro and Montevideo on his way to the conference in the Argentine capital indicated the success of Welles' work thus far. Roosevelt's speech at the opening session of the conference sought further to encourage the belief that the United States was prepared to take hemispheric equality seriously. He said, "We in the Americas stand shoulder to shoulder in our determination that others, who might seek to commit acts of aggression against us, will find a hemisphere wholly prepared to consult together for our mutual safety. Each one of us has learned the glories of independence. Let each one of us learn the glories of inter-dependence."[7] The test of these claims would come as the sessions of the conference unfolded, with Welles heading the American delegation. He acted tactfully and skillfully to tighten hemispheric bonds and, despite Argentine intransigence, achieved an agreement between the American republics to meet in times of crisis. This concord later provided the basis for the conferences at Lima in December 1938 and, more significantly due to the outbreak of war, at Panama in September 1939.

When Welles returned to Washington in early 1937 he was on the brink of becoming the second most important man at the State Department. William Phillips, then Under Secretary of State, had accepted the position of Ambassador to Rome, allowing Roosevelt to promote Welles. Although Phillips will reappear when Welles arrived in Italy in February 1940, his departure in 1937 brought to the fore the differences between Roosevelt and Hull. Suffice it to say at this point in the formation of Rooseveltian foreign policy that Hull disagreed with the choice of Welles as Under Secretary. This was somewhat predictable, given Welles' career to this point. Fundamentally, Welles was happiest and most effective working on his own under broadranging instructions from the President and independently of the Secretary of State, as he had done in Latin America. He was always well prepared and had proved his skills in the "dimly lit smoke-filled rooms" where decisions were made. In these circumstances, and given both his working and his personal relationship with the President, he had license to fully explore his directives. The one limitation to this, which was very much in evidence during the whole period under consideration, was the absence from Welles' diplomatic toolbox of the ability to resort to the use of military force. In a key respect this added to the pressure to undertake diplomatic moves regardless of their chances of success. It is also important to see the individual relationship between President and Under Secretary of State as facilitating personal diplomacy on behalf of Roosevelt. Both in Latin America and in Europe, Welles was operating very much at Roosevelt's behest, in addition to his task of representing the State Department and the United States more generally. Welles relished the opportunity to work with Roosevelt, describing it as a "joy." Welles wrote, "His mind grasped so rapidly all the implications of a new proposal, no matter how vast its scope, that crossing the t's and dotting the i's were usually unnecessary."[8] This background to Welles' early career and his contact with Roosevelt is important in illustrating why Welles was in a position to have a decisive impact on Roosevelt's foreign policy in the autumn of 1937. The personal relationship between the two was crucial and to provide a relatively minor example, Roosevelt made mention of his "old boyhood friend" in writing to Chamberlain to help explain the Welles mission itself in February 1940.[9] Welles would also be in a position (after the Welles mission had passed) to emerge as "one of the most important officials in the wartime Administration." According to historian Christopher O'Sullivan, Welles was "a man whose vision of the role the US would play on the global stage made him a central figure in America's transformation from a major power to a superpower, an architect of the coming 'American Century.'"[10]

Welles' main impact on Roosevelt's foreign policy in 1937 was as planner-in-chief of the proposal for a World Diplomatic Conference, to be staged in Washington on Armistice Day 1937. Although this was not held at that time, Welles' ability to step to the fore in providing policy direction was very much what Roosevelt needed from his Under Secretary in the aftermath of the hostile reception given to his Quarantine speech. Fervent criticism from those who saw the speech as involving the United States in overseas affairs had forced Roosevelt himself to adopt a low profile in foreign affairs. That historians have previously underplayed Welles' position in the formation of the conference plan in October 1937 reveals a lack of appreciation of his pivotal role in Rooseveltian foreign policy making. As Berle stated, the plan did have a heritage; the notion of a world conference had "been under consideration" in various forms within the Administration "since the summer of 1936."[11] Yet it was Welles alone who invigorated the prospect sufficiently for it to interest Roosevelt as a policy option. He proposed "holding a world conference under American auspices which would re-establish the rule of law in international affairs, and guarantee justice by granting all powers equal access to raw materials."[12] In other words, Welles hoped to inaugurate international acceptance of reciprocal trade, nonaggression, and mutual respect. These were principles that accorded well in Roosevelt's State Department, including with Hull, and that would be evident in various forms up to the time of the Welles mission. The declaration to other neutral countries on the day that the Welles mission was announced in February 1940 should be seen very much in this light. The adherence to "principles" of international conduct would enable the Administration to further its efforts to illustrate to the American people the common interests they shared with other liberal democracies. Roosevelt himself gave voice to this attitude in his weekly radio address following the Quarantine speech: "The development of peace in the world is dependent . . . on the acceptance by nations of certain fundamental decencies in their relations with each other. Ultimately, I hope each nation will accept the fact that violations of these rules of conduct are an injury to the well-being of all nations."[13]

It was on the basis that the proposal would further Rooseveltian foreign policy that Welles worked on the conference plan throughout October 1937.[14] Welles' understanding of the wider domestic implications of the plan was evident in his writing to Roosevelt to encourage him to pursue it. Welles stated that from "the standpoint of public opinion at home, I would think that your making this proposal four days before the opening of the Special Session of the Congress would put a very definite quietus upon those individuals who have been deliberately attempting to misinterpret your Chicago speech."[15] The Special Session of Congress Welles referred to had been called to address legislation backed up during the debate Roosevelt had instigated on increasing the number of Supreme Court justices. This added to the President's sensitivity to domestic criticism in October 1937. Nevertheless, as the month drew to a close Berle felt Welles' plan was likely to be put into practice. He noted on 28 October that he thought the Administration "should be able to get somewhere with it [the proposal]" and that the following week was "obviously the time" to act to take advantage of the significance of Armistice Day.[16]

It is important to consider the significance of Welles' role during this period. Welles had embellished a relatively vague idea from within the Administration and presented it as a distinct policy option. His ability to interpret Roosevelt's often imprecise instructions and then present a practical policy would be very much in evidence during the period from 1937 to 1940. Historian Kenneth S. Davis explains how the conference plan fitted into this practice. The plan offered an opportunity that "if nothing else [would provide] a grand theatrical gesture of a kind most attractive, as the Undersecretary of State well knew, to the large historic element of Roosevelt's personality."[17]

However, as events unfolded during the first week of November, Roosevelt drew back from carrying out Welles' proposal. Roosevelt signaled this by adding to Welles' draft, "Not carried any further. FDR." These words came to represent a postponement, with the plan being revisited in January 1938.[18] Two factors were material to Roosevelt's decision to temporarily abandon Welles' proposal, but guiding both was consideration of American public opinion. In the first place Roosevelt was sensitive to the wider international situation. He had aimed to use his Quarantine speech as an opportunity to put the spotlight on Japanese aggression in China. Therefore he initially welcomed the response of the League of Nations, which was to convene an international conference in Brussels in early November 1937 and sent a trusted associate, Norman Davis, as the American delegate. However, without the attendance of the Japanese, the Germans, and the Italians, the conference was dominated by the French and the British. This posed a particular problem for Davis, who was not authorized to enter into any political discussions for fear of appearing entangled in European affairs. This meant the British and the French were able to place the responsibility for the failure of the conference to do anything about Japanese aggression on Washington. The troubles in Brussels meant that the prospect of international cooperation, implicit in the Welles plan, was distinctly low. Roosevelt had said in early October that the conference could be "an example of one of the possible paths to follow in our search for means toward peace throughout the whole world."[19] Berle summed up the problems Roosevelt faced in early November: "The foreign news is bad. With Brussels in trouble I do not see that it is wise for the President to push Sumner's plan of an international conference."[20] The international situation worsened still further when, on 6 November, Italy joined the German-Japanese Anti-Comintern pact.

The second vital factor in Roosevelt's decision to postpone the conference plan in early November 1937 was the concern expressed by Hull. He was especially conscious of the Administration's standing in the eyes of the American public as the economy stalled in late 1937. The so-called Roosevelt recession had "wiped out most of the gains made since 1935."[21] With the prospect of the upcoming Special Session of Congress, Roosevelt knew he would need Hull's political kudos to deal with those on Capitol Hill. Hull's view on foreign policy was vital as was the relationship between himself, Roosevelt, and Welles through which American foreign policy was made.

Hull's concerns over the conference plan, which would reappear in his objections to the Welles mission over two years later, were essentially threefold: the views of the American people (with possible political repercussions in Washington), the sense of false security given to the democracies by American moves, and the possible antagonizing of the Axis powers by such moves. Hull said that Welles' proposal was "illogical and impossible" as it would "be fatal to lull the democracies into a feeling of tranquility."[22] Further, Hull was worried by the possibility of more isolationist criticism of the Administration should the conference mimic the strife of Brussels. Hull had become Roosevelt's Secretary of State at the outset of the Administration and would remain so until 1944. His appointment was based largely on his political experience. He was chosen "essentially for his influence with Congress," Benjamin Welles writes, "where, after twelve terms in the House and two years in the Senate, his prestige was high."[23] Yet he served under a President who had determined to direct his own foreign policy. While this may have become the case, the challenges facing Roosevelt at the beginning of his presidency meant the whole of the Administration was geared to the domestic arena. This in turn allowed Hull to stamp his own mark on American foreign policy that manifested itself in a program of reciprocal trade agreements. This program, and particularly the Anglo-American trade agreement of 1938, will be considered presently. Roosevelt understood how far reciprocal trade was Hull's "baby." He wrote to Welles shortly after the latter's appointment as Under Secretary that Hull "genuinely believes that if trade relations between nations can be broadened on lines and under conditions where it serves to advance economic welfare, existing political tensions would be thereby eased."[24] While this conviction sat easily alongside Roosevelt's views on foreign policy and the principles of international conduct that Welles sought to promote, personal tension plagued the relationship between Secretary of State and Under Secretary.

The friction between the two can be traced to Welles' appointment and sprang from the differing styles of the two men. When Roosevelt was faced with the prospect of finding a new Under Secretary in early 1937, Hull wanted the job to go to "his" man, Walton "Judge" Moore. Hull had been frustrated by Welles' conduct during the advancement of the "Good Neighbor" policy, particularly by his unorthodox communication with the President. Roosevelt resolved the controversy with Hull by reviving the long-dormant position of Department Counselor for Moore. While these beginnings did not necessarily bode well for a harmonious working relationship, Welles' conduct in the position hardly helped to effect a seamless transition. As was typical of him, he threw himself into the work with little effort made to ingratiate himself with his colleagues.[25] This meant, in the same way that he often felt about others, that he was "either liked or disliked with no middle ground."[26] Hull often found himself in the latter camp, as "Welles' close ties to FDR, his growing authority, and the publicity he was attracting exacerbated Hull's jealousy."[27] Welles' authority had manifested itself in an internal staff review of the State Department, which saw his followers obtain key positions, and the publicity sprang from the prominence of his second wife in Washington social circles.[28] For the man from Tennessee the difference in style and outlook was often stark in the period from 1937 to 1940 and would be especially so in January 1940 at the time of the Welles mission. The tension did not escape the notice of the rest of the Department, but Berle surmised, "The only attitude one can take is to endeavour to make sure that the two men, neither of whom wishes to indulge in personal considerations at all, continue a smooth working program."[29] This was certainly the case during the period under consideration here, as there was a mutual respect for each other's professionalism. Welles' close friend Drew Pearson summed up the difference in approach of the two men: "Sumner moves with lightning speed and Hull only wants to concentrate on one thing at a time."[30]

The strain between the two was often played out in relation to Roosevelt. A prime example of this can be seen in the preparation for the neutrals' announcement in the run-up to the Welles mission. Welles wrote to Roosevelt on 12 January 1940 that he had given "the Secretary of State a memorandum a few days ago for his consideration."[31] As if to justify this enquiry, Welles included in the rest of the sentence reference to the fact that Roosevelt was present when Hull said that he had been too busy to deal with it. "As he said when we were with you," Welles continued, due to his being "so swamped recently with his Ways and Means Committee hearings he has not had a chance to go into it or talk over the problems involved with you." Hence Welles sent a draft directly to the President—"I am sending you a copy of this memorandum, thinking that you may have time to give it some thought before I have the opportunity of seeing you at lunch on Monday." This episode shows perfectly how Welles would bypass Hull in taking matters directly to Roosevelt. While this may seem a less than satisfactory way in which to operate his State Department, Roosevelt was not overly concerned as long as the Department continued to function. Indeed, Roosevelt welcomed the caution that Hull counseled and sought it for that reason. This was typical of his presidential style, in that he was prepared to see subordinates operate in a "competitive" fashion. In short, then, the differences between Hull and Welles will be a recurrent feature of Rooseveltian foreign policy making from 1937 through to the Welles mission, and indeed beyond. Thus as 1937 drew to a close the Welles plan for a major diplomatic conference had illustrated, first, the capacity of Welles to develop ideas in league with Roosevelt; and, second, the problems this raised with Hull. Before considering the key events of the two years leading up to Roosevelt's decision to embark on the Welles mission another theme requires attention: the influence of Great Britain on the thinking of the Roosevelt Administration.

The importance of Anglo-American relations in Rooseveltian foreign policy became evident in early 1938, when Sumner Welles' plan for a diplomatic conference was resurrected and presented to the British.

On 11 January 1938 Welles called on Ambassador Ronald Lindsay at the British Embassy. His task was to present to the British the terms of a plan prescribing that "essential and fundamental principles . . . should be observed in international relations."[32] Such sentiment represented the values Welles had hoped to promulgate in his earlier conference plan. The document detailing the plan, which he left at the Embassy, went on to call for "limitation and reduction of armaments" and equal access to raw materials, which were both favorite themes of the Roosevelt Administration. Further, and of particular relevance for Anglo-American relations once war had broken out in September 1939, the plan called for respect of neutral rights in wartime. "In the unhappy event of war, rights and obligations of government, both on land and at sea, . . . may be delivered by existing international agreements, and laws and customs of warfare whose observance neutrals may be entitled to require." Accompanying the document Welles gave to the British was a letter from Roosevelt to the British Prime Minister Neville Chamberlain. It was composed by Welles and reflects the Under Secretary's desire to see something come from this proposal:

> I have felt warranted in addressing to you this communication because of my considered belief that unless the nations of the earth strive by concerted effort to come rapidly to a renewed agreement upon those fundamental principles which the experience of the past, and the best judgement of present time, demonstrate as being wise and salutary in the governing of relations between states, world peace cannot be maintained.[33]

This expression of worthy sentiment was typical of Welles' efforts to use grand gestures of diplomacy to further policy. Beyond the value of these terms the reasons for the redeployment of the plan are not clear.[34] Although the domestic situation had improved after the Special Session of Congress, Roosevelt's capacity to act in foreign affairs had been strengthened only marginally.

The controversy with Japan over the *Panay* incident and its peaceful resolution during December 1937 had illustrated to the American people the potential dangers prevalent in involving themselves in world affairs.[35] The overwhelming desire for a diplomatic outcome, with congressmen inundated with letters from concerned constituents, buoyed the Administration's desire to promote a diplomatic agenda. For Welles the concept of the plan had never entirely died despite the passing of Armistice Day, and he was ready to take it up again in early 1938. Although his plans therefore overcame Hull's objection, the Secretary of State did insist that the British government should be approached before the plan was presented to other nations. Hull's motivation here was to defuse American responsibility and to avoid embarrassing the

British. In short, his concerns of the previous autumn. It is important to remember, though, that the significance of this proposal is also to illustrate the state of Anglo-American relations in January 1938.

From the outset Chamberlain was against the American plan. Despite the words of Lindsay, urging "very quick and very cordial acceptance," Chamberlain argued that it would be inappropriate to proceed with the plan.[36] He explained his reservations in a letter to Lindsay: "My fear is that, if the President's suggestions are put forward at the present time, Germany and Italy may feel constrained to take advantage of them, both to delay the consideration of specific points which must be settled if appeasement is to be achieved, and to put forward demands over and above what they would put forward to us if we were in direct negotiations with them."[37] Clearly Chamberlain was concerned that any American move would "cut across" his own plans to resolve the tension in world affairs: the policy of appeasement. Lindsay was thus in something of an invidious position in relaying London's lack of enthusiasm. Welles later wrote that Chamberlain's response came "in the nature of a douche of cold water."[38] Roosevelt was left with little choice but to accept Chamberlain's objections and, although this correspondence did have repercussions in other areas later in the year, not to proceed.[39] However, the situation was different in February 1940, when Chamberlain's objections to the Welles mission, although heeded to an extent, were not sufficient for the mission to be dropped.

The British Prime Minister's lack of enthusiasm for the American approach requires explanation. It is inescapable not to attribute his negative response to Welles' plan, at least in large part, to his wider views of the United States. Chamberlain looked across the Atlantic with a mixture of disappointment and unease. Based on his examination of Chamberlain's time as Chancellor of the Exchequer, historian Greg Kennedy assesses Chamberlain's attitude to the United States in stark terms. His "view of the United States as untrustworthy, unimportant and marginal in the British strategic foreign policy process, as well as his jealous, petty and uninformed view of the nation as a whole, continued to plague attempts by the Foreign Office, Admiralty and other government bodies at manufacturing closer Anglo-American strategic relations throughout his career."[40] It was perhaps unsurprising then that Chamberlain was not disposed to welcome the move from the Roosevelt Administration. For his own part, Chamberlain told an American relative in early 1938 that his efforts to engage the United States had been met with "more than one disappointment."[41] However, this fails to reveal that Chamberlain was a man with a supreme belief in his own abilities and the plans that flowed from them. He wanted to deal with the United States only on his own terms and when it did not interfere with his own plans. Chamberlain was right, though, in identifying the strength of isolationist opinion as a problem in Anglo-American relations: "[T]he isolationists there are so strong and vocal that she [the United States] cannot be depended on for help if we should get into trouble."[42] His perception of Washington's unreliability was his overriding concern. More widely, many in London looked to the record of the United States since the Versailles Conference and saw naked self-interest in pursuit of commercial interests. Further, the United States had exhibited a lack of responsibility in conducting international affairs at various conferences, notably the London Economic Conference of 1933. Thus a proposal for an American diplomatic conference did not appeal to Chamberlain in early 1938.

Moreover, Chamberlain was also doubtful about Washington's decision to propose the plan in such a manner. As shall be evident again in early 1940, Chamberlain was not receptive to Roosevelt's penchant for personal diplomacy. He had written in September 1937 on the visit of the American financier and presidential adviser Bernard Baruch that he was "another of the unofficial Ambassadors who so frequently come over here from the USA with proposals of their own devising but without any official authority for them."[43] Although Welles' approach in 1938 certainly had official backing, the scheme lacked practical application in British eyes. Chamberlain's Home Secretary Sir Samuel Hoare wrote that the Cabinet was "deeply suspicious not indeed of American good intentions, but of American readiness to follow up inspiring words with any practical actions."[44] It was the reliance on good intentions and respect, explicit in Welles' approach, that added to the skepticism in London.

In contrast, the Prime Minister's answer to increasing tension in early 1938 rested on what appeared to be the tangible attributes of bilateral appeasement of the aggressors. The term "appeasement" is a weighty one and is often viewed with hindsight as an appalling miscalculation.[45] Yet it was a broadly accepted and popular policy in Great Britain during 1937 and 1938.[46] Historian David Dutton suggests appeasement "was based upon the notion that there must be a point, and a not too distant one, at which those being appeased would become satisfied and where a new status quo could be constructed on the basis of lasting peace."[47] This was in turn based on the "liberal attitudes of a generation which believed the lessons of the Great War spoke for themselves." While this may sound idealistic, Chamberlain was a practical man who dealt with Hitler or Mussolini only because they were the characters he was forced to contend with. At the beginning of 1938 Chamberlain sought to appease the Italian leader with recognition of his conquest of Abyssinia and, as his letter to Lindsay states, he feared Welles' plan would scupper this.

The appeasement policy posed particular problems for the Roosevelt Administration in two areas. First, the bilateral nature of the process meant that the British appeared to be "in league" with the dictatorships. For the

Administration this hampered its portrayal of the democracies as standing for values that were in line with American ones. Here again the influence of the American people was evident in how far the Roosevelt Administration could "associate" itself with those appeasing the Axis. The second concern for those in Washington was typically given expression by Welles. In a letter he composed on behalf of Roosevelt for Chamberlain he urged the British to consider "the harmful effect" the issue of recognition could have "upon the course of Japan in the Far East and upon the nature of the peace terms which Japan may demand of China."[48] Welles and Roosevelt realized both their extremely limited influence and the possibility that existed for Chamberlain in trying to influence Mussolini in early 1938. Welles informed Lindsay that the "President regarded recognition as an unpleasant pill which we should both have to swallow and he wished that we should swallow it together."[49] Welles nevertheless appreciated the different approaches: "His Majesty's Government wished to swallow it in a general settlement with Italy and the President in a general settlement involving world appeasement." This assessment provides a succinct précis of the state of Anglo-American relations in the aftermath of the proposal of the Welles plan in January 1938.[50]

The launch of Welles' diplomatic initiative in January 1938 illustrated the differing approaches of the Roosevelt Administration and the Chamberlain government to their security concerns, the legacy of which was to be felt in the run-up to war. However, it is worth considering that at the beginning of 1938 Chamberlain's Foreign Secretary Anthony Eden held a different view of Washington from that of his Prime Minister. Eden was enjoying a brief sojourn in the south of France when Welles spoke to Lindsay on 11 January 1938. He was called back to London by Sir Alexander Cadogan, then Permanent Under Secretary, but did not arrive before Chamberlain had responded to Roosevelt. The letters he then wrote to Chamberlain explain concisely his view of the American initiative:

> I really do not feel that this initiative of President Roosevelt need necessarily injure the attempts which we are making to improve relations with Germany, nor even have any repercussions on the conversations which I know you are so anxious to start with Italy. It may be that you think that I exaggerate, but I truly believe that with the world as it is now, it is almost impossible to overestimate the effect which an indication of United States interest in European affairs may be calculated to produce.[51]

Eden's tone is almost one of desperation in imploring Chamberlain to consider the positive effects that might flow from the American proposal. Chamberlain did not acquiesce, and Eden wrote again the next day:

> The decision we have to take seems to me to depend upon the significance which we attach to Anglo-American co-operation. What we have to choose

between is Anglo-American co-operation in an attempt to ensure world peace and a piecemeal settlement by way of problematic agreement with Mussolini.[52]

This attitude would not have been out of place within the Roosevelt Administration itself: the proposal was worth considering even if it was not likely to succeed. However, Chamberlain disagreed, and the difference in opinion resulted in Eden's resignation from his position in February 1938, to be replaced by Lord Halifax.[53] Although he returned to Chamberlain's government as Dominions Secretary at the outbreak of war, had Eden remained as Foreign Secretary then British policy toward Washington might have been more agreeable in the months preceding the conflict.

Instead, Chamberlain's objections to Welles' proposal meant it was stillborn and, although its sentiment would be evident in Administration thinking up to and including the Welles mission, it was not to be revisited in this form. With Eden gone from the Chamberlain government in February 1938, Anglo-American relations were in a difficult state. During the time leading up to war in September 1939 the relationship would shift only marginally between increased understanding and further frustration for both. Anglo-American relations were strained over key issues such as neutrality revision in the summer of 1939 and were dislocated over their responses to the acts of aggression being perpetrated by the Axis powers during 1938 and 1939. In short, the transatlantic relationship was hardly harmonious. This episode in early 1938 helped establish a pattern in relations between Washington and London over the next two years with the United States exerting only a marginal influence on events in Europe and Chamberlain seeking to both avert war and prepare Britain for it. The Anglo-American relationship will thus be considered after a brief summation to the conference plan, as this chapter examines the period up to the onset of war, in order to provide further contextual background to the Welles mission.

In his memoirs, Anthony Eden surmised that the American diplomatic proposal of January 1938 sprang from "a combination of the President's instinct and Sumner Welles's knowledge."[54] This assessment is accurate in identifying the personal relationship at the heart of this move. It was Welles' dynamism that moved the proposal to center stage first in the autumn of 1937 and then again in early 1938. His involvement in drafting the proposal, presenting it to Roosevelt, and then personally informing the British Ambassador illustrates his conviction in deploying the scheme. This proactive role would be evident again at various key points during the following two years leading up to the Welles mission. That nothing came of the proposal in 1937 or 1938 caused Welles to lament the opportunity that had passed. He wrote in his memoirs that the situation at that time "was still fluid" in Europe and that such "an appeal by the President . . . might well have rallied a still vocal public opinion in Europe sufficiently to have changed the course of the events of the next two years."[55]

It is only with hindsight that such an appraisal can be made, and that was certainly not available to Cordell Hull at the time. His objections to Welles' plans were rooted in his belief that the proposal would lead to frustration both within the United States and among other nations. From a domestic point of view Hull was worried that the failure to live up to the promise of an Armistice Day move would fuel criticism of the Administration. On the international stage, the failure of such a move could affect his program of reciprocal trade agreements, as well as creating further disenchantment with the United States among the democracies. Historian Arthur Schatz has characterized Hull's belief in "economic disarmament" as "the promotion of world peace through international economic recovery."[56] This would not have been helped by another interwar conference that failed to produce results. The memory of the distinct lack of international harmony at the Brussels Conference in November 1937 was to the fore in Hull's objections. Hull's concerns that the Welles proposal would precipitate trouble in the international arena were shared by Chamberlain. The Prime Minister was preoccupied with his policy of appeasement and saw the Administration's move as liable to "cut across" it.

The Anglo-American relationship that Welles' plan impacted upon was accurately summarized by Ambassador Lindsay at the beginning of 1938. On 7 February 1938 Lindsay wrote explaining the state of the American Administration and the implications for Anglo-American relations. His sage words were to accurately reflect the conditions in which the relationship operated during 1938 and 1939:

> What brings America closer to us is the identity of American aims, desires and policies with our own. The totalitarian governments have got themselves into such a position that they can hardly take any major action in any field which does not make that identity more patent. If we try to push or pull the Americans forward they inevitably resent it, because they must take their measures in their own American way. Fortunately the President and his Administration are far-sighted and are doing all the pushing and pulling that they think practically possible. If only we had time enough we should merely need to be candid, tactful and prudent, and the totalitarians would do the whole job for us. . . . American opinion is a distressing spectacle for at first glance one can see practically nothing but rampant isolationism, except in some limited circles and in Congress it is very bad. Yet, though I try to avoid wishful thinking, I do believe that it is not really quite as bad as it seems. A large part of the press is very sensible and there is widespread genuine friendliness towards us, and universal dislike of totalitarian systems. There are many elements in the situation favourable to us, and with such an emotional people a dramatic incident might have astonishing results.[57]

Lindsay's analysis presents a number of erudite points. Clear, succinct identification of the principles that Great Britain was standing for would help the Administration's efforts to paint a favorable portrait of the democracies for the American people, as would greater distance in relations with the totalitarians. The Ambassador further suggests that to try to "maneuver" the Americans before they themselves are ready, before they have done it the "American way," would be highly counterproductive. Lindsay acknowledges that the Administration was making some headway against "rampant isolationism," the nonentangling element, and that it was not as strong as might at first be supposed. Importantly here, Lindsay alludes to the dual trends of U.S. public opinion. Finally, Lindsay's analysis identifies that time was on Britain's side in the very long term, that the Dictators would make the job easier, and that a "dramatic incident" could have "astonishing results." This was eventually to prove the case when the Japanese attacked Pearl Harbor in December 1941. The impact of Lindsay's pronouncement in London was perhaps not high, considering that its addressee Eden was about to resign and Chamberlain was in the process of declining Roosevelt's approach, but its content was relevant to issues in the Anglo-American relationship.

Lindsay was clearly aware of the pressures that the American Administration was operating under vis-à-vis the American people in late 1937 and early 1938. This prevented overt political intervention in foreign affairs and increased the appeal for Roosevelt of a move such as the Welles proposal: the *grand design* meant he could circumvent accusations from critics of meddling in overseas politics. A proposal that sought to promote respect for international relations would, in the words of Eden, "put obstacles in the way of Hitler and Mussolini by the only method open to Roosevelt."[58] The Welles plan charted a path within the constraints of American public opinion by avoiding damaging political entanglements and thus the criticism that would have followed from the Administration's opponents. That the President of the United States had at his disposal a relative lack of foreign policy tools, and that he had to consider moves that stood little chance of outright success, reflects the nonentangling views of the American people. Eden understood this and later lamented Chamberlain's response to the Administration's proposal, which failed to look at broader aspects of Anglo-American relations. Eden wrote that Chamberlain "did not look beyond the Roosevelt plan itself, which admittedly might have failed, to the beneficial consequences which might have flowed from it, even in failure."[59] This analysis could equally be applied to a number of moves from Washington in the following two years, up to and including the Welles mission.

In sum, then, the Roosevelt Administration's consideration of Welles' plan for a diplomatic conference on international relations in late 1937 and early 1938 illustrates key issues for this analysis of the Welles mission. The dynamism of Welles, the caution of Hull, and the objections Chamberlain raised to reveal the state of Anglo-American relations were all to have a determining influence on the course of Rooseveltian foreign policy during 1938 and 1939, and indeed during the Welles mission itself.

This chapter will now move on to examine the events of 1938 and 1939 in the light of these themes, to provide contextual background to the main focus of this work: the impetus behind, and intentions of, the Welles mission.

The greatest challenge for Rooseveltian foreign policy in the 18 months before war broke out was for the United States to exert any kind of peaceful influence that might prevent full-scale hostilities. The constraint of nonentanglement imposed by the American people meant that Roosevelt had to be almost exclusively reactive when it came to dealing with the aggressors. Where he could be proactive was strictly limited, and the Ingersoll mission of January 1938 and the royal visit in July 1939 illustrate the length to which Roosevelt's foreign policy operated in the margins. These efforts exemplify the extent to which the Administration had to go to circumvent nonentangling opinion. The concern for the views of the American people was evident throughout the period and manifested itself in the events to be discussed in the rest of this chapter.

The Munich crisis of the autumn of 1938 represented the clearest challenge made by Hitler's Germany to the democracies to that point. The role Roosevelt and his Administration played in the resolution of the crisis was minimal and reactive. Yet, in view of the pressures outlined above, this was to be expected.

The Roosevelt Administration's reaction to the consummation of the Anschluss in March 1938 and then the spring crisis over Czechoslovakia had been negligible and provided a guide to the events of the autumn.[60] Jay Pierrepont Moffat, the Chief of the State Department's European Division, acknowledged this: "British reaction to what has been going on is the key to the whole situation and with each day that passes it becomes clear that England is willing to surrender Eastern Europe to German ambitions."[61] To the American people the policies of London and Paris looked like surrender to "peace at any price," with the British and French looking as if they were conspiring with Hitler over the fate of Eastern Europe.

Tensions in Europe continued to mount during the late summer and early autumn of 1938. The Munich crisis that saw Germany absorb the Sudetenland region of Czechoslovakia has given rise to much debate within historical circles; however, its importance here is to reveal the different approaches of those in London and Washington.[62] Chamberlain was at the forefront in preventing any armed conflict in September 1938. His hands-on approach, the famous flights to Germany, and his role in exerting pressure on Czechoslovakia to accept Hitler's demands were crucial in avoiding open conflict. In contrast, the role of Roosevelt was far removed, but his approach illustrates again the pressures of American opinion, the limited diplomatic tools at his disposal, and how in times of crisis Welles came to the fore.

In what was to become common practice for the Roosevelt Administration at times of heightened tension, Roosevelt chose in September 1938 to send diplomatic messages to Europe. On 26 September 1938 messages urging "continued negotiations" were sent to Prague, Berlin, London, and Paris, and the next day messages were addressed to Mussolini and Hitler appealing for peace to prevail.[63] The carefully worded messages represented the limit to which Roosevelt could act to influence events in Europe. They were aimed at least in part at the ongoing education of the American people about the dangers posed by the Axis powers to the United States. Welles was at the forefront of this diplomatic process. He overcame Hull's opposition to the appeal process by arguing that the President of the United States had to make some contribution at such a critical time.[64] As he would do at various instances up to January 1940, Welles took Roosevelt's desire to have some sort of input and presented a practical option that, crucially, did not incur nonentangling criticism. Berle understood the wider purposes of the appeals as he suggested that Roosevelt's messages had "only one chance in a thousand" of influencing European events but would nevertheless help present the stark reality of the situation to the American people.[65] The recurrence of such odds would not preclude Roosevelt from undertaking moves in foreign policy during the period under consideration in this work. The same odds would be quoted in January 1940 in relation to the Welles mission. In September 1938 time would prove Berle's odds to be overly generous. As the fate of peace in Europe was in the hands of Chamberlain and Hitler, those in Washington, as they would do almost a year later in the run-up to war, waited and watched.

The Munich crisis played a minimal role in Anglo-American relations. Although information was passed between the two capitals Chamberlain felt vindicated in his view that "words" were all anyone could expect from Washington at a time when *he* was dealing with the "real" issues. For Roosevelt the episode confirmed, as historian Barbara Farnham has suggested, that Hitler would need to be stopped at some point in the future.[66] Yet the outcome in Europe made Roosevelt's task of illustrating to the American people the distinctions between the democracies and the Axis all the harder.[67]

This sentiment was very much in the mind of the Roosevelt Administration when Hitler's aggressive designs on the whole of Czechoslovakia became clear in March 1939. The German leadership had orchestrated a crisis that facilitated the occupation of Bohemia and Moravia by German troops. The response from London and Paris was to guarantee the independence, as distinct from the territorial integrity, of Poland.[68] Not surprisingly, the response of the Administration in Washington was less decisive and was handled by

Welles. In the immediate aftermath of this act of aggression Roosevelt considered a full break in diplomatic relations with Berlin, but such a dramatic reaction was moderated by Welles. Over the next few days Welles fashioned the American response with clear consideration of the domestic situation. Moffat explained that Welles was fearful "of impeding progress on the reform of the neutrality legislation," which was then being considered in Washington and will be discussed presently.[69] Welles was reluctant to consider a complete severance of relations with Berlin because he believed in the value of maintaining a dialogue of some sort, something that would be evident in the summer of 1940 when he was seeking to pursue Italian neutrality. Welles sought to consider the wider foreign policy implications of any move. He argued that there was more merit in keeping American representation in Berlin than in risking an open diplomatic spat with the Nazis. An open breach with Berlin might see a move toward stricter isolationism among the public and increased difficulties for neutrality revision in Congress. This line convinced Roosevelt, and a few days elapsed before the Administration responded publicly to the passive absorption of Czechoslovakia. Welles composed a low-key statement using typically American language and terminology. It condemned Germany for "the acts which have resulted in the temporary extinguishment of the liberties of a free and independent people."[70] The use of the word "temporary" indicates that Welles did not want to preclude options in conducting relations with Germany. Welles' role here, in both using open language and endeavoring to remove emotion from diplomacy, illustrates how he sought to present policy to Roosevelt that maneuvered around any criticism that the Administration was involving the United States in European matters.[71]

Although Roosevelt had not severed relations with Berlin, Welles' statement was not the only American response to German aggression in the spring of 1939. Roosevelt had learned from the British Embassy that they believed "the absorption of Czechoslovakia has clearly revealed Germany's intentions. It marks the first departure from the Nazi racial theory and there is little reason to suppose that it is not Germany's intention to extend over other countries in Europe, notably Rumania and Poland, a control equivalent to that obtained over Czechoslovakia."[72] To counter this worry Roosevelt wanted to complement Welles' statement of condemnation in a manner that would prevent isolationist criticism. Moffat recorded that Roosevelt's "ideas are running along the line of a message to Hitler and Mussolini asking them if they will guarantee him that their troops will not invade a whole series of neighboring countries."[73] This came to fruition in a presidential appeal for "nonaggression" addressed to Hitler and Mussolini on 14 April. Roosevelt offered the "good offices" of the United States in return for ten-year nonaggression pledges against 31 named countries.[74] The appeal ended in idealist language: "I hope that your answer will make it possible for humanity to lose fear and regain security for many years to come."[75]

Welles was again crucial to formulating Rooseveltian foreign policy. With the legacy of his conference plan evident, the nonaggression appeals hoped to illustrate to the American people Germany and Italy's aggressive intentions and lack of respect for international relations.[76] This was helped somewhat by the dismissive response Hitler gave to the proposition in a speech in the Reichstag late in April. Moffat recorded afterward that "the conception of Germany as merely reuniting scattered Germans under one flag has given way to the idea of empire, power, living room, colonies and wealth."[77] It was this idea the Administration could use to further distinguish the differences between the democracies and the Axis to the American people. Roosevelt explained this to his Treasury Secretary and confidant Henry Morgenthau. Roosevelt was overgenerous in offering odds of "one in five" that the appeal would meet with at least a considered response in Europe, but in the conversation Morgenthau learned of what Roosevelt was aiming at. Morgenthau stated, "[A]nd if they turn it down, then you will know exactly where you are at"; the President responded simply, "[T]hat is my whole point."[78] In this straightforward phrase Roosevelt revealed the Administration's wider motive of continuing to inform the American people by clearly identifying the Dictators with aggressive policy aims and so associating the Allies with a "clear call for liberty."[79] Further, the practice of pursuing policy with an expected outcome based on a negative response from Hitler and Mussolini, and that response serving the Administration's goal, is clear.

The significance of these appeals in April 1939 is in further revealing the character of Rooseveltian foreign policy and Welles' role in implementing it. During the drafting process and once the appeals were made Roosevelt knew the chances of a positive response were minimal, but, as he explained to Morgenthau, this did not prevent its undertaking. Clearly, the presentation of the differences between the Dictators and the democracies to the American people was important for the Administration. The role Welles played in the draft further illustrates how he interpreted Roosevelt's desires and how he operated between Roosevelt and Hull. Hull was unconvinced of the value of the appeal process, as he stated that he "had little confidence" in "the direct appeals to the heads of foreign government," whereas Roosevelt believed the United States had to make some move.[80] Moffat and Berle both noticed how this played out in April 1939. Although "the idea was essentially the President's and the first draft entirely his," Moffat wrote, "the final draft was prepared by Sumner Welles."[81] Berle added that in his own opinion the Under Secretary's final version "immensely improved" on the President's initial draft.[82] Moffat was evidently aware of Hull's disapproving views, as he concluded Welles produced a solution that "very cleverly was halfway between the President's and the Secretary's thesis."[83] Berle was also alert to "the obviously growing tension" between Hull and Welles and concerned that, since "the crisis is forward, and getting worse, there must be no possible shadow which will impair the effectiveness of the Department."[84] The dedication of both men ensured that this did not happen, but the differences in approach were becoming starker. Welles' belief in these appeals reflected his desire to keep policy options open. An appeal might not achieve anything, but it was also unlikely to fatally damage the state of U.S. relations with Rome or Berlin and would again show the values that America stood for without overtly antagonizing isolationist sentiment. The quoting of odds by Roosevelt reflected the feeling that the United States was working in the margins in trying to influence events in Europe, which would again be evident when further appeals to Europe were considered in the final days of peace in the late summer of 1939. In similarly orientated language, Lindsay summed up the value of the April appeals. The Ambassador "thought it was the last trump card and would be a comprehensive and sound guide in the future for all peacefully disposed nations."[85]

The appeals may have appeared to be the last trump card in the spring, when Berle was not alone in thinking "the chance of getting off without a general war is not great," but as the summer progressed and tension rose the Administration again considered what it could do.[86] The answer was to be provided by Welles in both policy and practical terms. In August 1939 Roosevelt left the heat and humidity of Washington, and Hull followed suit. This meant Welles was Acting Secretary of State and in position to coordinate American policy. Berle stated that Welles had been left by Roosevelt "very wide authority indeed to do what was necessary to prepare for neutrality in case of trouble."[87] Welles was proactive in the preparatory task and telegraphed Roosevelt on 17 August requesting authority to begin "informally the steps which should be taken by this Government in the event that war broke out."[88] Welles was again working without recourse to Hull and directly with Roosevelt. The steps Welles took as Acting Secretary involved him overseeing a series of "technical conferences" with other departments. This meant "everything is reasonably well organised in advance but, of course," Moffat recorded, "if war should come there would be hundreds of new situations which have not been foreseen."[89] These meetings amounted to Welles' practical contribution to the preparations for war, but his policy input is entirely more important in understanding the nature of Rooseveltian foreign policy immediately preceding the outbreak of war and its relevance to the Welles mission.

While in charge of the department Welles composed a series of appeals to be addressed to Europe's leaders. The first was sent to the Italian monarch Victor Emmanuel III on 24 August, followed by appeals to Hitler and the Polish President Ignacy Mosicki the day after. The text of the appeals called for restraint, but their impact was utterly negligible as Europe hurtled toward war. This was anticipated by the Administration. The aim of the appeals, like those sent in April, was to illustrate to the American people that the Nazi regime was unreasonable and posed a threat to democratic values. This was clearly understood by those in the State Department. "I don't think that any-one felt there was more than one chance in a thousand that such messages would affect events," Moffat acknowledged, "but it seemed that the chance should be taken and above all that the record should be abundantly clear."[90] It was at this point that Berle remarked that the appeals would resemble a misplaced "valentine," but to reiterate the outlook within the State Department the "one certain thing in this business is that no one will be blamed for making any attempt, however desperate, at preserving peace."[91] This would enable the Administration to illustrate to the American people the lack of respect the Axis powers had for reasonable American initiatives and reveal further their aggressive tendencies. Moffat lamented the problem the Administration faced, after the failed attempts to revise the neutrality legislation (to be dealt with presently). The American people, he recorded, "have heard the cry 'wolf, wolf' so often that they do not appreciate the dangers involved."[92] Instead, with contingency plans in hand, those in Washington were forced to wait for news from Europe as peace expired. "There really is not much for us to do other than wait," Moffat wrote "what trumps we had were long since played."[93]

The impact of this appeal and the Administration's responses to the crises precipitated by the Axis powers in the period between the end of 1937 and September 1939 were marginal to the unleashing of war. Nevertheless, these appeals reveal crucial aspects of Rooseveltian foreign policy in the lead up to the Welles mission. First, Welles' role in influencing the drafting and drive behind these appeals was critical. The Under Secretary understood the severely constricted policy options open to the Administration. Welles also saw how these moves might help in bringing home to the American people the full extent of the dangers the Administration perceived in the aggressive designs of the Axis powers. Welles shared this understanding with Roosevelt, who gave final approval for the appeals to be sent after returning to Washington early from his fishing trip.[94] The second aspect of importance in this process is how these moves were embarked upon by those knowing full well that in its stated goal it was highly unlikely to be successful. Nevertheless, Roosevelt and his State Department felt that these moves should be consid-ered because their *failure* would further illustrate the dangerous state of affairs facing the American people. Accepting that the Administration's efforts would have only minimal chances of success, Berle neatly surmised the underlying motive behind pursuing policies expected to fail: "[T]he President wishes to be sure that he has left no stone unturned to prevent a war."[95] This attitude of seeking to explore every last option to avoid catastrophe would be replicated at the time of the Welles mission.

The impact of this sentiment on Anglo-American relations caused much disquiet in London at the time of the Welles mission, but its prevalence in Administration thinking, alongside Washington's wider consideration of American public opinion, had already caused noteworthy areas of disharmony in Anglo-American relations from the beginning of 1938. The inability of the Administration to revise the neutrality legislation in the summer of 1939 was a considerable disappointment. Yet in other areas, and at the same time, there was an increasing sophistication to the Anglo-American relationship. This was particularly notable within elements of the British Foreign Office, and the conclusion of an Anglo-American trade agreement can be seen at least in part as having resulted in improved relations. The areas of harmony and disharmony will now be considered.

The transatlantic relationship of the latter part of the Second World War has been much vaunted as a "special relationship," but there was little sign of that in the aftermath of Chamberlain's scuppering of the Administration's January 1938 approach.

However, the conclusion of the Anglo-American trade agreement in November 1938 for political rather than explicitly economic reasons is significant in revealing common interests. The trade agreement between London and Washington was signed at the White House on 17 November 1938 and had both obvious economic and more subtle political features to it. In economic terms, compromise was made on both sides, and for the British this meant change to the principle of Imperial Preference.[96] Yet it was the political aspects of the agreement that ensured its conclusion in the aftermath of the Munich crisis in 1938. Sir John Balfour, the Head of the American Desk, was already well aware of this at the beginning of the year. He wrote, "[I]t must always be borne in mind that the commercial advantages of the agreement may be relatively inferior to its political importance."[97] According to Keith Feiling, Chamberlain too was aware of the potential for the accord in two areas: first, it "would help educate American opinion to act more and more with us"; and second, "it would frighten the totalitarians."[98] While this reveals Chamberlain's knowledge of the potential, it also reveals that he wanted to utilize the agreement in support of his own policies. Nevertheless, the agreement between London and Washington had an important symbolic dimension. Lindsay was most aware of this and saw the meaning of the agreement as "being a well-timed gesture of solidarity between the two countries."[99] These words were endorsed by the Foreign Office, who saw the agreement as a commitment "to a continuance of the liberal system." It was the wider commitment that was of particular value to London, the Foreign Office adding that "the U.S. Administration are, through Mr Hull, even more certainly committed to such a system."[100] Thus the signing of the Trade Agreement between the United States and Great Britain at such a moment, despite some technical problems that would ensue, meant they shared a mutual interest in the preservation of at least one aspect of international relations.[101]

Yet the harmony of interests at the agreement's conclusion betrayed a long and hard negotiation process during which differences between London and Washington were evident. Hull's role in overcoming such difficulties requires some examination. As explained previously, Hull was a firm believer in the Reciprocal Trade Agreement program and saw an agreement with Britain as integral to this. Historian Tony McCulloch states that the "initiative in improving [trade] relations came from Washington rather than London and was largely the responsibility of Cordell Hull."[102] Yet it had taken until March 1938 for negotiations with Britain to begin formally and by early autumn Hull was exasperated by the lack of progress. Hull told Lindsay that he was "greatly discouraged [by] the lack of interest of the British Government in [the] broader features and objectives of the program to promote trade and peace . . . but only its very narrowest dollar and cent objectives."[103] Clearly, Hull had a wider agenda than simply that of "dollars and cents." He saw the successful resolution of an Anglo-American trade agreement as an indicator to the American people and the Dictators of shared beliefs between Great Britain and the United States.[104]

Although the focus of this book is on the motivations and objectives of the Welles mission and sees Roosevelt's relationship with Welles as crucial, Hull's place in American foreign policy is well illustrated here. His views on reciprocal trade were widely held in the State Department and in many ways complemented Welles' ideas on international relations. Moffat acknowledged as much in January 1938. "The developments of our trade agreement program," he wrote, "will automatically put economic pressure on Germany and in this we have a ready forged weapon to hand to induce Germany to meet general world trade and political sentiment."[105] Unfortunately this "weapon" would prove unsuccessful in countering Germany in 1938 and 1939. Nevertheless, Hull's dedication to pursuing reciprocal trade represented another of the options open to the Roosevelt Administration without the risk of incurring public rancor. Furthermore, the attitude of reciprocity would be evident in the neutrals' declaration Hull made on the same day Roosevelt announced the Welles mission in February 1940.

The swift conclusion of the agreement after the Munich crisis indicates that the imagery of Anglo-American cooperation was paramount. Such harmony was also evident in the face of increasing tension in the summer of 1939 when a transatlantic barter deal was concluded. In less than eight weeks a deal was completed that saw strategic exchanges of American cotton for

British rubber and tin. The speedy conclusion of the deal illustrates a number of key developments in the transatlantic relationship, at a time when the revision of the neutrality legislation was still in doubt. In complete contrast to the protracted negotiations that had preceded the signing of the Trade Agreement the previous November, the speed with which matters were dealt with reflected the intensified threats Britain was facing and the wider implications the conclusion of such a deal could have. From the outset Lindsay urged London to adopt a "forthcoming attitude" toward the proposal first put forward by American Ambassador to London Joseph Kennedy. Lindsay saw "any serious achievement in this line" as having "[a] useful effect in Congress."[106] This was understood in the Foreign Office, as one official wrote that it would be "clearly desirable" to conclude a deal "with a view to the increase of good will" that may follow.[107] Although the deal eventually covered relatively trivial matters, and was undoubtedly hastened by the increasing likelihood of war, the fact that Britain was prepared to compromise its tangible assets in favor of the influence of American public opinion was an important development and showed that London was becoming increasingly aware of the political pressures under which the Roosevelt Administration operated. The trading of palpable British assets in return for acts of American goodwill and assistance was a process that became vital to the survival of Britain during the war.

The importance of the successful conclusion of the Trade Agreement and then on a lesser scale the barter deal was that in one area of economic relations a harmony of interests was emerging as the crisis deepened. However, there was not wholesale progress, and increasing understanding across the Atlantic would not be sufficiently strong to overcome nonentangling opinion in Congress in the summer of 1939. The resultant failure of the Roosevelt Administration to successfully revise the neutrality legislation would be a blow to Anglo-American relations.

The process of neutrality revision had begun in March 1939 and would represent the limits to which the Administration could operate in the face of nonentangling public opinion in the United States. The dispute between the Administration and its opponents particularly those on Capitol Hill centered on Roosevelt's desire to revise the legislation in favor of allowing presidential discretion, and his opponents worried that this would precipitate involvement in the impending conflict. Hiram Johnson, a key opponent of the revision, went as far as to write that Roosevelt wanted "to knock down two dictators in Europe, so that one may be firmly implanted in America."[108] The debate that then ensued in the spring and summer of 1939, facilitated by the committee-hearing process, was lengthy, heated, and complicated even by Washington standards. Twin drives for revision in both the House and Senate, and the Administration's initial endeavors to take a low profile, meant there was plenty of opportunity for those opposed to revision to make their mark. The end result was failure of the Administration's bills. In June 1939 Johnson wrote to his son that the opponents had "whipped the Administration in the Senate Committee on Foreign Relations upon the Neutrality issue." The outcome of the hearings was "exactly what Roosevelt and Hull did not wish," as the legislation was made to be "impartial and applicable to all alike."[109] This meant the Administration had nowhere left to turn, and with the end of the congressional session approaching, the neutrality legislation was left unrevised and so lacking presidential discretion.

The significance of this episode to Administration foreign policy and Anglo-American relations was not lost on Roosevelt. After the Senate had voted down the Administration's bill he asked Morgenthau to send word to London that the "situation is a legislative tangle" but "we hope it will come out all right."[110] Roosevelt then added with a further gambling reference that he would wager an "old hat" "that Hitler when he wakes up and finds out what has happened, . . . will be rejoicing." Whatever Hitler's response, those in London knew that the Administration's failure meant there would be little assistance in this area coming from Washington as tension increased. Although Lothian later stated that the debate had shown "a wide sympathy with the Allies," he concluded that it also revealed an equally "unanimous determination that the United States must be kept out of war."[111] In short, then, the debate epitomized the dual trends within the American population with the nonentanglement element winning through. This would limit Rooseveltian foreign policy to making nominal appeals for restraint in the late summer of 1939 as war approached. Indeed, the significance of this episode is in illustrating the extent to which Roosevelt's policy options were constrained by nonentangling opinion. Once war broke out the pressure to remain aloof from Europe would remain an important element in Roosevelt's decision making behind the Welles mission.

By the outbreak of war Roosevelt was accustomed to working within the constraints predicated by American public opinion. The Welles mission of February and March 1940 would illustrate succinctly his efforts to work both within and outside these constraints. However, although certain of the Administration's policies, notably the appeals process, were very visible, Roosevelt also employed more oblique methods to further his policy aims. In drawing upon two examples, the Ingersoll mission (January 1938) and the royal visit (July 1939), this study will point to a covert political agenda that Roosevelt was able to deploy.[112] Having a range of objectives for any single policy was very much part of Roosevelt's presidential style, seen in no more stark terms than in my analysis of the impulses and objectives for the Welles mission itself. Less obvious, ulterior motives were often pursued through somewhat obscure channels and with indirect means, but they do represent an important part of the way in which Roosevelt operated. That these channels often involved the appointment of individuals at Roosevelt's discretion allowed him to maintain a close personal hold on his policy and manage the public profile of such moves. The mission of Captain Royal E. Ingersoll should be seen in this light. In late December 1937 Roosevelt was seeking to offer a response to Japanese aggression in mainland China while also encouraging closer Anglo-American relations and all without irking nonentangling sentiment. Roosevelt saw an opportunity to do this in the realm of naval relations in the aftermath of the *Panay* incident. Local Japanese forces, acting without authority, had attacked the *USS Panay* and a British ship, the *HMS Bee*, in the Yangtze River on 12 December 1937. Although the initial reaction of both governments was caution and a pacific settlement emerged with Tokyo, Roosevelt seized upon the occasion to promote some coordination of policy with Great Britain in the Far East.[113] He decided to dispatch Ingersoll, the Navy's Director of Planning and later during the war Commander of the Atlantic Fleet, to London late in 1937.[114]

Anthony Eden, still Foreign Secretary until the disagreement with Chamberlain that would see him resign in February 1938, was delighted at the prospect of Ingersoll's mission. This was because Eden was aware of the potential benefit such an approach could have for the wider Anglo-American relationship. He speculated to Lindsay that "the President was doubtless thinking aloud and feeling his way towards a plan" that if nothing else indicated his "good will." Ingersoll soon arrived in London and, when the first round of conversations began on 1 January 1938, the British sought clarification of the purpose of the talks. Ingersoll stated that Roosevelt believed the time had come to coordinate British and American naval planning in the Far East "more closely."[115] The talks were progressing "very satisfactorily" when Eden cabled Lindsay on 4 January, and he thought it might be feasible to "informally . . . discuss all possibilities."[116] He saw the Ingersoll conversations as an opportunity for communication with a personal representative of Roosevelt that should be taken advantage of, not necessarily for immediate reward but for the sake of future relations. Ingersoll himself was aware of the potential in his mission but was also conscious of not allowing the conversations to stray too far. After Ingersoll's conversation with Lord Chatfield, the First Lord of the Admiralty, on 3 January 1938, Chatfield recorded that Ingersoll felt that their conversation "had ranged further than was really under consideration at the time."[117] This awareness, even for the matters discussed, is indicative of the limits to the mission. An overt political dimension to the discussions could have caused considerable problems in Washington, and so the talks that continued with members of the Foreign Office and the Admiralty until 14 January remained very much on a technical and operational level. The result was "an informal agreement on joint action in the event of war with Japan" and nothing that could have been called a commitment by critics of either party.[118]

Even in the aftermath of the visit, sensitivity surrounding the matters discussed was evident in London. The Foreign Office quizzed Lindsay over the wording of a press release, as they were worried that if they misconstrued the Americans' aims then those in Washington "may get [the] impression that we are trying to belittle what they have been doing for naval co-operation." Significantly, the Foreign Office added, "That is the last thing we should wish to do."[119] This is a noteworthy admission of the consideration of Washington in Foreign Office thinking. Eden concluded that the visit was "interesting," as "much useful work has certainly been done" but realized this was not necessarily in terms of commitments but in terms of establishing a working relationship.[120] Further, the field of naval relations could be presented in national security terms and so was unlikely to draw fire from opponents in either state.[121] That is not to overstate the impact of the Ingersoll mission on the Anglo-American relationship. Nevertheless, it was indicative of Roosevelt's preference for personal diplomacy in circumventing the dangers of direct political channels. The same can be said of Roosevelt's handling of the royal visit in the summer of 1939.

The genesis of the visit of King George VI and his Queen had come almost a year earlier, when Roosevelt learned of the couple's intention to visit Canada. If carefully portrayed as an apolitical visit, Roosevelt saw it as an opportunity to further the understanding of the values he felt the United States and Great Britain shared without risking domestic criticism.

The President was himself the driving force behind securing the first visit of a British sovereign to the United States. In August 1938 Roosevelt wrote to Buckingham Palace, inviting the royal couple to add a stop in the United States to the planned visit to Canada. In doing so he revealed explicitly that in his eyes the visit would have an underlying political aspect: "I think it would be an excellent thing for Anglo-American relations if you could visit the United States." To prevent the royal couple from appearing aloof, Roosevelt intended them to stay at his own house in Hyde Park, New York. The President stressed the benefits of a trip to upstate New York in a second letter to London: "The simplicity and naturalness of such a visit would produce a most excellent effect."[122] The effect that Roosevelt wanted was to encourage a belief in the American people that they shared values with the United Kingdom.

Those in London saw the potential of such a visit. King George VI wrote to the President in the aftermath of Munich agreeing to visit the United States and exhibiting an understanding of the potential political benefits: "I can assure you that the pleasure, which it would in any case give to us personally, would be greatly enhanced by the thought that it was contributing in any way to the cordiality of the relations between our two countries."[123] Lindsay in Washington shared the view that a trip would assist the cause of the Anglo-American relationship: "[N]othing but good could come from it."[124] Both parties then recognized the potential of a royal visit to Washington for furthering the cause of Anglo-American relations.

The care with which Roosevelt orchestrated the visit is evident in the discussion surrounding a potential stop in Chicago as part of the itinerary. Lindsay had considered that it might help the underlying motive of the visit were the royal couple to venture beyond the East Coast. However, Roosevelt was very wary of sending the royal couple to the venue of his Quarantine speech, and home of the Hearst Press with its anti-Roosevelt agenda. He wrote to Buckingham Palace: "I am not in the least bit insistent on it if you decide to forego it." Roosevelt's lack of encouragement for the couple to "go west" reflected his twin desires not to incite any criticism for the visit as being political and to ensure the couple had time to visit Hyde Park.[125] The time in upstate New York was duly scheduled for the last two days of the North American trip. The first two days of four, following the visit to Canada, were to be spent between Washington and New York, where the royal couple would visit the 1939 New York World Fair.

When King George VI and Queen Elizabeth arrived in the United States on 8 June 1939 they received a rapturous welcome from the American public.[126] The visit to Washington caused quite a "hullabaloo," with Moffat noting that "today virtually all work stopped. The visit of the King and Queen was made the occasion of an unofficial but nevertheless complete holiday for the entire city."[127] It was after a busy day at the World Fair that the couple arrived at Roosevelt's house in New York on 10 June 1939. It was here that Roosevelt sought to fulfill the promise of the visit. In two private conversations Roosevelt attempted to impress upon the young King, as he had done with other British citizens he encountered, the need for British preparedness.[128] When King George VI reported to London that Roosevelt had broached the idea of transferring some old destroyers to Britain (a foretelling of what would happen in the summer of 1940), the suggestion was discounted and the King was seen as having been the victim of one of Roosevelt's "grand stories," rather than in receipt of a possible policy.[129] Indeed the inexperienced monarch later felt let down by such remarks from Roosevelt, although they were never intended as a portent of American aid to Britain at that stage. Nevertheless, the visit to Hyde Park did fulfill Roosevelt's desired aim of presenting the royal couple to the American people. Roosevelt's undoubted charm and the ambience of the setting meant the royal party could genuinely relax by the swimming pool in the summer sunshine. According to the British Consul General to New York, reports of this scene "undoubtedly revealed a new and appealing side of royalty to the American public."[130]

Lindsay agreed that a positive impression had been formed by the royal visit. "The truth is that the impression Their Majesties have created," the Ambassador wrote, "has been deep and has extended to the broadest strata of the population of America."[131] Bar those with an opposition agenda, the American press was wholly supportive of the visit. *The New York Times* used extravagant language to sum up the views of many in the aftermath of the trip: "We stand together on fundamentals, whatever our opinions as to transient policies . . . the mass of us, on both sides of the water, stand firm in our longing for a world in which there shall be assurances of peace and in which the spirit of man shall have room to grow toward a creative freedom."[132] Despite this attitude, Lindsay realized that the visit and the enthusiasm for the royal couple themselves would not be realized in political terms, at least in the near future. He wrote that it was far from certain that the visit would "materially influence the minority of the Senate who are opposing the amendments of the neutrality law desired by the Administration."[133] Unfortunately for London, Lindsay was proved right at the beginning of July, as outlined above. Nonetheless, Lindsay's observations succinctly illustrate the dual views of the American people.

The royal visit showed that Britain could not count on any sympathy from the American people translating itself into a weakening of the nonentangling element of American opinion. This was confirmed by Berle, who wrote, "I cannot conceive that any very deep political results will flow." Instead, he observed, "[E]verybody liked the King and Queen and the only broken hearts are those of the large group of people who wished to get a little closer to the King than they did"; nevertheless, crucially, Berle concluded, "[B]ut none of that is important."[134] Senator Borah agreed with Berle as to the prospect of influencing American attitudes: "Their visit, in my opinion, will have in the long run not the slightest effect upon the American people in formulating their judgement upon the great matters which concern the United States."[135] At least in the short term Borah was right, as the failure to revise the neutrality legislation proved.

Although it would come up in conversation when Welles met the royal couple in London in March 1940, the importance of the episode for this tome lies in illustrating the efforts Roosevelt made to circumvent political opposition and to increase understanding within the American people of a harmony of interests with Great Britain. Although Roosevelt might have been disappointed in his desire to see a wider improvement in Anglo-American relations resulting from the visit, the "effect" he was looking for—of producing a cordial and sympathetic effect in the American people—was largely achieved. That the visit did not aid the immediate cause of influencing the revision of the neutrality legislation in the summer of 1939 would have been of little surprise. The visit is important, though, as additional evidence of Roosevelt's investing the Administration's efforts in policy directions where tangible outcomes were unlikely. In other words, the Administration's efforts with regard to the royal visit and the Ingersoll mission represented policy operating in the margins as far as achieving direct outcomes was concerned. This sentiment would be evident in Roosevelt's motivations for the Welles mission in early 1940.

In this work's examination of the Welles mission, this chapter has argued that, during the period from the consideration of Welles' conference plan in the autumn of 1937 to the outbreak of war in Europe in September 1939, four key themes of Rooseveltian foreign policy are evident that have a broader influence on the mission itself.

The first element is the integral role played by Sumner Welles in formulating U.S. foreign policy. At important moments during 1938 and 1939—in January 1938, September 1938, in April, and then again in August 1939—as international tensions rose, it was Welles who was the key player in drafting and implementing the Administration's policies. Anthony Eden later wrote of Welles: "I have known no man in the United States who had a clearer perception than he of the course of international diplomacy in the last years before the Second World War."[136] Welles was able to forward his view because of the unique position he had in Roosevelt's Administration. The Under Secretary, whose background closely mirrored that of the President, had an almost uncanny ability to turn Roosevelt's ideas, of which he had many, into definite policy options. These skills, and Welles' own ambition, meant that he was able to develop Roosevelt's loose instructions and incorporate elements of his own agenda. Having fulfilled this task in Latin America, Welles was in a position in the autumn of 1937 to offer a plan for an Armistice Day conference. After playing a crucial role in 1938 and 1939 Welles had strengthened his standing in interpreting Roosevelt's ideas by the beginning of 1940. The legacy of the content of Welles' Armistice Day conference plan should not be underestimated. Although the link is direct to the reincarnation of the plan in January 1938, it fed indirectly into wider State Department thinking. The appeals for restraint, Hull's work on reciprocal trade, and then the declaration to neutral powers on 9 February 1940 should be seen in this light. In short, then, Sumner Welles was a key influence on American foreign policy both in substance and in being at the right hand of Roosevelt, whereas Hull was able to follow his own policy and counsel caution to his President.

This practice fitted in well with Roosevelt's administrative style. He encouraged subordinates to pursue individual projects to further U.S. interests even if they appeared to have been given the same remit. "Knowing the President fairly well," Berle explained, "I know that anyone who acts in his name is permitted to go right ahead. He never disavows anyone. As matters go along, he will eventually take a stand."[137] Berle's analysis alludes to how Roosevelt, while not concerning himself with the detail, would manage various policy moves and be prepared to act when he thought the time was right. Historian Warren Kimball writes of Roosevelt that "different officials and agencies seemed to have responsibility for the same task and policies" and that this suited Roosevelt because it "often worked to make him the referee and thus concentrate power in the White House."[138] This was crucial for the manner in which foreign policy was made in the Administration, particularly with regard to the way Welles operated, although it also applied to Hull and his pursuit of the reciprocal trade program.

Indeed, it is important to consider the standing of Hull in the Administration, as this is the second theme evident in this period identified in this work. Roosevelt valued his words of caution, and in the case of both the conference plan and the Welles mission they were to some degree heeded. Hull's worries remained constant throughout the period and centered on how any American move in foreign affairs would be viewed, first by the American people, and second by those overseas. The latter worry in itself contained two elements: the reactions of the democracies and those of the dictatorships. Hull knew full well that the United States was not in a position to intervene in any meaningful manner in the escalating hostility in Europe, and felt that U.S. interests would be best served by not venturing into European affairs. He viewed Welles' plans, throughout the period, as likely to antagonize the Axis powers, frustrate the democracies, and confuse the American domestic audience.

American foreign policy was limited in its practical ability to influence events overseas, and this was constantly in the mind of both Welles and Hull. The dual trends in American public opinion predicated careful policy formation by the Administration. The precise handling of the royal visit is one example of how Roosevelt operated under these pressures. Furthermore, Roosevelt's personal influence reveals a broader desire to remove the political pressure of public opinion by keeping a close rein on foreign policy moves. However, these efforts were recognized as being conducted with only the slightest odds of success. Indeed, while Europe headed toward conflict, the policies emanating from the Roosevelt Administration had next to no impact in Europe.

The far from harmonious state of Anglo-American relations is the last area of relevance highlighted in this chapter. Chamberlain exhibited a lack of understanding of the complexity of American opinion and how it informed U.S. foreign policy. In turn this meant cooperation between Prime Minister and President was minimal. Chamberlain's retort to Welles' plan at the beginning of 1938 reflected this. The implicit cooperation and harmony of interests on which the Welles plan was based meant Roosevelt had little choice but to listen to London. It is important to note that at the time of the Welles mission Roosevelt again received a negative response from Chamberlain and that the Prime Minister's objections were to affect the mission's evolution, but in very different circumstances the mission was nevertheless put into operation. The explanation of why Roosevelt pursued the mission will continue to be explored in the following chapters.

However, it is important to remember that Chamberlain was not the only dynamic in the Anglo-American relationship. Other British protagonists, notably those in the Foreign Office, especially Eden before his resignation and Lindsay in Washington, were becoming increasingly sophisticated in their understanding of the ways in which Rooseveltian foreign policy was being made. David Scott of the American Desk at the Foreign Office, in March 1939 accurately surmised the influence that the American people had in determining how Britain appeared in the United States. He wrote, "[A]ny compromise by us with the Dictators over a fundamental principle or moral issue would do this country untold damage in the United States." The crucial implication here is that if Britain were to appear to be in league with the Axis powers, then the Administration had less flexibility in conducting foreign policy. The Foreign Office's Chief Diplomatic Adviser Robert Vansittart expressed how the United Kingdom needed to act to secure American favor: "if we have no more Munich's" British prospects in the United States will be much the stronger. "We really lost the USA over that," he continued, "but if we now make it clear that henceforth we really are going to stand up, we can have much confidence in the attitude of the USA." In a typically dramatic tone he ended, "It is our only chance."[139] Relying upon any aspect of the attitude of the United States was more than Chamberlain was comfortable with. In evaluating the Anglo-American relationship in the two years preceding the outbreak of war, it must remembered that where there was progress; in concluding a Trade Agreement, there was also disappointment in the failure to revise the neutrality legislation in the summer of 1939. The temptation is to look back at these events from the high-water mark of the special relationship during American participation in the Second World War and stress the aspects leaning toward cooperation, but a qualification must be added that the path to any special relationship was fraught and far from straight. The transatlantic relationship can thus be described as one reflecting both a harmony of interests in certain areas and differences in others that were to be exacerbated to the point of "minor crisis" once war broke out.

A closing insight on the force of opinion that the Administration was compelled to address, circumvent, and maneuver around can be seen in the Ludlow Amendment at the end of 1937. So while the Administration was considering a plan for international cooperation, those on Capitol Hill were considering an amendment to the American Constitution that would take the authority to declare war out of the hands of Congress and give it to the people in the form of a referendum. "This episode was a striking indication of the strength of isolationist sentiment in the United States," Hull wrote after the Ludlow Amendment had been defeated by 209 votes to 188. He lamented that "the Administration had to exert its whole force to prevent—barely to prevent—approval of a policy designed to take one of the most vital elements of foreign policy, the authority to declare war, out of the hands of the Government."[140] The extent to which the Roosevelt Administration and its foreign policy were conditioned, if not entirely determined, is clear. At the end of 1937 this was a portent for the moves described in this chapter. The influence it exerted over the role of Sumner Welles, Cordell Hull's cautionary counsel, the "long odds" of Rooseveltian foreign policy moves, and the fluctuating status of Anglo-American relations will be central as this work now considers how Roosevelt's motivations behind the Welles mission emerged during the period from September 1939 to the beginning of 1940.

CHAPTER 2

WAR AND PEACE— ROOSEVELTIAN FOREIGN POLICY AND THE "PHONY WAR": "LIKE SPECTATORS AT A FOOTBALL MATCH"

THE OUTBREAK OF WAR IN EUROPE at the beginning of September 1939 cast a considerable shadow over the Atlantic and onto Roosevelt's foreign policy. How the United States was going to operate in relation to the war naturally became the focus of American foreign policy makers. The war was to be an important influence on the themes already identified in the development of Roosevelt's motivations for what became the Welles mission in early 1940.

This chapter maintains analysis of the key themes that were recognized in the opening of this work. Welles was again at the forefront of various aspects of Administration foreign policy, most notably in Latin America, and Hull's cautious counsel was felt as the Administration pressed for revision of the neutrality legislation and dealt with difficulties in Anglo-American relations and with various "peace moves." Further, the limited nature of American foreign policy, which manifested itself in the practice of making policy liable to have only negligible influence, can be seen in a lack of activity predicated by the neutrality legislation and the wider nonentangling influence of American opinion. Yet typically the neutrality revision had an ulterior motive to furthering American national security, as the provision of cash and carry would clearly benefit the Allies because of their need for armaments and

British naval power. A disposition toward those fighting the Axis, although not openly acknowledged, is hinted at with such a motive. Indeed, one might have suspected that revision would help to further harmonize relations with the United Kingdom. However, other issues in the Anglo-American relationship, such as disputes over the rights of neutrals, ensured that by the end of the year relations between Washington and London were on the verge of a minor crisis.

These four important themes—the individual role of Welles and separately Hull, a limited foreign policy, and Anglo-American relations—were augmented by two further elements worthy of consideration in this work's investigation of the Welles mission. The first was the continuing influence of American public opinion on the Administration's policy deliberations, seen perhaps most markedly in the neutrality revision campaign. The onset of the conflict had little influence on the dual trends evident in American opinion. The levels of interest in events in Europe remained high, but so did the aversion to any involvement. Someone who observed this and who provided a crucial commentary to the ongoing phenomena was the newly appointed British Ambassador to Washington, the eleventh Marquess of Lothian. Appointed because of his belief in the value of closer Anglo-American relations, it was Lothian who wrote that the American people watched the events in Europe in the autumn of 1939 "with all the keenness and intimate knowledge of the personalities and the moves in the diplomatic game characteristic of spectators at a football match."[1] Tellingly, though, Lothian added that once they realized they were not watching "a gigantic football show but a game in which the footballs were immensely destructive bombs," the American people were struck by a "wave of emotional pacifism" that reinforced the desire to remain separated from events in Europe. The importance of stressing this here is that despite the start of the war the Administration still had to frame its policies within these parameters.

The second element that was to be an important consideration for the Administration after war was declared was that the possibility then existed for the conflict to be ended, in other words, the chance to secure a "peace." Opportunity to prevent full-scale fighting seemed to emerge as popular talk of peace proliferated. A number of international businessmen with contacts within the Nazi regime approached Roosevelt to assess whether the United States could "mediate." The importance of these individuals, and of others (such as the King of the Belgians and the Queen of the Netherlands) who propagated "peace moves," lay not in the merits of their moves but in their contributing to a war of nerves that replaced the reality of fighting during the "phony war." Yet these moves prompted consideration by the Administration of the issues at stake, and here Hull's caution against any move that could incur criticism is clearly evident. Nevertheless, the details of various peace moves covered in this chapter are important in illustrating the discussion of "peace" that took place during the hiatus of the "phony war." The link between the conversations that took place in Washington in the autumn of 1939 and the motivations for the Welles mission are not explicit, and thus, require the careful consideration provided in this analysis.

Also brought on by the advent of war was the interest of the Roosevelt Administration, and particularly Welles, in the kind of peace that the world was heading for at the end of the struggle in Europe, whenever that might be. During the first few months of the war a noticeable change took place in Roosevelt's attitude to the possibility of American involvement in any settlement: from total disregard to contemplation on American terms. It was from this environment that the Welles mission was to emerge at the turn of the year, but it is important to acknowledge that as this story unfolds, American national interest was paramount. The Administration wanted to see whether they could ensure that any settlement would serve the interests of the United States. Any sort of victory for Nazi Germany would not do this, and this should be considered when contemplating the Welles mission as an outright peace mission.

This chapter will explore Welles' individual contribution in Latin America before turning to the ways in which the themes outlined above are evident in the course of the campaign for neutrality revision. The chapter will then look at the difficulties that engulfed the Anglo-American relationship before assessing the impact of the peace moves of the autumn of 1939. The importance of this chapter is in illustrating what can be considered the medium-term motivations that were at play, heightened by the onset of war after September 1939, in Roosevelt's thinking behind the Welles mission. This will then lead into chapter 3, where the longer-term themes and immediate motivations meet the objectives for the mission.

In the first few weeks of the war in Europe, Welles fulfilled a key task for the Roosevelt Administration, which was to make good the promise of the "Good Neighbor" policy and ensure for the U.S. security in the Americas. With war declared in Europe Welles pressed for a Pan-American conference to be convened. It had been agreed at the conferences in Buenos Aires (December 1936) and Lima (December 1938) that whenever a threat existed to the continent the nations of the Americas would meet.[2] Under these auspices, 21 republics convened in Panama at the end of September 1939. Welles was at the head of the American delegation, and he had three aims to put forth.[3] The first two were relatively straightforward: an economic plan to help Latin American economies affected by the war and measures to stop Axis subversion. The third, a neutrality zone, was to prove the most controversial not just at the conference but also in Washington and indeed in Europe for a number of months. It was designed to be "a prohibition against belligerent operations within 300 miles of North, Central, or South America or the Caribbean islands."[4] Welles was able to oversee the successful adoption of the zone at the Panama conference because of his skills in dealing with the delegates. However, in Washington the concept of the neutrality zone was questioned by Hull. The Secretary of State's concern was over the legality of such a move and arose against the background of unease in his relationship with Welles. The Under Secretary had been communicating directly with Roosevelt, and Hull was again removed from their conversations. Hull stated later that "the hemispheric neutrality zone was frankly an experiment, the idea of the President, seconded by Welles."[5] That such a plan originated with Roosevelt and was fashioned by Welles fits into the analysis provided here. Further, while practical applicability of the zone was doubtful, its wider purpose was to further differentiate between the Allies and the Axis. Roosevelt hoped that a clear moral difference could be established in the eyes of the American public between the Allies, who would respect the zone, and the Axis, who would not.[6]

However, when it came to respecting the zone or securing operational advantage, none of the belligerents paid much attention to the concept of a neutral zone. The most famous case of "abuse" of the zone came in December 1939, when the German pocket battleship *Graf Spee* was trapped in Montevideo harbor—clearly within the 300 mile zone. (This incident will be discussed later in this chapter with regard to the state of Anglo-American naval relations.) The general lack of respect for the neutrality zone evidently irked Welles, as he mentioned it to Winston Churchill in his final dinner with members of the British government in London in March 1940. His comments at that juncture reveal the wider purposes of such a zone in view of the influence of American opinion. Welles asked Churchill why the British did not publicize their respect for the zone, as they "would lose nothing and gain much from American sentiment."[7] Clearly much had happened in the intervening months between the introduction of the zone and Welles' conversation in London, but the Under Secretary's concern further reveals the importance accorded by Welles and the Administration to the rights of neutrals at times of war. Although this was to feature in the disputes of the "phony war" in the bilateral relationship between Washington and London, the rights Welles was seeking to protect were evident in his address to the delegates in Panama in September 1939. He stated, "[I]t is our common desire to take under consideration the complicated question of our rights and duties as neutrals, in view of the outbreak of general war in Europe, with a view to the preservation of the peace of our respective nations and with a view towards obtaining complete respect on the part of all belligerents for our respective sovereignties." The desire to influence events as a neutral nation was clear and came with some conviction: "Our influence for peace and for the reestablishment of a world order based on morality and on law must be unshaken and secure."[8] Such sentiment reveals how far neutrals' rights, to include respect for international law and liberal economic polices, were part of the Administration's conception of the U.S. national interest. They had been evident in most of the Administration's policies in this period, including Welles' conference plan and, in February 1940, the invitations to other neutral nations to discuss neutral rights.

The significance of this episode in relation to the Welles mission is evident in a number of areas. In completing the promise of the "Good Neighbor" Welles was again able to prove to Roosevelt that he was the man to call on to secure American interests. The personal contact between the two and Welles' familiarity with the area put added distance between Hull and Welles. The Secretary of State was concerned that the neutrality zone would be unenforceable, would be liable to abuse from the belligerents, and therefore would be likely to incite criticism in Washington as a measure that risked the United States' neutral status. This worry again illustrates Hull's concern for the Administration's standing in the domestic arena. However, the latter concern did not really materialize in the aftermath of the zone's introduction, as the Administration spent October 1939 campaigning for revision of the neutrality legislation, and this is where the chapter now turns.

The second campaign for neutrality revision in 1939, following the failed attempt in the summer, was successfully concluded with the restoration of the "cash and carry system" on 3 November. On that day the House of Representatives voted in favor (243 to 181)—following the Senate's (63 to 30) approval on 27 October. The story of neutrality revision sheds further light on some of the wider themes identified in this thesis in terms of the extent to which the Roosevelt Administration had to operate in the light of American opinion and how policies had ulterior purposes. To address both of these elements the Roosevelt Administration argued the case that revising the law would serve to improve U.S. security. Nevertheless, Roosevelt hoped to fulfill an unspoken goal and assist the Allied cause against Nazi Germany. As historian Irwin Gellman has stated, "[S]ince the British controlled the seas, the bill [for cash and carry] was in reality a form of indirect aid."[9] This campaign for neutrality revision was different from that of the summer in a number of ways. Most significantly, the revision campaign was given distinct leadership by the Administration when Roosevelt called for a special session of Congress in September 1939. There he made a bipartisan appeal in which he stressed that American security was his aim. He also challenged those who saw the Administration as warmongering: "[R]egardless of party or section the mantle of peace and of patriotism is wide enough to cover us all. Let no group assume the exclusive label of 'peace bloc.' We all belong to it."[10] Roosevelt knew full well that such language, and a bipartisan approach, would go down well with the American people. However, those ranged against revision were frustrated that the Administration had cornered this line. William Borah wrote, in the midst of the six-week debate in Congress, to his colleague Gerald P. Nye wanting the Administration to "admit that their ulterior motive in wishing to lift the embargo is to help Great Britain."[11] Such an admission was not going to be forthcoming given that the Administration presented revision as securing American interests despite the private acknowledgment that repeal would help the Allies most of all.[12] The important point here is that the Roosevelt Administration was pursuing an ulterior objective and one that assisted the Allies. Lothian's insightful analysis was clearly aware of this at the beginning of November. Having warned London that no one could "prophesy with certainty" as to the outcome of campaign, he reported that the result was "that the United States has decided to place its industrial resources behind the Allies, on the 'cash and carry' basis."[13] This fulfilled Roosevelt's desire to strengthen U.S. security and at the same time to help the Allies. Hiram Johnson, the Californian isolationist Senator and associate of Borah, acknowledged the Administration's success in straightforward terms: "It was a big victory for the President, and there is no question about that."[14] With this triumph for Roosevelt and its implicit assistance to the Allies, one might have supposed that Anglo-American relations would be on a high. However, as before the outbreak of war, different interests and misunderstandings characterized the transatlantic relationship during late 1939 and early 1940.

While the Welles mission itself was of great concern across the Atlantic during the period, other issues also served to add tension to the Anglo-American relationship. One key area of disquiet during the first months of the "phony war" was the question of U.S. neutral rights in the light of the Royal Navy's imposition of a naval blockade in the Atlantic. Most directly, disputes arose not only over the issue of "navicerts," the British system of approval for shipping to pass through the blockade, but also over British trading practices in the United States and censorship of mail. Hull, whose concern for free trade has been outlined previously, was keen to secure American neutral rights at the very outbreak of the war. Mindful also of tensions with Great Britain in this area during the First World War, Hull called Lothian in to see him on 4 September so as to avoid unnecessary "interference by Great Britain with American commerce."[15] Hull's insistence on establishing the American position was based on his awareness of the work the British Ministry of Economic Warfare (MEW) had undertaken during the 1930s. Despite considerable historical debate as to its effectiveness, the MEW had concluded "that economic warfare had contributed significantly to the defeat of Germany in the First World War," so much so that a blockade became "an axiom of British policy."[16] The importance of the blockade to the United

Kingdom was given expression by the Foreign Office as early as 3 September 1939. Cadogan put a need to "manage the naval blockade as effectively as possible, without doing serious harm to relations with the USA" at the top of a list of Foreign Office priorities.[17] This was a clear concern for those in the State Department such as Welles, Berle, and Moffat—"practically all those whom Hull identified as his 'principal associates.'"[18] Their apprehension reflected the unease felt by many Americans about Britain's conduct during the previous war of securing commercial advantage from wartime circumstances.[19] This injustice was not to be allowed to happen again, and American interests were to be defended stoutly. Moffat and his colleagues adopted the phrase "No help to Germany but no Dominion status for ourselves."[20] According to historian Robert Matson, those in the Administration had good reason to suspect the British. He wrote that Britain's reluctance to provide reasons for any refusal to issue a navicert was because it "had every intention of operating a clandestine blacklist under the cover of the navicerts system."[21]

After preparation during September and October, the issuing of navicerts began on 1 November 1939. The State Department's concern that the blockade was "open to considerable abuse" was confirmed almost immediately by Moffat. He learned that the British were "holding up cables to American businessmen just long enough to see that a British company get the contract." He termed the British conduct as "cavalier."[22] The importance for this work of this disquiet is that neutral rights were an important element of wider State Department policy. In both Welles' plan and Hull's economic program, the State Department had a track record, and they were keen to ensure that any conflict did not have too large an adverse impact on the United States. Those in the Administration, notably Hull and Welles, placed considerable stock in protection of neutral rights as a vital interest of the United States. The announcement that the United States had attempted to coordinate neutral opinion made on the same day as the announcement of the Welles mission, and indeed Welles' pursuit of Italian neutrality on his mission, illustrates further the importance of neutrals to the Roosevelt Administration.

Worse was to follow for the fate of Anglo-American relations when the issue of mail censorship compounded the blockade issue as the "phony war" progressed in the autumn of 1939. Indeed, when Welles arrived at Gibraltar the following February they were delayed by three-and-a-half hours, prompting the accompanying Moffat to record that "it was the treatment of the mails that seemed to annoy more deeply than the treatment of passengers or cargo."[23] The British had begun the war by examining limited amounts of mail, but by November they had begun full-scale searches of all American mail. This brought Britain's "imperial" hand directly into the lives of the American public and increased antagonism toward Britain. Of equal concern to the Administration was the fact that the censorship was carried out when the Royal Navy diverted American ships into the area designated by the neutrality legislation as a war zone. (Ships heading for Northern Europe were taken to Kirkwall in Scotland, while ships heading into the Mediterranean were stopped at Gibraltar). Lothian was again aware of this problem.[24] He cabled London at the beginning of January 1940 and stated, "The real American objection to Kirkwall arises from their fear that an American ship might be bombed or mined there with the resultant uproar in America. We should be the sufferers from such an uproar, not the Germans."[25] Clearly, the views of the American people, ever in the mind of the Administration, were crucial here. Hull was keen to emphasize this to Lothian in a meeting on 22 January. Hull explained, "There will soon reach a stage where the advantages of these discriminations and restrictions will be decidedly less than the bad reactionary effects in this country."[26] The "discrimination and restrictions" that Hull mentioned referred not only to American ships, passengers, and mail being diverted to British checkpoints but also to Britain's contravention of the 1938 Anglo-American Trade Agreement. At the beginning of 1940 Britain unilaterally announced that it was moving purchases of certain products away from American suppliers. Most notable of these supplies was the switch from American to Turkish tobacco, in order to save dollar resources and to cultivate a strategic ally. Unsurprisingly, given his belief in reciprocal trade, this move riled Hull. There was therefore considerable cause for acrimony in Anglo-American relations over neutral rights generally and specifically over the issues of the navicerts, mail censorship, and British purchasing. This did not escape the attention of Roosevelt. He wrote to Churchill on 1 February: "I would not be frank unless I told you that there has been much public criticism here," before suggesting, "[T]he general feeling is that the net benefit to your people and to France is hardly worth the definite annoyance caused to us."[27] This succinctly shows how the Administration saw the difficulties in transatlantic relations of January 1940.

The ill feeling in the Administration toward Great Britain drew upon that enmity evident in the American people during the "phony war." The fundamental issue was how far British conduct was affecting American interests and influencing American opinion. Hull concisely summarized the Administration's concerns when asking Lothian if it was necessary to "apply the slogan 'this is necessary to win the war' to a great variety of minor practices which would affect the United States."[28] The reasoning behind this was the impact that British practice was having on the American people. This view was shared by Assistant Secretary of State Breckinridge Long, who recorded in his diary in mid-February that "the sooner the British realize the effect their actions were having on the American people the sooner they could expect better relations with the American Government and better support from the American people."[29] Consideration of American opinion in the Administration should be no surprise, but Hull stressed to Lothian that it was the relatively minor issues such as mail censorship that were most "responsible for irritating expression in this country, and they influence public opinion [on] more major considerations."[30] It was the link between British practices and American opinion that influenced the Administration's ability to conduct its foreign policy, which, as seen in the neutrality revision, was disposed toward the Allies.

Conveying this understanding to those in London would not be easy, but in late January 1940, in the days before he learned of the Welles mission, Lothian's conduct revealed the delicate state of Anglo-American relations and his own belief in the value of the relationship. Lothian composed two key documents, which he sent to his close friend and Foreign Secretary Lord Halifax in London. The first, written on 27 January, made clear reference to the Administration's dissatisfaction with Britain, which he termed a "minor 'crisis' in Anglo-American relations."[31] The reasoning behind American exasperation, Lothian explained, sprang from "the feeling that we have been needlessly inconsiderate of American interests both private and public" and have "been trading upon her [U.S.] good will." Crucially, though, Lothian stressed that the annoyance did not take precedence over the wider sympathy for those facing Nazi Germany: "[T]he recent flare up against us does not mean that either the Administration or public opinion has diminished in the least its strong desire that we should win the war." Lothian concluded that in future Britain would "have to prove to the USA, which includes public opinion as well as the Administration, that any action we take affecting them is really necessary for the winning of the war." In short, then, Lothian suggested that Great Britain should consider American public opinion. He augmented this plea with an extensive document on the subject, entitled simply "US Public Opinion," at the beginning of February 1940. Lothian began with a passage clearly illustrating the importance of the role of the American population: "I say 'public opinion' deliberately because in this country, owing to the constitutional equality of status of the Executive and the Legislative, it is public opinion itself which is continually decisive."[32] Lothian gave his own opinion, which contained some guarded hope for the future and revealed again his belief in the value of solid Anglo-American relations: "Some of the best judges of American opinion are convinced that behind the surface facade of isolationism the people of the United States are slowly making up their minds that if their own future and a free civilisation are to be maintained they have got to intervene. That is my own conviction."[33] Lothian knew this was going to be a lengthy process, but his message did resonate in London: Halifax *red-penned* after reading it, "a very good despatch."[34]

The importance of considering the unease in Anglo-American relations during the "phony war" for this book can be seen in a number of areas. The status of Anglo-American relations is significant, if only in a relatively indirect fashion in this period, in examining Roosevelt's motivations in the lead up to the Welles mission. In simple terms, the outbreak of war did little to alter the Anglo-American relationship; there was sympathy for Britain as it stood up to Nazi Germany but still issues over which disagreements were evident, as there had been before. These differences of opinion culminated in the "minor crisis" in January 1940. The crucial point here is that this was *just* a minor crisis and nothing more. On the eve of the Welles mission Anglo-American relations continued to be fraught in certain areas but were not in a disastrous state. This is clear from the conversation Roosevelt had with Lothian on 1 February 1940. The purpose of the conversation was to inform the Ambassador of his intention to send Welles to Europe, but at its end Roosevelt mentioned the "minor crisis." Lothian reported that Roosevelt felt that "with a few mutual concessions there need be no recurrence of [the] recent little crisis in Anglo-American relations," with the Ambassador adding that the Administration "in no way wanted to impede our war effort."[35] To have remarked on the delicate state of the relationship at the end of such a conversation shows at the very least that the minor crisis was in Roosevelt's mind. Furthermore, his determination to press on with the Welles mission, despite the objections the British would subsequently raise, may well have come from a wider desire to secure American interests in the Anglo-American relationship. Nonetheless, Roosevelt's comment looked to concord in Anglo-American relations. The inference is first that he understood that in the final analysis Britain was at war, and second that the ongoing war effort would not be affected significantly by his proposal for Welles' visit to Europe. The full range of influences that Roosevelt considered for the Welles mission in his conversation with Lothian will be considered in the next chapter.

In other areas, notably Hull's concern for the standing of the Administration and his wider apprehension over American public opinion, a link between the difficulties experienced in Anglo-American relations and the Welles mission can be seen in the prominence given to the rights of neutrals. Given the heritage within the State Department in the principles propounded by Hull and Welles, the fight to secure acceptance of neutral rights was real and hard-fought. The technical issues of the blockade and navicerts were eventually resolved in what Robert Matson has called a "genuine compromise" after an Anglo-French mission held talks in Washington in the spring of 1940.[36] Yet those in London were beginning to understand why the Administration was so insistent on protecting these rights. Sir John Balfour, Head of the American Disk at the Foreign Office, concluded that, in addition to the mission to Washington, Britain needed to encourage "the good grace of powerful sections of American public opinion" because of their influence on the Administration. He added, in a candid admission, because upon such "goodwill we are in the last analysis dependent for victory."[37] The importance for Hull and others in the Administration of not drawing any criticism that they were favoring the Allies can be seen in the State Department's strong line on protecting neutral rights. This explains why neutrality revision was presented as primarily securing American interests. Furthermore, the involvement and views provided by Moffat are notable for their outlook on U.S. relations with Britain because he was to accompany Welles to Europe in February and March 1940. His task in Europe, albeit entirely secondary to that of Welles, was to explain the American view on neutral rights to those in London, and it certainly helped contribute to the work done by the mission in Washington to resolving the matter. This will be discussed in greater detail in chapter 5 during examination of Welles' time in London.

In summation then, the difficult state of Anglo-American relations, recounted in this work since the British dismissal of Welles' plan in January 1938, was not dramatically influenced by the outbreak of conflict in September 1939. Difficulties surrounding neutral rights did develop during the autumn. They caused sufficient disquiet for them to be in Roosevelt's mind at the same time as the Welles mission was being considered, but they were just one aspect of Rooseveltian foreign policy. Any connection between the disharmony in the Anglo-American relationship and the Welles mission remains largely indirect when considered in relation to issues raised by the peace moves of the "phony war" that might have involved possible U.S. intervention—in other words, the prospect of an American-brokered peace. This will now be considered in the period from September 1939 to January 1940. Nonetheless, it is worth emphasizing here that the disquiet of January 1940 was resolved amicably by the early spring, as the Welles mission took center stage and before the spring campaigns fundamentally changed the strategic situation.

Before examining the "peace moves" of the "phony war," and having considered the views of Lothian as Ambassador in Washington, it is worth considering the role played by the American Ambassador in London, Joseph Kennedy.

Having spent the summer of 1939 warning Washington of the destruction the war would bring, after only one week of war Kennedy wrote to Roosevelt imploring him to end the conflict. Kennedy considered that "it is entirely conceivable that the President can get himself in a spot where he can save the world."[38] In even more dramatic terms, he continued that the "situation may crystallize to a point where the President can be the saviour of the World." Kennedy's words alarmed the Administration, and most notably Hull. The Secretary replied insisting that the Administration saw "no opportunity nor occasion for any peace move to be initiated by the President of the United States. The people of the United States would not support any move for peace initiated by this government that would consolidate or make possible a survival of a regime of force and of aggression."[39] The vehemence in Hull's reply reflected his own caution against any American involvement in the European conflict. Nevertheless, it is worth noting that within a little less than five months Roosevelt would see an "opportunity" and the "occasion" to initiate discussion with Welles, of a "peace move," even if the Welles mission that resulted would be significantly qualified. This qualification would be underwritten by Roosevelt's belief throughout the "phony war" and beyond, and in common with Hull's views as expressed to Kennedy, that he did not want to see the "survival of a regime of force and of aggression."[40] Roosevelt was well aware of how far Kennedy's views differed from his own on the future of Europe and the threat posed by the Axis. Roosevelt told Henry Morgenthau, "Joe always has been an appeaser and always will be an appeaser. If Germany or Italy made a good peace offer tomorrow Joe would start working on the King and his friend, the Queen, and from there on down, to get everybody to accept it."[41] Given these views, Kennedy became increasingly marginalized during the autumn of 1939. By the time of his return to the United States in early December on health grounds he was far from being partner to the most intimate communications between London and Washington.[42] His fall from grace was illustrated by Moffat, who noted that "if Kennedy says something is black and Lothian says it is white, we believe Lord Lothian."[43]

All the time while the difficulties in Anglo-American relations were developing in the autumn of 1939, the consequential issue of the possibility of ending the war also existed. The prospect that a suitable basis for a peace settlement might be found was given added credence by the lack of actual fighting and the widespread acceptance that the "phony war" would end in the spring of 1940. It was in this atmosphere that a number of "peace moves" developed during the period, and they require both clarification and examination in relation to Rooseveltian foreign policy. This is important given that the Welles mission is so often considered a peace move in itself. This work considers that it did have at its genesis discussion of a peace settlement before the other objectives were considered. The peace moves themselves varied hugely in their scope, from the clandestine dealings of businessmen with contacts in Berlin, to an approach by the Royal households of the Netherlands and Belgium, to suggestions emanating from Berlin in both public and private that there was no need for the war to continue. To a greater or lesser degree these moves in some way involved Roosevelt as President of the United States.

The peace moves of the autumn of 1939 did have an influence on Roosevelt's thinking at the end of that year about what would become the Welles mission. The President alluded to the influence of some of the "peace moves" in broaching the subject of the Welles mission to Lothian on 1 February. He told the Ambassador that he had determined upon the Welles mission as a result of the peace moves he had been made aware of by "people who had seen Göring," alongside the "inevitability" of the spring offensive, which "would make peace much more difficult to obtain.[44] Therefore, it is possible to state that Roosevelt's consideration of the phony war's peace moves did contribute, together with the broader themes and objectives identified here, to his wider motivations and objectives for the Welles mission. Yet the term "peace move" requires some clarification. It was only their cumulative pressure and not *their* individual merits that came to influence Rooseveltian thinking. One further aspect that should be considered is that the moves considered here were in reality extremely unlikely to avert further conflict between Germany and the Allies. Roosevelt and the Administration knew this and understood that those moves that sought to utilize Roosevelt's position as head of a neutral United States carried huge risks for the Administration of appearing entangled in European affairs.

Therefore this section presents a brief insight into the most important of the "peace moves," so as to provide a full understanding of the environment in which the Welles mission itself was formulated. Key members of the Roosevelt Administration devoted time and energy to these peace moves, and special attention should be paid to a discussion amongst members of the State Department that took place on Sunday, 7 October in response to a speech by Hitler the previous day. It is here that this section begins.

Before moving on, though, it is important to consider that the discussion of peace led indirectly to thinking about what the war was being fought for and then in turn what the Allied war aims were. This had particular implications for the Administration in Washington in terms of illustrating to the American people what the Allies were fighting for, that is, a war to stop the threat posed by fascism and not one over territory in Eastern Europe. The importance of clarifying Allied war aims, albeit as a consequence of discussing peace, should be stressed, given that part of Welles' agenda in London and Paris aimed at assessing this.

A clear insight into Administration thinking on the state of the war and its propensity to consider playing an interventionist role is provided by the discussion that took place after Hitler's speech at the beginning of October 1939. The speech that was translated and broadcast across Europe purported to be a "peace offer" on the basis that neither the Allies nor Germany had anything to gain from continuing the conflict; Poland had already gone, and it would be sensible to resolve any further problems "before millions . . . are uselessly sent to death and billions of wealth destroyed."[45] In essence, then, it meant an acceptance of German domination of Continental Europe. With the Führer's words still fresh in their minds, the attitude of the

United States to peace was discussed by Hull, Moffat, Long, and Berle on Sunday, 7 October. Hull recorded that the purpose of the meeting was to cogitate over "the draft of a possible United States proposal," while Moffat recorded the aim as being to discuss "whether there existed any possibilities of the President offering mediation."[46] Such an agenda, where the United States' role in peace was being considered, was clearly a significant one. The conclusion to the discussion was that "the time was not ripe for mediation" because "nothing should be done that would prejudice . . . the Allies."[47] Nevertheless, it was felt that some preparatory work on "certain broad principles on which ultimate peaceful relationships would have to be built," Moffat wrote, "would at least focus the direction of people's thinking."[48] The propensity to consider all the options is clear. Hull's wider concerns as to an American role were evident as he was prompted to approach Moffat in order to "run over one or two points in the European situation." Moffat recorded that Hull was worried by the "rumours from abroad that the President will be encouraged to mediate," which made him "very fearful" on three counts: any offer of mediation by the President "would (a) not be successful; (b) would prove embarrassing to England and France, and (c) would tend to embroil us in Europe."[49] Hull's concerns are noteworthy here, as they align with those he raised in opposition to Welles' conference plan and would be replicated in his reluctance to support the Welles mission three months later. Prompted by Hull's ongoing anxiety, discussion continued in other quarters of the State Department. Long admitted to having given the matter "a good deal of thought" in the process of drafting "several memoranda . . . directed to the situation," for the President. However, Long left them in "rough" form as there was "no reason to believe that the President should at this time do anything."[50] Berle shared Long's view that the moment was not right "but the time might come and it might come very soon."[51] It is clear, then, that the State Department was considering a possible mediating role that the United States could play.

The discussion in Washington following Hitler's speech is important in illustrating key aspects of the Rooseveltian foreign policy-making process in the autumn of 1939 in the buildup to the Welles mission. First, evident again is Hull's caution over any U.S. involvement and how the American people would perceive this. The second important point is that the position of Great Britain was being considered. At a time when difficulties over neutral rights were emerging in the autumn of 1940 those discussing any settlement were clearly conscious of not wanting to "prejudice" the British position by making them appear as the obstacle to peace. A third aspect relates to the longer-term attitude of the State Department in being prepared to consider a full range of policy options. Here the linkage to preparing policy with its deployment subject to further modification is again evident: the "long shot." Indeed, the preliminary work that Moffat and Long considered here was complementary to both the issues involved in aspects of the Welles mission and in the embryonic postwar planning process that both men were involved with begun in early 1940 under Welles' chairmanship. What these features point to is a community in Washington, beyond solely Roosevelt and Welles, that was discussing the role of the United States in addressing the situation in Europe in the period leading up to the Welles mission.

The Administration's discussion of an American-mediating role throughout the autumn was in some degree prompted by, and subsequently maintained by, a number of "peace moves" that involved the exploits of some businessmen who attempted to encourage Roosevelt to mediate. Characters such as William Rhodes Davis, a businessman who had brokered an oil deal with Nazi Germany, and James D. Mooney, the President of the General Motors Overseas Corporation, made notable efforts to exploit their access to the Administration in Washington and their contacts in Berlin in the cause of "peace."[52] The peace that men such as these sought requires clarification. Their motivations are unclear, as well-meaning intent must be balanced against the realization that the ongoing war was not necessarily helping their business interests. Further, and more significantly for the success of any moves, there was a chance that these men were being "used" by the German authorities to gauge how far Roosevelt was prepared to involved the United States. Berle suggested that the Allies too were prepared to see how far the President would involve himself. "The air is filled with rumours," Berle noted, which he thought were "largely emanating from Berlin and allied sources."[53] What this meant was that it was known that these "peace moves" could be part of a German ploy and therefore were almost wholly discounted as providing any meaningful opportunity to provide a real settlement. Nevertheless, and as was evident in other foreign policy moves, Roosevelt saw a possibility of there being some value in keeping up with these moves as sources of information.

The significance of the exploits of these men for the Welles mission is twofold. In the first place, the exploits of these international businessmen added to the surreal atmosphere of the "phony war" in which peace was being discussed. The second aspect was that Welles, on his visit the following year, would meet with Göring who regularly appeared as the "peacemonger" in these moves. With regard to the case of James Mooney, the lengths the Administration went to in order to disassociate itself from his views in the spring of 1940 reveal that, once the Welles mission was truly under way, Roosevelt was convinced nothing could come from Mooney's efforts. Although discussion of the details of these moves would detract from the focus of this work, an examination of some of the key points can add weight to the analysis presented here.

An important element in the peace moves of the autumn of 1939, of particular relevance to those involving the escapades of the various businessmen, was the role of the Reich Air Marshal Herman Göring. In the rumor and counter-rumor of the peace moves Göring was often seen as likely to replace Hitler as Chancellor, who would in turn move to a purely figurehead position. This tale was relevant because it remained to some degree in the thoughts of those in the State Department. In the case of Davis' exploits in September and October, the businessman claimed that he had seen Göring and that the German wanted to end the war. Although Davis had had an audience with Roosevelt on 15 September and then met Berle once he returned from Europe, the Administration was clearly not impressed with Davis' activities. Berle wrote that Davis had tried to "counter a German intrigue with an intrigue of his own" and endeavored to portray "a set of views which he thought would appeal to Göring." Berle was under no illusions as to Davis' significance: "There is practically nothing in it; and no single statement which Davis has made really stands up under examination."[54] Berle's comments do reveal though that the Administration was aware that those in Berlin were seeking to use the likes of Davis to gauge the U.S. position. Hull too was aware of the activities of Davis and saw potential dangers for the United States. Having learnt from Harrison, the American Consul in Berne, that Göring was apparently ready to accept Davis, he cabled both Berne and Berlin to categorically deny any involvement. Hull wrote, "Davis does not in any way represent either the President or the American Government."[55]

The notion that Göring could be divorced from Hitler and somehow become the presentable face of the Nazi regime was maintained during the "phony war" by the exploits of Davis and others. From Berne, Harrison reported that if "peace might be possible [it] would strengthen the hands of Göring" in contrast to "Ribbentrop's argument that Great Britain and France desire only to crush Germany and do not want peace."[56] Harrison went on to say that he had learned of "the possibility of making [Hitler] a mere figurehead as 'the leader' and turning over the actual control of the government to Göring as Chancellor."[57] Berle returned to the possibility of a division between Göring and Ribbentrop in early December after the outbreak of the Russo-Finnish War.[58] Having surmised that a rift was "by no means improbable," Berle noted, "something curious is happening in Central Europe which I can only guess at." This curiosity arose because Italian planes had gone through Germany en route to Finland to assist in repelling the Russian invaders. Berle continued, with a further reference to Davis, "In endeavouring to explain this, I revert to that fantastic adventurer, W.R. Davis. His intrigues showed a distinct difference between Ribbentrop and Göring. The naval, propaganda and diplomatic machinery are in Ribbentrop's hands and are assisting the Russians. The army and air forces belong to Göring, and Göring is apparently favouring the Finns, in all left-handed ways. Whether this means that the German split on the Russian issue is beginning to appear, I do not know, but it is worth watching."[59] The British were certainly watching the events involving Davis and Göring. The British report confirmed that Davis had access to "high circles in Germany" and concluded that the "State Department regarded the whole thing as a Nazi plot to enlist neutral sympathy for a peace move based on alleged differences between Hitler and Göring."[60] That the State Department did not regard this move as anything more than a plot is clear.

It is important to note that it was not only through third parties that the Administration learned of Göring's peaceful leanings. In November Raymond Geist, the Consul General to Berlin, returned to Washington with a message from the German. Geist told Berle that Göring had called on him before he left Germany and had urged him to "persuade the President to try to make peace on the basis of the status quo."[61] Geist, an experienced diplomat, was frank in his assessment to Berle that there would be no prospect of a settlement, just that the Germans would "take what they have" and go on to build an "ever huger military machine." This raised the probability that the Allies would be overwhelmed and that America "should have to get into it." This was as unappealing a prospect as it was unrealistic for the Administration in the autumn of 1939, given the strength of public opinion against any actual involvement in Europe.

While contending with American opinion and securing revision of the neutrality legislation, Roosevelt was also keen to ascertain a complete picture of the situation in Europe regarding peace. His propensity to let matters develop before acting decisively, his preference for personal diplomacy, and his desire for information from Europe meant he was prepared to tolerate the likes of Davis even if they were "adventurers." In this phase Roosevelt recognized that what the various businessmen proposed stood next to no chance of achieving a peace but by taking on board their views he might learn something. To repeat the sentiment, evident in previous policy considerations: what harm could it do when the die was already cast?

Without seeking an exhaustive examination of the minute details, the case of James D. Mooney is illustrative of Roosevelt's involvement in the development of a peace move. Although Mooney operated without any official endorsement, the fact that Roosevelt met him on a number of occasions during the "phony war" and maintained a correspondence with him at the very least implied he would welcome news of Mooney's exploits. Nevertheless contradictions abound. Although during the spring and summer of 1940, and especially at the time of the Welles mission, the Administration made extensive efforts to disassociate itself from Mooney who even then talked of peace, Roosevelt did not wholly discount him: in 1942 Mooney became Director of Aviation Production in the Navy.[62]

Mooney's peace move began in the autumn of 1939. The businessman, who was effectively "the 'foreign minister' of the vast General Motors industrial empire," and a "veteran Roosevelt supporter with easy access to the White House," held a three-hour meeting with Göring in Berlin on 19 October 1939.[63] According to his friend Louis P. Lochner, during this meeting Mooney was told by Göring to go to the Allies and find out "what this war is all about."[64] Mooney proceeded to Paris and London where he met with Ambassadors Bullitt and Kennedy, before talking to Robert Vansittart at the Foreign Office in London on 26 October 1939. Even before, then, Mooney's proposal at the behest of Göring "for a meeting between British, French and German statesmen on neutral territory with a view to ending the war" was discounted by the Foreign Office.[65] Typically, Hull sought to distance the Administration from any association with such a move. He told Bullitt that he was "quite right in assuming that this government would not instruct you to urge that the French government accept Mooney's proposals. Please inform Kennedy."[66] The British were equally dismissive of the value of the suggestion Mooney brought. Having learned of the detail, Cadogan lamented, "No assurances, no promises, no signatures of the present regime are worth *anything*, Germany must do some *deed* as evidence of good faith" (italics in original).[67] Vansittart concluded that, despite his impression of Mooney as "an honest and reputable man," he "was being 'used' by Field-Marshal Göring."[68] This was the line the State Department had propagated to the British Embassy in Washington: Mooney had "been got at by the Germans and by Field-Marshal Göring in particular." Clearly, then, Mooney's moves were given little credence by Hull and those in the State Department. This was in some contrast to Roosevelt himself, who met Mooney again on 22 December 1939, listening "patiently and attentively" to the General Motors man recount his experiences of the autumn before stressing that he would not move until he thought the time was right.[69] By this stage, as will be explored in this chapter, Roosevelt's ideas were coalescing around the notion that there might be a role that he could play to assist in a peaceful settlement. The difference between Roosevelt and Hull reflected the former's desire not to discount any option and the latter's caution as to the risks. Roosevelt met Mooney again in mid-January 1940. On that occasion he left Mooney with a note stating he would welcome any information Mooney was able to learn, thus revealing that Roosevelt placed at least some value in Mooney's information. Crucially though, Roosevelt did not put himself in a position to be implicated by Mooney should the businessman be shown up to be operating wittingly or otherwise on behalf of the Germans.

The significance of Mooney's mission in the autumn of 1939 is not that he was undoubtedly part of a German "intrigue" but the degree of association Roosevelt had with him despite the State Department's efforts to discredit his efforts. This reflected to varying degrees Roosevelt's consideration of personal diplomacy, his desire for information, and his propensity to consider taking risks—policies with long odds of achieving a positive outcome. Although to differing degrees, these features would all be evident during the Welles mission itself.

Before concluding this chapter, it is worth considering other peace moves of the autumn of 1939. This is because the breadth of these moves illustrates that the issue of peace was very much on Roosevelt's agenda by December 1939 through his individual involvement and that of members of the Administration.

During October 1939 the Administration learned of possible peace moves under way in Belgium. Joseph Davies, the American Ambassador reported that there were "thorough-going efforts" happening in Belgium, "in connection with the German 'peace-offer'" of 8 October. He had learned of the presence of four "prominent and powerful German industrialists" who were "asserting with the greatest confidence that peace is now assured" and were there "making anticipatory business arrangements."[70] Although this merely prompted a reply thanking Davies for his report, the arrival of another tale that purported to be a peace move involving "businessmen" contributed to the discussion of peace in Washington. So too did the Ambassador's report on a three-hour conversation that he had conducted with King Leopold of Belgium. Davies suggested that the monarch thought that "there was still a slender hope for peace, but the only one who could do anything about it was FDR." Roosevelt responded personally and candidly to the King, admitting forlornly that "not a day passes without my trying to see if a favourable opportunity exists for some move that would lead to peace."[71] Clearly, Roosevelt was conscious of any chance that might exist for peace and his role in such a possibility. This became explicit in early November, when Davies reported a peace move initiated by the King of the Belgians and Queen Wilhelmina of the Netherlands. The two monarchs issued a statement saying that "as sovereigns of two neutral states" they were "ready to offer . . . good offices" to the belligerents. To this they added a somewhat desperate statement: "We hope that our offer will be accepted and that thus a first step will be taken towards the establishment of a durable peace."[72] Davies explained the desperation. He wrote to Washington that the two monarchs had learned that "Germany was going to invade Holland on Thursday [and] while there was scant hope that the joint efforts of the two rulers to obtain peace would be effective they nevertheless felt it imperative to make some effort."[73] Clearly in Davies' assessment the two monarchs shared the view of the Administration that the viability of a move did not preclude its undertaking. It would have been of little surprise that the move found little favor in Washington or London, where Chamberlain told Kennedy that "no peace proposal is practical just at this time."[74] Nevertheless, Davies alluded to the possibility that the Germans "were pressing the neutrals to assume active responsibility in pushing a peace offensive if they wish to prevent the horrors of the unrestricted war that otherwise is impending."[75] Although nothing came of the monarchs' appeal, this talk kept the idea that "the neutrals" could have a role to play alive in Washington.

Although Göring was the focal point of a number of the peace moves of the period he was not the only member of the German hierarchy who was associated with peace. Dr. Hjalmar Schacht, the former President of the Reichsbank and Finance Minister, came to the attention of the Roosevelt Administration after a conversation he held with Alexander Kirk, the American Chargé d'Affaires in Berlin.[76] Schacht had told Kirk that he "endorsed the view . . . that mediation by the President might bring about peace and indicated his sympathy with those groups in Germany which were dissatisfied with the present leadership."[77] The Reich Minister proposed that he be invited to the United States under the pretext of giving a public speech, in order to talk with the President. The Administration was not impressed. George S. Messersmith, an Assistant Secretary of State, wrote that both "the Secretary and Under Secretary were in agreement that . . . there could be no official sponsorship even of the most indirect character and that certainly no official contacts, such as [Schacht] had in mind, could be arranged." The fact that Schacht was given such short shrift by Welles is interesting, given that within three months he would meet the Finance Minister in Berlin. Messersmith's final thoughts on Schacht reflected awareness within the State Department that the peace moves may have been emanating from the German government with the aim of unsettling both the neutrals and the Allies. Messersmith concluded that "there was at least reasonable ground to believe, keeping in mind other information we have, that this move of Dr Schacht was a part of the general effort of the German Government to establish contact with other governments through unofficial agents who appeared to be acting entirely independently of the German Government and in fact in some ways in opposition to it."[78] The State Department's view was clearly that the German government was endeavoring to unsettle neutral opinion.

Roosevelt was aware of this sentiment when Welles approached him in early December with news of another peace move that was not associated with the German leadership. This time the overture came from Mr. Paul Van Zeeland, a Belgian who was a "leading spirit in refugee work."[79] The Belgian's proposal built upon a plan he had given to the Administration in June 1937, when he had accompanied the Belgian Prime Minister to the United States. The substance of his proposals was similar to that of the Welles Armistice Day plan of late 1937: an international meeting of those countries with an interest in establishing a lasting peace.[80] Having explained this to Roosevelt,

Welles suggested that the Belgian would "doubtless wish to have some public expression of support" for his idea to be put into operation. "Mr Van Zeeland's plan is on the whole good," Roosevelt's reply began, "but I think misses the *psychology* which is necessary to success" (emphasis in original). The Belgian's proposal, the President explained, would lead to "most people" regarding it as a "large series of small individual projects and would mentally miss out on the conception of the whole." Roosevelt lamented that "somebody has to breathe heart and ideals on a large scale into this whole subject if it is to be put into effect on a world-wide basis."[81] It was becoming more evident that the only person who could "breathe heart and ideals" into a settlement was the President himself. That Roosevelt was aware of a large volume of peace moves during the "phony war" was crucial in creating the atmosphere at the end of 1939 from which he considered instigating an American mission to Europe.

To emphasize the importance of the peace moves of autumn 1939 for the purposes of considering how they contributed to Roosevelt's motivations behind, and objectives for, the Welles mission, one needs to consider a number of factors. First, the sheer number of moves that emerged during the "phony war" meant most importantly that the issue of peace was never far from the agenda of those in the United States. A second crucial factor was the variety of sources from which the moves came, which meant that discounting them en masse was less easy. Although the State Department clearly overlooked those emanating from sources close to the German government, whether other of the peace moves were totally independent of any German intrigue was hard to judge amid the rumor and counter-rumor. Certainly Roosevelt was ready to consider sources of information even if they did carry increased political risk. The slight difference between the State Department and the President is explained by Hull's ever-present concern of the implications of even discussing the American role, as exemplified by the aftermath of the discussion on 8 October and Roosevelt's reluctance to rule anything out completely when faced with the prospect of the spring escalation. Furthermore and despite the considerable risk, Roosevelt did not entirely dissuade the likes of Davis and especially Mooney from appearing to speak on his behalf—he suspected they would anyway. As was the case when Welles endeavored to leave the impression in Berlin the following March that Roosevelt was actively considering making a move in order to prolong the "phony war," the President may have considered it worthwhile for Mooney and others to engage the Germans and try to instill the idea that he might make a move and thus forestall their plans for further aggression. This was certainly in the minds of some in the democracies. French Premier Edouard Daladier delighted in telling Bullitt that he was in receipt of a number of peace feelers emanating from German sources. Bullitt concluded that Daladier "was convinced that his pretence of readiness to consider German proposals had been the main factor in keeping the Germans from attacking this autumn."[82] While this may have merely been delusional on the part of the Frenchman, Roosevelt's actual belief in the value of Mooney's conversations in Berlin was not as important as whether the Germans placed any value on them. Ultimately they did not (the Germans even telling Welles when he arrived in Germany that the businessmen were an annoyance), but given the limited policy options available to Roosevelt the association with Mooney and the other businessmen was something he could entertain. Clearly, the situation in the autumn of 1939 with regard to the peace moves was confused. The variety of the moves stretching back to the first weeks of the war kept discussion of peace and the role the President of the United States could play in the mind of Roosevelt. It was from the mêlée of rumor that Roosevelt's ideas coalesced in December 1939 around the idea that the United States may be able to make a worthwhile contribution.

The latent pressure of the "phony war" placed the President of the United States at the nexus of consideration about how to end the war. With peace moves coming to the Administration's attention on a regular basis, and against a background of minor difficulties in Anglo-American relations and with American opinion inhibiting his options, at the beginning of December Roosevelt began actively to consider how he could address the situation in Europe.

Roosevelt was clearly thinking along the lines of some American involvement in a settlement: in other words, a peace move. He told Berle that he "proposed to make peace next Spring on the basis of having everybody produce everything they could; take what they needed; put the rest into a pool; and let countries which needed the balance draw it as needed, through the cartels." Although it was a "strange" tale, Berle lamented that Roosevelt's plan was "as good a way as any other; the conventional methods seem to be landing us precisely nowhere."[83] This certainly was a fantastic tale, and Berle's words reflected both Roosevelt's inclination for thinking aloud and also the feeling in the State Department, present in the last days of peace, that any American move could hardly make the situation worse.

The President articulated his thoughts on the situation he was facing in more considered terms, at a dinner meeting with Lothian on 13 December. Lothian's report to London contained a precise insight into what Roosevelt thought he might be able to contribute. The Scot, maintaining his propensity for sporting analogies, wrote that Roosevelt "evidently hopes that before his time is up he may be able to intervene as a kind of umpire." The Ambassador was well aware that this would cause alarm in London and qualified his analysis: "He clearly does not want another Wilsonian peace conference. He rather seems to think that if he were appealed to he could lay down conditions for an armistice. He is quite clear however that the time has not yet nearly come for this."[84] This last point of the time being "right" is a crucial one, yet the criteria that would mean the time was right were never clarified by Roosevelt. This was undoubtedly a deliberate ploy to leave the question open and avoid accountability in such a sensitive area, for Roosevelt knew the consequences of openly contemplating American involvement in any settlement.

Yet Roosevelt had begun to stir in terms of what actions he might take. The idea of a personal mission to Europe was seen in his proposal to Pope Pius XII that he should send a representative to the Vatican. The Pope, who had visited the United States in 1936 as Cardinal Pacelli, agreed to receive the President's chosen representative, Myron C. Taylor, the former Head of US Steel.[85] Taylor's mission ultimately proved inconsequential, although he did meet Welles when the latter was in Europe. Nevertheless, Roosevelt welcomed a further source of information from Europe, particularly in relation to Mussolini's position, and did not explicitly seek to discount the idea that he and the Pope might act in the future.

The nature of any peace move or settlement that Roosevelt was considering endorsing, proposing, or even just being associated with is worth clarifying. He told Lothian in their 13 December meeting that the nature of any future world order must be based on four essential freedoms. Although they would be famously championed over a year later in his address to Congress on 6 January 1941, Roosevelt explained the "four freedoms" to Lothian as being made up of the following: "a) freedom of religion; b) freedom for information, that is honest publications of accurate news, but not necessarily for editorial opinion; c) freedom from fear, namely excessive armaments and war, and d) freedom for trade and access to raw materials."[86] Although couched in typically grandiose Rooseveltian language, what these criteria do show is that the President's ideas were incompatible with those of the Axis on any future settlement.

The President's sensitivity to his position with regard to the American people was evident at the end of 1939. During the rest of his conversation with Lothian in mid-December, he lamented the problems he faced. The Ambassador wrote that "one of his greatest difficulties was to make the American people understand the tremendous risks that they themselves were running" and that any attempt to address this would "depend upon the political situation in the United States." In short, then, it is further evidence that the state of American public opinion was constraining Roosevelt's ability to act. The tentative nature of Roosevelt's engagement with the Vatican at the beginning of December should be seen in this light. Roosevelt's awareness of the dilemmas posed by American public opinion can be seen in his annual address to Congress at the beginning of 1940. He stated clearly to the audience on Capitol Hill and to those across the nation that there was "a vast difference between keeping out of war and pretending that it is none of our business."[87] He then went on to state that a peace was in the interests of the United States: the nation would "encourage the kind of peace that will lighten the troubles of the world, and by doing so help our own nation as well." Roosevelt ended by warning his countrymen, and in particular those convinced that the United States could remain aloof from events in Europe, of the danger posed by the Dictators. By using the example of an ostrich that buries its head in the sand, Roosevelt hoped that "we shall have fewer American ostriches in our midst [as] it is not good for the ultimate health of ostriches."

At the beginning of 1940 Roosevelt had no definite strategy for fulfilling any potential role in influencing events in Europe. It was at this juncture that his Under Secretary, alive to the kaleidoscope of different peace moves that kept discussion of peace to the fore, acutely aware of the limits on Administration policy and the wartime circumstances in which the Allies found themselves, came to prominence in devising Rooseveltian policy.

Welles was very much in tune with Roosevelt's thinking at the turn of the year. Ever since his return from Panama, where he had safeguarded hemispheric security, Welles had sought to increase both his knowledge of, and his influence upon, the Administration's policy toward Europe. Given his relationship with Roosevelt and the President's thinking on the possible role he and the United States could play, it was of little surprise that in early January 1940 the two individuals began to discuss the whole raft of issues that surrounded peace moves and a settlement. The first substantial evidence was the convening of a State Department committee to discuss the role of neutrals in postwar planning, with Welles as its chair. When the committee first met on 4 January, Berle recorded that Welles was fully prepared to deal with the issue of peace: "Sumner's mind moved smoothly and cleanly." The Assistant Secretary noted two aims of the committee, with the first clearly bearing the hallmark of Welles' Armistice Day plan of November 1937 and Roosevelt's subsequent proposals of January 1938. Berle recorded that the primary aim of the committee was "a conference of neutrals to be called here to discuss the maintenance of neutral rights"; the secondary and more consequential aim was "incidentally to suggest, if possible, some plan . . . which might be used as a nucleus for peace efforts."[88] This secondary aim implied an element of proactive investigation on behalf of the Administration and became clearer when the committee met again on 11 January. Berle concluded that the Administration was "about decided that the next thing to be done is to call a meeting of neutrals, in theory to discuss methods of maintaining their rights during the war period." Of more importance was the fact that this would lead to a "real and inevitable discussion [of] . . . whether mediation could not be proposed, together with possible peace terms, and with an insistence that the neutrals sit at the peace table with equal right."[89] The admission that a State

Department committee was discussing mediation and peace proposals at the beginning of January 1940 should not be a great surprise, given the discourse that was under way in Washington. Yet the stakes had been raised from the informal Sunday morning discussion in October; a committee had been formed with the State Department's key minds involved. The committee met again on 13 January. Breckinridge Long thought that they were investigating the "possibility of organising the neutrals for a peace movement." The committee "proposed that the President call a meeting of the representatives of groups of powers in Washington and that it be the basis for discussing a program which we would submit."[90] Clearly the heritage of the Welles conference plan was still in the mind of the State Department when addressing the trials of international affairs. Berle acknowledged this, as he considered the committee "an evolution of an idea which Sumner put forward several years ago."[91]

The significance of the committee was that the primary aim of a coming together of neutrals was directly addressed in early February, while the secondary aim of considering mediation and peace proposals was to be considered less directly through the Welles mission. Langer and Gleason neatly sum up the committee's role as the Administration preparing itself "with a positive program if any opportunity presented itself."[92] Welles played a key role in liasing between the committee and a President who was beginning to feel somewhat exasperated that catastrophe was around the corner in the spring while he was unable to influence events. Roosevelt told the Under Secretary in one of the pair's meetings in early January that "no possibility, however remote and however improbable should be overlooked." Most significantly, Roosevelt added, he had an "obligation to the American people . . . to leave no stone unturned."[93] It was at a brief series of unrecorded meetings in early January that the idea of a U.S. mission to Europe was first broached by the President and his close ally, the Under Secretary. Welles' access to the President's inner thoughts, his own views, and ambition put him in a position to illuminate Roosevelt's ideas and influence the outcome of Administration policy. As January progressed Roosevelt and Welles set in motion a mission to Europe, and this will be examined in the next chapter.

With a full appreciation of the limited means at his disposal and the desire to safeguard U.S. national interests, by the very end of 1939 Roosevelt was contemplating ways in which he could influence the European conflict. The prospect of the spring offensives drew ever closer and would certainly be detrimental to American security. In this environment Roosevelt's discussions with Welles at the beginning of January were the genesis of what became the Welles mission.

Before then, though, the themes that this book has identified were clearly at work during the autumn of 1939. Welles' ability to illuminate Roosevelt's line of thinking was critical during this period. Although at the end of 1939 the pair was on the verge of deciding on a mission to Europe, Welles' work in securing hemispheric solidarity should not be discounted. His effort pertaining to South America was vital in securing U.S. national interests within the Western Hemisphere. Clearly he was not at the very forefront of every aspect of Administration policy during the rest of the autumn, but the fact that he again came to the aid of Roosevelt at the turn of the year illustrates his importance in Rooseveltian foreign policy making. Hull too, in other vital areas, was crucial in formulating policy. His ongoing concern for American interests was clear in his caution over the discussion of American involvement in any peace and in protecting the rights of neutrals. This latter interest was long held, given Hull's enduring interest in reciprocal trade.

The unease Hull expressed on neutral rights, the discussion of peace, and the neutrality revision again reflected the inhibited nature of Rooseveltian foreign policy. During the early days of "phony war" the American people's sympathy with the Allies was reinforced as they saw them stand up to Nazi aggression. However, the lack of dramatic incidents as the autumn progressed meant that something approaching boredom set in; it was in the eyes of the American people a *phony war*. Furthermore, the lack of incident meant there was little evidence to support the President's case that there was a distinction between the Allies and Germany; instead it looked as though the war was simply over territory in Eastern Europe. The need to define the differences between the belligerents was prevalent in Roosevelt's thinking throughout the "phony war." It can be seen by his support of the hemispheric neutrality zone. Roosevelt's main achievement during the autumn of 1939 was the revision of the neutrality laws in early November. While this marked a real contribution to the cause of the Allies it was presented to the American people as a measure to help American security.

As had been the case during the previous eighteen months, during the last four months of 1939 the Anglo-American relationship was still fraught. Tension was exhibited most clearly in the dispute over neutral rights, which prompted the Administration to ask the key question of whether British policy was actually doing more harm than good in the eyes of the American people. The abrogation of the Trade Agreement, the inspection of American mail, and the navicerts were issues that brought British intervention into the lives of the American people, and those seeking to distance the United States from the European conflict were not slow to point this out. During the first four months of the war the initiation of the key personal relationship between Churchill and Roosevelt was crucial for its ultimate outcome, but in the short term the relationship between Roosevelt and Lothian would prove vital to ameliorating Anglo-American tensions. Lothian understood the constraints Roosevelt was working under but stressed in his communications to London, despite the difficulties he had to report, that it was the policy of the Administration "to help the Allies to defeat the totalitarians by every means short of war."[94] Lothian knew that this was not because Roosevelt happened to be sympathetic to the British plight but because he reasoned "that the United States would be in deadly peril if the Allies failed" and therefore "as being essential to the future of his own country [he] . . . would go to almost any length to secure the overthrow of Hitler and company." In short, Allied preponderance over Nazi Germany was in U.S. interests.

The intertwined relationship between the strain in Anglo-American relations and the influence of American public opinion was given expression by Roosevelt himself. In direct relation to how Britain could best present its policies to the people of his country, Roosevelt suggested, "[T]he most convincing approach to the American public was to admit the errors of the past" and, at the same time, point "to a change of heart in the present." Lothian understood this as he endeavored to convey to London the need for a clear definition of the British war aims as a measure to assist the President in educating the American people. Yet this would take time. Interestingly, when Chamberlain read of Roosevelt's suggestion for British action, instead of discounting it (as he might have been expected to), he lamented that "errors might only become 'errors' with the passing of time."[95] With Chamberlain's lament in mind, the upcoming Welles mission would reveal that Anglo-American relations still held scope for considerable misunderstanding.

To the mix of themes that illustrate the motivations behind the Welles mission the "phony war" added the prospect of peace. The expected spring escalation that might mean complete catastrophe added a somewhat surreal edge to discussions of a settlement. It was the collective effect of the "peace moves" in terms of both number and variety that meant Roosevelt could not avoid their influence. The variety of sources mitigated against completely discounting the moves, no matter how skeptical those in Washington were of the intent behind them. Nevertheless, Roosevelt himself did not decisively dismiss the notion carried by Mooney and others that he was prepared to listen to the peace moves. In doing this, Roosevelt considered, as Welles would in Europe the following year, that any doubt over the U.S. position might cause pause for thought in the minds of the belligerents. It is clear in retrospect that this was not going to work, but it reflected the unreal atmosphere of the "phony war," Roosevelt's desire for firsthand information and his propensity to consider policy without determined outcomes. In making such an estimation Roosevelt had to consider whether there were those within Germany who were genuinely interested in peace or whether they were merely feeding information to unsettle the Allies and key neutrals. Roosevelt's thinking on peace and any possible settlement evolved as the "phony war" progressed, from his categorical rejection of Kennedy's melodramatic appeals at the start of September, through the State Department's discussion of October and Roosevelt's thinking out loud at the beginning of December, to a point at the end of the year where he was prepared to do something. That he mentioned the various peace moves in the preamble to the Welles mission shows that they had at least a latent influence on his thinking. It is important to consider that at no point in his consideration of the issues surrounding peace did Roosevelt underestimate the seriousness of the situation facing the Allies. He told Davis in September "that the Germans perhaps had not realised the real situation in Europe. The British and the French were not fighting for Poland, primarily; they were fighting in order to have some assurances for the future against continual interruptions of peace."[96] Such a concise statement displays the foundation of Roosevelt's understanding of the issues at stake. Yet discussion of the issue of peace was difficult and risk laden. Vansittart's comments on what Britain's aims might be when considering peace illustrate the difficulties that surrounded the discussion of the whole subject: "[I]f we win, it is bound to be rather a drastic one, [although] it will be at least 1/10 as severe as if the Germans win. In other words, I hope that we shall be less severe and wiser in many respects than at Versailles, but more severe and wiser in others."[97] These sage words show the flux that surrounded discussion of peace.

The position of the Roosevelt Administration as 1939 drew to a close was neatly summarized by Berle. He captured the mood of the President: "My own private opinion is that the President's mind is working towards trying to summon a general peace conference before the beginning of the spring drives. My own mind is leaning in that direction. I agree that it is not ideal. But I do not see that it will be any more ideal, no matter who comes out top dog in the spring and summer fighting. In other words, I do not see that the situation is any worse for making peace now than it will be later."[98] The idea that the "phony war" provided an opportunity in which every possibility should be explored is clear. In short, Roosevelt was motivated, in the light of American public opinion and of a desire to secure U.S. interests, and underwritten by an acceptance of escalation in the spring, to explore the possibilities in Europe: a peace move of sorts. The pressures of the "phony war," the talk of peace, and the need to work within the constraints imposed by the American people provide a context for the President to consider a move in European affairs. From this atmosphere came the Welles mission. Its origins and immediate motivations, alongside the development of the mission's multiple objectives, will be examined in the upcoming chapter.

CHAPTER 3

"Wishing Welles": The Immediate Origins of the Welles Mission, January and February 1940

On the morning of 9 February 1940 Roosevelt informed the assembled pressmen at the 622nd presidential press conference that he had "only one thing of importance" to tell them. He then made public his intention to dispatch Welles to Europe in a press release of just three paragraphs (see appendix 1). Welles' goal for the mission was "solely for the purpose of advising the President and the Secretary of State as to present conditions in Europe."[1] Having read from the statement, Roosevelt declared to the press, "Now do not get didactic. You have to stand on this statement . . . Now that is the whole thing. It is all in one sentence."[2] Reality could hardly have been more different. Instead, Roosevelt, as has been illustrated in this analysis, was influenced by various motivations in considering the Welles mission. This chapter charts how during January and the first week of February 1940 the various factors that Roosevelt was conscious of at the end of 1939 came to bare alongside the objectives that the mission could achieve. This will in turn allow a full assessment of the mission's goals prior to Welles' departure for Europe on 17 February. In short, the mission's objectives by that point had become an exploration of the possibilities for peace, a desire for firsthand information from the protagonists, perpetuating Italian neutrality and the prolonging of the "phony war."

The chapter will begin by looking at the process of drafting the press statement that Roosevelt read out on 9 February. This process clearly reveals the longer-term themes that were involved in Roosevelt's thinking behind the mission: the influence of Welles, the concerns of Hull, the limitations on American foreign policy due to American public opinion, and the state of transatlantic relations. Beside the contending views of Welles and Hull as to what the mission should entail, influence from London was felt in a series of transatlantic exchanges that came to shape the draft and that reveal again the state of the Anglo-American relationship. This episode began on 1 February, when Lothian learned firsthand of the intended mission, and subsequently illustrates Chamberlain's opposition to the whole enterprise. This section highlights key passages of the dialogue that took place and draws out of them the relevant points. Importantly, it was at the meeting on 1 February that Lothian also learned that in Roosevelt's estimation the mission would have only a "one in a thousand" chance of influencing events in Europe. From the outset an acceptance that the mission stood little chance of succeeding was acknowledged as the mission's objectives developed in early 1940.

The chapter will then move on by examining the intentions of Roosevelt and Welles on the eve of Welles' departure for Europe. Their intent was seen in concise form in a series of letters the pair composed. Drafted by Welles on Roosevelt's behalf, these documents addressed to Mussolini, Daladier and Chamberlain explained Welles' mission, and provided a welcome from the President. It is notable that only three were composed. There was no message for Hitler, thus revealing that peace with Hitler's Germany was recognized as a virtual impossibility. In turn, such an omission hints at the existence of the other objectives that the mission had developed.

Assessments of Roosevelt's intentions in the first few weeks of 1940 were clouded still further on 9 February. Hull announced, later in the day, that the United States was approaching over 50 other neutral nations with regard to convening a meeting of neutrals. Though the heritage behind such a move can be seen in the policies forwarded by the State Department, and flowed out of the debate over neutrals' rights prompted by the war, it was left unclear as to how the neutrals' discussions would interact with the Welles mission. This move therefore also necessitates the explanation provided in this chapter.

As soon as Roosevelt had finished his press conference on 9 February, speculation erupted as to the President's *real* purposes. The conjecture was not confined to the press. With no more than Roosevelt's brief statement to go on and with less than 24 hours' notification (unlike the British), governments in Rome, Berlin, and Paris were left to ponder the President's intentions. Unremarkably, given that Roosevelt's announcement was received in both European government and press circles at such short notice, speculation in both groups ran along similar lines. This chapter charts the major areas of conjecture that emerged. These included parallels drawn with the activities of Colonel House and his trips to Europe during the First World War, and notions of the mission being a ploy by Roosevelt to secure a third term. Most importantly, the press and the European governments pondered whether Welles' trip to Europe meant a substantial U.S. "Peace Drive."[3]

That so many questions were raised by the prospect of Welles' mission (and would continue to be raised during its duration) was undoubtedly in Roosevelt's mind as he read from the press statement on 9 February. The ambiguity that surrounded the mission in fact served a purpose for Roosevelt and Welles, in keeping open the possibility that *something* might result from the mission. This fed into Roosevelt's and Welles' intention to prolong the "phony war" and the Administration's wider thinking in accepting "long odds" in pursuing policy.

In essence, then, this chapter is pivotal in tackling the central question considered in this book. It addresses the coming together in the first few weeks of 1940 of the longer-term themes that have been identified thus far. These were all present as Roosevelt, and Welles, put the mission into operation. That multiple motivations and possible objectives can be seen in Roosevelt's wanting to return to the *simplicity* of the mission in his 9 February press conference. His final words reiterated this. Roosevelt suggested, "You had better just stand on that language. That is all there is to say. Using the same old phrase I used before, do not try to break it down by impossible questions. The thing states the actual fact, the whole of the actual fact, and there isn't anything more. That is really the whole thing."[4] This chapter will show that there were "impossible questions," that there was considerably "more," and that this press release was definitely not "the whole thing."

The drafting of the press release poignantly illustrates the various influences on Roosevelt at the beginning of 1940. Two draft versions of the press release can be found in Roosevelt's papers, and they are presented here as appendices 2 and 3. In brief, the evolution from these drafts to the final statement shows that at the outset Roosevelt saw the mission as an opportunity to explore the possibilities for peace. The objections of both the British and Hull are evident as this objective is diluted and the word "peace" removed entirely. Also evident is Welles' influence, in particular in adding Italy to the itinerary. Lastly, the drafts show clearly the emergence of the publicly acknowledged aim of the mission: to advise "the President and Secretary of State as to present conditions in Europe."[5]

An exploration of the drafts in greater depth will now provide an answer to the central question of this work, namely Roosevelt's motivations and objectives for the Welles mission. Every sentence of each draft is vital in ascertaining the evolution in Roosevelt's thinking. Although both drafts are undated, the one with blank spaces and no name is the earlier draft and can be approximately dated to the last week of January, whereas the second draft, which is much closer to the final draft given to the press on 9 February, was drawn up on either 6 or 7 February. In looking at the first draft, its opening sentence illustrates two important things. The first is that the mission was conceived of by Roosevelt himself, with no mention of his Secretary of State. The second feature of the first draft is that Italy is missing from the tour itinerary and the mission was to be solely to the belligerent nations. This further strengthens the argument that at the outset Roosevelt wanted to address the issue of "peace," and this is confirmed in the draft's next sentence. Roosevelt's intention at this initial drafting stage to assist the cause of peace was clear. He wrote that it "will be the purpose of Mr _____'s mission to ascertain whether the governments of those belligerent powers will state for the confidential information of the President the basis upon which they would be prepared to make peace." This sentence is important because it is the one that was modified most between the first draft and the public announcement. The last two sentences in this draft reveal that concern for American public opinion was never far from Roosevelt's thinking, and that he sought to divert potential isolationist criticism by stating that no "proposals" would be made and his representative would merely be "reporting."

In turning to the second draft, its first significant feature is that Roosevelt had settled upon Welles as the man to undertake the mission. This was not entirely preordained. When Roosevelt had broached the idea of sending an emissary, on what he then described as a "fact-finding" mission to Europe, with Myron Taylor in early December, the President "had not decided whether it would be Welles, Berle or a 'businessman.' "[6] That Roosevelt had settled on Welles no doubt reflected the Under Secretary's keenness to undertake the task that will be considered presently. It is also important that, in deciding on Welles over Berle, he was choosing someone at least with Anglophile leanings over a dedicated Anglophobe, and in deciding against a businessman he was choosing to keep the mission official and close to him personally. The second significant development in this draft is the absence of the word "peace." If one reads under the crossing-out one can see that the word "peace" has been removed. The explanation for its removal will be provided when examining the influence of both Hull and the British, but it is worth noting here that, after consultation, Roosevelt was prepared to change the stated purpose of the mission. Further, that he took on board British concerns shows that, in spite of the developing goals of the mission and recent tensions with London, fundamentally Roosevelt did not want to compromise the British position.

The development of Roosevelt's ideas at the end of 1939 toward the design of a mission to Europe meant that the man who was to undertake the trip was able to exert a considerable influence on the formulation of the mission.

By the middle of January 1940, the idea of Under Secretary Sumner Welles undertaking a mission to Europe had been agreed between Welles and Roosevelt.[7]

Welles' influence on the drafts can be seen most clearly in the inclusion of Italy in the mission's final itinerary. This is significant, because Welles was to pursue the Italian neutrality once on the mission and then into the early summer of 1940. The handwritten inclusion of "Italy" in the second draft of the mission statement reveals that Italy was added to the itinerary at a relatively late stage. As Welles was away from the State Department for a few days at the beginning of the last week of January 1940 owing to illness, it is likely that Italy's inclusion came about upon Welles' return. Welles had a number of reasons for wanting to see a visit to Rome on the route of his mission. First of all, he wanted to include another neutral nation in his tour. This revealed a degree of political savvy. He wanted to mitigate any accusation from the Administration's opponents that the mission by solely visiting the belligerents was involving the United States in a European war. In arguing for the inclusion of Italy and subsequently in his pursuit of Italian neutrality, Welles was conscious that encouraging any sort of Italian involvement would remove sole responsibility from the United States. This could provide a "scapegoat," which he could point to, if the political implications of his mission became overly dangerous for the Administration.

This in turn reflected a view within the State Department that Mussolini had played a role in preventing war at the time of Munich and had tried to prevent war from breaking out in September 1939. Berle recorded in his diary only two weeks after the war had broken out that Mussolini might be "sympathetic" to "some neutral nation who might so act . . . as [an] arbitrator."[8] The notion that Welles might be able to encourage Mussolini to act as an "honest broker" would play to the Duce's ego, no doubt, but would also allow the Under Secretary to ascertain the strength of the Axis. Indeed the objective of gathering information on the state of affairs in Europe was perhaps strongest in Rome, as Ambassador Phillips had not seen Mussolini for a number of months. Welles was at the very least intrigued to learn in his initial conversations in Rome of Ciano's dislike of Ribbentrop and Mussolini's claim that he retained full liberty of action in the Axis. Indeed, the aim of exploring any division within the Axis was certainly something the German Foreign Office considered as a possible motivation for the mission, and this will be discussed in due course. In pursuing such a line Welles considered that any division between Italy and Germany would help limit the scope of the war and might assist the Allies.

Lastly, it is worth considering that Welles knew, given the belligerent status of the other countries he would visit, that adding Italy provided him with a greater opportunity to be able to produce a "positive" outcome from the mission, even if this was only a postponement of Italy's decision to enter the war. The prominence Welles gave to Italy in his final report and the efforts he went to in the spring betrayed a need to justify Italy's inclusion. Berle concluded once Welles had returned to Washington that "[t]he Italian position at the moment was determinative."[9] Again, although this may seem a grand claim, Berle knew full well that it was extremely unlikely to produce anything. His attitude, as it had been the previous September with regard to the last-ditch appeals, revealed this: "Fortunately, there is always liberty to dream, even if the result is nothing but dreams."[10] From Welles' own perspective then, and in keeping with the "neutrals' declaration," and with the heritage of Welles' own conference plan, Welles saw Italy as an opportunity to explore whether or not a neutral opinion could be mustered and exert an influence.

The wider strategic importance of Italy in relation to the war was also an important element for Welles. Benjamin Welles emphasizes this as he argues that Sumner Welles "won" Italian "inclusion" by stressing "the importance of Italian neutrality to Anglo-French control of the eastern Mediterranean."[11] In this area Welles was actually in line with British thinking. The Chamberlain government well understood the significance of Italian neutrality. In assessing Britain's position, in the weeks after war had broken out, Cadogan was pleased that, contrary to the fears of British strategic planners, who had seen war with either Germany *or* Italy *or* Japan as a precursor to war with them all, they were *only* facing Germany. In this sense, Italian neutrality was worth pursuing in order to "hold the Mediterranean open for Middle Eastern and Imperial reasons."[12] An article by Robert Mallet discusses the full range of efforts undertaken by the British to keep Italy neutral, including supplying oil to Rome, until Mussolini declared war on 10 June 1940.[13]

To return to early 1940 and Welles' influence on the formulation of an American mission to Europe: Welles' opportunity to affect the mission by including Italy is also explained by his close association with the President. As argued previously in this analysis, Welles had an almost intuitive understanding of what Roosevelt wanted to do. Roosevelt well knew that Welles' character made him suitable to undertake a mission that carried with it considerable political risks for the Administration. Welles was described by Harold Ickes, the Secretary of the Interior, as "a man of almost preternatural solemnity and great dignity. If he ever smiles, it has not been in my presence. He conducts himself with portentous gravity and as if he were charged with all the responsibilities of Atlas. Just to look at him one can tell that the world would dissolve into its component parts if only a portion of the weighty secrets of state that he carries about with him were divulged."[14] Welles' grave disposition and lack of emotion meant that Roosevelt had every confidence that his Under Secretary would not become a "football" to be kicked about by Europe's leaders.

Welles' own ambition to orchestrate Administration policy should not be ignored. While paying little more than lip service to his direct superior, Hull, Welles had become the State Department's expert on Latin American affairs. Gellman argues that as tensions rose in Europe Welles sought to extend his remit in that direction as well. "Already acknowledged as the department's Latin American expert, Welles intended to wear the same badge for European matters."[15] Despite his capacity for reticence in public, Welles was certainly keen to take on Roosevelt's plan for a mission to Europe. Ickes attributed the mission to Welles' personal ambition: "My guess was that the proposal emanated from Welles, who saw an opportunity to step out more towards the center of the stage."[16] Hull certainly saw it that way. He wrote later in his memoirs that "the President expressly stated to me that Welles had come to him secretly on several occasions and pleaded to be sent abroad on special missions. For this reason I feel satisfied that Welles had requested the President to send him on the trip in 1940."[17] Historian Arnold Offner agreed. He suggests that "Welles doubtless inspired his mission," based on his record of interpreting Roosevelt's ideas during his tenure as Under Secretary.[18]

On a practical level, Welles' influence in the last week before the public announcement was reduced owing to a brief bout of illness.[19] Nevertheless, Welles did meet with Lothian after the Ambassador had learned of the mission from Roosevelt on 1 February. The Ambassador wrote to Halifax on 2 February that Welles had said "that if [the] 100 to one chance of obtaining agreement did not come off he thought [the] only statement which [the] President could make would be that he regretted no agreement was in sight."[20] This would lay the blame for continuing the war on Germany and not with the British. Significantly, Welles' words allude to the multiple aims that he and Roosevelt saw in examining the "possibilities" for an agreement. While it is clear that an "agreement" for exploring possible peace terms was an objective for the mission, it is also clear that Welles thought the chances of obtaining satisfactory terms was extremely slim. Yet the Under Secretary saw a positive corollary, in allowing the Roosevelt Administration to elucidate to the American people the distinction between the British and the Germans, alongside the firsthand information he would gather.

Further, the manner in which Roosevelt and Welles communicated when Welles was in Europe served to concentrate his personal influence on policy making. That Welles would communicate with Roosevelt directly, without recourse to Hull, had become standard practice when Welles was in Latin America. It was not surprising for Berle to learn therefore that during the Under Secretary's mission, "Welles is reporting in cipher to the President; and the Secretary does not have the cipher; he learns what the President tells him."[21] In short, then, Welles' influence on the mission at this stage in its formulation was crucial. In terms of influencing the objectives for the mission, he successfully argued for the inclusion of Italy as a result of his relationship with Roosevelt. Welles' *The Time for Decision* stresses how it was he and Roosevelt who were the "directors" of foreign policy.[22] The Welles mission was a case in point. Yet Welles would not be the sole influence that would shape Roosevelt's concept of a mission to Europe in January and early February 1940.

Cordell Hull's impact on the Welles mission in early 1940 was minimal but at the same time significant. Although the publicly stated purpose of the mission was to inform the "President and the Secretary of State," it was only in the latter stages of the mission's formulation that Hull learned of Roosevelt's intention. Hull later recalled that Roosevelt asked him whether a mission "would be agreeable . . . in early February."[23] This is telling, given that the mission had already been under consideration by Roosevelt and Welles since early January. Some scholars have argued that Hull had no "inkling" at all prior to the announcement of the mission, but this seems incredibly unlikely given that Lothian learned of Hull's "doubts" and reported them to London on 6 February.[24] (This also helps date the second draft of the press release.) Whenever Hull did learn of the mission, it seems that he was presented with a fait accompli. Hull's memoirs confirm this: "[T]he President merely inquired of me whether I had any objection to Welles's going on the mission." Although Hull had "no objections" he did have "a few observations" for Roosevelt "if he really wished Welles to make the trip." Hull stated that the United States had "exerted all possible efforts, within the limits of isolationist opposition, to promote peace." Therefore the prospect of a "peace" mission would give false hope to those facing attack and encourage the aggressors in the war of nerves. Hull then supposed that "five hundred different rumours would inevitably arise as to the purpose and results of Welles's trip. These would create confusion in Europe and here at home." It is worth remembering at this stage how far these objections married up to Hull's concerns over Welles' Armistice Day plan of November 1937. In both instances Hull was worried that the move would serve only to give a false sense of security to the democracies and destabilize American opinion, neither of which Hull wanted to see. Hull's consideration of the domestic constituency shows how far he was liable to consider the influence of the American public, and Roosevelt knew this.

While Hull had been totally marginalized in the initial discussions behind the Welles mission in January, he did exert a notable if limited influence in early February. This can be seen in microcosm in the inclusion in the second draft of the press release of the word "commitments." Hull wrote in his memoirs that it was his influence that prompted the added insertion: "Mr Roosevelt, having in mind the comments I had made to him, emphasised that Welles was not authorised to make proposals or *commitments* in the name of the United States Government" (italics in original).[25] This reflected Hull's long-standing concern that the Administration should not appear to be in league with European powers in the eyes of the American people and Congress. Furthermore, Hull's anxiety over how far an explicit "peace" mission would upset the Allies fell in line with the objections the British would raise. These are to be discussed presently, but for Roosevelt to receive similar objections from both his Secretary of State and the British government could only have added to their impact on the eventual shape of the mission.

Herbert Feis, the State Department's Economic Adviser, commented in the spring of 1940 on how he saw Hull's influence in the State Department at this stage. He told Henry Stimson, the soon-to-be War Secretary, that the mission had "originated from the President and Welles" and that "Hull was not sufficiently in control of his subordinates and was devoting himself to specialities like the passage of the reciprocity legislation."[26] Feis concluded that "the Department was a little out of hand." Although this was a harsh assessment, it was in such an environment that Welles was able to operate independently of his superior. The differences between the two were clearly revealed in the Welles mission. Hull's memoirs state clearly how he felt about the mission: "I myself would not have considered sending Welles or anyone else of his official position to Europe on such a mission at that stage in the war."[27] Such sentiment was shared by the Chamberlain government in London. Having looked at the influence of both Welles and Hull on the formation of the mission, this analysis now turns to the influence Chamberlain exerted on the mission in early February 1940.

The Chamberlain government had a significant impact on the thinking of both Roosevelt and Welles in the week prior to the public announcement of the mission. As soon as those in London learned of the mission, following the meeting between Roosevelt and Lothian on 1 February, they sought to dissuade Roosevelt from pursuing it. The exchange of telegrams that flowed between London and Washington reveals much about the President's intentions for the mission and in particular his fluid approach to policy making. The ultimate effect of British objections, as with the influence of both Welles and Hull, can be seen in part in the press release that Roosevelt read from on 9 February. Chamberlain's protestations served to notably dilute the objective of exploring possibilities of peace.

Those in London first learnt of Roosevelt's intention to dispatch Welles to Europe after receiving a telegram from Lothian (No. 142), sent on 1 February 1940.[28] The meeting with Roosevelt that day began with the President alluding to the "peace" moves he had been made aware of by "people who had seen Göring" during the "phony war" and then turned to the "inevitability" of a spring offensive. Roosevelt explained that the escalation of the war "would

make peace much more difficult to obtain." The underlying influence of the
various peace moves of the "phony war" was clear to see in the President's
desire "to do something" in the early part of 1940, as was Roosevelt's objective at the outset to consider peace. Roosevelt confirmed his intention to
involve the United States in a possible peace move when he explained his
motivation to Lothian. He told the Ambassador that "in order to satisfy himself and public opinion here that every possibility of ending the war had been
[exhausted] he and [the] Secretary of State had decided to send Sumner
Welles to Europe." He then went on to state that Welles' objective would be
"solely to advise the President and the Secretary of State whether there was
any possibility of ending the war in the near future." These two statements
reveal in simple form Roosevelt's motivation and what he saw at this stage as
the mission's objective. That the latter subsequently changed should be of no
surprise, given Roosevelt's tendency to accept unfixed outcomes in his policy
making. Indeed, the desire to make sure every option had been explored to
avoid the war escalating is clear.

Had Roosevelt left the mission statement in such stark terms, then the
case for the Welles trip being solely a peace mission would be strong.
However, he immediately began to qualify the objective of the mission and so
inaugurated a process that would continue throughout the mission. First of
all, he stated that Welles would be "authorised to make no proposal . . . in
[the] name of United States and would report on his return solely to [the]
President and Secretary of State." Such a qualification indicated an awareness
of the political ramifications of such a move, as did Roosevelt's next comment
that the Welles mission "would be a public mission and not a private one like
Colonel House's." The allusion to Colonel House, who had been President
Wilson's roving eye during the First World War, was a line of speculation that
arose after the Welles mission was made public and will be discussed in
greater depth later in this chapter. Yet for Roosevelt to mention it at this stage
illustrates that he was conscious of the concerns that could influence Welles'
mission.

Lothian was certainly aware that the mission would arouse concerns in
London. The content of his telegram (No. 142) to London, beyond a
description of what Roosevelt had told him, reflected his desire to mitigate
unease in London. His first words in response to Roosevelt had already illustrated this clearly. Lothian wrote that the Welles mission would "produce a
profound effect in Europe of mingled hope and anxiety." Lothian then
pressed Roosevelt on what "possible basis" the mission could lead to peace.
Roosevelt countered that in his view any settlement "must include restoration
of freedom to Czechoslovakia and [the] Poles in some real form and guarantees that there would be no renewal of aggression during any of our life-times."
Such a statement allowed Lothian to conclude his telegram by stating that

Roosevelt's "ideas about peace were practically the same as ours." Nevertheless, Lothian's words would prove insufficient to placate British concerns.

Before turning to British unease and its subsequent influence on the mission's objectives, one can see further evidence of Roosevelt's propensity to consider policy on the basis of long odds. Lothian recorded from his conversation that Roosevelt foresaw many difficulties ahead for the mission and was therefore "not hopeful of [the] Under Secretary of State being able to find any basis of agreement which he or the Allies could accept." He acknowledged the likelihood as being "one chance in a thousand." Roosevelt then conceded that even in such a situation something could be achieved. He told Lothian that in such a scenario he would be able to "issue a statement . . . making it clear that Germany was the obstacle to peace and that Germans were being made to fight not for the security and integrity of their own country but for aggression." The audience for such a statement would be the American people, and Roosevelt's awareness of their importance to his foreign policy is clear.[29] Such a view of American public opinion also explains why Welles pressed those he spoke to for "peace terms" even when it was nonsensical to do so in terms of achieving a peace settlement. Nevertheless, it would enable him to clearly identify the different war and peace aims of the belligerents.

The first vestiges of influence that London exerted were seen in the initial response of the Chamberlain government to the prospect of the Welles mission. The arrival of Lothian's telegram telling of the mission caused a sensation in London. Cadogan's initial reaction was scathing; he called it an "awful, half-baked idea" and saw the mission as Welles coming "over here with a flourish of trumpets to collect data on which Roosevelt is to proclaim [the] basis of peace!"[30] The British response, in which Chamberlain himself was heavily involved, was a four-page seventeen-point refutation of Roosevelt's proposal. That it was sent within twenty-four hours of receiving Lothian's telegram (No. 142) illustrates the gravity of the concerns Chamberlain had. In simple terms, the British did not welcome the idea of Roosevelt intervening in Europe and specifically objected to the prospect of a publicly declared "peace mission." It is this reply that *The Foreign Relations of the United States* was unable to date when the volume was published in 1959.[31] The research undertaken for this volume has enabled a definite date of 3 February 1940 to be identified.[32]

The British reply, intended for Roosevelt himself, began in a diplomatic tone but, despite "appreciation" of Roosevelt's "motives," concerns dominated the telegram. This reveals a number of reasons why the proposed mission received a poor reception in London. The British objections began with the observation that the peace feelers that were coming out of Germany, and at the same time the "inevitability" of the spring offensive, were all part of the German propaganda campaign. The issues surrounding the discussion of peace that the Administration had been forced to consider during the autumn of 1939 were at the forefront of British minds in early February 1940. Chamberlain stated that it "must be realised that this war of nerves is directed not only against the belligerents but also against the neutrals." The concern of the British in this was that it might be "precisely the policy of the German Government to produce [the] impression . . . [that] they can mobilise world public opinion against the Allies who would be represented as being the sole obstacle to peace." This was the essence of Chamberlain's disquiet. He wrote, "I must frankly admit to a good deal of anxiety lest the effect of this move however carefully presented should be to cause embarrassment to the democracies from which Germany, still unconvinced of the failure of [the] policy of force, will reap advantage." It is worth noting here the similarity of such an objection to Chamberlain's response to Roosevelt's January 1938 plan for a diplomatic conference. In both instances he was apprehensive as to how Roosevelt's move would affect the British position in relation to Germany. Although the circumstances were very different, Chamberlain still saw the influence of the United States as only likely to complicate and frustrate his own policy. Chamberlain maintained this outlook in the rest of the telegram in February 1940. He quoted Roosevelt's phrase that any settlement "must include 'guarantees that there would be no renewal of aggression during any of our life-times' [as] the kernel of the difficulty." Chamberlain, mindful of his and the British people's experience of attempting to negotiate with Hitler, saw the "utmost difficulty in persuading people of this country" of the value of signing "*any* settlement . . . with Hitler or [the] present regime" (italics is in the original). The British response then poured further discouragement on the idea by highlighting the worldwide impact such a move would have, especially were its aim to be wholly disclosed: "The announcement of [the] mission of Mr Welles will of course produce a sensational impression throughout the world more particularly if it makes public [the] full purpose of this initiative." It is interesting to note that the British saw something of a distinction between the public and private goals of the mission. It is clear from Roosevelt's comments with regard to House that at this stage he wanted the mission to have a clear public profile. Nevertheless, a gap was to emerge between the public and private goals as was seen in the drafting of the private letters to three of the four leaders who Welles was to meet during the week before his departure. In fact the distance between public and private objectives for the mission would become another source of anxiety for the British government as Welles traveled toward London.

The overwhelmingly negative aura of the British telegram was compounded by Chamberlain's concluding remarks: "I earnestly hope that he will consider very seriously [the] possible side effects of a public announcement of [the] purpose of Mr Welles' mission." Clearly, Chamberlain did not want Roosevelt to pursue the mission.

Despite the swift reply by Chamberlain to Lothian it was not until the morning of 6 February that the Ambassador met Roosevelt. Lothian handed Roosevelt Chamberlain's response (No. 172) and waited until the President had finished reading. According to Lothian, Roosevelt's reaction, tempered by an overall disappointment, was an "appreciation" of Chamberlain's views "and general agreement."[33] That such an unfavorable response to his plan from those in London drew such a low-key response reflected in part the discussions Roosevelt had conducted with Hull in the intervening period. Hull had forewarned of doubts from the democracies, particularly along the lines Chamberlain highlighted.

Having heard Roosevelt's initial response, Lothian sought to assuage Roosevelt's disappointment. In keeping with the informal and friendly atmosphere that characterized relations between the pair, Lothian chose to disclose to Roosevelt the contents of a second document from London. The document (No. 173) was intended to provide Lothian with background information on the British view of "the President's new move."[34] Although it largely repeated the lines Chamberlain had composed (No. 172) in terms of establishing the British belief that the various "peace feelers" of the "phony war" had just been part of the "German war of nerves," it went on to stress the potential damage London foresaw in a public announcement of a peace mission. Lothian explained that the British had "for some time past been expecting a peace move to come either from the Italian Government, the Pope or from the President, though we had not foreseen that it would be so spectacular as a public mission from Washington, the object of which would be fully advertised in advance."[35] Clearly, to reveal such a passage was a sensitive tactic for Lothian. Nevertheless, it did achieve the response that many in London would have hoped for. Roosevelt understood the British objections as being primarily concerned with the public outlook of the mission. In essence, the British did not want the mission to be publicly acknowledged by the President of the United States as one of peace. Roosevelt told Lothian he was prepared to compromise on the publicly stated aim. Lothian reported "that in any published instructions to Welles [Roosevelt] would probably avoid use of the word 'peace' and simply send him on a tour of enquiry." From Roosevelt's point of view, in direct regard of the state of Anglo-American relations, the British were sufficiently important to discuss the mission with and then to take on board their views. Nevertheless, Roosevelt made it plain to Lothian that he was "clearly in favour of proceeding" with the mission.[36]

Lothian's reporting of this to London on 6 February helps further in dating the second draft of the mission's press release as being after 6 February, because the second draft sees the removal of the word "peace." Although David Reynolds does not attribute any date to this, he agrees that it was the influence of Chamberlain's disapproving telegrams (No. 172 and No. 173) that prompted this change: "Chamberlain's two messages obliged Roosevelt to couch his initiative in more cautious language, and he agreed to avoid the words 'peace' or 'peace initiatives.'"[37]

Also evident in Roosevelt's acceptance of British objections is the fact that the mission the President had initially envisaged at the turn of the year had already evolved. The objective of the mission, in public at least, would effectively be fact-finding. This change was a significant one, given Roosevelt's initial intention for the mission. Further, Roosevelt reveals again his capacity to incorporate the views of others into policy-making. This in turn illustrates that the mission was not inaugurated with fixed goals in mind. As had been the case with both Welles and Hull, the scope of the mission had been altered: in this instance thanks to British influence.

Yet in all Roosevelt's thinking on Welles' mission the influence of American opinion was never far from the surface. This became clear again as his meeting with Lothian drew to a close on 6 February. The Ambassador asked whether he "could make a purely private and personal comment" on the situation. In recognition of Roosevelt's potential influence he prefaced his comments with the observation that "the situation was one in which a little audacity might have tremendous results." Lothian went on that "it was clear to everyone that the United States could not afford to see Great Britain or France destroyed without grievous damage to its own national culture and interests. Was it not possible therefore for Mr Welles to make this fact plain to the German and Italian Governments?" Under such circumstances, then, "it might be worthwhile for the United States to make a proposal for ending the war." Lothian relayed Roosevelt's response directly to his friend Lord Halifax. He told the Foreign Secretary that Roosevelt "did not dispute that some such step was the right one to take but said however it was politically impracticable for him to do so."[38] The reason was American public opinion. After this exchange of ideas, Lothian reported that Roosevelt's "present intention is to carry it [the Welles mission] through."

News that Roosevelt intended to carry on with the Welles mission increased the vehemence and breadth of British objections. In a final volley of telegrams from London, Chamberlain made clear his intention that he did not wish Roosevelt to go ahead with the mission. He did this by introducing consideration of British involvement in the Russo-Finnish War. The Chamberlain government, along with the French, wanted to support the Finns in their war effort. According to Chamberlain's first telegram to Washington, they had just secured acceptance of the passage of war materials through Sweden and Norway to the Finns and the Prime Minister worried that the "action he [Roosevelt] proposes to take should interfere with the success of this plan."[39] In language almost identical to that which he had used to object to Roosevelt's diplomatic conference plan of January 1938, the Prime Minister sought to dissuade the President by suggesting that his plan would "cut across" the actions Chamberlain was planning to undertake. Again, the quick turnaround of telegrams in London is indicative of the anxiety the mission was causing the British, with the response to Washington being sent on 7 February 1940. Chamberlain was clearly trying to use the issue of French collaboration on aid to the Finns as another reason for Roosevelt not to carry on with the Welles mission. This was acknowledged by Sir Orme Sargent, the Foreign Office Assistant Under Secretary, who hoped that "the telegram which was drafted this afternoon explaining the intentions of His Majesty's Government as regards Finland will have the desired effect of making him modify his plans."[40]

A second accompanying telegram revealed how adamant the British government was in their disapproval of the Welles mission. It focused on the crux of the matter for Chamberlain: the potential effects of a publicly acknowledged peace mission. The telegram stated that if Roosevelt "is determined in any event to send Mr Sumner Welles on a mission I do hope that he may not think it necessary to make [a] public announcement on the subject. If he must make [a] public announcement, I hope a least it would not be in any form that would encourage the idea that the mission was part of a peace plan."[41] The escalating desperation in Chamberlain's words provide, again, proof of the substance of his objections: was Roosevelt going to provide Hitler with the opportunity to retain his conquests and raise questions as to why Britain was involved in the conflict in the first place?

The prospect of the mission raised this concern among many within the Foreign Office. David Scott, at the American Desk in the Foreign Office, feared that Roosevelt thought British defeat imminent and therefore that a peace offer was a way of "saving us from ourselves," while Cadogan concluded that "Mr Roosevelt's latest half-baked scheme" must be killed "by kindness—and firmness." The disquiet within the Foreign Office was given its most pointed expression by Sir Robert Vansittart, who referred to Welles at this point as a "grass snake." The analogy being drawn by Vansittart was that the Welles mission's appearance had proved startling to the British and that they might need to maneuver with caution, but that Welles was not expected to prove to be anything more than troublesome, against a backdrop of other more *lethal* animals.[42]

Confirmation of the British influence on the formulation of the Welles mission can be seen in Lothian's final meeting with Roosevelt before the 9 February announcement. The President sought to further allay British concerns by reconfirming that the "United States would have nothing to do with an inconclusive and precarious peace." He told Lothian that the "procedure he proposed to adopt would remove the [twin] dangers [the] Prime Minister feared." First, Roosevelt explained to Lothian that the "published purpose of the Under Secretary's visit would be merely to report to the President 'as to the present conditions in Europe.'" This would avoid the explicit use of the word "peace" that Chamberlain feared. Second, in order to tone down British worry over how the Welles mission might interfere with British plans for Scandinavia, Roosevelt said he would write to the monarchs of Sweden and Norway. He explained that he would tell them that he "did not think that there was a thousand to one chance of peace and that the mission was one merely of enquiry."[43] The understanding that Roosevelt had of the chances of peace is evident in his quoting of such long odds. While this may have been some solace to those in London, they were in the process of drafting a reply the next day when Roosevelt's "splash" came across the wires on 9 February. Cadogan's first reaction was that the announcement of the Welles mission was "not too bad."[44]

The Anglo-American exchanges of the first week of February 1940, alongside the influence of Welles and Hull, are crucial to understanding Roosevelt's motivations and objectives for the Welles mission. The President was motivated to address the situation of war in Europe although his objectives during this week were still not wholly finalized. That the British were able to exert a notable influence on the consideration of the mission is a testament to the fact that Roosevelt was not tied to fixed plans even a week before the mission was to be announced. Nevertheless, as is also clear, Roosevelt was not wholeheartedly dissuaded by British objections. The benefits Roosevelt envisaged, amplified no doubt by Welles, outweighed the potential costs of antagonizing the British government. This was because throughout, and despite other "minor" irritations in transatlantic relations, Roosevelt wanted nothing to do with a peace settlement that would allow Nazi Germany to continue to threaten Great Britain and thus, in Roosevelt's mind, the national interests of the United States in the future. This will be seen in microcosm by the simple fact that he neglected to compose a private letter to Hitler explaining Welles' mission.

Before turning to the detail of those letters, it is worth reiterating for its importance in this analysis Roosevelt's susceptibility to influence during this period. His approach to policy making was malleable, allowing deliberately for the views of a variety of people to be considered. During the end of January and beginning of February 1940 he was prepared to be maneuvered by Welles, to listen to Hull, and to accept a degree of British reservation. The significance of this approach is to dilute the accusation that the mission was one to find peace terms from the outset and throughout. Instead, although the Welles mission might have begun with this in mind, as is illustrated here, it was augmented by other objectives: the gathering of firsthand information, the prolonging of the "phony war," and the perpetuation of Italian neutrality.

As discussion of the Welles mission quickly circulated round the world after 9 February, Roosevelt and Welles stood firm in not adding any further comment in public. In private, however, Welles was busy composing a series of letters addressed to Mussolini, Daladier, and Chamberlain. But no letter for Hitler. The absence of a letter to the Führer is evidence that Roosevelt and Welles were not solely trying to engage with Nazi Germany in ending the war. Given the public silence from the Administration before Welles' departure, these letters provide further insight into the thinking of Roosevelt and Welles and their objectives for the mission. Welles originally drafted the letters on 12 February for Roosevelt's consideration. The cordiality that the pair wished to impart was typified by handwritten additions such as "Mon Ami Daladier" on the letter for the French premier and the suggestion to Mussolini that the pair should consider meeting. Similarly, the letter addressed to Number 10 began "My dear Chamberlain." Such a convivial tone is perhaps surprising, given the history of discord in the relationship between the two and the objections Chamberlain had raised to the mission during the first week of February. Nevertheless, the letter explains in concise terms, and with allusion to his personal relationship with Welles, Roosevelt's objectives before Welles left for Europe:

> My dear Chamberlain: Sumner Welles, my Under Secretary of State, and an old boyhood friend will give you this. What you tell him will be maintained in the strictest confidence and will be told solely to myself and to Cordell Hull on my talk with him on his return. At this grave moment I deeply hope this exchange of views may be of real value towards a peace which is neither "inconclusive nor precarious." Enough said. My warm regards, faithfully Roosevelt.[45]

The qualification to Roosevelt's initial objective of early January of exploring the possibilities of peace is significant, as is his desire for information. Both reveal the evolution of other objectives for the mission. Roosevelt had already expressed in clear and concise terms that Welles was not interested in peace at any price in his 8 February conversation with Lothian. He had told the Ambassador that the "Under Secretary would have private instructions that [the] President was not interested in [a] truce or unstable peace, and that anything like a successful attack on France or England would inevitably bring the United States nearer war."[46] The latter admission (in conversation with Lothian) was evidently unlikely to come to fruition in terms of U.S. belligerence, given the state of American opinion, which Lothian fully understood, but it is indicative of Roosevelt's state of mind and certainly points to events such as the Destroyers-Bases Deal later in 1940.[47]

As a brief glimpse of the days between the public announcement of the mission and Welles' departure for Europe, the drafting of these letters illustrates further that the mission had evolved from its initial conception to a qualified exploration of the situation in Europe. Thus while Welles "explored the possibilities of peace" on his mission—a peace that was to be neither "inconclusive nor precarious"—he was not solely aiming at finding acceptable peace terms but at utilizing such discussion for the other objectives outlined in this work.

The breadth of purpose in Rooseveltian policy making in early 1940 was further exemplified on 9 February. Less than an hour after Roosevelt had ended the press conference that announced the Welles mission, Hull declared that the United States had invited over 50 neutral nations to consider issues raised by the war. This enterprise was designed to sound out neutral opinion on the foundations for a "sound international economic system and at the same time world-wide reduction of armaments" in the postwar world.[48] Such a proclamation, to many at the time and since, clouded further the purposes of Rooseveltian diplomacy in early 1940. To enlighten, the importance for this study lies in two main areas. First of all, the neutrals' conversations reveal the continuation of the diplomatic heritage within the Roosevelt State Department from which the Welles mission also came, and, second, the Administration realizing the dangers of irking nonentangling public opinion, sought to portray themselves as looking to the postwar world. A related but lesser point is that by announcing the conversations on the same day as the Welles mission, the Administration was endeavoring to mitigate any accusation that they were interfering in the current conflict by pointing to the neutrals' conversations as being compatible with the neutrality legislation.

Roosevelt explained to Lothian the purposes of the conversations on 1 February, when he first announced his intention to dispatch Welles. The President stated that the conversations would not be concerned with "terms for ending of war but rather to elicit neutral views as to principles which should underlie [the] final peace including reduction of armaments, [and] a sound international economic system."[49] Robert Dallek expressed the purposes in more forthright terms by stating that the conversations hoped to see an "organisation of neutrals" sit "at the peace table with equal right."[50] The neutrals' proposal should be considered as congruent with longer-term concepts deeply ingrained in both the Roosevelt Administration and the State Department agenda. The antecedents to the neutrals' conversations can be seen in the State Department's vociferous support of neutral rights in relation to British practice after the outbreak of hostilities, and in the recent history of both Hull's preoccupation with free trade and the heritage from 1937 of Welles' plan for international relations. .

The political dimensions of the conversations, most notably the possible connection to the ongoing war, were understood by the Administration. Hull included in his statement of 9 February that "matters involving present war conditions are not a part of these preliminary conversations."[51] It was during the run-up to the neutrals' conversations that the example used in the first chapter to illustrate Welles' explicit bypassing of Hull took place. As regards substance, Welles' involvement reveals the political conditions the Administration was operating under. He wrote in January that it would be "understood that before any actual meeting in Washington took place, all of the governments mentioned would have agreed upon [a] concise and detailed agenda and would have been afforded an opportunity, through diplomatic channels, of reaching an agreement as to the general lines of the recommendation to be formulated."[52] Welles added further qualification as late as 5 February, which revealed his own desire to provide order in international relations and the longer-term, postwar, justifications for the neutrals' conversations. He wrote posing the questions as to "whether moral cooperation between neutral states would be of service in bringing about the formulation of standards of international conduct, and the solution of other problems related thereto, which they would hope to see observed in any post war period."[53] The desire to present the neutrals' conversations to the American people as essentially apolitical is evident.

That the Administration was politically aware of any fallout from the neutrals' conversations was not surprising, and neither should it be a surprise that Roosevelt failed to draw distinct lines between the conversations and the Welles mission. *The Daily Telegraph* posited, "[I]t is not possible yet to know whether Mr Welles's mission and the American conversations with neutrals are designed to merge into one another."[54] Given Roosevelt's desire to stimulate interest within the American people on foreign affairs issues without risking political criticism, it is entirely probable that he would have been happy that the *New York Times* banner headline the next day read "Roosevelt Sounds Neutrals on Peace," coming as it did above news that Welles was going to Europe.[55] That the matter was being used in some part to deflect possible criticism of the Welles mission is evident from the fact that although 55 nations initially responded to Hull's enquiries by the middle of March the Administration acknowledged that the opportunity to make any progress had passed.[56]

Nevertheless, the neutrals' conversations should be seen as part of the efforts Roosevelt made in early 1940 to do something about the war in Europe, with the Welles mission as a focus, compatible with American public opinion and before the spring escalation. In some respects the conversations again represented the "what harm can it do" element of Rooseveltian foreign policy making. Court historians William Langer and Everett Gleason conclude that the attempt to organize "a neutral front . . . remains in many respects simply a remarkably picturesque manifestation of American indecision in the face of a war which our people and our Government could neither wholly ignore nor resolutely embrace."[57] The importance of being in step with American opinion is evident in the endeavor to build a consensus of neutrals, alongside the belief within the State Department, held by Welles especially, in the value of a "code of conduct" in international relations. Establishing a case for international norms stretched back through the Roosevelt Administration and would extend into the future as part of the extensive efforts toward postwar planning undertaken in Washington. In February 1940 that lay in the future. The immediate focus for the Administration was the Welles mission.

The reaction in the State Department to the announcement of the Welles mission and the neutrals' conversations reflected their acceptance of the limited options open to the Administration because of American public opinion. In other words, those who had become accustomed to Roosevelt undertaking policy moves with long odds saw the Welles mission in this light. Berle, who had expressed this sentiment on a number of occasions, wrote that the mission was merely "a variation on a procedure we have thought of before."[58] Moffat, meanwhile, who was to accompany Welles on the odyssey to Europe, initially saw the mission as a "last effort . . . to restore peace" but agreed the process was not particularly novel.[59] Assistant Secretary Breckinridge Long offered his own assessment of the mission: "It will be a very important trip—that is, it may be. If Sumner can find any willingness on the part of the various responsible officials of any of those Governments to cease hostilities, it will be important, but if he does not find any such situation, it will probably mean that the war will continue on ad infinitum."[60] Reaction within the State Department to Roosevelt's announcement reveals that they saw the mission as being in line with previous policies: that some initiatives were worth pursuing even if they might not seem to be successful.

While opinion in Washington was largely supportive, the views of those in the American diplomatic corps ranged from wholehearted support to vitriolic condemnation. William Bullitt fell into the latter camp. The Ambassador to France returned to the United States on 9 February and learned of the mission only in the evening press. He told Ickes at a dinner meeting the next day that "he did not relish the idea of Welles's going over and, in effect, superseding the regularly accredited diplomatic representatives."[61] Although Bullitt was apparently "seething with anger" by the time he met the President soon afterward, Roosevelt pacified him somewhat with talk of a Cabinet position. Despite this, Bullitt refused to return to Paris until Welles had returned to the United States and let it be known to the French Ambassador that if he had known of the mission before "he would have opposed it."[62] Thus Bullitt, still smarting from his pacification in the White House, helped in ghostwriting the *Chicago Tribune* article entitled "Welles' Peace Trip Scuttles Peace at Home," which castigated the mission prior to Welles' departure.[63] In conversation with Long before he left, Welles blamed Bullitt's "vitriolic tongue" for the press stories that "indicated that he and the Secretary had had some dispute" over the mission.[64] Welles claimed that "Bullitt had taken the trouble to go the Capitol and to talk to a number of Senators and that they arranged a story of this nature to go to Chicago and to appear in the Chicago papers so that it would not have the earmarks of a Washington story."[65] Such concern reveals an understanding on Welles' part, rarely expressed during the mission because of his reluctance to discuss it, of the potential for the mission to be misconstrued.

Whereas Bullitt met news of the mission with outright anger, Joseph Kennedy confronted it with something approaching resignation. Kennedy had become increasingly disenchanted with his role after the outbreak of war and was back in the United States convalescing at the time of the announcement. It was probably of little surprise to him, therefore, that Roosevelt had seemingly ignored him. According to Michael Beschloss, Kennedy saw the mission as "merely another instance of personal humiliation by the White House," which in turn gave "more evidence to Whitehall that Roosevelt had no faith in his Ambassador."[66]

Interestingly, as well as Kennedy and Bullitt being in the United States at the time of the announcement of the Welles mission, so was Joseph Davies, then the Ambassador to Belgium. He was on holiday in Florida on 9 February and wrote to the President the next day. He was full of praise for Roosevelt and Welles in undertaking the mission. His letter began by stating that "the appointment of Sumner Welles for this exploratory mission in Europe is timely and splendid. Sumner is just the man to get an objective perspective and procure it simultaneously from the principals involved." Notwithstanding this, Davies was not optimistic about the prospect of the mission providing a settlement: "I have little hope that any peace discussion will fructify or even germinate now. The principals involved are too far apart—their real or avowed purposes too extreme and too set in passions. . . . Nevertheless it is worthwhile. If there is one chance in a thousand it is worth a try." It is important to note that Davies, physically removed from the State Department, recognized that despite the dangers involved—the long odds—the mission was "worthwhile." Furthermore, Davies considered that by endeavoring to explore the possibilities for peace "it will renew the faith of the liberty and peace-loving people the world over in the fact . . . that you are doing everything within human power to try to stop this terrible tragedy."[67] This was a crucial point, as Davies understood that "exploring the possibilities for peace" actually provided an opportunity to achieve other goals, including illustrating to the American people the differences between the Allies and Germany.

That Davies' views were most clearly in line with the Administration reflects the state of the relationships Roosevelt had with Bullitt and Kennedy. Relations with both had broken down during 1939. As the Ambassadors moved further away from the Administration's line—Bullitt to the point where he was promoting the idea that the United States would defend France and Kennedy becoming increasingly defeatist—Roosevelt became more and more likely to question the information he received from the two capitals. He had told Morgenthau in October 1939 that Kennedy was "just a pain in the neck" because of his readiness to accept appeasement, while Bullitt was equally troublesome. Morgenthau recorded Roosevelt stating the "trouble with Bullitt is in the morning he will send me a telegram 'Everything is lovely' and then he will go out to have lunch with some French official and I get a telegram that everything is going to hell."[68] Roosevelt saw some consolation in the autumn in that the "only thing that saves the information is I know my men." By the turn of the year it seems that his patience with biased information had worn thin. The disenchantment with Kennedy in particular was no secret and may have fed into the questioning Roosevelt received from the press within minutes of the announcement of the Welles mission. Roosevelt was asked whether his information from London and Paris was satisfactory, and "if he needed a new reporter?" to which he responded that he had "excellent" information from each country. Significantly, though, Roosevelt went on to say, "It might be a good thing to get somebody to see all the conditions in all the countries so that one mind would be able to cover the situation instead of having four separate minds reporting on separate things."[69] To add support to such an argument Davies wrote to Roosevelt stating that "no single Ambassador assigned to a European post" could have conducted the mission he proposed.[70] In summation, Roosevelt clearly did see the mission as an opportunity to hear firsthand information on the European situation from a single trusted source: gathering information was a clear objective for Welles. While this was the only publicly acknowledged goal, in the immediate aftermath of the 9 February announcement, both the press and the foreign governments whom Welles was intending to visit were still endeavoring to clarify the mission's purpose.

There was a good deal of similarity between the views on the mission of the world's press and those of the governments in Europe. This is in part logical, because the paucity of information supplied by the Roosevelt Administration meant that those in Europe looked to the press for clarification. In short, none of Welles' destinations particularly relished the prospect of the Under Secretary visiting Europe. The lines taken by the press and those in Europe focused on the following areas: the real chances for peace, Roosevelt's official objective, consideration of the Welles mission as a domestic move and part of a possible campaign for a third term, exploring the strength of the Axis, and analogies with Colonel House's mission to Europe. In examining these views, concise evaluations of how far any of these lines were actually involved in Roosevelt's thinking will be provided in this section.

To many, the mission was simply a "peace move." Various papers and individuals shared the view of the *New York Times*, which saw the Welles mission as the "President's long-awaited 'offensive for peace.' "[71] This was a concern to all the governments in Europe, but it was most evident in French opinion. Indeed, French alarm in this area was largely to mirror that of the Chamberlain government in respect of a "peace" move disturbing domestic opinion. With Bullitt unaware of the enterprise, the French government had been taken by surprise by news of the mission and it was not enamored with the prospect of Welles' arrival. Robert Murphy, the American Chargé in Paris, learned this the day after Roosevelt's announcement. M. Charveriat, the Director of Political Affairs at the French Foreign Office, explained the French position with faint praise that bore the hallmarks of a begrudging acceptance. The French government had two observations: the first, a formal welcome; and the second, an expression of "reserve as to the purposes of the visit" for fear of disturbing Allied public opinion.[72] Similarly, William Strang of the British Foreign Office learned from the French Embassy in London that, although the mission would officially be welcomed, Allied war aims had already been proclaimed and "the President's initiative was likely to be a cause of disturbance in the public opinion of the Allied countries."[73] In this scenario the French sought to publicly play down any "peace-making" rumors about the mission and instead stress its fact-finding aspect. A press release through the semiofficial Havas Agency stated that Welles' purpose was not as "a mediator or even as a messenger between the different capitals but to make a general report to Washington on war conditions."[74] The rest of the French press largely followed this line—agreeing with Roosevelt's stated purposes.[75] The British Ambassador to Paris Sir Ronald Campbell concluded that news of the mission had "aroused considerable interest and some anxiety."[76]

In Germany the mission prompted equal levels of curiosity about Roosevelt's published objective. Kirk reported from Berlin that "although the official reserve on the matter of the visit . . . still continues there is reason to believe . . . that [Welles'] impending arrival in Berlin has aroused the greatest interest in the highest government circles here."[77] This was an accurate assessment as, in accepting that Welles would be afforded an invitation, von Ribbentrop queried Roosevelt's "intention and objective" for the mission by making enquiries to Hans Thomsen, the Chargé in Washington.[78] Thomsen suggested that it was the desire for specific information that had prompted the mission. This was because "the American Government . . . has been surprised and confused by the course of the war and the international power situation to date and has not yet been able to reach any definite conclusions."[79] It is also worth noting regarding the German calculations that Thomsen reported to Berlin that he thought Welles had been chosen because he was "especially suited" to the mission "owing to his sharp attacks on the Versailles Treaty and its consequences for Germany."[80] Welles, along with many in the department, had criticized the Versailles settlement as sowing the seeds of the war they were then facing. German press coverage of the announcement was minimal: restricted as it was to perfunctory coverage the next day and no editorial comment. This was hardly surprising, given the extent to which the Nazi party influenced all aspects of the media.[81] An official reaction to the Welles mission similar to that emanating from Berlin could be found in Rome. Press reports in Italy were superficial, with little comment. Although Count Galeazzo Ciano, the Italian Foreign Minister and son-in-law of Mussolini, said he and the Duce would be "happy to receive" Welles, Ciano's expression of enthusiasm on behalf of his father-in-law would prove unfounded.[82] The *New York Times'* Rome correspondent provided a more balanced view in reporting that news of the mission was "received with . . . scepticism"[83] In this respect, all four of the countries on Welles' itinerary had something in common in their initial responses to the mission. None was wholly sure that Roosevelt's stated aim of gathering information would not be a precursor to a dramatic peace move. This prospect was something that Welles would privately endeavor to cultivate in Europe, in Berlin in particular, and so he and Roosevelt were not keen to dispel this line in the aftermath of the public announcement. Nevertheless, the reaction in both the press and the foreign governments of looking to the possibilities of peace and the gathering of information had been and, alongside the other objectives, would continue to be part of Roosevelt's thinking behind the mission as a whole.

The influence of domestic politics, and particularly of electoral considerations, on Roosevelt's thinking was a further area of speculation that arose in each of the European capitals. Roosevelt's sensitivity to the views of the American people had become broadly known. In London, Scott had brought this matter up in Foreign Office discussion of the Welles mission. He stated that "if the President can somehow stop the war his own domestic position will be enormously strengthened." Scott added that "to do him justice, I don't believe he would set his own personal position before what he thought were our interests [but] we should remember how passionately he must wish for another Democratic term to carry on the work of the New Deal."[84] Vansittart, who had already called Welles a "grass snake," was not so charitable. He stated after Welles' time in London that "President Roosevelt is ready to play a dirty trick on the world and risk the ultimate destruction of the western democracies in order to secure the re-election of the Democratic candidate in the US."[85] After the announcement, the *Times'* New York correspondent reported that "most people [in the United States] are inclined to regard it simply as an election manoeuvre."[86] Lothian added weight to this, reporting that the "week-end press" had seen the mission as "primarily connected with home politics in the presidential year."[87] Clearly, the 1940 election was being considered as potentially important in trying to second-guess Roosevelt's thinking. Such views were shared by Germany and France. Hans Thomsen reported to Berlin from Washington that the Welles mission and the neutrals' declarations together "unquestionably fit in well with Roosevelt's domestic political strategy for the impending presidential election campaign, in which he will endeavour to play up his election for the third time as unavoidable and enforced by circumstances."[88] Bullitt reported to Ickes the contents of a message he had received from Daladier about the Welles mission. The telegram "was to the effect that either the President had sent Welles to Europe as a matter of domestic policy, or he didn't know as much about the European situation as Daladier had hoped and believed. In either event, the President had gone down in Daladier's estimation."[89] Across Europe, then, there was a concern that Roosevelt was motivated by domestic factors in launching the Welles mission. For Roosevelt himself, American public opinion was always his first consideration, but he was also practiced in trying to maneuver around its vagaries.

Although it is beyond the direct focus of this study, the issue of the third term provided a tantalizing backdrop to events in Europe.[90] For a man who often spoke of retiring to his family home in Hyde Park, New York, Roosevelt had not yet decided whether to run for an unprecedented third term in early 1940.[91] Although he fully understood that if the United States could exert any influence to avoid the spring onslaughts it might benefit any Democratic candidate, Roosevelt was also aware that overt involvement in European affairs would add to calls that he was entangling the United States. As such, it was a question of perspective, and with the likes of Senator Hiram Johnson suggesting that Roosevelt's motive was to put the President "in intimate touch with the war, in order that he may do his part as an undisclosed Ally of Great Britain," Roosevelt had to tread carefully.[92] On 10 February Johnson was quoted in the isolationist *Chicago Tribune* as saying the "bombshell . . . is a coolly calculated scheme to take us further in . . . easing us a little bit forward to war."[93] Roosevelt wanted to avoid such accusations. In stressing the information-gathering role and Welles' public silence on his trip the Administration sought to address the two perspectives of the mission: either involving the United States directly in Europe or being purely for domestic show.

Roosevelt explained his own views on the third-term issue to Morgenthau at the end of January 1940. Morgenthau recorded that Roosevelt did not "want to run unless between now and the convention things get very, very much worse in Europe."[94] That events would unfold in such tragic fashion during the spring of 1940 led to Roosevelt's accepting the calls of "We Want Roosevelt" at the Chicago convention that summer.

Returning to the speculation surrounding the Welles mission in mid-February 1940, one factor that would certainly develop as one of Roosevelt and Welles' objectives for the mission was the assessment of the strength of the Axis between Berlin and Rome. The possibility that the Welles mission was aimed at testing the bonds of the Axis was immediately picked up on by those in Berlin. Kirk included in his report information that had been intimated to him on collaboration between the two Axis powers in the face of the Welles mission: "It is said that particularly close contact with Rome is being maintained in regard to the significance and possible consequences of his [Welles'] mission."[95] German concern was well founded, as Welles, having established Italy as part of the mission, sought to try to preserve Italian neutrality once in Europe. Historians Stanley Hilton and Elizabeth Wiskemann agree. Hilton states that "Italian neutrality" was a "related objective of the Welles mission," while Wiskemann argues that Welles "intended to counteract Germany's pressure upon Italy to join the war."[96] This work has argued that consideration of Italian neutrality became an increasingly important objective during the early months of 1940. The importance that Welles laid on Italy during the latter part of his mission, in his report, and into the spring of 1940 is testament to this and has not been explored previously. Nonetheless, the significance of Italy at this point is that the Germans saw the potential testing of the Axis as a possible motivation of the mission, and therefore "a source of no little concern."[97] In fact both Ribbentrop's hastily arranged trip to Rome while Welles was in London (March 11–12) and the Brenner Pass meeting (18 March) can be attributed to some degree to the Welles mission. Both events will be considered more fully in the course of later chapters.

A further line of speculation, and one that Roosevelt was evidently aware of, was the historical parallel between the mission of Sumner Welles and that undertaken by Colonel House some 25 years earlier during the First World War. House had been sent to Europe in January 1915 and then again early in 1916 by President Woodrow Wilson. House's purpose was to "sound out the governments of the warring powers" and therefore help Wilson in his search to "discover a means of ending the war," which would therefore save "America from all possibility of being sucked into it."[98] That Roosevelt was aware of his history is shown in his initial meeting with Lothian on 1 February. The President made a point of telling the Ambassador that "the Under-Secretary of State's mission would be a public mission and not a private one like Colonel House's."[99] Roosevelt explained this again to Breckinridge Long: "There would be no 'Colonel House business.' Whatever [Welles] did was to be done openly."[100] This distinction was only explained explicitly in private;

thus it is not surprising that the press and those in Europe were quick to make the link. The *Chicago Tribune* immediately charged Roosevelt "with following in Woodrow Wilson's footsteps" by attempting to "deal" with the Europeans.[101] The British Embassy in Paris reported that the French press had made the connection between House and the possibility of an early peace. "Many newspapers recall Colonel House's visit during the last war," Campbell wrote, but he continued that "the general tone is that there must be nothing in the nature of mediation between the belligerents with a view to an early and inconclusive peace."[102] The allusion to House could also be found in Berlin. A cable from Kirk met Welles when he arrived in Rome. It "indicated that the Germans would talk to Sumner Welles more freely if he came to Berlin after London and Paris." Kirk explained that this was because "the memory of Colonel House was still strong, and particularly his habit of repeating in London what he heard in Berlin."[103] The sentiment of this telegram confirmed what Kirk had cabled to Washington on 14 February. He stated then that there was "the definite impression that if the Under Secretary proceeds directly from Rome to Berlin and concludes his journey in Europe by visits to England and France the purpose of his visit will be coloured in the minds of the German authorities."[104] Stanley Hilton agrees with this argument, noting that the Germans were "especially eager to have Welles make Berlin his last stop . . . since any rumoured peace proposals would more than likely be attributed to the first countries he visited."[105] According to Kirk's words and Hilton's analysis, Germany did not want to become associated with any peace proposals. This augured well for those who feared Germany might exploit the Welles mission for their own purposes. The link between the missions of Welles and House was a logical one for the casual observer to make, given the parallels that the two were sent to a warring Europe by Democratic presidents while the United States was neutral. However, the reality was that House had a considerably more invasive brief, while owing to the pressure of American opinion Welles could not appear to be transferring information or making any proposals of his own.

Concluding the analysis of the speculation that surrounded the Welles mission in the immediate aftermath of the 9 February public announcement is problematic. The difficulty lies in making clear assessments between what was more fictional (the third-term issue) and what had a semblance of fact in relation to Roosevelt's thinking (such as the gathering of information). The reality was that Roosevelt and Welles did not have entirely fixed objectives for the mission to achieve. Furthermore, it should be remembered that Roosevelt and Welles were not entirely unhappy with the rumor and counter-rumor that surrounded the mission. They made no effort to publicly clarify the stated goal of the mission from 9 February until Welles had returned to Rome in mid-March. As the goals of prolonging the "phony war" and perpetuating

Italian neutrality became stronger during the course of the mission, the more conjecture that surrounded the mission the better for the aim of making people think that Roosevelt might act when Welles returned to Europe. As long as the mission was presented as being not overtly entangled, that is, not like the House mission, then it had the potential to achieve something from its developing goals. Had the mission been solely one to successfully explore the possibilities for peace with Germany, then the lukewarm response the mission received across Europe, alongside the views of Hull and Great Britain, would have fundamentally undermined that objective at the outset. Clearly, Welles and Roosevelt were considering other goals for the mission.

Before concluding this chapter it is worth considering, with a view to the development of the mission's objectives over the course of Welles' time in Europe, Roosevelt's retrospective explanation for the mission. He did this notably in describing his motivations to Long on 12 March, and then again, in a more oblique fashion, in discussion with Canadian Prime Minister Mackenzie King in late April. Crucially, these episodes further illustrate the flexible approach Roosevelt had to the Welles mission, how he was prepared to embark on policies while acknowledging that they may have only a marginal influence on events, and the overall evolution of the mission's objectives themselves. Roosevelt told Long that he would tell him about the history of Welles' visit, and his first comments are critical in illustrating how the Administration was prepared to embark on policy that was likely to be marginal in influencing events. Long recorded that Roosevelt "figured [the mission] could not do any harm and might do some good."[106] Roosevelt's words stress further the belief he and his colleagues had that although the Welles mission might carry certain risks, when set against the prospect of a forthcoming German offensive the risks were worth taking.

Roosevelt then went on to explicitly acknowledge that prolonging the "phony war" was in his mind with regard to the Welles mission. With the prospect that "the Germans might launch a spring offensive about now," Roosevelt explained that if "Welles' visit would delay that offensive or possibly prevent it, it would be worth a great deal. If it prevented it altogether, that would be fine. If it delayed it a month, that would be so much the better. Even a week would mean a lot, because it would help England and France to get additional supplies during that week." Clearly, prolonging the "phony war" was something Roosevelt was considering and can explain Welles' focus on this in the latter stages of his mission. Long concluded that the President wanted the Allies "to have as much time as they could have before the German attack commenced in all its ferocity, in order that they might be in a better position to defend themselves." With this objective in mind, Roosevelt advanced the "only other reason he sent Welles abroad." Long recorded that this was "to find out what he could from Mussolini and from Hitler." In this

Roosevelt's desire for firsthand information, specifically on the state of the Axis, is clearly evident. Interestingly, Roosevelt was rather dismissive of the rest of the mission, as Long quotes him as calling the stops in Paris and London "just 'window dressing.'" Roosevelt explained to Long that Welles "had to go there to balance the picture," but "what he had gone to Europe for really was to get the low-down on Hitler and get Mussolini's point of view." Clearly a dearth of information from the two Axis capitals was influential in Roosevelt's mind at this point. It should be acknowledged that this conversation between Long and Roosevelt took place on 12 March, when Welles was in London. Undoubtedly, Roosevelt's thoughts were therefore influenced by what he had heard from Welles in their entirely private communications on what the latter had learned in Rome, Berlin, and Paris. That he considered Paris "window dressing" at this stage is entirely compatible with the paucity of significant information Welles accrued in the French capital. Furthermore, for Roosevelt to say the "only" other reason he sent Welles was to gather information is in direct conflict with the contents of the private letters he composed, where exploring the possibilities of a suitable settlement are clearly stated. Plainly for Roosevelt the focus of the mission had changed by 12 March. The exploration of the possibilities for a peace that was neither "inconclusive nor precarious" had been relegated from its position in January as the initial objective in relation to that of gathering information and the prolonging of the "phony war." The flexibility that had been part of the mission from the outset is again clear, as is Roosevelt's capacity to retrospectively justify the mission's purpose.

Roosevelt expressed similar sentiment on Welles' visit to Paris and London being "window dressing" and stressing the information-gathering role in Rome and Berlin, in discussing the mission with Mackenzie King once the phony war had ended in Europe. The Canadian recorded in his diary that Roosevelt would tell him "the whole story," before going to note that "so far as England and France were concerned, there was nothing really to say, except they had received Welles in the best manner possible."[107] Roosevelt then recounted the positions of Mussolini and Ciano, before explaining to King how Welles had been harangued in Berlin. Absent from this account is any allusion of the mission's aims other than an account of the information Welles had gathered in the Axis capitals. This is hardly surprising since German troops had invaded Scandinavia at the beginning of April. Nonetheless, the explanations Roosevelt provided after the event to both Long and King illustrates the differing emphases throughout the mission. This will continue to be examined in upcoming chapters.

When Welles set foot on board the SS *Rex* bound for Naples on 17 February 1940, the initial purpose of the mission he was embarking on had been augmented by other objectives. This meant the goals of the mission had evolved significantly during January and early February, and in both process and concept this evolution reflected the themes that this work has identified in Rooseveltian foreign policy: the influence of Welles, the concerns of Cordell Hull, the limitations on American foreign policy imposed by American public opinion, and the views expressed by the Chamberlain government. As Benjamin Welles acknowledges, "Roosevelt was a man of infinite complexity, . . . and the Welles mission an example of multiple motivations."[108] At its genesis the concept of the Welles mission was the exploration of the possibilities for a peace that was neither inconclusive nor precarious. The initial drafts of the mission's press release, together with the development of Roosevelt's thoughts on the contribution he could make up to the end of January 1940, make it clear that this was his opening idea. That this early design was then to be subject to modification was typical of the way policy was made in the Roosevelt Administration.

There were three key influences on the drafting of the mission all laid over the underlying influence of American public opinion. First of all, Welles' enthusiasm for the project undoubtedly helped Roosevelt's idea crystalize as January 1940 progressed. The second and third influences, Hull and the British, each provided qualifications that tempered the goal of exploring peace possibilities. In doing this, the objections raised helped broaden the mission's scope. It is clear that when Roosevelt consulted with both Hull and the Chamberlain government, despite the negative, almost derogatory tone of the communications from London, he was prepared to listen to their suggestions and then incorporate them into the evolving mission. This is vital in illustrating that Roosevelt did not approach the mission of his Under Secretary to Europe in a dogmatic manner. The exception that both he and Welles adhered to, along with other members of the Administration, was official silence on the mission as it progressed. From the 9 February announcement until Roosevelt made public the contents of Welles' report at the end of March, the official silence was broken only by a reiteration of the public statement of the mission in Rome the day before Welles left Europe. Given the intense interest in the mission, it would have been easy for "Administration sources" to let information about the mission enter the public domain. Instead, the conjecture that ensued in the absence of any official word was actually part of Roosevelt's and Welles' goal of endeavoring to prolong the "phony war." Any doubt that took hold in Berlin or Rome as to the future conduct of the United States might contribute to this. Ultimately, of course, it would not. German plans for the escalation of the war were signed two days before Welles arrived in Berlin, and by early June Mussolini would be sufficiently wedded to Hitler to declare war on the Allies.

It is crucial to acknowledge that Roosevelt and Welles knew the mission stood a minuscule chance of achieving both its initial aim and those that had augmented it. Even when the mission was publicized as being one of gathering information, talk of the mission assisting the cause of peace remained. It was this confluence that Lothian reported to London on 13 February 1940. He wrote of his assessment of the opinion of the American weekend press that having "decided upon inclination to give [the] mission a chance, although this is regarded as one in a thousand, hope is expressed that the mission will at least not do harm."[109] It is significant that Lothian, who had seen firsthand the development of the mission in the first week in February and who had been told by Roosevelt and Welles separately of odds of "one in a thousand" and "one in a hundred" respectively, used the phraseology in reporting to London. The idea of the mission being a long shot was clear.

The publicized goal of the mission—gathering information—was sufficiently broad for Roosevelt and Welles to allow any positive developments to be considered successes but at the same time any unhelpful outcomes to be presented as beyond the scope of the mission. Welles' suggestion of Italian inclusion, then the prominence he gave to Mussolini's comments elsewhere in Europe, the high profile of Italy in the conclusions to his final report, and the appeals made to Rome in the spring reveal how the quest for Italian neutrality developed and how Welles sought to pursue it as *something* that could be achieved from his mission. The breadth of what the mission might achieve is clearly exemplified by Welles' hopes for including Italy on the mission's itinerary. Most importantly, Welles sought to preserve Italian neutrality and so limit the scale of the war. More generally, he saw an opportunity, also noted by others in the State Department, to build a neutral block of opinion upon which recognition of a code of international principles could be based. That Italy was still a neutral at this stage was also in his thinking, as discussions with Italy could help dilute accusations that the Administration was intervening directly in the conflict.

Concern for such accusations reflected both Roosevelt's and Welles' understanding of the constricting nature of nonentangling American opinion. The American people did not share the dangers Roosevelt saw in the situation in Europe. This was the major factor in why Roosevelt and Welles professed at the outset that the mission was to be both in the public domain and restricted to gathering information. By being able to point to such a limited goal, as Welles did in the sporadic press conferences that he convened on his mission, the Administration was able to claim that it was not involving the United States in the war in Europe and that it was acting in accordance with the neutrality legislation. Furthermore, the mission's publicly stated objective should not be underestimated. Firsthand information from a trusted confidant would give the President a clear account of the situation and the personalities involved such as he did not have from Rome or Berlin, and allow him to more fully assess the information he was receiving from Paris and London.

As a final conclusion, then, the initial concept behind the Welles mission evolved into a broader mission with a number of objectives in a relatively short space of time—just six weeks at the beginning of 1940. Crucially for this analysis, the mission would continue to evolve. Roosevelt's thinking in late January 1940 was clearly subject to a number of influences, which makes drawing distinct conclusions as to why the Welles mission was undertaken at the time and in the manner it was, a very complex matter. In essence, though, the continuing analysis presented here reveals that against the background of the "phony war" the Welles mission resulted from Roosevelt's awareness of the pressures of the various peace moves, constrained by American public opinion, and his view that the early part of 1940 provided a window of opportunity before the spring escalation. In this environment, Welles was able to provide the impetus and energy that became a diplomatic mission to Europe. The disapproval of the British government and the cautious words of Cordell Hull dulled the objective of directly exploring peace terms, but Roosevelt and Welles pressed on with the mission, believing the other objectives would still be worth exploring. Yet Welles had not lost complete sight of the idea of exploring peace terms before he arrived in Europe. They were worth pursuing, both for their own sake and for the purpose of understanding more fully the position of the belligerents. Welles never acknowledged as much because of his concern that it would appear as though he were in league with the belligerents—the House analogy. Nevertheless, and unbeknowingly, the British in a telegram notifying the Dominions of the Welles mission succinctly pointed to a possible outcome that Roosevelt and Welles had considered for the mission. The telegram stated that "in spite of these dangers, the Under Secretary's visit may serve a good purpose if he can convey to the President a clear picture of the issues which are at stake, and assure him of the determination of the Allies to achieve the aims which they have set before themselves and have publicly proclaimed."[110] Such a statement would have been music to the ears of Roosevelt and Welles. For the pair, every last possibility of avoiding the expected catastrophe in the spring had to be thoroughly explored, even in the full knowledge that the odds were stacked against their making any positive impact on events in Europe.

CHAPTER 4

HOPE, DESPAIR, FRIENDS—WELLES IN ROME, BERLIN, AND PARIS, 17 FEBRUARY– 12 MARCH 1940

As WELLES TRAVELED TOWARD EUROPE IN MID-FEBRUARY, the mission that both he and Roosevelt had devised had developed sufficiently from their initial concept so that Welles would be able to forward a number of objectives in his conversations in Europe's capitals.[1] This chapter examines the objectives Welles had for his discussions in Rome, Berlin, and Paris. The next chapter will deal with his time in London.

Welles' time on the continent of Europe provided the opportunity to explore the breadth of the mission's objectives. The investigation of the possibilities of peace, both for their own sake and because it allowed an assessment of the combatants' war and peace aims, was considered along with the gathering of information and the objectives of perpetuating Italian neutrality and prolonging the "phony war." Nevertheless, it is unrealistic to expect that Welles, in each of the over 20 official conversations he had, would address each of these objectives in precisely the same manner. The evolution of the mission up to this point indicates that Welles himself was a key dynamic and had considerable scope to mold the mission. Its evolution can be seen in which elements Welles stressed within the spectrum of his objectives as he progressed through Europe. In some respects his emphasis reflected the reality of conducting conversations with assorted individuals in a variety of environments. In Rome, unsurprisingly, given that it was his first stop, Welles had the full breadth of the mission to explore. This meant stressing the potential benefits of neutrality in terms of Italo-American cooperation and encouraging Mussolini to believe in his post-Munich image as a peace broker, in the hope that he might seek to fulfill such a role before the spring catastrophe. These were points he would reiterate when he returned to Rome at the end of his mission. Welles' emphasis in Berlin became more focused than the broad range of objectives he pursued in Rome. After his time in the German capital the discussion of peace in its broadest sense was solely for the purpose of assessing war and peace aims. Roosevelt and Welles, having acknowledged at the outset that any accommodation with Hitler was a very unlikely prospect, certainly did not see peace with Nazi Germany as possible after Welles' time there. That the Administration had already largely discounted the prospect of a stable and lasting peace with Hitler is evident in the lack of a presidential letter to the Führer. Instead in Berlin, Welles, having heard tirade after tirade about the injustices done to Germany, sought to prolong the "phony war" by presenting an ambiguous position over whether Roosevelt might then make some "move" upon his return to Washington. In the French capital, Welles' emphasis in conversation was to ask about the possibilities of peace with a view to gathering information with a particular stress on assessing French resolve. Throughout all of his conversations Welles knew he was working with long odds. In revealing that Welles had different emphases in the different capitals, this book illustrates further how within the breadth of the mission's objectives, it continued to evolve, even once Welles was in Europe.

Tracing the evolution of Welles' thinking when in continental Europe is acknowledged to be somewhat problematic. Evidence of Welles' personal thinking at the time is scarce. His private views on how his mission was progressing were revealed in only a few documents, and in these instances Welles' solemnity must be remembered. There is no record of the private communications he sporadically had with Roosevelt. While details of the communications between Welles and Roosevelt are impossible to know, this analysis has explained the intimate working relationship that the pair established as part of the longer-term themes at work in Administration policy making. Indeed, the bilateral line of communication reflected the pair's desire to limit the possibility of any sensitive political aspects of the mission entering the public domain. The full detail of the mission—its breadth of objectives—had to remain private to best enable their chances, acknowledged as being remote, of a positive outcome.

Although the direct focus of this work looks at the day-to-day activities of Welles, the other themes that it has utilized to provide an analytical framework should not be forgotten as underlying aspects of the mission. In the case of Hull's role, the direct and private communication between Roosevelt and

Welles meant Hull was not to the fore as the mission progressed. Crucially, the fact that Hull, named as one of the two recipients of Welles' findings, should be left out of the most sensitive communication epitomizes the state of that triumvirate relationship in early 1940. With regard to American public opinion, the control that Welles and Roosevelt exerted over the mission in avoiding making any comment reveals the extent to which they both tried to prevent it becoming a source of criticism for the Administration. When the Administration did feel the need to comment on the mission it was only once Welles had returned to Rome in March and it was in direct response to suggestions that Welles was about to forward a peace move. Somewhat paradoxically, Welles, Roosevelt, and Hull found themselves in agreement in proposing a statement reiterating the 9 February declaration. This episode will be dealt with in due course in chapter 6. Regarding relations with London, little can be said about Welles' time on the continent. The British, having been somewhat reassured by Roosevelt's presenting the mission as not being a public peace move, still had concerns about what Welles might privately have to offer. Whereas for those in London Welles' time in Rome, Berlin, and Paris meant watching and waiting, for the Under Secretary himself his time in those capitals was crucial in attempting to further the breadth of the mission's objectives.

To reiterate: the aims of the mission continued to develop once Welles was in Europe. As his first meeting began in Rome Welles had the full spectrum of the mission's objectives in mind, but as he traveled to Berlin and then Paris the objectives evolved subject to what he had learned and what was then possible. In Berlin the prospect of any peace settlement, acknowledged as being remote, became nonexistent. This did not mean that he stopped a line of discussion that focused on possible peace terms, as this allowed him to gather explicit accounts of French, and then British, war aims and their conviction in fulfilling them. As Welles traversed Europe he hoped at the very least that while he was talking the guns would lie quiet.

Welles began the mission on 26 February 1940 with conversations in Rome with Mussolini and his Foreign Minister, Count Ciano. These two meetings were significant for the mission because in both cases Welles learned potentially valuable information that might further the objectives of his mission.

The first meeting was with Ciano and took place on the morning of 26 February.[2] While the subject matter of the conversation ranged from the poor state of Italo-American relations, through the neutrals' conversations, to the proposed Rome Exposition in 1942 and was indicative of Welles trying to engage with the Italian, the meeting's importance lay in two areas. The first was the way Welles presented to Ciano the goal of his mission and the second was that Ciano revealed views on the Axis with Germany and on Italian neutrality. The latter gave Welles cause for hope in addressing the wider goals of the mission.

In describing his mission to Ciano, Welles revealed the interpretation of it that he wanted to portray in Italy. A discrepancy between the 9 February public statement and what Welles said is clear. The Under Secretary told Ciano that he was "to report to [the President] upon the present possibility of the establishment in Europe of a stable and lasting peace—that was the only kind of peace in which my Government was interested." Welles then added, "The President is not interested in any precarious or temporary peace which would, in essence, be no more than a patched-up truce." This second sentence is crucial in illustrating that the only type of peace the Administration wanted was one that would be stable and lasting. However, paradoxically, it also shows that Welles was prepared to let Ciano believe that in broad terms Roosevelt was considering a settlement as an objective of the mission. In view of the objections of Hull and Chamberlain this goal had been qualified but not entirely discounted at this stage.

Welles' next comments further reveal the limitations on his mission brought about by the objections of London and Hull, and in this case they match the published statement. Welles added that he "was not empowered to offer any proposals, nor to enter into any commitments." Ciano's response was to welcome those guidelines, as he "doubted whether the moment was propitious for any effort of that character." These were potentially devastating words for the Welles mission had it been only solely to ensure peace, instead the concord that was evident during the rest of the conversation helps show, on the surface at least, that Welles was most interested in maintaining a dialogue with Ciano. Furthermore, Welles made a notable effort, as he would with Mussolini later and then when he returned to Rome, to praise Ciano's diplomatic efforts. Welles used glowing terms in stating that he had been "privileged to follow from a distance his [Ciano's] brilliant career." The normally reserved Welles went further in saying that he had seen with "much admiration" Ciano's efforts "to prevent war at the end of August, and since that date, to limit the spread of war." Such flattery was part of Welles' attempts to encourage continued Italian neutrality. If the Italian camp could be engaged sufficiently for them to think they may have a crucial role to play in any peace, then one of Welles' objectives might be more possible. This aspect of Welles' conduct, in perhaps a more desperate fashion, would be evident again when he returned to Rome at the end of his mission.

The most important information that Welles discovered in this first conversation of the mission came from Ciano's views on the Axis and Italian neutrality. In the case of the former, Welles recorded that throughout the discussion Ciano "made no effort to conceal his dislike and contempt for Ribbentrop or his antagonism towards Hitler. He did not hide his anxiety with regard to Germany and his apprehension with regard to her military power." Such a revelation was welcome news to Welles in his quest to gauge the Italian position in the Axis. Furthermore, Welles considered that one of Ciano's chief interests was "to maintain a balance between the Allies and Germany so that Italian neutrality may be preserved and so that when peace negotiations are undertaken, Italian claims may receive preferential consideration." Again this type of information was valuable to Welles in seeking to preserve Italian neutrality. That this was in his thinking had been evident from his first words to Ciano. He had opened by stating that "in the interest of civilisation itself" the "two great neutral influences should pull together, and not apart" for "the construction of lasting and sound peace foundations." Welles recorded that Ciano "heartily concurred" with such a suggestion.

In order to provide a thorough analysis of the significance of this conversation it is necessary to understand the character of Ciano. The Duce's son-in-law was a political chameleon in his ability to appear sympathetic to his immediate audience. While Welles stated in his report that Ciano "could not have been simpler nor more frank in the expression of his views"[3] in their meeting, the Italian had himself set out to appeal to the Under Secretary. Ciano wrote in his diary, published in 1947 with Welles providing the foreword: "I gave him [Welles] a humane turn to our conversation and this impressed him, because he was not expecting it."[4] Such duplicity was typical of Ciano and manifested itself in his tapping of the phone conversation Welles had with Roosevelt upon the former's return to Rome in March. Questions exist as to how far Welles believed in Ciano's apparent readiness to listen to the Under Secretary. This is especially relevant given that Welles later wrote of Ciano that "of all the men possessing high authority within the Axis governments, he was the only one who made it clear to me, without subterfuge and without hesitation, that he had opposed the war, that he continued to oppose the war, that he foresaw nothing but utter destruction for the whole of Europe through the extension of the war." However, this assessment was countered by Welles' knowledge of "Ciano's total inability to change the course upon which Mussolini had embarked."[5] Furthermore, that Welles wrote in his report in March 1940 that Italy will move as Mussolini alone decides, suggests he was indulging in his own intrigue in trying to encourage Ciano to think that Italy might have something to gain from their talks. Nevertheless, the tenor of Welles' record of his conversation with Ciano suggests he saw the meeting as a positive one. That Welles' tone indicates this even after Ciano had dismissed the prospect of any American intervention suggests that he regarded what else the Italian said as important information for furthering the range of the mission's objectives. In essence, then, the meeting between Welles and Ciano was intriguing. Each was trying to engage the other without revealing his motivations; in Welles' case the range of objectives his mission had developed; and in Ciano's, his knowledge of Mussolini's ultimate power over Italy's policy. Welles' understanding of Mussolini's preeminent position would become evident in the Under Secretary's next meeting on 26 February.

Though Welles' meeting with the Italian leader was conducted in a civil manner, in private both parties acknowledged that little of substance was achieved.[6] In Ciano's estimation the meeting with Mussolini "went badly," with Welles leaving the Duce's office "more depressed than when he entered it."[7] Nevertheless, the discussion began on a cordial note, with Welles presenting Mussolini with the personal letter the Under Secretary had composed on behalf of Roosevelt. The poor state of Italo-U.S. relations, along with the fate of the international economy, postwar disarmament, and Washington's neutrals conversations, provided a substantial introduction to the meeting before Welles' mission was broached. Such a wide-ranging opening illustrates again the range of subjects Welles was seeking to talk about in order to engage the Italian government.

In specifically raising the purpose of this mission Welles repeated the interpretation of its goal that he had given to Ciano earlier in the day. He stated that his goal was to report "on the present possibilities of the establishment of the bases for a permanent and stable peace in Europe" and that he brought with him no proposals. Mussolini's response immediately betrayed his commitment to the Axis, as he stated that German claims in central Europe must be settled together with Italian claims in the Mediterranean.[8] Despite such a settlement being clearly at odds with the Roosevelt Administration's ideas for a just and lasting peace, Welles then asked the Duce outright whether he considered it possible "for any successful negotiations to be undertaken between Germany and the Allies for a real and lasting peace?" Given what Mussolini had said previously, his answer of "an emphatic 'Yes'" is perhaps remarkable. Nevertheless he quickly followed this by stating, "I am equally sure that if a 'real' war breaks out . . . there will be no possibility for a long time to come of any peace negotiation." Such a statement can only have added to the feeling in Welles' mind that time was an issue in the "phony war." Having lasted an hour, the meeting ended with a "particularly cordial handshake" and an agreement that on his return through Italy at the end of the mission Welles would have a further meeting with Ciano and Mussolini. This meeting would illustrate how far Welles had by that stage dropped consideration of peace from the mission's objectives and was focusing on preserving Italian neutrality.

Also in evidence on this first day of the mission was Welles' ability to reset its parameters by asking Mussolini for "his suggestions as to any conversations which I might hold in Berlin." The Duce replied that he "believed that what I would be told there would be very similar to the opinions which he had expressed to me."[9] In asking this question, Welles was exhibiting the license he had to move beyond a strict interpretation of the 9 February announcement, which stated that he carried no proposals. This would be in evidence to varying degrees during the rest of the mission.

Despite the prospect of further meetings, the Italian view of this meeting was not positive. Ciano recorded in his diary that Mussolini was "not impressed by Welles' personality."[10] Richard Bosworth's well-received biography states that in private Mussolini was "scathing about Welles and his President, dismissing the exchanges with his visitor." This Bosworth attributes to Mussolini's judgment that "Americans were eternally superficial, while Italians judged matters in depth."[11] That the Duce was not impressed by the Under Secretary is significant, as it illustrates further the duplicitous character of the Italians. Mussolini's comments throughout the meeting were revealing of his own self-importance and his capacity to provide what he thought his audience wanted to hear.[12] While Welles saw some hope in the prospect of further conversations with Rome, Mussolini was not going to let the Under Secretary distract him from his devotion to the Axis. This would become clearer when Welles returned to Rome in mid-March.

In the American camp opinion was more positive. Phillips wrote that Welles' visit prompted "the official 'tap' . . . which was turned on or off by Mussolini as he saw fit, [to be] turned slightly towards a more friendly approach to the United States."[13] Welles, in a telegram reporting on both conversations to Roosevelt and Hull, clearly saw some reason for optimism in pursuing the broad objectives of the mission. Observing that "Mussolini received me in a very friendly manner," Welles pointed out that he believed "it wiser for me not to telegraph the more secret of the views expressed" on the Italian view on the prospect of a settlement. Clearly he believed he had been given some privileged information, and in direct contravention of what he had just written Welles continued that "Mussolini stated emphatically that he believed that such a possibility [of a settlement] existed."[14] What Welles could have considered more secret than this is not clear, but that this was not considered the most secret information indicates here that finding a peace settlement was not Welles' top priority. Furthermore, these comments were reported as point six in an eight-point memorandum and were in themselves given no extra comment. The remit of the other points covered in the telegram further reveal the extent of the mission's goals. To report on the prospects for peace alongside international economic prospects and even the proposed 1942 Rome Exposition illustrates at the outset of the mission that Welles and Roosevelt did not see a settlement as an overriding objective but as one aspect of the mission. This was crucial as it shows how far the mission had moved away from Roosevelt's initial conception of searching for a settlement and the incorporation of other objectives.

It was of little surprise, then, that Welles did not make more of his conversations in Rome in his telegram to Washington. Mussolini had said that negotiations involving the Nazis and Italy could prevent further armed conflict, but only on terms incompatible with Administration policy: Italian control of the Mediterranean and German preeminence in Eastern Europe. Yet Welles pursued Mussolini and Ciano's comments later on during the mission in order to address the objective of prolonging the "phony war." The belief that Mussolini acting as conduit might provide the parties with something to discuss was preferable to further escalation of the fighting. Set against previous difficulties in Washington's relationship with Rome, Welles' meetings with Ciano and Mussolini did augur some degree of hope. That Welles had found the Italians prepared to enter into discussion meant the mission was not "stillborn" in Welles' eyes and that the possibility existed to further its broader goals.

While Welles was considering how he could further his mission in his private conversations in Rome, in the glare of the world's press he was content to respond with "no comment" when asked about the mission. Moffat's previously unseen diary of the mission tacitly acknowledged at the outset that the press would be a key consideration for the Administration. He wrote that the press had been ordered to follow Welles "night and day" so that they could "report in a friendly, objective, or hostile manner according to the politics of their editor."[15] Berle also recognized that the press would have to be considered on the mission. He had learned that the "*Chicago Tribune* is sending along a man to write [Welles] up as unpleasantly as possible and make political capital against the Administration."[16] The importance of this was recognized by Welles, who remained tight-lipped on his mission. Although this earned him the title of "Sumner the Silent" among the following press, his taciturnity in public meant that those in London and Paris learned very little of the mission.

The British Ambassador Sir Percy Loraine, exhibiting the concern the British still had over the mission, was keen to rectify this and learn what Welles was doing in Rome. He had met Phillips in between the American's two appointments on 26 February and immediately reported back to London on Welles' meeting with Ciano. Although no detail was disclosed, Loraine wrote that the interview had apparently been "most satisfactory," with Ciano "at his best; friendly, charming, informative and lucid."[17] Loraine was able to meet Welles in person the next day at an informal lunch at the American Embassy in Rome. Although Welles had told Phillips that he wished to avoid all social engagements on his visit because of "the nature of [his] mission, as well as because of present conditions in Europe," the Under Secretary did end up in conversation with Loraine and the French Ambassador.[18] Despite Loraine later recording that he "would make no attempt to pump [Welles] about what had been said to him on the Italian side," Moffat recorded that the Ambassador "without preliminaries" did ask Welles "what Mussolini had said to him."[19] Welles' response reveals that he would not divulge any detail of his conversations. He stated "that he would no more tell him what Mussolini had said to him than he would tell Mussolini what the British Minister talked about." Moffat stated that this left Loraine "apparently puzzled."[20] Interestingly though, Loraine still filed a report to London that stated Welles' conversations had been "instructive and that he had been received . . . in a very friendly and cordial way which, in the case of Signor Mussolini had been rather unexpected."[21] That Welles talked with both the British and French Ambassadors, albeit at an informal luncheon at the Embassy perhaps reveals a certain disposition toward the Allies, especially as the German Ambassador had not been invited. Crucially, though, as Welles pushed on with his mission's objectives he certainly did not divulge any details to the diplomatic corps in Rome before moving on to Berlin.

Welles spent two nights in Zurich en route to the German border, where he was met by a special train that took him to Berlin, arriving on 1 March 1940. Welles' time in Berlin would see the prospect of reaching any kind of stable and lasting settlement with the Nazi regime, acknowledged from the outset as being remote, being discarded as one of his objectives. Having listened to various Nazi officials, particularly Ribbentrop, Welles knew privately that they were bent upon war as a means of achieving their aims. (Importantly, though, he would keep "exploring the possibilities for peace" on the rest of his mission, as a means of learning what the belligerents were fighting for and assessing their commitment to the fight.) The Nazis' fervor for war was evident throughout Welles' time in Germany. On the eve of his visit, Hitler had a memorandum prepared to circulate to all those who would meet Welles. The document explained the reasons why Germany was at war and why no peace was possible. It also meant there was no prospect of Welles finding acceptable peace terms with the Nazi regime. The memorandum read, "All statements are to be avoided which could be interpreted by the other side to mean that Germany is in any way interested at present in discussing possibilities of peace. I request rather that Mr Sumner Welles not be given the slightest reason to doubt that Germany is determined to end this war victoriously and that the German people—and their leadership—are unshakeable in their confidence in victory."[22] The Nazi regime clearly did not contemplate finding any arrangement with Welles and were clear in the message they wanted to send.

The Under Secretary's first meeting in Berlin revealed the distance between the American and his hosts. Welles met Joachim von Ribbentrop, the German Foreign Minister, on 1 March and began with the same assessment of his mission that he had presented in Rome.[23] He told Ribbentrop that his mission was designed to facilitate "the President's desire to ascertain whether there existed any possibility of the establishment of a sound and permanent peace in Europe." Ribbentrop's response, which lasted "for more than two hours," was an account of "Germany's participation in European history, as he saw it, from January 30, 1933, the day Hitler became Chancellor." He began by stating that there was no feature of German foreign policy that "conflicted" with the interests of the U.S. government. Welles recorded that he had to restrain himself from interjection at this point, as he feared that "violent polemics" would ensue, given Ribbentrop's "obviously aggressive" stance. Included in the German's analysis was the mention that it was the British who had rejected Hitler's October "peace offer," and a remarkable analogy: Ribbentrop stated that "Germany wished for nothing more in Europe than what the United States possessed through the Monroe Doctrine in the Western Hemisphere." The two-hour tirade ended with Ribbentrop stating that only once the English desire "to destroy Germany is killed, once and for all" could there then be peace.[24]

By this time, and in a somewhat exasperated state, Welles said he "would not attempt to speak at any length, but . . . could not refrain from making certain comments upon what the Minister had said." That Welles did not attempt to respond in any detail indicates that, however distasteful the German, Welles did not want to become involved in a "spat" that could have jeopardized the rest of his time in Germany, or the wider goals of his mission. His meeting with Ribbentrop confirmed to him that in Germany his main priority must be to leave the impression that, upon his return to Washington, Roosevelt might make some gesture. It was again a long shot, but there was no prospect of discussion with the Nazi regime. Welles' limited response to Ribbentrop was nevertheless a straightforward assessment of the poor state of American-German relations. The reason, according to Welles, was the gross violation of international law, human rights, and common decency perpetrated by the German government. Further, Welles could not let the meeting end without redressing Ribbentrop's comments on the "Monroe Doctrine." Welles suggested in forthright terms that if "the Minister desired to use the term 'Monroe Doctrine' as synonymous with the term 'sphere of influence'; whether political or economic, he should find some more accurate synonym." After a brief riposte from Ribbentrop, which he again ended by stating that there could be no peace "save through German victory," to avoid the potential for even more heated exchanges Welles "terminated the interview" after an uncomfortable two and three-quarter hours.

Welles' private observations about Ribbentrop show that he saw little prospect of ever being able to have a civil conversation with the Reich Foreign Minister, let alone reaching an agreement with his government. In a rare instance of Welles' personal views being evident, he wrote of Ribbentrop: "[He] has a completely closed mind. He struck me as also a very stupid mind. The man is saturated with hate for England, and to the exclusion of any other dominating mental influence. He is clearly without background in international affairs, and he was guilty of a hundred inaccuracies in his presentation of German policy during recent years. I have rarely seen a man I disliked more." Clearly, Welles was appalled by Ribbentrop. It is significant also that, throughout the pair's conversation, both men used Dr. Schmidt as an interpreter, despite the fact that, having been Ambassador to London and a traveling wine salesman in North America, Ribbentrop spoke English, and Welles spoke adequate German. The use of the interpreter is symbolic of the distance between the two men.

Welles' next meeting on 1 March, conducted in entirely more civil circumstances, has two important features for this analysis. The meeting was with Welles' German counterpart Ernst von Weizäcker, and although it was of little consequence because Weizäcker was entirely marginal in Nazi policy-making, Welles learned of Hitler's directive for conversations with him. Weizäcker told Welles, at no little personal risk, that he had "been strictly instructed not to discuss with you in any way any subject which relates directly or indirectly to the possibility of peace."[25] This was valuable information for Welles regarding the rest of his conversations in Germany. The second important aspect of this conversation was that, in breach of his remit, Welles stated to Weizäcker that although his conversations in Rome were confidential he "felt entirely able to tell him [of his] impressions after talking with the Duce." Such impressions were obviously subject to Welles' interpretation but reveal how far he was seeking to utilize Mussolini's comments as a means of prolonging the "phony war" and assessing the strength of the Axis. Based on Mussolini's judgment that the "basis for a just and lasting peace could still be found before it was too late," Welles asked Weizäcker whether an approach from the Duce would receive a "favorable reception" in Berlin. Although he gave no direct answer, Welles concluded after Weizäcker's comments "that if the Duce approaches Hitler directly and secretly, it will have a decisive influence"; however, "if Ribbentrop knows of the approach, he will do his utmost to block it." Ribbentrop's position as a proponent of war was clear to Welles. Weizäcker wrote of this exchange that he had objected to Welles' line because it was not his "business to discuss peace actions," clearly revealing his concern to appear to be conforming to Hitler's directive.[26] According to Welles, the interview ended in an emotional state with tears in Weizäcker's eyes and a hope that Welles' mission might see "an absolute holocaust . . . avoided."[27]

The next day, Welles met Hitler at the new Chancery building. The conversation would signal the end of any prospect of the Welles mission inaugurating a lasting and just peace. The meeting began with Welles, repeating as he had done the day before, that his mission was for the purpose of examining the grounds for a "just and lasting peace" and that any information would be retained for the President and Secretary of State. Welles also spoke in his opening of Mussolini's comments that "the foundations of a just and lasting peace might still be laid."[28] In doing so he was trying to assess the nature of the Axis; however, Hitler ignored Welles' opening. Instead, in much the same vein as Ribbentrop and in accordance with his own directive, he explained how it was the British who had set out on a destructive path by declaring war and refusing his October "peace offer." Hitler by contrast was merely trying to reunite all the German peoples. Although other issues were discussed, including Hitler's claiming to be in agreement with the Roosevelt Administration's principles on free trade, the theme returned to Germany as the victim in the war. Hitler's final words illustrated his commitment to the conflict: "I can see no hope for the establishment of any lasting peace until the will of England and France to destroy Germany is itself destroyed."[29]

At the end of this conversation with Hitler, Welles knew that there was no chance of the founding objective of the mission—exploring the possibilities of peace and finding the basis for a just and lasting settlement. This original aim had been weakened by the objections of Hull and the Chamberlain government, and it was now dealt a mortal blow by Hitler in Berlin. Langer and Gleason in *The Challenge to Isolation* agree. They suggest that "to all intents and purposes, . . . the major objective of the Welles Mission had failed . . . when the Under Secretary left the German capital."[30] However, while this analysis agrees that the exploration of peace was *a* major objective it was not *the* major objective, and so Welles still had additional objectives to pursue on his mission. In Berlin this meant cultivating the belief that something might come of the mission, and, more broadly prolonging the phony war, preserving Italian neutrality and gathering information for the President. An air of resignation that acknowledged that the Nazis were hell-bent on war can be seen in the rest of Welles' time in Germany. It was evident the next day as Welles met first of all with Rudolph Hess, the Deputy Head of the Nazi Party. Their meeting was of little consequence. After Welles' introduction as to the purpose of his mission, Hess merely reiterated from a "typewritten memorandum" the points that Welles had already heard from Ribbentrop and Hitler: the Allies were bent on the destruction of Germany and only military victory could guard against this. Welles wrote afterward that it was "entirely clear that either the Chancellor or the Foreign Secretary had dictated the course which the conversations to be had with me by the members of the German Government were to follow."[31] Once Welles was aware that "Hess was merely repeating what he had been told to say," the Under Secretary "made no attempt to set forth any views of my own" or record "any detailed account of this conversation."[32] Welles did record much of the detail of his next conversation as it was with Reichs Marshal Herman Göring, who had been the focus of much of the talk of peace the previous autumn.

In order to see Göring Welles endured an open-topped car journey of an hour and a half in freezing temperatures to his latter's country retreat, Karinhall. Welles' aims for this conversation were to assess Göring's standing in the regime in the light of the autumn rumors and, once he had found out that Göring was propagating the same message as the rest of the Nazi regime, to endeavor to play up the possibility that Roosevelt might act in the future. After his introduction, when he again referred to Mussolini's opinion that "there was still a possibility of a firm and lasting peace" in the hope of testing the Axis, Welles was once more subjected to the familiar recital of German foreign policy under the Nazis.[33] Although, in contrast to Welles' opinion of other high officials of the German regime, Göring was "simple, unaffected and exceedingly cordial," the subject matter of the conversation did not fundamentally change.[34] Göring carefully outlined how the British had continually rejected Hitler's efforts toward an "understanding" and that it was they who were fighting a war of destruction, not Germany. As elsewhere, the conversation discussed other matters, including the recent neutrals declaration by the United States—on which Welles found Göring amenable, but only after a peace settlement in which Germany's aims had been satisfied.

Welles' objective of trying to instill in Göring's mind the possibility that Roosevelt might act can be seen in the subtle differences between the German and American accounts of the final exchanges of the meeting. The German account ends with Welles declaring that he was leaving with "the hope that some way could still be found to avoid the tragedy of a war of annihilation." He then apparently said that he "would be glad" when he arrived back in Washington to indicate to the President "that there was still some hope of peace."[35] The significance is that Welles' own version does not mention either of these propositions. By pursuing such a line, the Under Secretary hoped that the prospect of U.S. involvement might cause pause for thought before Germany considered escalating the war. This could help achieve one of the mission's objectives, that of prolonging the "phony war." Welles' words also reveal something of his diplomatic style, no doubt drawing on the experience learned in the smoke-filled rooms of South America, in intimating that the President might be ready to act under his advice and thus increase the perception in Göring's eyes of Welles' importance. Welles' own account ends by recording a statement from Göring that is considerably more downbeat, offering no hope of anything other than war: an entirely more realistic assessment. "I fear that when you visit Paris and London you will realise that there is no hope for peace," Welles recorded of Göring. The German continued, "You will there learn what I now know, and that is that the British and French Governments are determined to destroy Germany, and that no peace, except on that basis, will be considered by them."[36] While it is possible that both accounts were embellished in order to further their individual aims, given the congruence of the accounts up to this point there seems little reason to suggest that this was the case. Instead, the subtle variance reveals Welles' acceptance that delay was the best he could hope for from Germany.

Before Welles departed from Germany he met briefly with Hjalmar Schacht, the former Reichsbank President. This meeting, though it contains an extraordinary tale of intrigue prefaced by Schacht's statement that if what he said became known he would "be dead within a week," reveals further that Welles was not desperate to achieve a peace at all cost.[37] Schacht outlined an apparent plan by a group of leading generals to depose the Hitler regime, which could be furthered if Schacht could visit the United States. Welles responded by dodging the question, as he was no doubt aware that the State Department's view of Schacht was hardly complimentary. "To understand him," Messersmith had written in January 1939, "it is necessary to realise that his dominating characteristic is his ambition to play a great role, to be in the public eye and to have his outstanding merit recognised."[38] With this in mind, Welles ended the conversation by disassociating himself and restricting himself to the statement that he "could not undertake to question any course which he [Schacht] might determine to lay down for himself."[39]

Welles' final opportunity to promote the view that Roosevelt might act after his return to Washington came when Ambassador Hans Dieckhoff, the erstwhile German Ambassador to Washington, saw Welles and Moffat off at the station. Dieckhoff subsequently recorded that Welles "expected his trip to be successful if only Europe remained quiet 'in the next four or five weeks.' "[40] In making comments like this Welles, knowing that a settlement with the Nazi regime was nigh on impossible, was trying to implant the idea that his mission would result in an initiative from Roosevelt, in the hope that this might prevent the onset of any German offensive. It seems that Kirk was in league with this idea. After calling on von Weizäcker the next day Dieckhoff concluded that Kirk had stated in "unmistakable terms" that "at the end of Welles's trip some kind of initiative by President Roosevelt could be expected."[41] That Dieckhoff evidently put some faith in this line is clear from his composed report on the return to Berlin of James D. Mooney, one of the businessmen who had been involved in a peace move the previous autumn. Mooney had returned to Berlin in early March, erroneously believing that he had presidential endorsement after briefly talking again with Roosevelt in January 1940. Nevertheless, Dieckhoff recorded that if "any American initiative can lead to results, it is that of Sumner Welles, but not of Mooney."[42] Welles' activities had evidently raised the prospect that Roosevelt might consider some move. Historian Ralph de Bedts agrees that Welles had delay as an objective of his mission. He writes, "Given the likelihood that the so-called 'phony war' might not last forever, Roosevelt seemingly hoped that the mission might throw any Nazi offensive plans off balance."[43] The notion of prolonging the "phony war," on the basis that the Roosevelt Administration might "act" at some point in the future, is a key aspect of the analysis that this work proposes. That it was a deliberate tactic in Germany is supported by the fact that leading comments of the type Welles made there cannot be found in his discussions in Paris and London and are seen only in vague terms when Welles returned to Rome. Faced with the prospect of either capitulating to Nazi dominance of continental Europe or witnessing complete carnage across Western Europe, and in the full realization that it was unlikely to influence events, Welles saw this as worth pursuing as he progressed through Europe.

The substance of Welles' meetings with the Nazi government had been predetermined by Hitler's directive. This meant that he was unable to utilize Mussolini's comment that a "settlement" was still possible in order to engender a discourse that might prolong the "phony war." Instead, Welles, having been subjected to a party line entirely incompatible with the Roosevelt Administration's views, was left to propagate the view that something might flow from his mission upon his return to Europe. The notion that time was running out was clearly in the air while Welles' party was in Berlin. Moffat was told by a former colleague in Berlin that "the moment the spring really comes anything may happen." The Belgian diplomat, well aware that U.S. intervention would be wholly unlikely, expressed to Moffat views very much akin to those Welles was disseminating. Moffat recorded of the Belgian: "Even if it's not true, let the Germans think that you might come into the war. . . . It's the only deterrent possible."[44] The futility surrounding the mission was brought to the fore for Welles facing the Nazi government. In fact, the day before Welles arrived in Berlin, Hitler had authorized plans to invade Scandinavia. As Welles left Germany on the evening of 3 March and returned to neutral Switzerland, battle plans were being drawn up.

After resting for two days in Switzerland, Welles headed for Paris on board the Simplon-Orient Express. From his conversation with an unexpected traveling companion it is possible to gain a rare insight into Welles' personal views about his mission and its multifaceted nature. On board the train was Ambassador Joseph Kennedy, heading for London to prepare the ground for Welles. Although Kennedy's is the only account of this meeting, and his views on the fate of Europe were by this stage significantly divergent from those of the Administration, his record of the conversation is worthy of analysis. Kennedy had passed through Rome briefly, on his way to Milan to board the train, and had called on Phillips. There he had learned two things. First, and in accordance with what Welles himself had ascertained, that Mussolini "was still strong for Hitler" while "the rest of the Italian Government group . . . from Ciano down were pro-Ally . . . none of them had that fortitude of character that would lead them to take positions in opposition to what Mussolini might want."[45] The second piece of information that Kennedy relayed was news that the Germans had approached the Pope with a request that Ribbentrop be accorded an audience. As the two Americans pondered this seemingly surprising move, Kennedy concluded that "it seemed patent . . . that the reason for Ribbentrop's visit was his [Welles'] own visit to Berlin." Perhaps such a conclusion reveals Kennedy's hope that Welles' mission had influenced policy in Berlin. The reality of Ribbentrop's trip to Rome was that it was an opportunity for Germany to tell Mussolini that Italy's position was alongside Germany and in the war.[46] Although unknown at the time, this conformed with what Welles had learnt in Germany and how he responded to Kennedy on the train to Rome. He told the Bostonian that, although he had told Hitler and Göring of Mussolini's willingness to see "a negotiated peace" and that the Duce was prepared to "use his influence to attempt to bring one about," they had responded in a negative fashion. This prompted Welles to again quote long odds in relation to his mission. Welles stated he was "sceptical about immediate results," Kennedy's account states, and "that the chances of peace seemed about one out of a thousand." Nevertheless, Welles hinted at the wider objectives of the mission: he "believed that in any event his mission would have some value in consolidating official American opinion on the war and its issues." Such an assessment, albeit subject to Kennedy's interpretation, is significant in revealing the other objectives of the mission and specifically the influence that American opinion had on Administration policy formulation. Yet there was little time for further reflection as the pair soon arrived in the French capital with Welles "eager to do the rounds in Paris."[47]

When Welles arrived in Paris he was back among friends. He knew Paris well, had met many French politicians government before, and was well informed of events in the French government owing to the efforts of Ambassador Bullitt. Despite Bullitt's success in conveying a general picture, Welles' conversations in Paris were conducted with an emphasis on gathering information. In particular, his discussions were aimed at ascertaining French commitment to pursuing their war aims, their postwar plans, and the state of relations with Rome. Welles also maintained the silence that had typified his mission. At this time, he had two motives for this: first, in Europe Welles wanted to prolong the belief that the mission might result in something; and, second, in the United States he wanted to avoid any accusations that he was bringing with him from the Axis capitals any "terms" for the Allies. The memory of House was still strong.

Welles began his time in Paris by meeting the elder statesman of French politics, President Lebrun, on 7 March 1940. The conversation proved largely inconsequential because of the President's frail mental and physical state. Welles recorded that the Frenchman had great trouble remembering "with any accuracy names or dates, or even facts."[48] As in Italy and Germany, Welles' meetings in Paris followed quickly on from one another, and his next appointment was an entirely more significant meeting, with Prime Minister Daladier. Given that they had met previously, it was hardly surprising that Welles characterized their conversation as "exceedingly frank and entirely informal." He began as he had done elsewhere by stating that he brought no proposals, "much less any commitments," and explained that Roosevelt had sent him "in order to ascertain whether there was still any hope that a basis for the negotiation of a peace of the right kind could be found." Welles asked the Prime Minister for his views "as to the possibilities for the negotiation now of a just and lasting peace," adding that it was his "very definite impression" that the Duce "believed that there was still time for the establishment of such a peace."[49] In Paris, therefore, as in Berlin, Welles was keen to mention Mussolini in the hope that raising the Italian's name might trigger memories of his role at Munich. This might in turn lead to a reduction in tension between Paris and Rome and the preservation of the "phony war." Unsurprisingly, Italy provided the focus of Daladier's response as he recounted in glowing terms Mussolini's conduct during the Munich crisis. Daladier suggested that "the real difficulty . . . was an adjustment between Italy and Great Britain," not with France, as he saw no reason for not acquiescing to various Italian demands in the Mediterranean. Daladier continued in this tone as he stated that "there was every reason why the really German peoples of Central Europe should live under German rule, provided they so desired." Daladier's comments reveal that elements of appeasement were still alive in the corridors of power in Paris. Welles drew this conclusion, stating that the "Prime Minister made it very clear to me that he did not believe that political or territorial adjustment would create any insuperable difficulty in reaching peace." Furthermore, and equally significantly, Daladier "made it clear that whatever he might say in public, he would not refuse to deal with the present German regime." Although Daladier's comments alluded to the possibility of achieving a settlement, Welles, who knew that any "just and lasting" peace with the Nazis was impossible, was more concerned with ascertaining how far the French willingness to "deal" reflected a lack of conviction. Had he still been set upon reaching a settlement he would surely have made more of Daladier's comments. Welles continued to investigate French belief further by raising the much-discussed issue of disarmament. He pondered, "How could any actual step towards disarmament be undertaken by France or by England unless they were confident that Germany and Italy were in reality disarming at the same time?" Welles, in order to *test* French resolve, followed this by declaring that "the United States would not assume any responsibility . . . which implied as a potential obligation the utilisation of

American military strength in preserving the peace of Europe." This line, for entirely practical reasons to do with the strength of nonentangling opinion in the United States, had been one that the Administration had taken with both the British and the French in preceding years. It reflected a view that the Allies must "stand up and be counted for" in the fight against the Axis and not be seen to be relying on the eventual involvement of the United States.

This meeting with Daladier is significant for understanding Welles and his mission by the time he reached Paris. Though Welles was in familiar surroundings and discussing familiar subjects, this conversation reveals that he was not purely concerned with securing a peace from the mission. Had this been his priority at this stage Daladier's comment that in private he would be prepared to "deal" with the Nazis would no doubt have prompted more consideration. Instead, Welles sought to broaden the discussion in order to assess the state of Franco-Italian relations and to assess the government's commitment to defeating Nazism.

In discussing Italy and Mussolini at some length, Welles implicitly revealed that after Berlin he saw Italian neutrality as becoming a more important objective of his mission. If the mission could alleviate tensions in Franco-Italian relations from the French point of view, then it would remove one of Mussolini's justifications for entering the war, and so prolong the "phony war." To this end, Welles welcomed the comments of M. Leger, the Secretary General of the French Foreign Office, who under obvious prompting from Daladier stated, "in the most categorical manner," that "every possible consideration was given from now on to the sensibilities of both Mussolini and Ciano." This was encouraging for Welles as he sought to preserve Italian neutrality.

Familiar as they were to him, Daladier seems to have taken on board Welles' words on hardening Allied resolve. The British Embassy in Paris recorded the next day that "M. Daladier considered it essential to demonstrate the strength of the Allies' organisation, financial and economic, their determination to win, and their confidence in doing so without external aid."[50] This is important for Welles' mission, as it had intended to assess Allied resolve. The importance for the Allies of not appearing to be waiting for the Americans was understood by those in Paris and London, and, paradoxically perhaps, this would encourage American support for their cause. The "audience" for this resolve was American opinion that was skeptical of the reality of the conflict that the spring might bring.

Of further relevance for comprehending Welles' conduct on his mission was that in talking to Daladier he continued to use the same format for his conversations that he had with the Germans and Italians, even when confronted with an old acquaintance. In doing this he did not tell Daladier any *more* about his mission's progress than he had told Hitler in Germany. Welles was fully aware that he could not be seen to be giving any advantage to a particular party, and this meant not appearing to favor the French, especially as he had just come from Berlin. Here the memory of Colonel House is evident. In essence, Welles' conversation with Daladier simply represented a further opportunity to gather information on the French position.

Welles' meetings the next day took in a range of French opinion yet ultimately proved of little consequence. Of more importance was a brief press conference he held on 8 March, at which he maintained his public "silence" in stating that he would repeat nothing he had heard thus far on his mission. The day began with a meeting with the President of the Senate, Senator Jeanneney, who recounted with "Clemenceau"-style vigor how France had been forced into war with Germany three times during his life. M. Herriot, the President of the Chamber of Deputies, sought to portray himself to Welles as someone who had tried to mediate across the Rhine for years but had been deceived by German trickery. He was thus convinced that "the German people were themselves the cause of the present situation, and not their leaders alone." Welles found Herriot "utterly pessimistic, completely without hope, and without an iota of any constructive suggestion or proposal with regard to the possibility of any lasting peace." In contrast to this he found the Deputy Prime Minister M. Chautemps ready to discuss peace. Proposing an agreement on territorial questions in the East, and with a practicable plan for disarmament and the maintenance of French security, Chautemps was prepared to "strongly recommend . . . entrance upon negotiations . . . rather than a continuation of the war." A last meeting in the day with the Minister of Justice M. Bonnet proved merely to be an opportunity for the Frenchman to justify his role in the negotiations with Germany over the previous two years.[51]

Welles' day was not over though as he took the opportunity to reiterate the public objectives of his mission. The purpose of such a reiteration at this stage of his trip was to state for the mass ranks of the press, many of whom had not followed him to Berlin, that he would not be revealing what he had learned in Rome or Berlin in his conversations in Paris. At the American Embassy Welles reaffirmed that his mission was "solely to be able to give an account to the President of the present situation in Europe. Consequently he could not either directly or indirectly make any allusions to the information he had been given or to the views which had been expressed to him."[52] During Welles' time in Germany the press had become insatiable for information, and Welles sought to mitigate the prospect of a sensational story emerging from the rumors by making this statement. Nonetheless, such a story did emerge on the eve of Welles' departure from Europe and would require a further pronouncement of the mission's stated goals. In Paris, Welles handled the press with no little aplomb and typically dry humor: as Murphy, the

Chargé to Paris, recorded, "The Under Secretary's clear-cut statement to the journalists that he would say absolutely nothing about what he has seen and heard and what he thought about what he had seen and heard left them tongue tied before his smiling invitation to ask him any questions that they thought he might answer."[53] Although Murphy reported that Welles' approach had "clicked" with the French press, after he had returned to Washington a photograph taken in Paris was to cause Welles and the Administration momentary discomfort. At the time, Welles' party was content with the press coverage they were receiving. Moffat wrote in his account of the mission after seeing numerous "personal titbits" about the party that "on bigger things, the press has been surprisingly good."[54] At this stage at least, Welles' silence was serving the wider purposes of not letting the mission appear to be entangling the United States in European intrigue.

Welles' most significant meeting in Paris took place the next day (9 March) with Treasury Secretary Paul Reynaud at the Louvre. This meeting was important because the Under Secretary found Reynaud to be a kindred spirit on the issue of economic diplomacy. He wrote in his report of Reynaud that he had a "greater grasp of foreign relations, and . . . a keener mind, than any other member of the present French Government."[55] In this meeting Hull's influence, although he was many miles away at the time, could be felt on the course of the mission. When the meeting turned to the economic difficulties that were bedeviling American relations with the Allies, Welles urged Reynaud to continue French purchases of American tobacco and other agricultural products. Despite the cordial mood Reynaud could not agree wholeheartedly to Welles' request, using much the same argument that the British had used that the French were conserving dollar resources for future purchases.

Hull's influence could also be seen in Welles' presentation to Reynaud of a memorandum on principles of U.S. foreign economic policy. The document, which was in effect an economic addendum to Hull's 9 February announcement, stressed access to raw materials and free markets: "Healthy international commercial relations are the indispensable foundation of well being and of lasting peace between nations."[56] These were familiar points to Welles, who, as seen in his conference plan for November 1937, was very much part of the Administration's efforts to forward a principled agenda for the conduct of international relations. Reynaud welcomed the State Department memorandum in rather contradictory terms—"emphatic acquiescence"—but nevertheless announced later in the day that the terms were part of the principles that France was fighting for. Such a statement was intended to reach an American audience and provides more evidence of how the Administration sought to encourage the Allies to acknowledge that they were fighting for values akin to American ones.

Regarding Welles' immediate mission, as many of his compatriots had already commented to Welles, Reynaud suggested that it was the future of French security that was at stake and not necessarily the immediate issue. He believed that the "political and territorial issues now at stake could be solved without any considerable difficulty through negotiations between the Allies and Germany" but that "[t]he real problem was the problem of how France could obtain security and insure herself against a repetition of German aggression."[57] Here was the dilemma that Welles heard throughout Paris and that was the *real* issue for the French. Expression of such a predicament would be replicated when Welles arrived in London.

Before leaving Paris for London, Welles also met the exiled Polish leadership then in Paris. The significance of this meeting is that it illustrates further that the mission no longer had debate over acceptable peace terms as a central objective. Had this been the case, the meeting with the Poles would have been important. Instead, the meeting with the leadership of the country that had precipitated the Allied declaration of war was entirely more symbolic than substantial. The Prime Minister General Sikorski impressed Welles as a man of "character, of integrity, and of patriotism," but the conversation focused on the Pole's accounts of German atrocities. Moreover, Welles found Zaleski, the Foreign Minister, "profoundly pessimistic."[58] To orchestrate any peace settlement of the European war Poland and the Soviet Union would have had to be involved, as more than half of Poland was in Soviet hands. Stanley Hilton considers Moscow a "significant omission" from Welles' itinerary.[59] As it was, the meeting with the Polish leadership was of little consequence for the mission, except in illustrating that it had evolved well beyond its embryonic objective.

In essence, Welles' stop in Paris was far from momentous. This was of little surprise to the Administration in Washington, as they knew more about the French government than the others Welles would visit; elsewhere the Under Secretary had more to learn. Nevertheless, Welles' time in Paris is important in revealing more about the conduct of his mission and its breadth of objectives. He evidently made a good impression in Paris, as the British Embassy reported him to be "a man of the highest character, extremely loyal and of great honesty of purpose." However they added quite aptly that "[h]is is very honesty might lead to some naïveté."[60] Indeed, Welles' adherence to preserving his almost "saintly" neutrality meant that he did not disclose any of the broader objectives for his mission in Paris. With the memory of Colonel House clearly in mind, it is certainly notable that when among friends in Paris Welles did not disclose the details of his conversations in Berlin and Rome. In focusing on the role of Italy and Mussolini, he hoped to dampen tensions between Paris and Rome and so preserve Italian neutrality. Furthermore, in talking of Allied war aims Welles had endeavored to impart the familiar Administration line that the Allies needed to take on more responsibility in order to elicit greater support from the United States. What Welles learnt from a cross-section of French opinion was that the heart of the matter was the recurrent problem of security against German aggression. While not revolutionary news, this was fulfilling the information-gathering objective of his mission, with particular reference to what the French believed they were fighting for.

French opinion of Welles after his time in Paris was largely positive. Gone were the initial French concerns that Welles' trip would be a German propaganda coup: instead, and with the preface that Welles had "refrained from giving any information" to the French authorities, they concluded that "his sympathies were definitely on the side of the Allies, and that what he had seen of Germany had not pleased him." In relaying this information to London through the British Embassy, the French Foreign Ministry felt that Welles had "not been taken in by Herr Hitler and that his impression of Herr von Ribbentrop was definitely disagreeable."[61] Although largely accurate, "disagreeable" does not do justice to the vehemence of Welles' dislike of the German Foreign Minister.

As Welles left Paris on 10 March for London, his mission continued to fulfill the goal of gathering firsthand information for Roosevelt and had the capacity, through its continuation at the very least, to further two others: the prolonging of the "phony war" and the perpetuation of Italian neutrality. The lack of attention in Paris to a potential peace settlement, even after a number of people had mentioned it as a possibility, reveals further that Welles no longer saw this as a primary objective of the mission. Welles was by then using the discussion of "peace terms" to facilitate dialogue in pursuit of the mission's other objectives.

The two weeks from 26 February to 10 March that Welles spent on the continent of Europe allowed him to explore the breadth of objectives that his mission had developed since its initial conception in January and subsequent refinement in Washington in early February. Through contact with Europe's statesmen the mission evolved further, with different emphases becoming evident in Welles' conversations. Welles himself was the major influence on the development of the mission as he moved through Europe. Having been entrusted with the mission by Roosevelt, he had license to explore what he thought possible within the spectrum of objectives.

In Rome, Welles found in Ciano a genial and friendly disposition; someone whom he could talk to, but he knew the extent of the Foreign Minister's influence. Although written with hindsight, Welles described Ciano's "efforts" to maintain Italian discretion as "futile." Welles attributed this to Ciano's obsequiousness toward Mussolini: "Count Ciano was a man who lacked neither personal dignity nor physical courage, yet I have seen him quail at an interview with Mussolini when the Dictator showed irritation." Welles sums Ciano up as an "amoral product of a wholly decadent period in Italian history."[62] Nevertheless, Welles considered Ciano to be the most accommodating member of the Axis governments that he met. Though perhaps not surprising given his impressions of many of the Nazis, Welles' positive reportage of Ciano also reflects the lengths he was prepared to go to produce a positive outcome from the mission. The subject matter Welles considered in Rome—most notably his direct question to Mussolini as to whether peace was possible and Mussolini's positive response—reflected his ability to operate within the scope of the mission's objectives. Even though Mussolini's terms (for Italian dominance in the Mediterranean and German dominance in continental Europe) were far from palatable, Welles saw some value in discussing Mussolini's desires in that it maintained a dialogue that he hoped would prevent the early escalation of conflict. In the light of the long odds—the "one in a thousand chance" that Roosevelt had mentioned—that Mussolini had not dismissed Welles and in fact had provided grounds for further discussion did provide some glimmer of hope. Equally, if not more importantly, Mussolini's words provided something that Welles could use elsewhere—in Berlin, to test the bonds of the Axis, and in Paris, and then London, to test Allied resolve. Lastly, in Rome Welles hoped he could encourage Mussolini to believe that he might again be pivotal to peace in Europe and act as the "honest broker." Such a course of action might help preserve Italian neutrality. Welles later told Kennedy that Mussolini was "essential to the cause of peace," although he recognized fully, as he would in his report, that "[Mussolini] has got to get what he wants."[63] Though Welles' aims in Rome seem unrealistic in view of events during the rest of 1940, mindful of the intention of the Administration to "leave no stone unturned" Welles was attempting to further a range of objectives that he acknowledged stood little chance of halting the slide to war.

In Berlin, however, Welles' scope for furthering his mission was inhibited by Hitler's directive. This effectively signaled an end to the mission's chances of exploring the possibility of peace. Personally, Welles found the Nazis distasteful and was left in despair by their aims. Although he thought Göring spoke "rationally," this was only in comparison to Hitler, who, he considered a "really . . . cruel man," and Welles was almost apologetic in suggesting he had "reacted badly" to Ribbentrop.[64] Welles' disgust with the Nazis meant he resolved to try to leave in the minds of certain Germans the idea that his mission might produce a significant outcome. This was only ever a long shot. What is crucial is that Welles continued to talk about the conditions for a peace in Paris, London, and then back in Rome, because this provided a vehicle to explore the other objectives of the mission. Had he considered peace a real prospect after his time in Berlin, then the comments he heard—from

Daladier particularly—in Paris would surely have interested him more. Welles' priorities in Paris were to assess the French government's commitment to their war aims, the state of French relations with Rome, and to a lesser degree their postwar plans. Continuing to pursue the line of conversation he had had in Rome and Berlin allowed for this and countered any charges of "favoritism," that is, that he had changed his stance when among the Allies. He further sought, as the Administration had done during the months preceding the war, to reinforce French resolve. However this could not be openly acknowledged by Welles for fear of appearing entangled in European affairs. It is very difficult to see Welles' success in achieving these objectives in Rome, Berlin, and Paris as anything other than largely peripheral. Importantly, Welles at the time was not in a position to assess his success, but, as has been seen, "success" was not a prerequisite for Administration policy to be considered.

Evident in the first three legs of Welles' mission was the Under Secretary's understanding that he needed to keep interest in the mission going while avoiding controversy. He appreciated Roosevelt's desire "to do something" and so operate within the dual trends of American public opinion in early 1940. Welles was able to discuss wider ideas of security that accorded with the State Department's principles for international relations. Also obvious during the first three stops of his mission is his ability to push at the point of least resistance and so attempt to achieve something along the broad front of the mission's objectives. The wish to perpetuate the "phony war" and Italian neutrality was evident as was Welles' desire to gather firsthand information, especially in Rome and Berlin. The continuing interplay and development of the mission's objectives would be very important in London as too would Welles' own understanding of the state of Anglo-American relations. In London the Chamberlain government waited with some trepidation for the Welles mission to arrive.

CHAPTER 5

"THE GRASS SNAKE" ARRIVES: WELLES IN LONDON, 10 MARCH– 13 MARCH 1940

WHEN WELLES ARRIVED IN LONDON ON 10 MARCH, the objectives for the mission that he had embarked on had already evolved notably. In London this would continue in light of his quest for information. Having heard from Daladier that he might consider a settlement with the Nazi regime, Welles pressed those in London on what it would take for them to contemplate peace with those in Berlin. He did so not for the purpose of genuinely exploring peace with Hitler's government after his time in Berlin but in order to inform Roosevelt about the British government's war aims and their commitment to them. This fulfilled Welles' objectives as he saw them by this stage of his mission. The British government's intention on the eve of Welles' arrival was to impress upon the Under Secretary their steadfast commitment to the war in order to dispel any notion that Welles' may have had that they would be prepared to accept peace with Hitler's regime.

As Welles landed in London, relations between the Roosevelt Administration and the Chamberlain government were far from harmonious because of the minor crisis of late January and tension caused by the disclosure of Welles' intended mission at the beginning of February. While these tensions were somewhat mitigated by the British influence on the mission's objectives—notably the removal of the word "peace"—and by Welles' silence on his mission thus far, Chamberlain's government still harbored concerns as to what Welles would have to say on the issue of a settlement. Through the course of the conversations Welles undertook, these worries were somewhat alleviated but never completely dispelled and were augmented by concerns over Welles' conception of disarmament and security. The net effect of Welles' time in London was largely neutral in terms of a positive or negative influence on Anglo-American relations. Nevertheless, one can see a hint of accord between the United States and Great Britain in one area despite the difficulties that arose. Jay Pierrepont Moffat arrived in London, having limited his efforts on the mission up to that point to meeting a number of diplomatic colleagues across Europe. In London his presence was important, because in a semiofficial capacity he met a number of representatives of the Foreign Office and the Ministry of Economic Warfare. The latter were a significant audience for Moffat as he presented the State Department's concerns over the British economic practice that had prompted the minor crisis of early 1940.

With Welles in London, this chapter continues to consider the spectrum of the mission's objectives against the backdrop of the themes this book has explored. Naturally, Welles continues to play a prominent part in this analysis, and, given the circumstances, so does consideration of Anglo-American relations. It is important also to remember that the concerns of Hull and the limits to American foreign policy continued to be relevant to Welles in his discussions. A number of Hull's anxieties in particular would be replicated by the British. Further, Welles was conscious of not appearing to exhibit any favoritism to the British for fear of being cast in a "Colonel House mold" and so continued to remain silent about the progress of his mission to the press.

This chapter will also continue its analysis of the interaction of Welles' objectives. In London his emphasis was on the most straightforward one: the gathering of information, with a particular focus on information that revealed British war aims. This focus fitted in with the recognition that the exploration of peace for the purpose of resolving the conflict was nonsensical after Welles' experience in Berlin. Likewise, there was little value in pushing the case for Italian neutrality in London, although this would definitely be reinvigorated when Welles returned to Rome. Furthermore, Welles' objective of prolonging the "phony war" in London served only to increase tension in Anglo-American relations. British second-guessing of Welles' motives did little to dispel the notion that his mission might produce something. In an indirect fashion this helped Welles to sustain the doubt he wanted to engender in the minds of those whom he had met in Berlin as to his ultimate course of action. In this environment, the gathering of information was Welles' most achievable goal.

To support the analysis, this chapter will chart Welles' numerous conversations in London and consider the emphasis of those discussions. This will be of particular relevance in his two meetings with Chamberlain (11 and 13 March). The records of Welles' meetings in London are drawn from two main official sources and a third, personal account. The British Foreign

Office records illustrate succinctly the initial worries that Welles' visit prompted in Whitehall. They also acknowledge that, although Welles contemplated the discussion of peace with the Nazi regime, he found the prospect entirely distasteful. The Welles report published in *The Foreign Relations of the United States* mirrored that in his own memoirs, *Time for Decision*. It differs little from the British account in substance, though it uses less specific and political language and gives only rare glimpses of Welles' personal views. The main difference between the two accounts lies in who introduced the points of discussion. The British account emphasizes that Welles was the instigator of key issues, especially in his first meeting with Chamberlain and Halifax, whereas Welles' account is less clear. Halifax after meeting Welles on 11 March went as far as to suggest that Welles had introduced the "general outline of [a] plan" based on the principles of international conduct.[1] In view of Welles' practice elsewhere, it is reasonable to assume that, after his customary introduction and with his diplomatic experience in play, he did introduce issues and then manage the debate where he thought it possible and practical. The Welles report though, reflects the fact that he did not want to be accused of bringing "proposals" to the discussions for fear of exceeding the published stipulations of his mission and risking criticism for the Administration. The third account of Welles' conversations in London comes from Joseph Kennedy. It was written based on original notes almost 20 years after the mission took place. Despite the passage of time, in his account the Ambassador's slant on the course of the "phony war" is clear, that is that Great Britain was doomed and peace with Germany was better than the prospect of communism in Western Europe. With views so divergent from those of the Administration in Washington, it is no surprise that in contrast to the other two accounts it is only Kennedy's that maintains discussion of an imminent peace during Welles' time in London. The distance between Kennedy's views and Roosevelt's outlook only reinforces his requirement for firsthand information in London. Nevertheless, it is an account worthy of attention, given the moments of personal insight it provides. In brief, the Foreign Office records reveal British uncertainty; Welles' account, political awareness; and Kennedy's, his personal interpretation.

Having traveled to Paris with Welles, Kennedy then continued on to London. While Welles was preparing to depart for London the Ambassador met with Chamberlain and Halifax.

The initial concerns the British had about the mission are clear, as is an appreciation that the mission had not become a rallying point for any peace move. The Prime Minister explained to the Ambassador that he had initially been "very much concerned" by the prospect of the mission. However, after the transatlantic discourse of early February "it had been made so clear by Washington" that purpose of the trip was not to make a peace proposal that he had been put at ease. Furthermore, Chamberlain thought that "Welles had handled the trip in such a masterful fashion as to allay any suspicion or unrest that might be in the mind of anyone."[2] Chamberlain's words acknowledged that the mission had not turned into a coup for Hitler that might have seen Welles arrive in London with a "peace plan" from the Führer. In Kennedy's own account of this conversation his conclusion amplifies this line and supports the view that Welles' aim was to assess Allied resolve. Kennedy recorded that Chamberlain was "happy . . . believing that [the mission] would help to make more articulate for America and the rest of the world the war aims of the belligerents."[3] Such an assessment mirrored the one the Chamberlain government had dispatched to the Dominions in early February and shows a sophisticated degree of understanding of the Administration's position. Nevertheless, as far as preparing the ground for Welles' arrival was concerned, this conversation revealed that British concerns, though effectively reduced, still existed.

Kennedy's assessment of the mission on the eve of Welles' conversations further reveals his opinion of the original motive behind the mission and of the nature of the man who had sent Welles to Europe and his Administration in Washington. According to Kennedy, Welles had told him that "there's nothing . . . that Roosevelt would like to do more than make a dramatic move for peace. If he sees anything in my report to encourage him in such a move, he will jump for it, Hull notwithstanding."[4] Even with Kennedy's own bias, the sentiment of this further confirms that the mission's original objective, as conceived by Roosevelt and Welles in early January, was to explore the possibilities for peace. However, these comments also illustrate that Hull, who had opposed the mission from the outset, would act as a constraint on any action. Welles' awareness of his own responsibility in this process is obvious. He had to exploit his information-gathering role in order to present Roosevelt with as complete a picture as possible.

11 March was a typically busy day for Welles on his mission, with three important meetings. The first was with Lord Halifax, the second with the King and Queen, and the third with Chamberlain. However, Welles' day had already been eventful by the time of his first meeting that afternoon. His day had begun with a press conference at the U.S. Embassy, where his awareness of his mission's presentation was again evident. He prefaced the questioning from the hundred or so eager pressmen with his familiar statement of purpose: "[H]e was in Europe solely to report to President Roosevelt on the present situation." Welles then stated, "I would like to emphasise that I have no proposals to make and no commitments to offer in the name of my government. I am here solely on a fact-finding mission." Clearly this was far from the truth, but Welles sought to maintain this as the public explanation. His response to the questions raised revealed that he was steadfast in this. The

vast majority of enquiries found Welles responding with "no comment," which prompted the *New York Times* to remark that he was living "up to his reputation for reticence."[5] Welles continued to be conscious, as exhibited in this press conference, of the public perception of the mission. In London, as he had done in Paris, despite the familiar surroundings, Welles wanted to make sure he could not be accused of being too "friendly" with the Allies, for two reasons. First, such kinship would bankrupt the tenuous aim he had of leaving in the minds of the Germans the notion that the United States might act; and second, it would appear as though Welles was in league with the Allies. Neither scenario would help him further his mission's broad goals in view of what he saw as the pressing time factor.

After finishing the press conference, Welles had a lunch meeting with Kennedy at which the latter's standing in London became clear. Kennedy told Welles that he had not been invited to accompany him to Buckingham Palace that afternoon. Having just that morning dealt with the press, Welles was only too aware of what they would make of this. "Some of them will interpret it to mean that you and I have had a row. Others will say that the British want to put something over on me and have left you out because they know you are on to them. And still others will say that the British are sore because Kennedy said the United States must keep out of the war and so they are going to snub him. Any one of these interpretations will raise hell in the United States and can have serious repercussions, more so to the English than to us. I can't see them being so stupid and I will telephone Cadogan right away."[6] Welles managed to sort the situation out, as Cadogan explained that it was simply an administrative error, but the Under Secretary's concerns illustrate his anxiety over the way the mission was viewed, particularly in the United States. Although explained away by the British as an administrative error, it seems likely that they wanted to prevent Welles' meeting with the King being tarnished by Kennedy's defeatist views. Kennedy's opinions on the outcome of the war meant that those in London, as well as those in Washington, no longer used the American Embassy as a key channel of communication. Nevertheless, Kennedy had established a close relationship with the Royal couple during his time in London, and this was evident in the meeting Welles had at Buckingham Palace that afternoon.

Though not as important as the conversations Welles would have with members of the government, his discussion with the King reveals two significant features. First, on both sides there were happy reminiscences of the royal visit of the previous summer, with Welles stating he had "never known of a more completely successful visit" as it had engendered a "very genuinely friendly feeling on the part of many millions of my fellow-citizens."[7] The second and more important aspect of this conversation was a memorandum prepared by the Foreign Office for the King on the line to take with "Mr Sumner

Welles on the subject of dealing with Germany."[8] This was likened "to a Ministry of Information propaganda briefing" but reflected a clear-cut statement of Britain's position.[9] This was the type of statement Welles was keen to hear, but it was unfortunate that the King's difficulties in communicating meant that Welles characterized the meeting as "rather strained, with occasional lengthy pauses."[10] Nevertheless, the document stated that there were two clear difficulties in "dealing with Hitler": first, "his complete unreliability"; and second, "his limitless ambitions." These points prefaced three "concrete obstacles to peace." In turn, the Foreign Office document pointed to Germany's refusal to consider "restoring independence to [the] Poles and Czechs and [a] deliberate policy of extermination in Poland," the absence in Germany of a readiness to "agree to either disarmament or liberal trade system," and the "abandonment of [the] doctrine of force." At this point the memorandum put forward the British side of the case, asserting that the country had "no wish for, or expectation of, any gains from the war," unlike the Germans who hoped to "dominate Europe, if not the world." Finally, the Foreign Office message sought to expound the view that the British public was "united in its firm resolution" to fulfill the previously stated aims of defeating Nazi Germany and restoring Polish sovereignty. This last point was one that Welles would hear throughout his time in London—British commitment to their war aims—and it would help him fulfill his goal of fact-finding. It is all the more unfortunate, then, that such a concise statement failed to be fully conveyed to Welles because of the King's difficulties in communicating. In Welles' other conversations in London the *difficulties* that arose in the exchange of views were far more to do with substance than with the manner in which things were said.

The importance of Welles' meeting with Halifax, besides its role as a prelude to the Under Secretary's meeting with Chamberlain, lies in a number of areas. As a procedural point, Welles began his meeting with the same introduction he had used elsewhere: he and his government wanted nothing to do with a "patched-up peace."[11] Also as he had done elsewhere, he then discussed Mussolini's role and his claims in the Mediterranean. This drew a particularly robust response from Halifax, in keeping with the line the British government wanted to take with Welles.

Significantly for the development of the mission's objectives, this first meeting with Halifax saw Welles press the issue of British war aims. He questioned how far Britain was fighting against fascism and Hitler's regime and how much they were fighting for a settlement to territorial issues in Eastern Europe. While any distinction here may seem nonsensical, it is worth considering how important it was for Welles to be able to declare to the American people that the British were not fighting a war for territorial acquisition. Welles' report of this conversation emphasizes that Halifax spoke "in great detail" of the efforts he and Chamberlain had made to placate Hitler.[12] Each time, the pair was met by "new and more far-reaching demands," and "what was far more intolerable" was Hitler's "utter disregard [for] the solemn agreements into which he had entered." This led the Foreign Secretary to state that "peace could not be made except on the basis of confidence, and what confidence could be placed in the pledged word of a Government that was pursuing a policy of open and brutal aggression, and that had repeatedly and openly violated its solemn contractual obligations." While his report refrained from adding any comment at this juncture, Welles' remarks the previous day to Kennedy reveal that he understood the British predicament. He preempted the Foreign Secretary's line by telling Kennedy that there was "no confidence anywhere," leaving the British to believe that "Hitler lied yesterday and that he will lie tomorrow." Welles added, "I confess, I agree with them."[13] Though a note of caution should be sounded, given that this came from Kennedy's personal account, Welles would not have disclosed such a view in anything other than a private conversation for fear of suggesting that greater American assistance was waiting around the corner. A concern that precisely married up to one of those Hull had previously expressed.

In his conversation with Halifax, and in subsequent conversations, Welles also sought to ascertain what Britain was fighting for by talking about the principles of security and disarmament leading to a settlement that divorced the territorial issues from the political ones. This was familiar fare to Welles, given the heritage of his Armistice Day plan, but it was also familiar to the Chamberlain government. The lack of faith that the British had in such principles after their experience in the interwar period gave them considerable cause for concern in assessing Welles. Vansittart wrote after reading Halifax's record of the meeting that what disquieted him most was Welles' "naïveté in regard to disarmament," about which he thought the Under Secretary talked in a "glib and facile way."[14] Nevertheless, Welles did press the issue by asking "whether disarmament was not the real key to the problem, because it seemed to [him] that a real disarmament must tend towards the reestablishment of confidence."[15] In doing this Welles sought to use the broad issue of disarmament as a tool for the purposes of drawing out longer-term British war aims. Views on how far disarmament was integral to providing security against future aggression would provide Welles with an assessment of what the British were fighting for in early 1940.

Welles' emphasis on disarmament as a means of providing security was again to the fore when he met for the first time with Chamberlain later on 11 March 1940. Before then Welles raised the matter of how far Hitler was the cause of Britain's belligerence and in so doing raised more concerns for the British. Nevertheless, the meeting began with Welles handing Chamberlain a personal note from Roosevelt.[16] As Chamberlain read the note the Under Secretary restated the purpose of the mission in his customary preamble.

The conversation opened with Welles seeking further information on Chamberlain's aims in the war. He stated to Chamberlain that he had come across the strong conviction in Germany that it was "fighting a war of self-preservation," as they were convinced that Britain was trying to "destroy the Reich."[17] This may have been augmented by Kennedy's assessment of the British position, recorded at the time by Moffat. The Ambassador had learned that Chamberlain "is determined not only that it will not make peace with the present 'gang' in Germany, but will not make peace on terms that would enable any German Government or the German people to say they had won the war."[18] Welles wanted to know whether Britain felt she was fighting Germany as a whole or the Nazi regime in isolation. The Prime Minister rejoined that the United States "might take as a premise the positive assurance that England had no intention of destroying the German people, nor of impairing the integrity of the German Reich." Such an assurance would help Roosevelt draw distinctions in the eyes of the American people between the British and the destructive policies of the Nazi regime. In discussing Hitler's "gang," Chamberlain stated "flatly that so long as the present Government of Germany continued there could be no hope of any real peace."[19] This was because of the "impossibility of trusting Hitler."[20] It was clearly the Nazi regime, the one that Welles had found so appalling, that was the crux of the matter. Kennedy lamented later that day that because the "the only peace Chamberlain thinks will work is his peace and that calls for the end of the Hitler regime" that this "offer" would not allow Welles much "to work on."[21] While clearly revealing Kennedy's belief that the mission was intended to find a settlement, his comments reinforce the view that for the British it was Hitler's regime that was the reason for the war.

In contrast to Kennedy's conclusion, Chamberlain deduced that Welles' line of argument on Hitler was a precursor to the Under Secretary's suggesting the Führer could be moved to a "figurehead" position. While such rumors had been prevalent during the autumn in Washington, Welles had seen nothing in Berlin to suggest this was either likely, or more importantly, palatable to American sentiment. Chamberlain nevertheless felt Welles had "made up his mind" that for a settlement to be achieved Hitler would "nominally retire but remain a leading personality in Germany."[22] Such a solution, Chamberlain had explained to Welles, would allow Hitler to claim that "he had come out of the war without loss of prestige" and would be "unacceptable to the Allies." Chamberlain stated that the "Allies had gone into war to convince Germany and the world that force did not pay," and any solution that allowed "Herr Hitler to retire from the nominal leadership of Germany," would enable "Hitler to claim that it did." Welles' line in discussing

Hitler's position had clearly irked Chamberlain and raised a concern over his mission.

Chamberlain was also disenchanted with the next line of discussion Welles had introduced. Welles had sought to assess Chamberlain's view on future security through disarmament. Chamberlain's response reflected British disillusionment with this issue, as he said "he had been over the subject so many times but never with fruitful results."[23] The differences in opinion between Welles and Chamberlain over this issue as applied to the future of central Europe dominated the rest of the conversation. British assessments made in the immediate aftermath of this meeting reveal how they viewed Welles and this agenda.

Both Halifax's notes and Welles' report refer to the different conceptions of disarmament by drawing parallels with the "old story of the chicken and the egg." Halifax stated that the interview "turned upon whether disarmament could proceed, or at any rate be the agent for restoring confidence, or whether it would be the effect of such confidence being in fact required. After comparing the controversy to that of " 'the hen and the egg,' Mr Welles said he was inclined to agree with the first (disarmament leading to confidence); the Prime Minister argued vigorously for the second (confidence being a precursor to disarmament)."[24] Such divergent starting positions meant Chamberlain told the War Cabinet two days later that "Welles was aiming at the impossible," in suggesting "that the necessary sense of security could be obtained by general disarmament."[25] Chamberlain was totally at odds with Welles' view; the Prime Minister thought it was inconceivable "to secure disarmament first and security second. The exact reverse was the case." The differing points of view also reflected the different ideas on how to tackle the issues of the day that had soured relations between London and Washington at the onset of the crisis.

Just as troubling to the Chamberlain government as Welles' views on disarmament was that the Under Secretary "seemed to have in mind [a] general outline of [a] plan." After having listened to Welles, Halifax summarized the points made to him. The Foreign Secretary saw four features in Welles' comments:

a) That the Germans should agree to withdraw their troops from Poland and Bohemia within an area to be agreed by discussion.

b) That inasmuch as paper assurances and signatures were valueless, a scheme should be found for rapid and progressive disarmament of the belligerents. This is to be accomplished by progressive destruction of offensive weapons on land and in the air, and of factories devoted to the production of such weapons, and the creation of an international air force.

c) That, while this process was continuing up to a point to be agreed, armies would remain mobilised and the blockade would continue.

d) That there should be associated with this general layout a plan of economic reconstruction.[26]

When outlined in a manner such as this Welles' points of discussion take on the appearance of a "plan." Yet Welles was at pains to point out that in London, as elsewhere, he had "no proposals" of his own. Welles' explanation of his conduct in his report was that he was "merely exchanging views in order to try and get as clear a knowledge as I possibly could of his [Chamberlain's] point of view and that of his Government."[27] Welles was introducing ideas of security and disarmament in order to prompt British views and so further ascertain British war aims. Welles' son wrote that his father had "pressed his 'security through disarmament' formula" in his meetings on 11 March.[28]

It should be of little surprise that Halifax's assessment of Welles' "plan" caused concern in London. Having overcome Roosevelt's desire to use the word "peace" for fear of it embarrassing the Allies in early February, it seemed that his Under Secretary was ready to make a proposal that would end up leaving the Allies in just such a position. Chamberlain explained to the Cabinet that he suspected Roosevelt "would make some attempt to bring the war to an end, even if that attempt should be embarrassing to us."[29] This was a considerable setback to the semipositive outlook Chamberlain had explained to Kennedy on the eve of Welles' arrival in London.

Also of significance, although not so controversial, was Welles' raising of economic issues. Having discussed economic matters with Reynaud it was hardly surprising that the Under Secretary should want to glean the views of the British on this subject. This had implications for discovering British war aims as well as supporting the wider State Department program. Welles suggested that disarmament could lead "towards the rebuilding of economic security which in turn always made less likely the urge towards military conquest."[30] This was a fundamental and recurrent feature in the foreign policy of the Roosevelt Administration.

In essence, discussion of disarmament had vexed Chamberlain. It was ground that had been covered numerous times in the interwar period, and, without a dramatic shift in the American position that would see U.S. involvement, Chamberlain saw Welles' line as a waste of time. Vansittart wrote that American suggestions of disarmament were "entirely worthless" unless the United States were "prepared to go to war with anybody (i.e. Germany) who may be found (as they would be found) infringing any disarmament clauses within a short while." Of course, the United States was not in a position to act in such an enforcement role. The British diplomat concluded that Welles' "suggestion is merely playing ostrich, and all this is far too serious for the participation of ostriches."[31] Such an assessment identified a key weakness in American foreign policy from the British point of view: the retreat from responsibility.

In discussing the role of Hitler, Welles was endeavoring to establish how far the German leader was the basic reason why Britain was fighting, but this line resulted only in concerns arising in the Chamberlain government. Given Welles' personal experience of Hitler, it is inconceivable that he favored the continuation of his regime. Yet in discussing Hitler's role Welles was making himself look unsophisticated in the eyes of the Prime Minister and others in Britain. This was important, as it left Chamberlain with the impression that Welles would present Roosevelt with a proposal for ending the war, at a time when Welles considered the possibility of a meaningful settlement to have passed. The Prime Minister would have one more chance to impress his objections upon the Under Secretary in a meeting later on 13 March.

Before Welles met Chamberlain and Halifax again, he had the opportunity to canvass a wide variety of opinions in London. The importance of these conversations with members of the Cabinet, the opposition, and other leading figures lies in a number of areas. First, the consistency with which Welles approached his meetings is evident; this was even the case when he met old acquaintances such as Eden, who had stayed at Welles' Maryland mansion during his visit to the United States the previous year. The second feature of these discussions is the range of sources from which Welles was able to gather information. Related to this was his capacity to relay to Roosevelt after the mission the characters of the individuals he had met. Given Roosevelt's penchant for personal diplomacy, such information was potentially valuable. His opinion of Churchill as an "impressive character," for example, made its way back to the President, although that was accompanied by an assessment of the future Prime Minister's state of inebriation.[32] During the vast majority of the conversations on 12 March, as throughout his whole time in London, Welles heard of Britain's unswerving commitment to prosecuting the war.

The leaders of the opposition parties showed a solidarity of purpose with the government when Welles met them. When he asked Clement Attlee and Arthur Greenwood, the Leader and Deputy Leader of the Labour Party, what it would take to bring about security, Attlee made it clear that he wanted Germany to learn the lesson that force would not prevail. Welles recorded that the pair "saw no way out except the defeat of Hitler."[33] Although the Liberal leader Sir Archibald Sinclair spent an hour with Welles, the meeting served only to reinforce the British position. Welles was again given the same message: "There can be no compromise with Hitler."[34]

On this day of reaffirmation, a dissenting view from the government's line came from Mr. Bruce, the Australian High Commissioner, as he presented the views of the Dominion governments. The Australian presented Welles with a memo on the issue of peace and posed the question of what was the more practical, "a cooperative or an enforced peace settlement?" This line of thinking, with its implied reference to the inadequacies of the Versailles settlement, was simply filed in Welles' notes.[35] Had peace still been a priority for Welles, then he could have used this opportunity to enlist the support of the Australian in his efforts. He did not. It is not surprising, therefore, that the Under Secretary noted Bruce's views to be "widely divergent from the opinions held by the majority of the members of the British Government."[36]

Welles had little respite on this busy day, as he was soon the guest of honor at a lunch hosted by the Chancellor Sir John Simon at 11 Downing Street. An array of ministers and dignitaries had been assembled and spoke on various facets of the war effort.[37] The conversation was cordial as Welles explained to his host the Administration's concerns over American public opinion and, implicitly, how this influenced his own mission. According to Simon's account, Welles was worried that many American people were "afraid that if they gave the Allies any assistance, even financial, they would ultimately be dragged into the war."[38] This was of course a crucial concern for the Roosevelt Administration and a constant consideration for Welles. Welles explained that this desire among many of his countrymen rationalized their wanting to see an end to the war. Such a proposition troubled Simon. Exhibiting the resolve his government wanted Welles to hear, he told the American that he "should realise the strength of [British] resources, and should not go back to Washington with the impression that peace proposals, the real object of which was to reassure American fears, would serve also to save us from destruction." They simply would not.

Of further note is the fact that Lord Chatfield, the Minister for the Co-ordination of Defence and one of the other lunch guests, sent his impressions of Welles to Lothian in Washington. "I must say I like the look of him," Chatfield recorded, "and he gave me a good impression of honesty of purpose, and I feel sure that his visit will have been of great value and will put the President in a wonderful position to know the European outlook from all quarters."[39] Chatfield was evidently impressed with Welles and correctly surmised the broader aim of Welles' mission, that of relaying information to the President. The tone of Chatfield's assessment of Welles contrasted sharply with that of Chamberlain. This can be explained in part by Chatfield's relationship with Lothian. The Ambassador had primed Chatfield as to the nature of what the United States wanted from Britain, namely information with which to educate the American people. Lothian had told Chatfield as early on in the war as 15 September that he needed "any facts and figures" in order "to bring home the real issues and the real facts to Roosevelt and other leaders here."[40] He implored Chatfield to comply with his request by stating, "Believe me, there is nothing more important you can do than to equip me with the facts and the arguments which will bring home to the United States the real situation which confronts us." Chamberlain's concern, on the other hand, was that supplying information to the Americans would fail to produce tangible help.

After lunch Welles moved on to appointments with first Eden and then Churchill; both had returned to the government at the Dominions Office and the Admiralty respectively upon the outbreak of war. Welles began the discussions with Eden by asking whether he "saw any way out of the existing deadlock." Again, the government line was in evidence. Eden responded that the only solution to the crisis was "the defeat of Germany and the establishment of a regime in that country in whose good faith it would be possible for other nations to have confidence." Welles further pressed Eden, stating he "could not believe that it was past the wit of men to devise some method of avoiding so terrible a fate for civilisation."[41] He continued by repeating his proposal that disarmament might be able to provide a solution. He asked Eden whether it was "so impossible to visualize a continuation of mobilization on the fronts, while stage by stage a scheme for disarmament was worked out under international supervision?"[42] In pursuing this line Welles was trying to assess just how far Eden would be prepared go to avoid the spring onslaught. The answer, Welles learned, was a further reiteration of British resolve. His chronicle shows that Eden "had no belief that any disarmament move could be considered until after Germany had been crushed, and taught that 'war does not pay,'" adding in conclusion, "Mr Eden's conviction is that nothing but war is possible until Hitlerism has been overthrown."[43] To Eden such a view seemed to disappoint Welles, as he recorded that Welles seemed "depressed by the refusal to believe in the possibility of an arms agreement in the present conditions."[44] Although it was conceivable that the American had been disappointed with Eden's response, his report exhibits no such intimation. Instead, he concluded that the meeting had been particularly cordial with Eden "as charming and agreeable as always" and had shown further evidence of British resolve.[45]

Having spoken with Eden, Welles called on Churchill at the Admiralty. While Welles had used the opportunity provided by his conversation with Eden to further press his thoughts on disarmament, Churchill dominated the discussion to such an extent that he spoke without a pause for over two hours. Churchill, complete with "cigar and highball," evidently impressed Welles, as he included in his report that Churchill spoke in a "cascade of oratory, brilliant and always effective, interlarded with considerable wit."[46] Welles wrote later in the month that Churchill was "one of the most fascinating personalities he had ever met."[47] A wide variety of subject matter was covered in Churchill's oratory, although he concentrated on events in the Atlantic. In view of the united front the government wanted to present, Churchill emphasized that the German naval campaign was not having a huge impact on British shipping. Instead, he explained that the convoy system was now "functioning perfectly," the German magnetic mines had been overcome, and a new invention "had eliminated the danger of submarines, as in any sense a serious menace to England's ability to continue her provisioning, and her export trade."[48] Of course this was far from the truth as the Battle of the Atlantic was to show. Welles' report of the meeting concludes by referring to the sentiment he had heard from all those he had met that day bar Bruce. The Welles report states that Churchill thought there could be "no solution other than outright and complete defeat of Germany; the destruction of National Socialism and the determination in the new Peace Treaty of dispositions which would control Germany's course in the future in such a way as to give Europe, and the world, peace and security for 100 years." Such an assessment would be in accord with the pronouncements of the man who within two months would be Prime Minister, though in March of 1940 Welles' estimation of Churchill served only to present a further example of British resolve.

After talking to a future Prime Minister, Welles began the next day by talking to a former Prime Minister. Welles meeting with David Lloyd George was far from significant, as Welles knew that Lloyd George was peripheral to policy making in London. Although Welles found the Welshman to be in broad agreement with his own thoughts for security and disarmament, the conversation did not dwell on these topics as they turned to the quality of the leaders in the democracies.[49] Lloyd George felt in contrast that "the totalitarian governments, and I include Russia among them, have brilliant leadership whereas the democracies have none. There is only one exception," the Welshman stated, "and that is Mr Roosevelt." He continued by declaring that his only "real quarrel with him is that he was not born an Englishman."[50] On that note the meeting ended, and Welles moved on to a more important meeting at the Treasury.[51] There he met Sir Horace Wilson, the Treasury's Permanent Secretary. The subject of this was an American proposal flowing on from Hull's 9 February announcement for "unofficial Anglo-U.S. cooperation to consider post-war economic problems."[52] The Administration saw this as an opportunity for "the exchange of data and suggestions," as long as there was "no publicity and no suggestion made that they [were] engaged in any joint activity." The American desire to keep any cooperation low-key is shown by Kennedy's concern that nobody should go from Great Britain to the United States "in the near future unless it was quite clear that the person who went could go quietly."[53] Wilson recorded that this was because it might "look as if we were from this side following up Mr Welles' visit to Europe." Although Welles was keen to stress that there should be no formal links, given his concern for postwar planning he was favorably disposed to the prospect of Anglo-American cooperation as he "thought there would be advantage in the two committees informally exchanging ideas whether by visits personally or by means of memoranda." Although these ideas were followed up by an exchange of letters, the significance of the meeting between Welles and Wilson for this work is that it is not mentioned at all in the Welles report.[54] Viewed alongside the efforts of Moffat in London, which will be dealt with shortly, this meeting reveals that Welles was endeavoring to further Anglo-American understanding albeit in secret and on a limited issue. Such efforts suggest that Welles' mission was not likely to produce results that would fundamentally affect the interests of Great Britain, such as his return to Washington with a peace plan that condoned Germany's acquisition of Eastern Europe. However, this was the fear that Chamberlain held, reinvigorated somewhat after his first meeting with Welles (11 March), when he again met the Under Secretary (13 March). Before this it is pertinent to recall the importance of the variety of other people Welles met in London. His own consistent preface and then the consideration of the disarmament question were designed to draw out statements of what Britain was fighting for and about British commitment to their aims. In the variety of meetings he had, the British resolve shone through. Nevertheless, and not just because of the dissenting views of Bruce and Lloyd George, Welles was able to assess a range of opinion and gauge the character of those he met. His aim of gathering information on present conditions in Europe was being fulfilled.

Welles' final meeting in London was again with Chamberlain and Halifax, on 13 March. The importance of this meeting was that it presented Chamberlain with the opportunity to further stress the British determination to carry on with the war. It is notable that Chamberlain took the lead in this meeting in endeavoring to do this. As for Welles, this discussion allowed him to learn more about the British view of the situation in Europe.

Chamberlain began the meeting by attempting to reaffirm to Welles the strength of British resolve. He handed Welles a letter intended for the President, which stressed this. It stated that Welles now knew "exactly how the situation" looked to him. Rather paradoxically, Chamberlain's hope that Welles' mission "may have fruitful results, if not immediately, yet in time to avert the worst catastrophe," belied his concern that Welles would suggest something to Roosevelt when he returned to Washington.[55]

Chamberlain then told Welles directly that he had given great consideration to what the Under Secretary had said during their previous meeting. He felt he had to emphasize at the outset "the impossibility of proceeding on the assumption that disarmament could by itself breed confidence, where in fact the opposite was in his judgement true, namely that only from restored confidence could you get disarmament." Chamberlain underlined the problems he foresaw in discussing disarmament. He pointed out that "the distinction between offensive and defensive weapons was one that was very difficult to draw . . . the only practicable method of advance was to endeavour to pursue progressively . . . qualitative limitation."[56] Rather optimistically, Welles' report suggested that although Chamberlain felt these were significant problems theoretically, they "could be solved, but he had not discovered the solution."[57] This typifies Welles mindset of seeking to leave options open rather than close them.

Carrying on Chamberlain again took the lead in stressing to Welles that complete destruction of Germany was not part of British war aims. Chamberlain told Welles that he wanted to make it "definitely clear" that it was not "a war objective either to destroy the German Reich or to subjugate the German people." This was of definite value to Welles for the purpose of tackling the misconception amongst the American people that the war was about territory in Eastern Europe. Chamberlain then went on to suggest that, in order to illustrate that destruction of Germany was not one of Britain's aims, the British Empire could "bind themselves not to attack Germany by a formal undertaking given to the United States."[58] In asking Welles for his views, he immediately added, quite contrarily, given his proposal, that "this would impose no responsibility on the United States." The British record states that Welles saw "no objection to it from the point of view of the United States. He would submit it to the President." In typically less committal language the Welles report states that he would simply communicate Chamberlain's suggestion to Roosevelt, adding a qualification that he assumed "the latter would wish to see the text of any suggested declaration before reaching any final opinion."[59] As was evident elsewhere on his mission, Welles was aware of the potential domestic political implications of his mission, and it is clear that he was mindful of not appearing to have discussed any notion of American commitments. However, he did fulfill the pledge to discuss the matter with Roosevelt. In early April, in almost the last hours before Germany struck, Roosevelt's response illustrated again the constraint imposed by the American public's fear of entanglement. This will be discussed in the final chapter.

Welles continued to press on the question of how far the Nazi regime was the root cause of Britain prosecuting the war. He asked Chamberlain directly whether, on the optimistic assumption "that satisfactory arrangements could be reached for the restoration and future status of Poland, Bohemia and Moravia, and supposing that other provisions could be drawn up in regard to disarmament which made for security on the lines discussed, would the British Government feel it still impossible to deal with the present regime?"[60] His response was to suggest that such a transformation would be in the nature of a "miracle" and that "he did not believe that a miracle would occur."[61] Chamberlain continued that "so long as Hitler or his group remained in control of Germany," there would be no prospect of Germany entering "into any arrangements which would offer any real guarantee of security to the Allies."[62] This was the essence of the British position. Significantly, Welles' account adds that Chamberlain stated that if "a miracle did occur, and there seemed a practicable plan of security offered, he would not discard such an opportunity of striving for a real and lasting peace merely because the present Nazi regime remained in power."[63] Although Kennedy would later see this as offering the prospect of peace, it was certainly not intended that way by Chamberlain. Welles' assessment reflected his own desire not to preclude any option.[64] In fact, Welles saw Chamberlain's comments in terms reminiscent of those applied to his own mission. Kennedy's account states that, having likened being able to find any accommodation with Hitler to a miracle, Chamberlain said, "I am perfectly willing to see a miracle happen and willing to pray to God that it might," to which Welles' response was to say that "the chances are one in a thousand, better, one in ten thousand, but there is a chance and therefore I must explore every possible angle."[65] In less colorful prose the British account agrees that Welles offered such odds: "one chance in ten thousand."[66] Such sentiment exemplifies what Welles saw as the quintessential nature of his mission: to explore every last opportunity for resolution ahead of the spring offensives, no matter how forlorn, in fulfilling the breadth of the objectives of his mission. The British acknowledgment that Welles considered any proposals to have only a one in ten thousand chance of any type of success gave them some hope that Welles' mission would not result in embarrassing the Allies.

The conversation then broadened out, under Chamberlain's direction. It turned first to Germany's colonial desires. Chamberlain suggested the "creation of a broad colonial belt through Africa," which would provide an open trading block and emigration rights.[67] Welles concluded that if Chamberlain's proposals were enacted there could "be no further basis for the German complaint of discrimination in the colonial field." That this matter was raised by Chamberlain suggests that he wanted to present a further unpalatable aspect, particularly in the eyes of the American people, of any settlement to Welles. That colonial matters were discussed is notable, given the American commitment during the Second World War to overseeing the end of colonial rule—which formed a key element of American postwar planning.

The second topic that Chamberlain introduced in broadening the discussion with Welles was the role of Russia. Having stated that the Russian triumph in the Russo-Finnish War had "profoundly modified" the Allied position, Chamberlain asked Welles whether his "plan contemplated bringing Russia into the situation."[68] Welles' response to the question was negative but implicitly acknowledged Chamberlain's observation that he had a plan. He stated that if "they came in that might be all to the good, although it would increase the intrinsic difficulty of mutual confidence particularly in the realm of inspection." Interestingly, Welles added that the Russians "are not essential to the scheme," continuing that "Russia has not demonstrated her ability to become much of an offensive force in Europe and an international body could consequently easily deal with whatever offensive threat Russia might make. Russia, moreover, because of her difficulties with Japan is unlikely to want to come in." The British account of this part of the conversation is notable for mirroring this line but fails to mention a "plan" or "scheme." It states that there was merely "some discussion as to the reactions of the Russian attitude toward any possible disarmament in the West. It was generally admitted that no system of inspection could operate in Russia and that the attitude of Russia would in turn be greatly affected by that of Japan."[69] This is important, because even those who had considered Welles' ideas of 11 March to constitute a plan did not see all of Welles' comments in this light. In this sense they were using some discretion in assessing Welles' different lines of discussion. Nevertheless, the implications of Welles' comments on Russia were significant, as there is no mention of Russia in the Welles report. While he may have considered Russia to be beyond the focus of the mission, it is also possible that he along with many in the United States at that time did not consider Russia to be integral to a solution to Europe's woes. His assessment of Russia's capabilities, although perhaps right on "offensive" attributes, was dismissive of the traits that would ultimately be so vital to Allied victory in the Second World War. Welles' analysis of Russia augments Hilton's view that Russia's omission from the tour itinerary meant that the mission did not aim at a universal settlement.[70] This historian agrees with him, but Hilton fails to go on and consider the full range of objectives the mission had developed. Russia's omission was very significant if the mission had been solely to explore peace: but it was not, and although the breaking of the Nazi-Soviet Pact might have assisted in prolonging the "phony war," the Soviet Union was very far from ever being considered as integral to the Welles mission.

What Welles did consider as integral to his mission was his interest in Italian neutrality. Although only briefly considered in London, Welles' desire to pursue this when he returned to Rome is evident from his quizzing of Chamberlain on the meetings Ribbentrop had conducted in Rome on 10 March. Although they had "no certain news," the British Ambassador in Rome had seen nothing that would indicate Mussolini had any "intention of leaving the fence on which he . . . rested."[71] For Welles, as he prepared to leave London and return to Rome, this request for information reveals again that he saw Italy as potentially important in furthering the mission.

Welles' and Chamberlain's discussion came to an end after an hour and a half, with an official dinner imminent. Yet the range of topics discussed reflected an important episode in the course of the Welles mission. Chamberlain stressed to Welles the British resolve to overcome the Nazi regime. The core of the British view was that "Herr Hitler personified a system and method with which the British Government had learned from bitter experience it was impossible to make terms."[72] In taking the initiative in this conversation, he tried to dispel the worries he and other members of his government had about what they conceived to be Welles' plan. He was happy to broaden the scope of the discussion by talking of Russia and the colonial question in order to dilute Welles' focus on producing (and presenting obstacles to) any settlement. For Welles, this conversation concluded his formal talks in London with a final reiteration of British determination to prosecute the war. This was central to Welles' search for information, particularly in assessing British and French aims. Although he undoubtedly welcomed British resolution in private, given his distaste for what he had seen in Berlin, Welles' report reveals no opinion either way. The absence of opinion and neutral language about his talks in Britain exhibited his commitment to present Roosevelt with a straightforward account of the conditions in Europe. Despite this, Welles did take on board the message the British were pressing home. He would tell the Italian King in Rome that he had not found "intransigence in France or England, but merely the determination, and a very cold determination, to fight to the finish."[73] Clearly, the British approach had been well impressed upon Welles.

Welles' final conversations in London were less weighty and took place at a dinner convened in Downing Street.[74] Welles found himself seated between Chamberlain and Churchill, with discussion focusing on the American neutrality zone around the Americas. Given that Welles had been crucial to the introduction of the zone the previous autumn, he explained "the background and the workings of the 'chastity belt' around the Americas" and asked why the British did not publicize their respect for the zone, as they "would lose nothing and gain much from American sentiment."[75] Without an answer being given the conversation moved on as Welles was given a guided tour of Downing Street by his host. Welles ended his account of his time in London by quoting Chamberlain's last words to him. They repeated the sentiment of the Prime Minister's letter to Roosevelt, and ended with Chamberlain saying he has "has all my admiration, and I shall hope to see you here again in happier days."[76] On this note, Welles mission to London ended.

Before leaving the London episode of the Welles mission it is important to consider that Welles was not the only American who held high-level discussions in London. Jay Pierrepont Moffat, the State Department's Chief of the European Division, had spent most of the previous two weeks engaged in low-level discussions with members of the diplomatic corps in the European cities he visited. In London, the significance of his discussions showed that the Welles mission had an important ulterior purpose. His role was to help ease the tension in Anglo-American relations that had prompted Lothian to record that Roosevelt had mentioned a "recent minor crisis" at the end of January 1940.[77]

Lothian was very much aware of the importance of Moffat in this role, as evidenced by his communication of 29 February 1940. He wrote, "I am sure I need not emphasise the desirability of every attention and courtesy being paid to Mr Sumner Welles . . . but I hope Mr Moffat will not be overlooked. We are very dependent on the latter's good offices and he would I am sure appreciate any kindness that can be shown him by his opposite numbers in the Foreign Office."[78] This was taken on board by the Foreign Office, as illustrated by the fact that when Cadogan and Halifax were discussing the arrangements for Welles' stay on 9 March, their first point related to Moffat. Cadogan wrote, "It is important from the point of view of the relations between our Embassy in Washington and the State Department that Mr Pierrepont Moffat should be included so far as possible."[79] Moffat was therefore considered in British arrangements, with R.A. "Rab" Butler being detailed to entertain him on the evening of 11 March and the American being invited to attend the final dinner at Downing Street.

Moffat evidently enjoyed the evening hosted by Butler. He wrote in his diary that the "dinner was excellent, and the talk good." Moffat was also impressed by his host, whom he described as having "an interesting mind . . . clever, quick, and intensely ambitious."[80] During the evening, Moffat spoke with R.S. Hudson of the Board of Trade about the issue of British purchases of Turkish tobacco (in preference to American tobacco). This had been one of the factors that had given rise to the difficulties earlier in the year, and Moffat, although understanding of the reasons, was disappointed to learn that the British had no intention of altering this practice. The efforts the British made in entertaining Moffat led the American to visit a number of London clubs on 11 March before retiring in the early hours having eaten "bacon sandwiches with the Duke of Devonshire and his son." These efforts to entertain Moffat continued the next day, and it was not until after a dinner laid on by David Scott of the Foreign Office that Moffat got to speak with the Earl of Drogheda, the Deputy Director General of the Ministry of Economic Warfare.[81] Moffat saw this as his opportunity to put across the American, and in particular the State Department, point of view. Outlining the concerns over the denial of navicerts, a possible British blacklist, and the inspection of the mail, he reserved his and his department's gravest worry until last. Moffat asked whether it was really necessary to apply the label "it is necessary to do this to end the war" to British actions when it was often used merely to cover "administrative conveniences." He feared that it was "like raising the cry of 'Wolf, Wolf' and that if it were used too frequently in a lightened sense it would not be listened to" when it was really warranted.[82] In following this line of argument Moffat was entirely in line with the State Department. Given that Moffat's meeting gave him the opportunity to operate as a mouthpiece for such views in London, historian Robert Matson proposes that Moffat's "firm enunciation may have been the most significant, if unintended, result of the Welles Mission."[83] While this overstates the case, Moffat's performance on the mission might certainly have contributed to the resolution of the "minor crisis" and so to an improvement in the general state of Anglo-American relations.[84]

Welles' discussions in London had at best perplexed the Chamberlain government and had at worst revived their suspicions of Washington, which they hoped had been overcome in early February. Any assessment of Welles' impact upon his return to Washington was difficult for London to gauge in early March. Like the rest of the world, the Chamberlain government would have to wait and see what Roosevelt would do when Welles arrived back in the United States.

Nonetheless, initial British reaction to Welles was variable. Vansittart was ferocious in his views. He stated that "Mr Sumner Welles emerges more and more clearly as an international danger. His idea of security via disarmament first is nonsense, and I am glad that the Prime Minister dealt with him so firmly on all grounds, though I regret that he [the Prime Minister] even contemplated the possibility of gradual disarmament with this Germany, for until the Germany not only of Hitler but of the military caste has been disposed of, disarmament is not only a delusion but a death-trap." This was vitriolic enough but he continued in an even more scathing manner: "Mr Sumner Welles' chief crime towards common sense and humanity is that he has now gone so far as to want us to make peace with Hitler."[85] In some contrast to Vansittart's views were those expressed by Campbell in Paris. After briefly meeting Welles in Paris during his stopover en route back to Rome, the Ambassador said Welles "had been immensely impressed by the conversations which he had with the Prime Minister, Your Lordship [Halifax], the First Lord of the Admiralty and others." Campbell saw these comments as "rare pearls" and recorded that Welles had given "the impression of having left London with quite different ideas from those with which he arrived."[86] This augured some hope that Welles had been convinced by the government's line.

The British were further encouraged in their belief in the aftermath of Welles' mission that the Roosevelt Administration would not embarrass them by a speech Roosevelt delivered on 16 March, while Welles was back in Rome. The speech was broadcast nationally in the United States and its timing and text illustrate that Roosevelt wanted nothing to do with any "inconclusive" peace. Roosevelt's opening stated clearly his foundation for peace: "Today we seek a moral basis for peace." He continued, "It cannot be a sound peace if small nations must live in fear of powerful neighbours. It cannot be a moral peace if freedom from invasion is sold for tribute. It cannot be an intelligent peace if it denies free passage to that knowledge of those ideals which permit men to find common ground. It cannot be a righteous peace if worship of God is denied."[87] Roosevelt's final sentences added to these sentiments: "These are the highest of human ideals. They will be defended and maintained. In their victory the whole world stands to gain; and fruit of it is peace." Having made no public utterance on the ongoing conflict since the announcement of the mission and having been kept informed of Welles' findings, Roosevelt could have been in little doubt as to the affect of such a speech.

Roosevelt's speech was a fillip to the British in the aftermath of Welles' time in London. Halifax cabled Lothian in Washington to suggest the Ambassador make a special point of telling Roosevelt that his speech had been greeted with "pleasure and admiration" by Chamberlain in Parliament on 20 March.[88] Halifax went on to say that "the President's speech came at an appropriate moment when all sorts of rumours are abroad of the possibility of a patched-up peace." Halifax also admitted the tactics the government had adopted when Welles was in London. He wrote they had "endeavoured to put to him frankly [their] point of view," and Halifax concluded that Welles had been "glad to receive" such straightforward views. The Foreign Secretary's concluding words reveal an air of greater confidence in London that Welles' mission would not result in any move by Roosevelt that would compromise the Allies: "It is inconceivable to us that a peace fulfilling the conditions so well defined by the President himself would be signed with the present rulers of Germany." Lothian agreed with the sentiment of his friend. His final comments to Hull revealed again the fear that had surrounded the whole enterprise, as he stated that the British government was "especially glad that Mr Welles had come and gone without any development of a dangerous or harmful nature."[89]

More reflection on Welles' mission can be found in a Foreign Office minute prepared once Welles had left Europe. It began by suggesting that Welles' views seemed "to have been to some extent affected by Mussolini's influence, to have been impressed in Berlin by Germany's pretended invincibility, and to have been spoon-fed by Mr Kennedy as to the prospects of general financial ruin." While reflecting British awareness of Kennedy's views, they concluded with a degree of hope that what Welles told them "may have reflected his own impressions rather than the President's mind." The Foreign Office thought Welles "had in mind to suggest that the President should put forward an outline for peace which would not require the elimination of Herr Hitler's Nazi regime but which would give security to the Allies." The British felt "Mr Welles appeared disappointed at receiving the impression from all his interlocutors here that his ideas on disarmament were impractical in present circumstances." The Foreign Office attributed Welles' disappointment to the fact that those whom Welles met "spoke strongly to Mr Welles and he was left in no doubt as to our position, but we cannot tell what effect we produced on him, or whether we disabused him of some rather serious misconceptions." This was the ultimate dilemma that the British faced in the aftermath of Welles' mission—how far did Welles truly believe in the points he had discussed? They had not learned Welles' views over and above what they had gleaned from his line of argument: while indicative, they appreciated that it was not definitive and an element of doubt remained. The Foreign Office memorandum concluded that despite the British efforts "there is still some risk that Mr Welles may advise the President to make some attempt to bring the war to an end even if that attempt should prove embarrassing to the Allies."[90] Had the British learned that Welles had taken such a strong sense of British resolve away with him, as he explained to the Italian King, then they would no doubt have been pleased, yet even after Welles had left, the British were still not completely clear as to what the final outcome of his mission might be.

When Welles left London and headed back to Rome he still had a range of objectives to pursue. Notably, he would seek to further Italian neutrality and prolong the "phony war." However, when in London Welles' pursuit of his objectives was largely focused upon gathering information. His conversations had two emphases that facilitated clear declarations of British aims. The first was to enquire about how far Hitler and the Nazi regime were the root cause of Britain's fighting the war, and the second was to push the British on their views on disarmament. Welles was successful insofar as he left London with a definite view that the British were fighting against Hitler's regime and what it stood for. This, along with what he had learned on the continent, achieved Roosevelt's objective of one man being able to gather information from each capital. Regarding the other objectives, Welles paid them scant attention in London, which reflected his belief in trying to leave options open. The pursuit of peace was no longer relevant once he had arrived in London, except in the realms of the "miracles" Chamberlain had spoken of. That Welles had openly acknowledged the lengths of the odds he was dealing with—"one in ten thousand"—is crucial in revealing that, no matter how desperate a hope, Welles was going to explore every last opportunity to succeed. Kennedy, even with his hope that the war would end imminently, acknowledged the odds: "The chance was still, however, one in a thousand."[91] The same could be said of Welles' other objectives in his time on the continent, although in London, perhaps unsurprisingly, Italian neutrality and prolonging the "phony war" were not priorities. But when Welles returned to Rome, both would again be important.

In regard to his conduct in London, Welles remained conscious of how his mission continued to appear, particularly to the American people. As had been the case when he arrived in Paris from Berlin, Welles still did not want to appear to be in league with the Allies. This sprang out of his own stoic character and the residue of feeling within the State Department that the British were taking advantage of the war to the detriment of American interests. This was seen in Welles' concern for the absence of an invitation to Kennedy for his meeting with the King, which was more to do with how that would appear in the press rather than the value he placed on any contribution Kennedy might make. The problem here was that the element of doubt that Welles' approach left in his conversations, which he hoped might serve a purpose in Berlin, served only to increase anxiety in London. This example betrays the double-edged complexity of gauging Welles' motivations at every stage of his mission and again the attitude that in these circumstances policy should be tried even if its outcome was unfavorable.

The concerns raised by Welles' mission in the Chamberlain government were the major result of the American's time in London from the British point of view. The lines of discussion on the Nazi regime and disarmament took on the appearance of a "plan" to many of the people whom Welles met. Such an assessment was not unreasonable but was definitely not Welles' professed intention. But, as with much of Welles' time in London, it was subject to understandable misinterpretation by the Chamberlain government. Any "plan" caused concern, as the British found it incongruous to talk of disarmament making possible a lasting peace with the Nazi regime. This meant that the mission failed to improve mutual understanding in Anglo-American relations. Nevertheless, the semiofficial role that Moffat adopted, in addition to the unofficial talks Welles held on postwar economic problems, reveals a predilection in certain areas for accord. However, this did not extend to Welles disclosing the full breadth of the mission's goals to the British when he clearly felt a greater understanding with them in comparison to the views he had encountered in Berlin. Instead, as Welles headed back to Rome, concerns remained in London. The welcome given in London both to the speech by Roosevelt on 16 March and to Welles' reiteration of the mission's purpose in Rome two days later reveal the continuing anxieties. It is to Welles' return to Rome, and continuing convolution of his conduct and objectives, that this book now turns.

CHAPTER 6

INCREASINGLY
FORLORN: WELLES
HEADS HOME
VIA ROME

ONCE BACK IN ROME WELLES called upon the full range of his diplomatic skills and experience in pursuing the mission's objectives. His priorities, with the likelihood of the offensive shortening as every day passed, were to prolong the "phony war" and perpetuate Italian neutrality. Welles attempted to achieve these by maintaining a dialogue with Ciano and Mussolini that encouraged them to think of themselves as potentially pivotal to peace. Further, Welles hoped that the fact that he was still discussing Italy's role might engender some doubt as to what might happen at the mission's conclusion. This proved impossible as Mussolini set out to test how far Welles was prepared to involve the United States in the conflict in Europe. When Welles declined Mussolini's offer to discuss the American's views with Hitler, any doubts in the minds of Mussolini over the American position were dismissed. Welles knew he was in no position to make any commitment to European security on behalf of the United States in the spring of 1940. Mussolini's offer in mid-March revealed the limitations that "exploring the possibilities of peace" had in terms of Welles creating the impression that the United States might play a part. In this situation Welles' attention focused on the gathering of information in an environment where catastrophe appeared imminent. Pervading Welles' time back in Rome was a sense of urgency concentrated by an acceptance that the "phony war" would soon end. The world's press saw the announcement of Hitler's and Mussolini's meeting at the Brenner Pass on 18 March (just hours before it took place) as a precursor to escalation. Welles also learned from Donald Heath, a staff member of the

American Embassy in Berlin who had traveled to Rome to speak to Welles personally, that in Germany as elsewhere "the imminence of an offensive probably against the Maginot Line, is more and more generally accepted."[1] Welles understood this pressure. He wrote later that Mussolini's view of the situation was that "the minute hand had reached one minute before midnight."[2] The aura of impending doom brought with it a sense of responsibility for Welles to make sure he had explored every last option and gathered every last piece of information. This adds to the complexity evident thus far, in deciphering the key tenets of his conduct.

The intentions of the Roosevelt Administration at this time were shown in a speech Roosevelt delivered on 16 March. At the same time that Welles was meeting Ciano in Rome, Roosevelt proclaimed, "Today we seek a moral basis for peace."[3] Such a peace—one that was "neither precarious nor inconclusive"—was incompatible with what Roosevelt knew Welles had heard in Berlin. The terms laid out in this speech marked an emphatic acknowledgment by Roosevelt that he had not received anything from Welles that could lead him to fulfill the conceptual aim of the mission; simply put there was no opportunity to exploit in the name of peace. Publicly, of course, the mission continued to be "solely for gathering information," something that was reconfirmed by the Under Secretary himself the day he left Europe.

This chapter will outline Welles' diplomatic maneuverings in Rome and his efforts to maintain cordial relations with Mussolini and Ciano in order to perpetuate Italian neutrality. The conversations held between them will be scrutinized for this purpose, and in doing so the duplicity of Mussolini and especially Ciano will become clear. The chapter will also assess the way the mission appeared to the American people and how this continued to be important to Welles and the Administration in Washington. The reiteration of the mission's public goal on the eve of Welles' departure from Europe served to illustrate this succinctly. Also evident here, and rather like Britain's ongoing worries, are Hull's continuing concerns. The Secretary of State's disquiet became more acute as the mission drew to a close, and this will be examined toward the end of the chapter. In an important sense then, as in chapter 3, this chapter sees the ongoing themes of the work interwoven with the objectives of the mission. In particular, the goal of Italian neutrality is emphasized, as well as the concern for American opinion. The final aspect of this chapter addresses the report that Welles composed for Roosevelt. It was almost exclusively narrative in recording the conversations Welles had around Europe and therefore was very much in line with Welles' publicized goal of information gathering. Ultimately, the report presented Roosevelt with little scope for maintaining any notion that the mission could have any further outcome. He thus told the world's press that the mission would not be heralding any further move from Washington. The impact of the mission, as was always likely to have been the case, was negligible.

Welles' efforts at prolonging Italian neutrality began again as he met Ciano on 16 March. He hoped to engage both Ciano and Mussolini with the prospect that they had a role to play in a settlement. Alongside a good deal of personal flattery of the pair, Welles entirely overstated the reception Mussolini's ideas had received elsewhere. Welles clearly considered Italian neutrality as his priority—his only hope—when back in Rome.

The compliments and the embellishments began immediately. Welles opened his conversation by stating to Ciano that he "had been looking forward for many days to [his] return to Rome, and to the opportunity of having further conversations with him."[4] He continued, "[O]ne of the outstanding impressions that I have gained on my trip is the confidence felt that the Minister and the Duce would do everything possible on behalf of Italy to further the reestablishment of peace." Such comments were far from the truth of what he had heard elsewhere. However, and more accurately, Welles went on to explain that he had found in London and Paris "a complete determination on the part of [the British and French] governments to continue the war to its bitter end." In telling Ciano this, Welles was endeavoring to raise doubt as to Germany's invincibility and stress that Italy would face a resolute and prepared enemy. Ciano, although proclaiming that he was "by no means convinced of Germany's ability to win" a decisive victory in 1940, concluded from Welles' remarks that if the Allies "fight truly on this road, they are on the way toward defeat."[5] Nevertheless, in suggesting this Welles might well have been influenced by an assessment that Moffat learned of Italy in London. Butler had told the diplomat that "Italy did not want to join the Allies in war, but did want to join them in the peace."[6] While maybe reflecting more hope than expectation, Butler's words alluded to suspected weaknesses in Italian military forces and to the dangers Italy would face in a Europe dominated by Berlin.

It was to his time in Berlin that Welles then turned. He recounted how he had been told in Berlin of Allied intentions to destroy the Reich but that when he had visited Paris and London he had found that this was far from the case. Ciano replied that he knew this to be true. He went on, no doubt much to Welles' satisfaction, to tell him of Ribbentrop's visit to Rome while Welles had been en route to London. With the preface that he would speak "frankly, and of course solely for the information of the President," Ciano told Welles that throughout Ribbentrop's conversations in Rome he had stated "that Germany was determined to undertake a military offensive in the near future; that she was not considering any solution short of a military victory as a means of obtaining peace, and that after German victory peace would be laid down by German 'Diktat.'"[7] Such a stark assessment certainly helped Welles to gauge the situation in Europe. Ciano continued and in doing so tried to portray himself as a moderating influence. Welles recorded that Ciano had tried "as he had at Berchtesgaden, to persuade Ribbentrop that the reasonable objectives of Germany could be achieved by negotiation." Crucially, Ciano went on to say on that basis he had "mentioned" Welles' mission. Ribbentrop's response shows how little the Germans were actually considering Welles' mission. Ciano said that "Ribbentrop had brushed to one side all references of this character, and that he had talked in very loud and violent terms of German power and of German military strength." This exchange within the Italo-German conversation was relevant to Welles' information-gathering role. What this also shows is that the Welles mission had registered on the Nazi agenda. That it was pushed to one side so readily, though, reveals that the mission did not serve to encourage talk of peace but almost certainly helped to hasten German planning for war. Also evident in this passage were Ciano's less than complimentary interjections on the Nazis and on Ribbentrop in particular. Having heard this, Welles turned the conversation to one aspect he had pressed in London.

In introducing talk of disarmament, Welles was doing so for subtly different reasons than he had done in London. Whereas in London he was trying to extract statements of British aims, in Rome Welles was trying to find terms that might entice Ciano to prolong the hiatus. He stated that what was needed was "agreement upon measures of real disarmament," and this drew Ciano "immediately" into saying that he "quite agreed." Welles continued with the aim of using the disarmament question to preserve the "phony war." He pondered whether "the brink of the precipice upon which they were now poised might prove to be an incentive to all peoples to strive towards a real and actual disarmament, and the means of practical security which that alone could afford." Welles' record shows that Ciano made no direct response to his plaintive suggestion. Instead the conversation moved on in a fashion that augured some hope for Welles.

Ciano suggested to Welles that he delay his departure from Rome. The reason, he said was that "word from Berlin would probably be received before noon on March 19 and that he would meet . . . to give me the last word that he had before I departed." Though the value of the information that Welles was waiting for was already in question in the American camp, such a proposition was welcomed by Welles, as it would enable him to gain the most up-to-date picture possible before he left Europe. In response to an enquiry from Phillips as to the nature of the information Ciano was to receive, the Italian "refused to specify." Furthermore, personal opinions of Ciano were not wholly complimentary. While his report saw Ciano as accommodating, Welles was aware of his playboy image.[8] Moffat went further, as he found the Italian to be an "open and rather disengaging snob" who had "eyes and ears for nothing but the ladies." Nevertheless, Moffat did observe that Ciano was able to turn off "his frivolous side as though he . . . pushed an electric button."[9] Such an assessment alludes to Ciano's duplicity, which would be in evidence again during Welles' time in Rome.

Having received Ciano's suggestion that he wait in Rome for further information with some satisfaction, Welles was less pleased with the offer he received in his next meeting with Mussolini. Investigation of this illustrates two things: first, that the Welles mission had a minimal effect upon the Axis in terms of them pausing for thought; and second, the clear limitations to Welles' exploration of peace. In essence, the offer amounted to Mussolini asking whether he could tell Hitler the content of his conversations with Welles. Welles endeavored to stall and stated that he would need to speak with Roosevelt. In that conversation that took place later that day, Welles argued that allowing his views to be discussed would be tantamount to appearing to have had his own proposals and to be entangled in Europe's diplomacy. Roosevelt agreed and declined Mussolini's request.

Nonetheless, the meeting on 16 March began in a genial atmosphere. After the Duce had welcomed Welles "with the utmost cordiality and in a very friendly personal way," the conversation started with his asking Welles for the "impressions" he had formed on his tour. As ever, Welles began by stating that the views expressed to him were intended solely for the President and the Secretary of State. Nevertheless, Welles stated that elsewhere he had told his audience that Mussolini still saw a settlement as possible. Clearly overstating the facts, Welles continued that he had found "on all sides" confidence in Mussolini and Ciano desire's to work for peace.[10] To this Welles added that "it seemed to [him] that the influence of Italy towards this end might consequently be very great."[11] This flattery worked, as it had done earlier in the day with Ciano, insofar as Mussolini interjected to say that this was true and he "had done everything possible to avert the present war." With this contrived adulation out of the way, Welles returned to Mussolini's opening enquiry and within the self-imposed "limitations set forth" outlined his impressions.[12]

Welles' opening reflected his own views. The American recounted that everywhere "the fundamental demand was for security; not a fictitious nor illusory security but a security which involved a real disarmament." He then went on to say, with little basis in fact given what he had heard in London, that territorial questions in Europe "were by no means insoluble problems."[13] Such an assessment aimed to engage Mussolini, and it certainly did so. Mussolini responded first by telling Welles of the imminent meeting he was to hold with Hitler at the Brenner Pass. In repeating Ciano's appraisal, he continued that during Ribbentrop's recent visit the Reich's Minister had insisted that "Germany would consider no solution other than a military victory and that peace negotiations were impossible."[14] In the light of this, Mussolini believed "that the German military offensive was in fact very close, and that it would be undertaken within a number of hours rather than within a number of days." Having set this scene, Mussolini then asked Welles whether the American would authorize him "to communicate to Hitler the impressions [he] had formed with regard to the possibility of a negotiated solution of territorial and political questions in Europe." Welles' response illustrates clearly the limits to his mission. The American knew the mission could not entangle the United States in direct discussions between Europe's belligerents. Welles stated that he was "not empowered to give . . . such authorisation and that [he] would require specific instruction from the President of the United States before [he] could make a reply." Welles did go on to say he would ask Roosevelt over the telephone and inform Ciano of the result later in the day.[15] By stating that he would need to consult with Roosevelt he was trying to build in some delay and possibly engender doubt over the eventual outcome of his mission.

Mussolini's proposition crystalized the mission's limits. In endeavoring to draw out from Mussolini consideration of the possible role Italy might play, the Italian's proposal had overstretched Welles' license to operate. He knew he was not in a position to agree to Mussolini's proposals. Welles duly rang Roosevelt later on 16 March to discuss the "chief points" of his conversation with Mussolini. This was the "first and only telephone call" Welles made to Roosevelt during the course of the mission, and it reflected the sense of urgency that Mussolini's proposal was dealt with.[16] This urgency reflected a concern that the proposal would involve the United States in the war. Welles urged Roosevelt to decline the offer, as he knew full well that American intervention between the belligerents was too risky for his government in Washington. Roosevelt agreed with Welles' advice against authorizing him "to agree to permit Mussolini to convey to Hitler any impressions . . . with regard to any possible territorial adjustments."[17] Consideration of the views of the American people was still very much to the fore as Welles explained his recommendation. He feared that "the impression would inevitably be created that the President was participating in the determination of such bases for a political peace as might be offered by Hitler." Welles ended his counsel by returning to his long-held views on disarmament as a means of providing security. Welles stated that security was the "fundamental issue, since security involved real and actual disarmament of the kind which would make it possible for men and women to go back to constructive work, with a consequent increase in living standards, and with a consequent immediate opportunity for all of those economic readjustments which are indispensable to a durable peace." In such literary terms the conversation ended, but it is interesting to note that this sentiment was repeated by Roosevelt in his speech later that day. The speech laid out plainly the type of settlement the United States wanted to see. The British government particularly welcomed Roosevelt's declaration.

Nonetheless, Mussolini's offer had succinctly illustrated the constraints under which the Welles mission took place. Both Roosevelt and Welles knew that the mission could not appear to involve the United States in European affairs, and when an opportunity arose here it was declined. Moffat understood the gravity of what Mussolini's offer meant to the Welles mission. He noted that thus far "our task has been relatively easy: henceforth, it will require all S.W.'s acumen to prevent becoming entangled in German designs and Allied counter-designs."[18] This opinion reveals a number of important elements. First, Moffat's concern that Welles was facing a situation in which he was placed between Berlin and the Allies. The second aspect is the use of the word "entangled," as it alludes to Moffat's understanding of the appearance of neutrality that the mission had to maintain. Perhaps most telling, though, was Moffat's revelation that he thought the mission up to that point had been a relatively straightforward task, which can only mean that he thought it had not been intended to produce a peace settlement—by any reckoning a complex task. This episode shows that the founding aim Roosevelt and Welles had in January 1940 for the mission—of exploring the possibilities for peace—had been fulfilled, and their decision to decline the opportunity to do anything more than "explore" illustrates the limits of the mission.

Mussolini's motive in making the proposal seems to have been to test how far Welles was prepared to involve the United States. When Ribbentrop had visited Rome on 10 March Mussolini had learned from the German that "the visit of Sumner Welles to Berlin produced nothing new."[19] This left Ribbentrop to ponder, "In Germany people are asking what Roosevelt actually meant by that step." Mussolini postulated to Ribbentrop during their meeting that the whole Welles mission "must principally be a question of an internal American matter." In these circumstances it seems likely that Mussolini was endeavoring to probe how far Welles' mission was just that or a genuine peace move. Welles' negative response confirmed to Mussolini that he, and his Axis partner Germany, did not need to take note of Welles' mission.

Interestingly, in Welles' report he ends coverage of this conversation with Mussolini by noting that the Duce said something "very significant." Welles recorded that Mussolini stated "that while the German-Italian pact exists he, Mussolini, retained entire liberty of action."[20] Mussolini was clearly trying to impress upon Welles his importance in the Rome-Berlin Axis, and this no doubt reflected his desire to "to impress his visitors rather than listen to what they were saying."[21] However, Welles was fully aware that Mussolini was almost wedded to Hitler at this stage. Ciano had told him that morning that

"Mussolini was definitely 'pro-German.' "[22] With hindsight unavailable to Welles at the time, this would become obvious at the Brenner Pass meeting. Welles dined informally with Ciano later on 16 March and told him of Roosevelt's decision to decline Mussolini's offer. Welles was somewhat surprised that Ciano "expressed emphatic approval" of the President's decision to resist the Duce's suggestion. Ciano believed it dangerous for the United States to be involved in "the formulation of any terms of political adjustment which might be considered by Hitler."[23] In endeavoring to return Welles' flattery, Ciano continued by agreeing with the American's analysis that "security" was the key problem facing Europe. Ciano also stressed to Welles, as Mussolini had done, that the forthcoming Brenner Pass meeting might be a precursor to the outbreak of fighting. Welles learned that Hitler was insistent upon the meeting taking place on the 18 March and lasting for no longer than an hour.[24] Time was clearly of the essence during Welles' return to Rome. The postdinner conversation ended with Ciano informing Welles that even if war were imminent, "close, friendly, and continuing relations between Italy and the United States would prove of inestimable value when the time came for laying the foundations of a decent and enduring peace."[25] Such words were to ring entirely hollow as, within weeks, Italy declared war on the Allies. Ciano's duplicity is clear with hindsight. In early May 1940 he visited Albania to meet with "General Carol Geloso, commander of Italian military forces there, and ordered him to prepare for war."[26]

Interestingly, Ciano recorded in his diary what he considered to be the most important result of his meetings with Welles. His assessment was that Welles' information led him to conclude that "in London and Paris there does not exist any of the uncompromising attitude which their speeches and the papers indicate."[27] Here again Welles efforts may have had unintended consequences. While Welles had tried to suggest that the Allies were resolute in prosecuting the war, Ciano interpreted these comments to reveal a fear within the Allies of Nazi Germany.

Though Ciano might have been guilty of misinterpretation in making his assessment of Allied resolve, his capacity for outright duplicity was also in evidence. In agreeing with Roosevelt's directive that the United States should not become involved, Ciano was drawing on a phone tap of Welles' conversation with Roosevelt.[28] His diary shows that he had listened to the entire discussion, which allowed him to gain an accurate insight. Ciano's precise assessment of Welles' mission was "that Roosevelt does not wish to commit himself beyond a certain point, and certainly not before he has carefully examined the results of his colleague's European mission."[29] It is perhaps ironic that Ciano's capacity for deceit had allowed him to make a true evaluation of Roosevelt's predicament as the spring of 1940 approached.

Welles had utilized the license given to him to operate independently by Roosevelt on his mission thus far, but Mussolini's offer had raised the prospect of direct U.S. involvement. Welles would have to use the acumen that Moffat said he would need in order to dispel the notion. However, Welles' hope that his mission might act as a brake to the escalation in Europe was not compatible with a clear declaration that there would be no U.S. involvement. This was to be the dilemma Welles would face during his final days in Europe, and it was one that he made little progress in addressing.

Having spoken to Roosevelt on the telephone, Welles followed this up with his first telegram to Washington since his time in Paris. Welles' explanation for this was "the urgency of the situation," underlining that time was pressing upon his return to Rome. The significance of this telegram here is that Welles stressed his information-gathering role, even after he had received Mussolini's offer. That Hull would receive the telegram was undoubtedly in his mind here, given he had recently spoken to Roosevelt. Welles began by stating that after his conversation with Mussolini he "had thereby been encouraged in [his] search for information."[30] Welles did turn to the prospect of "peace" but only as point seven of the memorandum. He foresaw two possibilities. First of all, Welles thought that as a result of the Brenner meeting "Mussolini may convey to the Allied Governments peace terms which would prove entirely unacceptable and which might be couched in the nature of a German ultimatum." Welles immediately considered how such a move should be dealt with in order to remove any notion that he or the United States had been party to any knowledge of this. His suggestion is prefaced by an implicit acknowledgment of the importance he placed on maintaining Italian neutrality. Welles wrote, "I would suggest that the Secretary issue a statement saying that while the President greatly appreciated the particularly cordial and friendly reception accorded me by the Duce and by Ciano, as well as the opportunity they have given me of procuring the information which the President sent me to Europe to obtain, nevertheless neither the President nor I have been consulted in anyway with regard to the peace terms nor were the President nor I in anyway apprised of their nature before they were made public." Welles followed this immediately by saying that such a statement "would immediately kill the impression which would presumably be intentionally created that the President's step in sending me abroad had favoured a drive of that character." This absolution from involvement in any peace drive illustrated Welles' own concerns and those he knew Hull harbored over his mission being perceived as an outright peace drive. The second of Welles' options was his last point and painted a bleak picture for Europe: "A second alternative is that Hitler actually is determined upon a military offensive in the immediate future and will consider no alternative. End."

This telegram helps further in elucidating Welles' approach upon his return to Rome in March 1940. The objective of gathering information is clearly outlined, as by implication is the prominence he gave to Mussolini. The distance Welles wished to put between the Administration and the prospect of a peace move provides further evidence of the dangers he perceived in his mission's image being tarnished by association in the eyes of the American public. Further, the realism with which Welles tackled the prospect of German aggression shows that in March 1940 he was fully aware of the threat posed by Nazi Germany. That Welles understood all these factors at the time was crucial as he sought to fulfill the objectives for the mission. Once Welles had fulfilled the conceptual purpose for the mission that Roosevelt and he had considered at the turn of the year, and the possibilities of peace had been explored to no avail, the other goals of the mission came into sharp focus.

For Hull the concerns continued, and in some respects became more acute, as Welles' mission drew to a close. He confessed to Lothian that "the problem of defeating the peace offensive which had been developing towards the end of Welles' mission had given him great anxiety."[31] Hull continued that he thought the situation was precarious, as the American people were "asleep on the central issue to-day as Great Britain had been in the past." Further, Hull was worried by the constant press attention Welles was receiving, even if no headline-grabbing story had resulted thus far. Given these concerns, Hull welcomed Roosevelt's 16 March speech, which he saw as dispelling "the spread of the 'peace at any price' sentiment . . . which would be the equivalent of a German victory."[32] The term "peace at any price" was one that had quickly become associated with the discredited policy of appeasement and was of concern to many in the Roosevelt Administration. Berle, in agreement with Hull, wrote that he was "glad" Roosevelt made the "speech against the peace-at-any-price idea [because] if it has no other effect, it will indicate that Welles is not behind the peace-at-any-price move."[33] The concern for how Welles' mission was regarded by the American people remained.

While Hull continued to fret over the outcome of the mission in Washington, Welles continued his series of meetings by visiting the Pope at the Vatican. This meeting, and one with the Vatican's Secretary of State, Cardinal Maglione, took place on 18 March while Welles was waiting in Rome for news of the Brenner Pass meeting. Although aware that the Vatican held a unique position in Italian society, Welles also knew that the Pope had only marginal influence on Mussolini. The meeting touched on a number of important areas, but should be considered very much in the light of Welles' pursuit of continuing Italian neutrality.

Welles went into the meeting knowing the views of the Vatican on the prospect of peace and on Italy's role. Myron Taylor, Roosevelt's recently appointed representative to the Vatican, had told Moffat that the Vatican "did not believe the moment opportune for a peace conference."[34] They had "reluctantly . . . come to the conclusion that there must first be a further trial of strength." Clearly, the Vatican was not considering bringing about peace at that time. Of more importance to Welles at this stage was what Taylor had learned with regard to the Vatican's view of the Italian position. Taylor calculated the "principal preoccupation of the Vatican" as being "to keep Italy non-belligerent." This aim was in line with Welles' own thinking on how his mission could make a contribution to events in Europe. According to the British Representative to the Vatican, the Pope told Welles that "the President would perform a service of the highest value in the interest of peace by exerting his influence with Mussolini so that Italy would remain a non-belligerent."[35] A comment such as this at such a time, from a source with some independent perspective, may have further confirmed the importance of Italian neutrality in his thinking.

Important with regard to the future of Italy was Welles' direct enquiry as to the contents of the Pope's recent conversation with Ribbentrop. The Pope informed Welles that Ribbentrop had been most deferential, but this did not hide the German's central message. Throughout their conversation Ribbentrop stressed Germany's "determination to proceed with the war until she had achieved a military victory."[36] Welles also learned that Ribbentrop had endeavored to suggest that "a vast German offensive on the western front was imminent, perhaps only a few days away."[37] In bringing up the subject of Ribbentrop's trip to Rome, Welles was looking to find out about the possible end of the "phony war." Such information would clearly help his mission's objectives. Ultimately, though, there was little consequence to the meeting Welles held with the Pope, or the conversation he held later in the day with the much-respected Cardinal Maglione.[38] Italy was under the direction of Mussolini, who at that time was at the Brenner Pass agreeing to enter the war.

When Ciano returned to Rome to meet Welles on 19 March, the Italian was at his most deceitful. At the same time, Welles' behavior acknowledged that in this final episode of his mission gathering information was his main priority. His last act before leaving Rome was to reiterate this public goal of his mission.

Welles returned to the Rome Golf Club on March 19 to meet Ciano. The Italian described the meeting at the Brenner Pass as "no more than a domestic incident" for the Rome-Berlin Axis.[39] Despite claiming to speak with complete frankness to Welles, Ciano continued that he thought "the most important thing for [Welles] to learn was that there would be absolutely no change in Italy's non-belligerent attitude as a result of the meeting." This assessment is at complete odds with the actual facts of the Brenner Pass meeting, at which Mussolini agreed to join Germany in the war. Ciano's own account reveals his double-dealing nature, particularly his propensity to tell his audience whatever he thought they wanted to hear. His diary admits this, in revealing how he responded to the British Ambassador's enquiry about the Brenner meeting. "I put him at ease," Ciano wrote. "The Brenner meeting is no prelude to surprise in our policy. This is what he wanted to hear." While it might not have been a "surprise" that Italy would agree to join her Axis partner in the war, and although it did not take place immediately, Ciano was clearly not being completely frank with either the British Ambassador or Welles.

Ciano's next comments reveal further intrigue. Although stating correctly that the meeting had seen no German peace proposals or any request for "Mussolini to present any suggestions for peace proposals to the Allied governments," he continued with an entirely fatuous line. Ciano stated that he "very emphatically . . . believed that the time might come in the not distant future when Hitler would be receptive to the consideration of a negotiated peace." Under such circumstances "the initiative should be taken by the President of the United States, using Italy as its 'point of support' in Europe."[40] The first part of Ciano's comments here alludes to the possibility Welles had suggested in his 17 March telegram to Washington. That no proposals would be immediately forthcoming was welcome news to Welles as he sought to avoid the appearance of his being involved in peace negotiations. However, the second part of Ciano's comments that Hitler might be receptive to peace terms in the future was pure fantasy. Given what Welles had learned himself in Berlin, he knew this to be the case. His suspicions of Ciano can only have been reinforced. Indeed Roosevelt subsequently questioned in the spring in conversation with Mackenzie King, whether "Ciano even knew what had taken place."[41]

Ciano's duplicitous qualities are shown to an even greater extent in a monologue at the end of his final meeting with Welles, and the last of the mission. He made the hollowest of promises. Ciano asked Welles to tell Roosevelt "that so long as I remain Foreign Minister, Italy will not enter the war on the side of Germany, and that I will do everything within my power to influence Mussolini in that same sense."[42] History would soon prove this to be a complete lie.

Welles' time back in Rome exposes the delicate nature of the task he faced. He had tried to play up a possible role for the Italians and exploit both Mussolini's "liberty of action" and Ciano's dislike of the Nazis. This was done with a view to furthering Italian neutrality and limiting the scope of the war. Welles knew it to be a thankless task, given Mussolini's attraction to Berlin and his complete control over Ciano, but nevertheless in an increasingly pressured environment he saw some value in pursuing it. Ciano's final words to Welles perhaps allude to the dilemma facing the American. From a position of imminent disaster maybe something could be made of his comment that "nothing will be more gratifying to me than the opportunity to cooperate in the name of Italy with the United States in the cause of the reestablishment of that kind of just and durable peace in which the President believes."[43] When faced with the prospect of total war in Western Europe Welles would continue to exploit any last vestige of opportunity that Ciano's comments provided to preserve Italian neutrality in the spring of 1940.

Cordell Hull's concerns that Welles' mission would become associated in the press with rumors of peace became a reality during Welles' final hours in Rome. Welles had been followed on his travels in Europe by numerous members of the press, many of whom had accompanied him all the way from the United States. Welles, as has been seen, strictly limited his public utterances and so endeavored to restrict the rumors surrounding his mission. "Rab" Butler in London had referred to Welles as "carp-like," owing to his capacity for silence.[44] Such a tactic had served to successfully prevent sensational headlines appearing in the American press, but Hull continued to worry. Prompted both by continual questioning from the press in Washington and by Welles' telegram of 17 March, which had mentioned the possibility that he might receive peace terms from Hitler, Hull suggested to Roosevelt that he compose a message to Welles to stress the fact-finding nature of his mission. Roosevelt in typical fashion initialed "OK FDR." Hull then wrote to Welles that he thought it "hardly inconceivable that any peace proposal based on an ultimatum as to time and/or threat of force will be put up to you for either action or comment." This was clearly a prospect that worried Hull, as he continued, "I assume that within your function as fact-finder you would not be given peace terms for transmission to belligerents, except as data for our information."[45] Though Hull's words show that he was not party to the direct communications between Roosevelt and Welles, they also clearly reveal his concern that the United States should in no way be seen as intervening between the belligerents.

Hull's fear that amid the plethora of press rumors one would come to the fore came to fruition the very next day, while Welles waited in Rome. Herbert L. Matthews of the *New York Times* penned a story that prompted a flurry of questioning about the mission. Matthews wrote that Ribbentrop had delivered to the Pope an "eleven-point peace" program, which Welles had received from Hitler and then discussed with the Pontiff.[46] Considerably upset, Hull immediately cabled Welles and suggested that he issue a strong denial. The United Press had already added to Matthews' story by saying that the terms presented were "far from satisfying the desires of the Allies," and Hull wanted such stories to be dispelled.[47] The Under Secretary promptly followed Hull's suggestion:

> In order to allay the flood of rumours about my mission, I wish to state categorically that I have not received any peace plan or proposals from any belligerent or from any other government; that I have not conveyed any such proposals to

any belligerent nor to any other Government; nor am I bringing back to the President any such proposals. My mission has been solely one of gathering information for the President and the Secretary of State as to the present conditions in Europe.[48]

Angered by the story, Welles tracked Matthews down later in the day and told him plainly that the story contained "not one solitary vestige of truth." Moffat's diary confirms Welles' public reiteration of the mission's purpose. The account reads, "Welles issued a public statement that he had neither received nor proposed any peace plan whatsoever, and that his mission was what it had been [when] announced,—namely, fact-finding."[49] Welles' words in Rome provide further evidence of the appearance he and the Administration wanted the mission to have. This marked the end of his time in Europe.

Welles arrived in the United States on March 27 and proceeded straight to Washington to present Roosevelt with his report.

Welles' report reveals to varying degrees the multiple aims of the mission. The explicit mention of a section entitled "Italy and Peace in Europe" shows the importance Italy had assumed in Welles' thinking as an objective for the mission. Implicit to this and in Welles' conclusion is an acknowledgment that prolonging the "phony war" was on the verge of becoming impossible although anything that could be done to encourage its continuation might be beneficial. With regard to the original objective of the mission, Welles' conclusion reveals that there was now no prospect for peace between the belligerents. Throughout the extensive, 117-page report, Welles' skill at recording his conversations with Europe's leaders is self-evident. That this includes a conclusion of only two pages shows that Welles did not embellish his report with a host of personal views or recommendations. It reads as a remarkably neutral narrative and is replicated in *Time for Decision*.

The interesting aspects of the report for the mission's objectives lies in the section entitled "Italy and Peace in Europe."[50] Welles began it by stating that "Mussolini alone" would determine Italy's future. Welles' understanding of this is crucial. No matter what he thought about Ciano, he knew after his time in Rome that Mussolini was the one who counted. His subsequent efforts to further Italian neutrality in the spring of 1940 should be seen in this light. Welles saw a potentially pivotal role Mussolini could play but nevertheless did not see Mussolini as a man of real character. This became clear when Welles reported to Roosevelt that Mussolini remained "at heart and in instinct an Italian peasant. He is vindictive, and will never forget either an injury or a blow to his personal or national prestige. He admires force and power. His own obsession is the recreation of the Roman Empire. His conscience will never trouble him as to the way or the means, provided the method of accomplishment in his judgement serves to gain the desired end."

These are not the words of a man, who had placed faith in Mussolini being an agent of peace. Instead he saw Mussolini's position, particularly during his initial time in Rome, as one that could be exploited with the aim of preserving Italian neutrality and the "phony war." But he was far from hopeful as he considered Mussolini to be wedded to Berlin. Welles explained that if "Germany obtains some rapid apparent victories, such as the occupation of Holland and Belgium, I fear very much that Mussolini would then force Italy in on the German side—and I use the word 'force' advisedly." Of course the events of April and May in Northern Europe encouraged Mussolini in that direction.

Even after this assessment Welles did turn to his belief in the value of seeking to improve relations with Rome. That he saw any worth in this reflects his, and the Administration's, experience of seeking to explore every last opportunity: the one in a thousand chance. Welles reasoned that the "United States can make a very real and a very practical contribution towards the cause of peace by improving relations between the two countries." He noted that Roosevelt's letter to Mussolini had been "a powerful factor" in the warm reception he had received. If relations could be improved, then accord between Rome and Washington "would do much to prevent any possible entry of Italy into the war, and should a negotiated peace in Europe prove practicable, the ability of the United States through the President to maintain a friendly and confidential contact with Mussolini might in many contingencies prove of exceptional value." These comments again reflect Welles' desire to keep an option open no matter how seemingly distasteful. Overall, the inclusion in Welles' report of the section on Italy shows the emphasis that he placed on Mussolini and the role of Italy. Prefaced by an accurate awareness of Hitler's influence over Mussolini, Welles implicitly revealed the importance that prolonging Italian neutrality had assumed in the Welles mission, even if it were a hope against hope in the face of impending catastrophe.

Welles' report also reveals the Under Secretary's assessment that prospects for peace were absolutely minuscule. Although this section is perhaps tinged with his own views on the issues to be tackled in an eventual peace, the conclusions he draws are clear. Welles wrote for Roosevelt,

> I do not believe there is the slightest chance of any successful negotiation at this time for a durable peace if the basis for such negotiation is made the problem of political and territorial readjustment or the problem of economic readjustment.
>
> The basic problem I feel is the problem of security, inseparably linked to the problem of disarmament.[51]

In making this claim, Welles' understanding that security meant guarantees against future aggression is clear. On this basis, he saw disarmament as a potential method of establishing security, yet he did not lose sight of the importance of political issues; "they must be solved before any lasting peace can be found." His concluding remarks show further the extent to which he was endeavoring to find that one in a thousand chance of averting catastrophe. Even this was prefaced with a realization of the difficulties involved. "I do not underestimate the magnitude of the task of finding any hope of real peace so long as Hitler and his regime remain in control in Germany," Welles continued. "The only slight hope of peace, before Europe plunges into a war of devastation, or drags through a long-drawn-out war of attrition . . . is the agreement by the great powers of Europe upon some practicable plan of security and disarmament. This would be the 'miracle' spoken of by Mr. Chamberlain which would persuade Great Britain and France once more to negotiate with Hitler." Welles' belief that a miracle would be needed to avoid catastrophe was a tragically accurate assessment.

Welles had briefed Roosevelt and then Hull on the morning of 29 March. The President announced later that day in a press conference that peace in Europe was a "scant prospect."[52] Therefore, despite his assertions to the contrary ever since the mission had entered the public arena, such an admission implicitly acknowledged that exploring the possibilities for peace had been at least part of the thinking behind the mission. Nevertheless, Roosevelt opened the press conference by sticking to his publicly proclaimed line that the mission had not been meant to consider peace. He stated that Welles "had not received, nor has brought back to me, any peace proposals from any source." Still, even after the mission, concern remained that the United States could become entangled in peace negotiations. Such anxiety would continue through the spring as events unfolded in Europe. Crucially, Roosevelt continued his statement by pointing to what he saw as the justification for the mission. In this he stressed, predictably, the information Welles had collected: "The information which he has received from the heads of the governments which he has visited will be of the greatest value to this government in the conduct of its foreign relations." He qualified this to state that it was not information regarding any peace settlement but information relating "to the views and policies of the European Governments mentioned." Roosevelt then provided further justification by stressing the value of the fact that just one person, Welles, had been able to meet with so many different people. While also revealing his own penchant for personal diplomacy, in his next comment Roosevelt declared that he was "glad to say that Mr Welles' mission has likewise resulted, through personal contacts and through the conversations which he held, in a clarification of the relations between the United States and the countries which he visited and will, I believe, assist in certain instances in the development of better understanding and more friendly relations." Roosevelt's final point touched on peace: "Finally, even though there may be scant immediate prospect for the establishment of any just, stable, and lasting peace in Europe, the information made available to this Government as a result of Mr Welles' mission will undoubtedly be of the greatest value when the time comes for the establishment of such a peace." Interestingly, it is only at the end that the word "peace" is mentioned in connection with the Welles mission, and even then it is in dealing with the future peace and not the present. In looking to the future Roosevelt was in effect asking his audience, the American people, to think about what role the United States would have to play. In this sense the mission was fulfilling its role of informing the American people about the dangers the Roosevelt Administration saw in both the war and a settlement to it, which could injure U.S. interests.

Roosevelt's final comments added a salutation to his friend's efforts in Europe: "To Mr Welles go my thanks and full appreciation for carrying out this difficult mission with extraordinary tact and understanding and in accordance with the best American diplomatic traditions." Roosevelt refused to add any more at the press conference. Within two weeks of Roosevelt's announcement, the "phony war" would end with Germany's invasion of Scandinavia. Nonetheless, the themes that had fostered the Welles mission, and the objectives Welles pursued did create in various forms a legacy that will be examined in the final chapter of this work.

When Welles left Italy on 20 March he, in a better-informed position than the vast majority in Europe, suspected that the stalemate of the "phony war" was drawing to a close. He "feared . . . time would necessarily elapse."[53] The threat of the spring offensives had run as an undercurrent throughout the "phony war" and were now staring Europe in the face. Within two weeks of Welles presenting his report to Roosevelt, Hitler ordered German forces into Denmark and Norway, and a month later Germany attacked the Low Countries. The same day, in Whitehall, Churchill became Prime Minister of Great Britain. These events fundamentally altered the geopolitical landscape that Welles had faced. Nevertheless, against a backdrop of the expectation that the "phony war" would end in a matter of weeks with complete catastrophe, the perpetuation of the unreal stalemate and particularly of Italian neutrality remained important objectives for Welles.

This chapter has shown how in an increasingly pressurized situation the themes identified in this work became interwoven with the objectives of the mission. The emphasis once Welles was back in Rome was to perpetuate Italian neutrality and the "phony war." He endeavored to do this by continuing to talk to Ciano and Mussolini about an Italian role in any possibility of avoiding escalation. Welles was fully aware that this was unlikely to succeed, but he was familiar with operating in situations when the odds seemed "long." He wrote later that any "ability of the United States to arrest the catastrophe was tenuous."[54] Welles also knew upon his return to Rome that the fate of Italy lay in the hands of "one man, and one man only," that man being Mussolini. Despite Welles' efforts to engage with Ciano, he knew that Ciano "was wholly subservient" to the Duce. This should be borne in mind when this work turns to examining Welles' efforts to maintain Italian neutrality even after Hitler's attack on the West: they were aimed directly at Mussolini. Welles saw this effort, manifested in a series of appeals, as part of his responsibility to explore every possibility to avoid the cataclysm of full-scale war in Europe. In this aspect he was taking to the extreme the State Department's institutional memory of conducting policy knowing that any impact would be minimal. The theme identified, of Welles' position in Administration foreign policy making, is also evident here in the prominence Welles places on Italy as the mission culminated and into the summer of 1940.

The other objectives that the mission had initially developed had, by the time of Roosevelt's press conference, proved unattainable. This was always likely to be the case. With regard to the exploration of the possibilities for peace, this had been exhausted. Nothing approaching acceptable peace terms had emerged. Instead, Welles could barely contain his disgust with those he had met in Berlin. Equally, the goal of fact-finding had been achieved through Welles' thorough conversations as chronicled in his report. It was a surprise to no one, least of all Roosevelt and Welles, that it contained little groundbreaking information. The enquiry with regard to Allied war aims had provided Welles with a picture of what the Allies were fighting against: Nazi domination of continental Europe. However, it would take closer Anglo-American cooperation on infinitely more important matters over the upcoming months and years for a synergy to emerge on what the British, and subsequently the United States, were fighting *for*. In the end this was a set of values espoused in proclamations such as Roosevelt's Four Freedoms speech (January 1941) and epitomized in documents such as the Atlantic Charter (August 1941). In this light, the state of Anglo-American relations at the end of the mission was little different from what it had been immediately after Welles had left London. Roosevelt's speech of 16 March had further soothed some British anxieties, but many remained before the momentous events of the spring took hold. An instant of these anxieties will be examined in the final chapter.

During the final leg of the Welles mission and upon Welles' return to Washington, the continuing importance of American public opinion to the Roosevelt Administration is once more evident. Hull's heightened concern in the last days of Welles' time in Europe, as to the presentation of the Under Secretary's activities, reflected the nonentangling element of American opinion. Welles too was aware of this during his time in Europe and of the dilemma it placed him in. The dual trends within American opinion allowed, and indeed encouraged, the President on the one hand to consider the situation in Europe but on the other hand to steer clear of anything that the American public might regard as entangling. The line was thus very fine between accusations of being ensnared in European politicking and endeavoring to outline the challenges a European war posed to the United States. In public, the mission had to give the appearance that the United States was neutral, although this might have hampered Welles' ability to create doubt over the future course of American policy. As it was, Roosevelt's speech declaring that peace must have a moral basis, before his 29 March statement, can only have contributed to the belief in Rome and Berlin that they could discount the United States from their consideration. By that stage Roosevelt in Washington had learned of Welles' views of the Nazi regime and had told Long in their 12 March conversation (quoted here at the end of chapter 3) his retrospective motivations for the mission. Roosevelt saw no prospect of reconciling the issues at stake in Europe with his perception of the views of the American people at that time. Essentially he was hamstrung and was left to watch with no tools, diplomatic or otherwise, to affect Hitler's advance across Western Europe in April and May.

In the face of Nazi Germany's exploits in the spring of 1940, the final chapter of this work considers the legacy of the Welles mission in Europe and in Washington. Any legacy was, however, tenuous, as the events of the spring overwhelmed the margins at which the Welles mission operated. *The New York Times*, which had emblazoned news of the mission's announcement on its front page on 10 February, relegated coverage of Roosevelt's press conference of its end to page 5. Comment was restricted too. *The New York Times* article stressed that the mission would be of use at some nebulous point in the future, "When [the] Time Comes" and that the mission had ended in nothing more than a " 'a very handsome sentence.' "[55] Such an assessment illustrates the minimal impact—always acknowledged as being the most likely outcome—of the mission. The analysis of the mission's motives and objectives is consequently where the real diplomatic and political drama lies and thus has been the focus of this study.

CHAPTER 7

THE WELLES MISSION: A SHORT-TERM LEGACY TO THE ANGLO-AMERICAN RELATIONSHIP AND ROOSEVELTIAN FOREIGN POLICY

ROOSEVELT'S STATEMENT AT HIS PRESS CONFERENCE on 29 March 1940 that there was "scant immediate" prospect for peace proved tragically correct within two weeks. The spring and summer of 1940 saw a fundamental remapping of Europe's political geography that inaugurated four years of Nazi domination on the continent. Germany's attack upon Scandinavia (Operation Weserübung, 8–9 April) and then the Low Countries (Operation Gelb, 10 May), Churchill becoming British Prime Minister, Italy's eventual intervention, the capitulation of France, the drama of Dunkirk, and then the Battle of Britain all contributed to one of the most tumultuous six months in European history. Under such circumstances it is of little surprise that the mission of Sumner Welles has been ill considered. With the geopolitical landscape changed so dramatically in such a short space of time, the legacy of the Welles mission was overtaken in many respects. Any long-term impact amid the unfolding European war was negligible.

This final chapter begins with an examination of a number of episodes in the spring and early summer of 1940 that illustrate the continuing relevance of the themes this book has utilized in exploring the mission and the objectives that Roosevelt and Welles had for it. In one sense at least, then, this meant that the mission did produce a series of legacies. The key role played by Welles, the worries of Hull, the concept of policy being carried out in the knowledge that it would have only a minimal effect, and the influence of relations with Great Britain are all evident in the final phase of the mission's influence. The first episode under consideration concerns a series of appeals sent to Mussolini by the Roosevelt Administration. The chapter moves on to look at the continuing concern that Welles and the Administration had for the public's perception of the mission. It does so by looking at Welles' conduct in dealing with a photograph of him taken during his time in Paris. The capacity for misunderstanding in Anglo-American relations, which has characterized much of this analysis, including Welles' time in London, was again in evidence in the spring of 1940. This was particularly the case as the two governments exchanged views over the proposal Chamberlain had made in his second meeting with Welles on 13 March. Although the individual events that this chapter examines were of minimal importance when set against the events of the summer of 1940, they are crucial in illustrating the thesis that this work has presented. The Welles mission can be truly understood only if the longer-term themes that made it possible are considered alongside the objectives that both Roosevelt and Welles sought from it. This chapter will conclude by offering its final analysis of the Welles mission in terms of Rooseveltian foreign policy and the Anglo-American relationship at the beginning of the summer of 1940.

Roosevelt watched in dismay as German forces struck in the spring of 1940. His capacity to influence events was limited by the dual trends within American public opinion. In these circumstances he adopted a policy option that he had used before in times of increased tension—in April and August 1939. In those instances Roosevelt had sent appeals to key European leaders in the expectation not that they would avert disaster but that they instead might provide a momentary pause for thought and also indicate again to the American people those with aggressive intent. These were the same motives that Roosevelt had when he composed a series of messages for Mussolini in April and May 1940. The fast-changing environment meant each was different, but the underlying motivation remained the same as it had been when previous presidential appeals had been considered. The appeals, unsurprisingly, had very little impact on events in Europe. Ultimately, the case for persevering with efforts to preserve Italian neutrality was made redundant by Mussolini's declaration of war on the Allies on 10 June 1940.

As for Welles, although he quickly resumed his normal duties within the State Department upon his return from Europe, he did not forget the final section of his report—entitled "Italy and Peace in Europe." It was his desire to see Italy remain neutral and so to limit the scale of the war that governed his thinking in the aftermath of his mission. Welles at first opposed and then supported the series of presidential appeals destined for Mussolini. His change of mind reflected the lengths he was prepared to go to in order to preserve Italian neutrality. Having opposed the sending of the first appeal on the grounds that it would serve only to incense Mussolini and push him closer to Berlin, Welles sought to use subsequent appeals to reverse this.

The first of the appeals illustrates once more Roosevelt's disposition to try and assist the Allied cause. The appeal was prompted by a British request. Lothian told the State Department of British concerns over Mussolini's position following Hitler's conquests in Scandinavia.[1] In a meeting on 29 April the Ambassador told Hull that the "preliminary reverses" that the Allies anticipated in Norway might encourage Germany to entice Italy into the war. In the light of the Administration's "interest in peace and in keeping the war from spreading," Lothian continued by asking whether Roosevelt "might find something further to say to Mussolini that would be persuasive with him to keep him out of the war at least for the present."[2] Hull's response was non-committal, betraying his belief that there was little value in "these personal appeals."[3] His memoirs note that he "said so to the President on several occasions." Nevertheless, it seems that Roosevelt had already been thinking along these lines, as he had members of the State Department prepare a draft. Once he had learned of Lothian's request, the message was sent to Rome, where Phillips relayed it to Ciano on 1 May 1940.[4] The message, dressed up in typical Rooseveltian language, was a "warning not to enter the war."[5] The note cautioned that if the war were to spread, "some neutral states," that is, the United States, would have to review their position. Ciano confided to his diary that, despite its "polite phrases," the objective was "none the less clear" in providing a warning to Rome. Ciano described Mussolini as accepting the appeal with "ill grace" and his response as "cutting and hostile." Mussolini was not to be shaken from his allegiance to the Axis.

This reaction was precisely the basis of Welles' objection to sending the appeal. He had feared that to do so could prompt Mussolini into taking the decision to join the war. Moffat, Welles' traveling companion, shared this view. His diary recorded that Welles "and I argued very strongly that no message should be sent. After all, any message would imply that we disbelieved the assurances Mussolini had given Sumner Welles six weeks ago."[6] Although these assurances amounted to nothing substantial for the Administration, to send an appeal so shortly after Welles' return would indicate to Mussolini that the Americans placed little value in their conversations in Rome. Unusually, Welles found himself in agreement with Hull, although for different reasons, and in opposition to Roosevelt in arguing against this first appeal. Nevertheless, Roosevelt proceeded as a result of Lothian's direct request.

In the aftermath of the German attacks on 10 May, and despite Mussolini's abrupt response to Roosevelt's first appeal, the Administration looked again at the possibility. On this occasion Welles helped to draft the appeal that was given to Mussolini on 15 May.[7] The quick German successes in the Low Countries encouraged Welles to argue that another message might act to temper Mussolini's desire to enter the war. In accordance with this, the telegram was composed in an understanding tenor. Ciano noticed this, as he commented that the "tone is changed; it is no longer, as it was the first time, in a covertly threatening style."[8] Instead he noted that it was "rather a . . . conciliatory message." The text began with Roosevelt making "the simple plea that you [Mussolini], responsible for Italy, withhold your hand, stay wholly apart from any war and refrain from any threat of attack. So you only can help mankind tonight and tomorrow and in the pages of history."[9] Roosevelt's words, composed by Welles, were a clear attempt to encourage Mussolini to remain out of the war. Ciano confided to his diary that an appeal was likely to have little effect on Mussolini, "when he is convinced that he has victory in his grasp." Although Ciano called upon Phillips to relay Mussolini's "thanks to the President" and to assure him that the appeal would "be given the most serious consideration," Phillips was not positive in reporting back to Washington.[10] He wrote, "It is clear . . . that the Duce does not desire to receive me today." Mussolini had reverted to the stance he had adopted prior to the Welles mission, of refusing to see the Ambassador. Clearly, any notion of understanding Welles might have inaugurated during his own time in Rome had expired. Mussolini's refusal even to see Phillips indicated this and meant that any further appeals were only likely to enrage the Italian.

Nevertheless, a further appeal from Roosevelt followed on 26 May 1940.[11] The circumstances of this appeal reveal the desperate situation that the Allies were in, as it was prompted by a request from London and Paris. With German forces advancing rapidly through the Low Countries, the British and French were ready to consider negotiating with Mussolini. Frank Warren Graff states that Churchill and Reynaud asked Roosevelt to "say the British and French were willing to consider reasonable Italian claims."[12] Yet John Lukacs pointed to a subtle but crucial difference in the views of London and Paris with regard to Mussolini's role. He states that Reynaud's "main purpose was to try buying Mussolini off; Halifax's to try inducing Mussolini to mediate with Hitler."[13] Although both these views prompted the Anglo-French approach to Washington the distinction is crucial; "buying off Italy facilitated the war against Germany, Italian mediation meant its end."[14] Although the story of Halifax's readiness to consider a settlement with Hitler at the end of May 1940 and Churchill's refusal to do so is a fascinating one, it is beyond the scope of this study. Its relevance here is that the Allies turned to Roosevelt as they sought to influence Mussolini. Nonetheless, and sharing the outlook of the Administration, the British were not hopeful of the impact of an appeal. Loraine, the British Ambassador to Rome, was despondent as he felt no "attempt by Roosevelt would do any good," yet, the Ambassador suggested, "the situation could hardly be made worse."[15] With Mussolini refusing to see Phillips, the American delivered this third message to Ciano. The intention of the message, again composed by Welles, fitted very much with the objective he had pursued when on his mission of limiting the scope of the war. The telegram declared that Roosevelt's "sole desire in making this suggestion [was] to make a practical effort towards avoiding the extension of the war."[16] In more candid terms, Ciano considered Roosevelt's proposal amounted to an offer "to become the mediator between us and the Allies, making himself [Roosevelt] personally responsible for the execution, after the war, of any eventual agreements."[17] Phillips showed some agreement in stating the message "was an offer of mediation."[18] Crucially, though, Roosevelt and Welles were not preparing any American intercession. Graff regards this plea as "the next logical step in his series of appeals to Mussolini."[19] Having so carefully orchestrated the Welles mission to present the image that the United States was not going to become entangled in European affairs, the pair was not in a position to change their minds despite the trying circumstances of the spring of 1940. Notwithstanding the desperate pleas of Churchill and Reynaud, this appeal did not foretell any American involvement.

As the situation deteriorated for the democracies with Germany's armies continuing their advance, Roosevelt considered a final appeal to Mussolini, which was sent on 30 May 1940.[20] Welles was less involved in this one, and its language was decidedly more bellicose. This appeal amounted to a definite warning to Mussolini and cautioned him about the "traditional interest" of the United States in the Mediterranean. It went on to say "that Italy's intervention in the war would bring about an increase in armaments by the United States and a multiplying of help in raw materials and war supplies to the Allies." Nonetheless, the result was the same, with only Mussolini's level of annoyance rising. This was relayed to Phillips by Ciano. "America has no business in the Mediterranean," the Italian stated, any more "than Italy has in the Caribbean sea."[21] Ciano warned Roosevelt that any "further pressure . . . can only stiffen Mussolini's determination." This was precisely what Welles had feared at the outset of the appeals process. The Italian decision to go to war alongside Germany had already been taken. It had been agreed to in principle at the Brenner Pass meeting, and Ciano wrote in his diary the day before Roosevelt's final appeal arrived that the "decision has been taken. The die is cast. Today Mussolini gave me the communication he has sent to Hitler about our entry into the war."[22]

The significance of this series of appeals in the aftermath of the Welles mission lies in a number of areas. In the fluid situation of April and

May 1940, they reveal that Roosevelt was deeply concerned by the escalation of the conflict. His readiness to act in accord with the Allied cause is exposed again. Furthermore, the appeals, particularly the first and fourth, became clear warnings to Mussolini and risked antagonizing the Italian. Roosevelt's patience was about to break. It did so most clearly in the speech the President delivered on 10 June at Charlottesville, Virginia. Roosevelt declared of Mussolini's decision to join the conflict that day that "the hand that held the dagger has struck it into the back of its neighbour."[23] Roosevelt continued, promising that the United States would act, but adding the proviso that American security would also be enhanced: "We will extend to the opponents of force the material resources of this nation: and, at the same time, we will harness and speed up the use of those resources in order that we ourselves in the Americas may have equipment and training equal to the task of any emergency and every defense." The fact that Roosevelt pointed out that "at the same time" as offering assistance to those fighting the Axis, his policies would be increasing the security of the United States, reflected his long-held policy that accommodated American nonentangling opinion. Also reflecting a longer-term practice was the very process of delivering presidential appeals that were unlikely to influence their recipients. Again the influence of the American people can be seen, as the appeals served to provide a record of the Administration's efforts to avert war and in doing so point out the aggressive designs of the Axis powers. In regard to Welles, these appeals reveal a variety of salient lines that this work has put forward. Not only do the appeals and their drafting show his involvement in policy making, but they also reveal his desire to fulfill a legacy to his mission. By maintaining a dialogue with Mussolini, Welles hoped that Italian neutrality could help the cause of the Allies and limit the scope of the conflict. There is therefore no little continuity between Welles' pursuit of this during his time in Europe earlier in the year and upon his return.

The consideration of the American public that was evident in the appeals to Mussolini was already evident in the aftermath of the Welles mission. In dealing with a minor incident surrounding the publication of a photograph taken while he was in Paris, Welles maintained the Administration's care over the appearance of his mission to the American people. On 16 March the French journal L'Illustration had published a photograph showing Welles in discussion with Reynaud (see appendix 4). Little might have been expected of this, until the photograph came to the attention of the Press Section of the German Foreign Office in early April. The reason was the map that appeared in the background of the picture. The Germans were riled by the borders to the south and east that showed to Berlin's mind that Germany was divided. Protests were made to Alexander Kirk, the American Chargé in Berlin, that Welles had discussed territorial matters with the French: the implication of the map. Kirk had no answer, as Welles was traveling home at the time. Once Welles had arrived in Washington and delivered his report, he set about countering the stories that the picture had spawned in Europe's press. These stories claimed that Welles had overstepped the public goal of his mission. Such a reaction had been one of Hull's concerns since the mission had first been considered. Welles' response was categorical in its refutation of such allegations. He called the charges "fantastic nonsense," as at "no time during the course of my interviews in Paris or in any other capital I visited was any reference made to any maps. I never even looked at any map which may have been in Monsieur Reynaud's office."[24] This message was relayed to Berlin, and Kirk was then summoned to the German Foreign Office. There he was given a statement that the Germans did not "care" whether Welles "noticed the map or not" but that the picture had been published "showing Mr Welles, M. Reynaud and the map." The German announcement continued: what "would the world have said if we, on occasion of Mr Welles' visit in Berlin, had had him photographed with Ribbentrop and Göring with a map showing a drastic partition of England? This is not a question of 'Germany-Welles' but a question of 'war policy or peace policy.'" While this question might not have been entirely unreasonable, it was never answered, as wholly more serious events took place in the days following this meeting. Importantly, in regard to this study, that Welles had to issue a statement about the appearance of the mission even after he had returned illustrates that the Administration was still very aware of the political risks his mission had entailed. Even then, the Administration was conscious of the American public entertaining the thought that Welles had discussed political, entangling, issues.

As has been explored in this work, those in Chamberlain's government still harbored notable concerns over Welles' mission after the Under Secretary left London. Although these were mitigated by Roosevelt's speech on 16 March and the low-key statement he had delivered on 29 March, the possibility that the White House might act to expose the British position still existed. These concerns, revealing of the effect the Welles mission had in Anglo-American relations, were evident at the beginning of April 1940. Lothian reported to London the substance of a conversation he held with Roosevelt and Welles on 3 April 1940.[25] Roosevelt had begun the conversation by referring to the proposal Chamberlain had made during his meeting with Welles on 13 March. This scheme was for the British to give a territorial guarantee of Germany to the United States. The proposal had been made by Chamberlain in order to dispel the impression Welles had garnered in Berlin of the "unanimity of opinion in Germany," that the Allies saw the breakup of Germany as one of their war aims. Given his views on the likelihood of American commitments it is highly likely Chamberlain thought Welles' noncommittal response would be the last he heard of the matter. Nevertheless, the proposal suggested that the British "bind themselves not to attack Germany by a formal undertaking given to the United States."[26] Roosevelt's response to this suggestion was typical of the policy the Administration pursued in the late 1930s, in that it sought to bring a multilateral aspect to the offer and so allow the United States to retreat from the responsibility. Roosevelt's justification was that if Chamberlain's offer was directed to all neutral states because of "American politics" it would be more acceptable in the United States. In this light, Roosevelt had a prepared statement that outlined what he sought from such a policy. It bore the hallmarks of the foreign policy that emanated from the Roosevelt State Department in calling upon the need for security of "national unity and existence to all nations both large and small," the removal of armaments that prevented children having "a free and happy life," equal access to raw materials and markets, the abolition of offensive weapons, and the freedom of information. The influence of Welles is evident in these terms, as they would lead to the code of conduct in international relations that he believed in. Also implicit in this proposal was the aim that Welles had pursued when in London of gathering information on the British war aims. An alignment between British aims and the proposals the Administration was considering would have helped present the Allied cause to the American people. This was clear from Roosevelt's final statement: "The Allied objective in fact was security in the widest sense of the word for all nations. In this way only could all nations alike look forward to future generations living under some other regime than that of fear." Lothian's response to this was characteristically to point to the immediate issue facing his government: that is, the ongoing conflict. Although Roosevelt had prefaced his proposal by stating that it would not enter "at this stage into the question of possible peace terms," Lothian rightly pointed out that it would be well nigh impossible not to give "the impression that it was a proposal for peace." This was clearly of concern to Roosevelt and Welles. The latter immediately suggested an addendum to any proposal that the Allies "ought to make it clear that it [the proposal] is not concerned with the conditions of peace but solely to enlighten the nations including Germany about the fundamental basis of the new world which the Allies had in view." The concern for projecting a longer-term vision of what the Allies were fighting *for* is revealed again, particularly in light of Welles work as chair of Advisory Committee on Problems in Foreign Relations.

Lothian's report of this meeting caused much concern in London, reminiscent of that raised at the outset of the Welles mission. The report was first seen on 8 April by R.M. Makins, a clerk in the Central Department, who concisely described the British concerns.[27] He wrote that Roosevelt "has completely misunderstood the point of our proposal," given that "it was an essential part of the proposal that the undertaking not to attack Germany would be given by the Allies to the United States Government only, who would therefore accept—as a stakeholder—some indirect responsibility." Here, Makins identifies what seemed an intractable problem for the British in dealing with the United States. Cadogan added in a most succinct statement that the "principal snag" was that "the US will not act *alone*" (italics in the original). This left Makins to conclude that Roosevelt's suggested text was "nothing but the familiar demand that we should make [a] further statement of peace aims." That the British were aware of the Administration's desire is significant in revealing an understanding of the pressures Roosevelt operated under. However, the reticence evident in Makins' tone discloses a British distaste for Roosevelt's dependence on American opinion. On the other hand, for Roosevelt, repeated statements of British peace aims would help distinguish between the Allies and the Axis in the eyes of the American people.

The reservations the British had about Roosevelt's proposal were expressed in stark terms by Vansittart. Having read Makins' remarks he characterized Roosevelt's draft as "characteristically woolly" and the President's "references to disarmament, abolition of offensive weapons, etc. reflect[ing] the usual American naivete on these matters." Vansittart was adamant as to how the British government should react to Roosevelt's suggestion: "Let us now get on with *fighting* the war, which is the only effective form of propaganda. And do not let us get drawn into all this embarrassing rigmarole by these distant and inexperienced amateurs"[28] (italics in the original). This disenchantment replicated Vansittart's attitude toward the Welles mission, and so did his final concern. Repeating his suspicion that the upcoming presidential election was dictating Roosevelt's appeals, Vansittart suggested that "His Majesty's Government must on no account be influenced by tyros, even if these are influenced by electioneering notions." Those in the Foreign Office were clearly less than impressed with the President's counterproposal in the aftermath of the Welles mission.

At a time when Hitler's forces were making rapid progress in Scandinavia, Halifax's priority in dealing with Roosevelt's proposal was to remain engaged in dialogue with Washington. Makins wrote of Halifax that he "wished to keep President Roosevelt in play" in spite of the importance of the events in Denmark and Norway.[29] Cadogan shared this view. He wrote, "I should have thought we ought to send a [telegram] . . . I don't like leaving the President unassured (he might even do something foolish on his own)." Cadogan's candid admission demonstrated the potential that still existed for misunderstanding in Anglo-American relations. The worry for the Foreign Office, as it had been in early February, was that Roosevelt might act independently, and in London's eyes rashly, and so jeopardize British interests.

In order to forestall this possibility, Halifax authored a telegram to Lothian on 20 April 1940.[30] It questioned whether the President would want to maintain his proposal under the circumstances brought about by Hitler's successes in Scandinavia. Halifax wrote that in "the altered circumstances we presume that the President would regard a statement of the kind he suggests to be inopportune. A brutal aggression has just taken place and further attacks on inoffensive neutrals are very probable. In the circumstances a statement intended primarily to reassure the German people would be open to considerable misconstruction." Lothian was already well versed in conveying sensitive issues to the Administration and, owing to their personal relationship, to the President. At this point the matter was taken no further because of the force of events, as Hitler's military consolidated their conquests in Scandinavia.

Nevertheless, this episode illustrates the potential for misunderstanding in the Anglo-American relationship in the aftermath of the Welles mission. The British viewed Roosevelt's response to Chamberlain's proposal with suspicion and frustration. The possibility that the suggestion might prove to be a precursor to a further embarrassing policy drive from Washington still existed, and the terms the President offered were just a reiteration of those they had heard before. At the same time though, Roosevelt's suggestion was viewed as a relatively low-key and somewhat belated outcome of the Welles mission. That the proposal remained bilateral at that stage gave the British greater scope to manage any developments that Roosevelt might consider. In this sense it did not cause any wider embarrassment and so fulfilled the concerns held earlier in the year that Roosevelt would publicly compromise the British. Halifax's response of keeping Roosevelt "in play" revealed the approach the British were adopting by the spring of 1940 in dealing with the President. With the Welles mission having provided a portent, Halifax's and Lothian's responses to the proposal indicated that, despite the potential for exasperation in London, it was still in British interests to try to accommodate Roosevelt. This was because the British wanted to be in a position to check at the earliest opportunity any move by the Administration that they considered rash. As an outcome of the Welles mission this discussion over Chamberlain's proposal reveals how neither party was able to wholly grasp, in accordance with their own aims, the aims of the other. As David Reynolds suggests of Anglo-American relations during the summer of 1940, both governments were "engaged in an uneasy bargaining game" and were "exploring in a rather heavy handed way how best to obtain support from the other."[31] Support in various forms would ultimately be forthcoming because of the catastrophic events of the summer and not in any meaningful sense owing to any positive outcome from the Welles mission.

The events that have been analyzed in this chapter thus far, the presidential appeals, the response to the *L'Illustration* picture, and the Anglo-American exchange over Chamberlain's suggestion, have pointed to elements of the longer-term themes that are necessary in understanding the place of the Welles mission in Rooseveltian foreign policy. In straightforward terms these four themes were Welles' role, Hull's concerns, foreign policy being enacted with little prospect of influencing events, and regard to Anglo-American relations. Underlying them all was a concern for American opinion. Furthermore, of the objectives Welles had for his mission, the pursuit of Italian neutrality and the desire for clear assertions of British aims were still being pursued and providing a legacy to the mission. In the closing portion of this study, the themes that have allowed for this examination of the Welles mission will be considered in a final analysis of Rooseveltian foreign policy in the spring of 1940.

The governing principles of Rooseveltian foreign policy were altered little by the experience of the Welles mission. Roosevelt had believed since Munich at least that Hitler would ultimately have to be stopped in the only terms he understood: military force. At the outbreak of war he was ready to support the Allied cause against the Axis and to assist them as far as he could. For Roosevelt personally, Kimball writes, "the question was not whether America would aid Britain and the Allies, but to what degree."[32] Roosevelt's efforts to ensure revision of the neutrality laws should be seen as an indication of this. That he could go no further and offer direct assistance to the Allies reflected his realization of an ill-prepared American military infrastructure but, more importantly, the views of the American people. As explained at the outset of this volume, Roosevelt had to contend with dual trends in American opinion. Their influence on his foreign policy and on the Welles mission is manifest. After war had broken out in September 1939, Roosevelt pondered how to reconcile his belief in the need for Hitler to be overcome and his inability to influence events because of American opinion. The emergence of what became the Welles mission in early January 1940 is self-evidently complex. Yet the ultimate shape of the mission was determined by the themes that this work has identified. Each of these will now be considered in summary as this work reaches its conclusion.

The intervention of Sumner Welles was critical to the mission that emerged in January and subsequently developed in early 1940. Described as "the most Olympian of Roosevelt's advisers," Welles' relationship with Roosevelt was such that the pair was practiced in concocting policy and its direction.[33] Roosevelt's penchant for personal diplomacy facilitated this and is well seen in the Welles mission. Kimball remarks appropriately that "one of the characteristics of Franklin Roosevelt's long presidency was his emphasis on personal diplomacy, both in his use of personal contacts and in his desire to shape the broad, long-term direction of American foreign relations to meet his own criteria."[34] Through Welles, Roosevelt was able to garner valuable information on the individuals who were involved in the war in Europe.

From Welles' point of view, Roosevelt's style allowed him to develop the mission in conjunction with his own views on establishing principles of international relations. Having been vital to establishing the "Good Neighbor" policy during the 1930s, Welles' Armistice Day conference plan inaugurated this and he returned to these themes during the rest of his tenure as Under Secretary. At the time of his mission, particularly in London, Welles utilized ideas of disarmament and security to facilitate his gathering of information. In essence, the zeal and appetite that Welles brought to Roosevelt's initial idea was integral to the final outcome of the mission. His skills and experience were vital in the evolution of the mission and its objectives. Those attributes in Hull were, in a very different fashion, also fundamental to Welles' mission.

Cordell Hull played a crucial, if less direct, part in the Welles mission. The prospect of a member of the Administration departing for Europe worried Hull from the outset. He saw the potential to antagonize the democracies and, more importantly to him, endanger the standing of the Administration in the eyes of the American people. These concerns replicated those he had over Welles' Armistice Day plan, and in many ways Hull's views remained consistent during the period under consideration. Yet Hull's role in foreign policy making is subject to debate. While he was given presidential license to pursue reciprocal trade, he was not party to key elements of foreign policy making. Kimball has gone so far as to say that Roosevelt "consistently acted as his own Secretary of State" and so bypassed Hull, in delegating "the conduct of specific foreign affairs to men like Under Secretary of State Welles or Morgenthau."[35] Kimball concludes that the real reason Hull remained Secretary of State for so long, an unprecedented 12 years, was his "political influence with Congress." His appreciation of how Congress reflected the views of the American people made him an important asset to Roosevelt, and this should not be underestimated. Historian David Woolner examines the role that Hull played in formulating a comprehensive foreign economic policy, the legacy of which can still be seen in the form of the World Trade Organization. In short, then, Hull, throughout his time in office, played a critical if less than direct role in formulating Rooseveltian foreign policy. In the case of the Welles' mission, Hull's influence, important though it was, could be felt away from the central decision making of Roosevelt and Welles.

The influence of the dual trends within American public opinion permeated the Welles mission as they did the making of foreign policy at this time. In broad terms the underlying influence of the nonentangling attitude of the American people revealed itself in a number of interrelated aspects of Rooseveltian foreign policy making. First, foreign policy was set out without necessarily having fixed goals in mind. At the same time foreign policy was intended to have only marginal influence. The various appeals are the best examples of policy initiatives being undertaken in the full knowledge that their impact on their recipients would be minimal. These appeals also exemplify a third feature of how Roosevelt's foreign policy was influenced, that being a consideration of how any policy would appear to the American people after the event. In this regard, the continuing education of the American people as to the dangers posed by the Axis was served by policies that showed the latter to be hostile to American interests and values. All of these elements were relevant to the formation and evolution of Welles' mission to Europe in early 1940. For example, to varying degrees, in the minds of Roosevelt, Welles, and Hull, the appearance of Welles' activities in Europe were of concern. This manifested itself in a number of ways, such as Welles' silence to the press and the reiteration of the mission's public purpose prior to his departure from Europe.

The nature of the mission was also influenced by consideration of Anglo-American relations. That Lothian learned about the proposed mission ahead of its announcement, and ahead of the other nations that Welles would visit, reveals a disposition toward London within the Administration. The exchanges that followed between Washington and London, in light of the minor crisis, illustrate that there were considerable grounds for misunderstanding. Indeed, for Chamberlain himself the prospect of Welles' mission represented his worst fears about Rooseveltian foreign policy. Replicating his own concerns of January 1938 when faced with Roosevelt's plan for an international conference, Chamberlain shared with Hull the worry that Hitler would take advantage of the mission to the detriment of British interests. This possibility hung over the mission from the early days of February right through until the middle of April, without complete resolution in British minds. The discussion, in April, of Chamberlain's suggestion of giving assurances to the United States of British intent toward Germany, reveals that the opportunity for misunderstanding remained. That no more dramatic move from Roosevelt followed Welles' return to Washington was ultimately welcomed by many in London, although there was little scope to rejoice as Hitler's tanks rolled westward. Though the Welles mission did not herald a new era of Anglo-American understanding, and it certainly did increase unease in a number of quarters, it did not lead to lasting distrust in relations between Washington and London either. Indeed Roosevelt commented in the spring that Welles' time in London had "been most satisfactory."[36] The events of the spring and summer of 1940 overtook any possibility that might have existed for a lasting outcome in this area.

Pervading each of these themes was the Administration's concerns for American opinion. Nonentangling sentiment within American opinion made overt assistance to the cause of the democracies impossible during the period covered by this study. Roosevelt knew this and thus devoted his energies in circumventing its influence. To a greater or lesser degree all of the policy initiatives that have been examined here in the run-up to war, and the Welles mission itself, had to contend with it. In Roosevelt's view the American people had to be educated in a sophisticated and respectful manner to understand the threats he saw in Europe to U.S. interests. However, having been caught too far ahead of American opinion in the aftermath of the Quarantine speech, he was conscious that to implement bold policy initiatives could be counterproductive. In these circumstances the force of events provided the best form of illustrating to the American people the dangers to U.S. interests. That is why British and French collusion with Hitler at Munich did so much to damage the cause of the Allies in the eyes of the American people and why upon learning of Hitler's attack on Scandinavia in early April 1940 Roosevelt proclaimed it a "great thing" as it would force a "great many Americans to think about the potentialities of the war."[37] The ever-erudite Lothian had a keen understanding of Roosevelt's position. He wrote in the aftermath of Germany's invasion of Scandinavia that the "intrinsic ugliness of the aggression achieved effects that no Allied propaganda could have secured."[38] The impact of this, Lothian explained, would not be seen in terms of any "great movement towards intervention" but crucially in creating "a profound effect on American opinion in the sense that it has increased largely the number of those who feel that Hitlerism will inevitably in the end force the United States of America into the war in defence of her own vital interests." In simple terms, Lothian surmised, "The United States is ninety-five percent anti-Hitler, is ninety-five percent determined to keep out of war if it can, and will only enter the war when its own vital interests are challenged."[39] This analysis was what faced Roosevelt when composing his foreign policy in early 1940. As the summer wore on wider British understanding became more sophisticated, with Cadogan commenting in the immediate aftermath of Churchill's request for American destroyers: "I'm quite convinced that Pres[ident] will do all he can, but he can't go ahead of his public."[40] The rapid success of the German military, which saw them reach the English Channel by 20 May, heightened Roosevelt's consideration of these dual views. He dealt with them by focusing on rearmament; on 16 May 1940 he had called upon the nation to produce "50,000 planes a year," a total that was eventually exceeded by 100 percent.[41] Under the pressure of these dual trends it is understandable that Rooseveltian foreign policy was made with a view to it appearing nonentangling. This meant policy was accepted, by those orchestrating it, as not being able to directly influence events in Europe. The limits were appreciated by those around him: to paraphrase Berle's description of the appeals sent to Europe in August 1939, Rooseveltian foreign policy at times had the appearance of an ill-timed Valentine sent to an inappropriate recipient. Crucially, though, with regard to public opinion, the Administration was convinced that these moves had to be made, even if they bore the hallmarks of the naïvety Vansittart identified in the Welles mission. Theses themes provide the context of Rooseveltian foreign policy making, from which a direct analysis of the motivations and objectives of the Welles mission can proceed.

By the end of 1939, Roosevelt was motivated to consider what became the Welles mission. His comments to Berle and Lothian in early December show he was contemplating how he could act. Nevertheless, it is important to remember that it was not clear that this motivation would coalesce around the sending of his Under Secretary to four European capitals with a number of objectives in mind. The pressures created after four months of "phony war" were crucial here. The dual trends within American public opinion have already been explained, but added to these was the pressure of operating in a situation where spring offensives were accepted to be inevitable. Welles himself wrote later, "The prospects for the Western democracies already seemed very dark indeed, although not yet so hopeless as they became a few months later."[42] This increased the likelihood of considering policies whose effect was always likely to be negligible. The discussion of the issue of peace, exemplified by the dialogue in October among members of the State Department, should also not be overlooked. The postwar world was of clear concern to the U.S. Administration and the discussion of peace in Washington should be seen in this light. The emergence of a postwar planning committee in early 1940, the declaration to the neutral powers, and then Welles' subsequent career suggest how seriously the issue was taken. Concern in Washington for the postwar world also fed into the onset of the minor crisis in Anglo-American relations, which Roosevelt was clearly aware of at the same time as the emergence of the concept of a mission to Europe and contributed to Roosevelt's belief that a mission to Europe might be worthwhile.

During January 1940, as Roosevelt weighed up the different motivations, the objectives for a mission emerged. They were liable to evolve from the outset, and would continue to do so throughout the course of the mission and into the spring. To restate the objectives of the mission, the initial concept was an exploration of the possibilities of peace. From the start this was acknowledged as being a long shot and other objectives developed from this concept. Throughout the mission's course, and indeed the whole war, Roosevelt believed that U.S. interests were incompatible with any settlement with Hitler in the long term. Unless Hitler changed his policies in a comprehensive and fundamental way, something they knew was not going to happen, Roosevelt and Welles were not striving to achieve a lasting peace settlement with Nazi Germany. Gathering information from the European capitals that Welles visited may have been an obvious goal, but it was important for Roosevelt in deciding upon the mission, given the paucity of valuable information independent of national bias. Additionally, the concept of per-petuating the "phony war" became part of the mission. It reached most prominence in Berlin, where Welles hoped any notion of American ambigu-ity might influence German plans. Closely intertwined was the objective of seeking to encourage Italian neutrality, particularly by supporting any notion that Mussolini might be a force for peace. Of course this would prove unten-able, but Welles in particular saw the Italian angle as worth pursuing when faced with the prospect of catastrophe in Europe.

When the escalation of the conflict arrived in April and with it such fun-damental changes in the month that followed, the Welles mission ceased in many senses to have relevance for Roosevelt. His initial concept had proved untenable, as he suspected it would, and the breadth of the other objectives had not provided anything substantial, especially in the face of the German advance. In this sense, any chance of a legacy to the mission that could have influenced events in Europe had gone. This also means that this analysis ends at a time when a whole range of issues arise in Rooseveltian foreign policy and Anglo-American relations brought on by the war.

A final word on American public opinion, in acknowledgment of its enduring position in this analysis, can be drawn from Lothian. Acknowledging in the spring of 1940, with such dramatic events taking place in Europe, that any assessment of American opinion was "difficult to crystallise in a despatch because things are so fluid . . . and so constantly changing," he felt the views he had dispatched on 1 February on the nature of U.S. public opinion were still valid.[43] Lothian wrote to Halifax surmising the dichotomous attitude within American opinion: "The United States is still dominated by fear of involvement and incapable of positive action. On the other hand the war is steadily drifting nearer to them and they know it."[44] It is therefore somewhat ironic that the trauma that the Welles mission brought to many in London could have been avoided had Lothian's sage advice on the pressures under which Roosevelt operated, offered consistently since his appointment, been heeded more closely.

This book has presented a wealth of evidence and analysis to explain the influences behind Roosevelt's decision to undertake the Welles mission. While the precedents established in the examination of Rooseveltian foreign policy and Anglo-American relations can help toward an understanding of Roosevelt's decision to embark upon the Welles mission, it must be acknowl-edged that the detail of the conversations between Roosevelt and Welles in early January does not exist. In this light, Roosevelt's comments to Breckinridge Long in early March show him to have been content for the mission to remain between him and his Under Secretary. He told his Assistant Secretary of State that "he was the only person who knew why

Welles had been sent abroad, and he was the only person who would know what Welles had to say."[45]

Ultimately, though, the Welles mission was conceived by two individuals who did not commit to record their precise thoughts on all aspects of the mission. The later famous George F. Kennan, having accompanied Welles from the Swiss border to Berlin as part of the American Embassy delegation, later recalled his thoughts on the Welles mission. "I was never briefed on the purposes of Mr Welles' journey," Kennan commented. "I cannot recall that he ever spoke to me in the course of his trip; and I know no more of his talks with the European leaders than the official files would reveal."[46] This work has scoured those files and other sources. In posing the question of its motivations and objectives in the context of Rooseveltian foreign policy the true place of the Welles mission emerges. In the end, Welles' summation as the title of the chapter on his mission in *Time for Decision* as "a forlorn hope" is one I consider to be most apt.

Appendices

Appendix 1: Transcript of the Press Release of 9 February 1940

1. Given out at Press Conference: PSF File Feb 9, 1940

At the request of the President, the Under Secretary of State Mr. Sumner Welles will proceed shortly to Europe to visit Italy, France, Germany and Great Britain. This visit is solely for the purpose of advising the President and the Secretary of State as to present conditions in Europe.

Mr. Welles will, of course, be authorized to make no proposals or commitments in the name of the Government of the United States.

Furthermore, statements made to him by officials of governments will be kept in the strictist confidence and will be communicated by him solely to the President and the Secretary of State.

Source: President's Secretary File, Box 76, Franklin D. Roosevelt Papers. The Franklin D. Roosevelt Library, Hyde Park, NY.

APPENDIX 2: THE FIRST DRAFT OF THE MISSION STATEMENT

DRAFT

The President has today directed Mr. _____ to proceed to Europe to visit Germany, England, and France. It will be the purpose of Mr. _____'s mission to ascertain whether the governments of those belligerent powers will state for the confidential information of the President the basis upon which they would be prepared to make peace. Mr. _____ will be empowered to make no proposals in the name of the Government of the United States to the governments mentioned, but only to inquire what the peace terms of the contending powers may be and to report the statements he may receive to the President and to the Secretary of State.

In view of the confidential nature of Mr. _____'s mission, any statements which may be made to him by officials of the governments of Germany, England, and France will be communicated by him solely to the President and to the Secretary of State.

Source: President's Secretary File, Box 76, Franklin D. Roosevelt Papers. The Franklin D. Roosevelt Library, Hyde Park, NY.

APPENDIX 3: THE SECOND DRAFT OF THE MISSION STATEMENT

At the request of the President ~~and the~~ *U.S of S Sumner Welles*

~~Secretary of State~~) *The Under Secretary of State Mr Sumner Welles* will proceed

shortly to Europe to visit *Italy* France, Germany and Great *Italy*

Britain. This visit is solely for the purpose of advising

the President and the Secretary of State as to ~~whether~~ *present* *present conditions in Europe*

conditions in Europe.

~~or not there would seem to be any possibility of ending~~ ~~an~~

~~the existing war between those powers in the near future.~~

Mr. *Welles* will, of course, be

authorized to make no proposals *or commitments* in the name of the

Government of the United States.

Furthermore, statements made to him by officials

of governments will be kept in the strictist confidence

and will be communicated by him solely to the President

and the Secretary of State.

Source: President's Secretary File, Box 76, Franklin D. Roosevelt Papers. The Franklin D. Roosevelt Library, Hyde Park, NY.

APPENDIX 4: PHOTOGRAPH FROM THE
PHILADELPHIA RECORD SHOWING WELLES (RIGHT)
AND REYNAUD (LEFT) (MURPHY IS IN THE MIDDLE)

Source: Telegram No. 843 from Washington to Kirk (Berlin) 5 April 1940, 121.840 Welles Sumner/165b: General Records of the Department of State 1940–1944, Central Decimal File Box 297, Archive II, MD.

NOTES

INTRODUCTION: THE MISSION OF SUMNER WELLES TO EUROPE (FEBRUARY–MARCH 1940), ROOSEVELTIAN FOREIGN POLICY, AND ANGLO-AMERICAN RELATIONS, NOVEMBER 1937–MAY 1940

1. Stanley Hilton, "The Welles Mission to Europe, February–March 1940: Illusion or Reality?" *Journal of American History*, Vol. 58 (1971–1972), p. 94.
2. John Lukacs, *Five Days in London May 1940* (New Haven, CT, and London, 1999), pp. 40–41.
3. Key sources on Rooseveltian foreign policy that consider briefly the Welles mission include Robert Dallek, *Franklin D. Roosevelt and American Foreign Policy, 1932–1945* (Oxford and New York, 1995); William L. Langer and Everett S. Gleason, *The Challenge to Isolation, 1937–40* (New York, 1952); and Basil Rauch, *Roosevelt—From Munich to Pearl Harbor: A Study in the Creation of a Foreign Policy* (New York, 1950).
4. Langer and Gleason, *The Challenge to Isolation, 1937–40*, pp. 361–362.
5. Arnold Offner, "Appeasement Revisited: The United States, Great Britain, and Germany, 1933–40," *Journal of American History*, Vol. 64 (September 1977, pp. 373–393.
6. Naturally, Roosevelt has become the subject of many scholarly works. For primary sources on Roosevelt's foreign policy see Elliott Roosevelt (Ed.), *F.D.R: His Personal Letters, 1905–1928*, and *His Personal Letters, 1928–1945*, Vols. 1–2 (New York, 1947–1948); Samuel L. Rosenman (Ed.), *The Public Papers and Addresses of Franklin D. Roosevelt*, Vols. 1–15 (New York, 1938–1950); Samuel L. Rosenman (Ed.), *Complete Presidential Press Conferences of Franklin D. Roosevelt, 1933–1945*, Vols. 1–25 (New York, 1972); Edgar B. Nixon (Ed.), *Franklin D. Roosevelt and Foreign Affairs*, Vols. 1–3, First Series, January 1933–1937 (Cambridge, MA, 1969); and Donald B. Schewe (Ed.), *Franklin D. Roosevelt and Foreign Affairs, 1937–1939*, Vols. 1–14 (New York, 1979–1983). The major texts on Roosevelt's foreign policy and the Second World War, including those of a revisionist ilk, that have been most useful in the production of this work include Charles A. Beard, *President Roosevelt and the Coming of the War, 1941: A Study in Appearances and Realities* (New Haven, 1948); Rauch, *Roosevelt—From Munich to Pearl Harbor*; William L. Langer

and Everett S. Gleason, *The Undeclared War* (New York, 1953); James MacGregor Burns, *Roosevelt: The Lion and the Fox* (New York, 1956); Robert A. Divine, *The Reluctant Belligerent: American Entry into World War II* (New York, 1965); James MacGregor Burns, *Roosevelt: Soldier of Freedom* (New York, 1970); Warren F. Kimball, *Franklin D. Roosevelt and the World Crisis, 1937–1945* (Lexington, MA, and London, 1973); Frederick Marks III, *Wind over Sand: The Diplomacy of Franklin Roosevelt* (Athens, GA, 1988); Warren F. Kimball, *The Juggler—Franklin Roosevelt as Wartime Statesman* (Princeton, NJ, 1991); and Kenneth S. Davis, *FDR into the Storm—A History* (New York, 1993).

7. Sources on the Anglo-American relationship of the period include Ritchie Ovendale, *"Appeasement" and the English Speaking World—Britain, the United States, the Dominions and the Policy of Appeasement* (Cardiff, 1975); C.A. Macdonald, *The United States, Britain and Appeasement, 1936–39* (London, 1981); William Rock, *Chamberlain and Roosevelt: British Foreign Policy and the United States, 1937–1940* (Columbus, 1988); and, most recently, David Reynolds, *From Munich to Pearl Harbor: Roosevelt's America and the Origins of the Second World War* (Chicago, IL, 2001). Sources dealing with the Anglo-American relationship over a longer time frame include Alan P. Dobson, *Anglo-American Relations in the Twentieth Century* (London and New York, 1995); David Ryan, *The United States and Europe in the Twentieth Century* (London, 2003). Reading dealing specifically with the wartime "special relationship" should begin with Warren Kimball's coverage of the Roosevelt—Churchill communications; Warren F. Kimball, *Churchill and Roosevelt: The Complete Correspondence*, Vols. 1–3 (New York, 1984–1988); others of note include Joseph P. Lash, *Roosevelt and Churchill 1939–1941— The Partnership That Saved the West* (London, 1977); John Charmley, *Churchill's Grand Alliance: The Anglo-American Special Relationship 1940–1957* (London, 1995); and Warren F. Kimball, *Forged in War; Roosevelt, Churchill, and the Second World War* (New York, 1997). For sources on the interwar relationship see Brian McKercher, *Anglo-American Relations in the 1920's—The Struggle for Supremacy* (London, 1991); and Brian McKercher, *Transition of Power—Britain's Loss of Global Pre-Eminence to the United States, 1930–1945* (Cambridge, 1999).

8. David Reynolds, *The Creation of the Anglo-American Alliance 1937–1941: A Study in Competitive Co-operation* (London, 1981), p. 72. This work establishes the idea of "competitive cooperation" as its central thesis. Whereas this analysis aptly describes the economic underpinning of the Anglo-American relationship throughout the period 1937–1941, the diplomacy of the Welles mission in early 1940 requires a modified critique. The personal and diplomatic nature of the mission had little to do with "competition" or "cooperation"; instead the two parties were not in a position to compete or cooperate on the issues that surrounded the Welles mission. This again necessitates the contextual analysis provided here.

9. Reynolds, *From Munich to Pearl Harbor*.

10. Sources on Sumner Welles in addition to his papers include most notably Benjamin Welles, *Sumner Welles—FDR's Global Strategist* (London, 1997).

Two other recent texts were also helpful to this study: Irwin F. Gellman, *Secret Affairs: Franklin Roosevelt, Cordell Hull and Sumner Welles* (Baltimore, MD, and London, 1995); and Christopher O'Sullivan, *Sumner Welles, Postwar Planning, and the Quest for a New World Order, 1937–1943* (Columbia, SC, 2003). There is also Frank Warren Graff's *The Strategy of Involvement: A Diplomatic Biography of Sumner Welles—1933–43* (New York, 1988).

11. Sumner Welles, *The Time for Decision* (Washington, DC, 1944).

12. Memorandum by Rosenman for Roosevelt, 9 June 1944. Samuel Rosenman Papers (hereafter SRP), Box 4, The Franklin D. Roosevelt Presidential Library, Hyde Park, NY.

13. Nonentanglement had a considerable heritage in the United States, stretching back to the Founding Fathers. Among those committed to divorcing the United States from crises overseas were a number of leading Senators, who through the process of seniority occupied important congressional positions. Men such as William Borah, Gerald Nye, and Hiram Johnson were often supporters of Roosevelt domestically but "had the ability to arouse intense emotions in the country over alleged foreign exploitation of the United States." Dallek, *Franklin D. Roosevelt and American Foreign Policy*, p. 70. Furthermore, isolationists could count amongst their number: Father Charles Coughlin, a Detroit radio preacher, and the anti-Roosevelt William Randolph Hearst, the press magnate. It is significant that these two men were able to appeal to the heartland of "isolationism" in the Midwest through the written press and radio. The literature on Isolationist influence can be found in the following works: Wayne S. Cole, *Roosevelt and the Isolationists, 1932–1945* (Lincoln, NE, 1983); Robert A. Divine, *The Illusion of Neutrality* (Chicago, IL, 1962); and R. Powaski, *Toward an Entangling Alliance: American Isolationism and Europe, 1901–1950* (New York, 1991).

14. Memorandum by Adolf A. Berle, 22 August 1939. The Papers of Adolf A. Berle (hereafter ABP), Box 210, The Franklin D. Roosevelt Presidential Library, Hyde Park, NY.

1   ROOSEVELTIAN FOREIGN POLICY MAKING AND ANGLO-AMERICAN RELATIONS IN 1938 AND 1939—RELATIONSHIPS IN THE MAKING

1. Memorandum by Berle, 13 October 1937, ABP, Box 210.

2. Welles would eventually resign from his position as Under Secretary of State to prevent salacious rumors regarding his private life from being published. The rumors of homosexuality, propositioning, and drunkenness were in part true and were propagated by Welles' opponents. Welles' position became politically untenable, and despite their close friendship Roosevelt accepted Welles' resignation on 30 September 1943. For an in-depth account of this episode see Benjamin Welles' account: Benjamin Welles, *Sumner Welles— FDR's Global Strategist* (London, 1997).

3. Letter from Roosevelt to Welles 15 March 1915. The Franklin D Roosevelt Papers: The President's Personal File (Hereafter FDR PPF) Box 81 Franklin D. Roosevelt Presidential Library, Hyde Park, NY.

4. During one period when he was out of the service he turned to scholarship. This resulted in a two-volume history of the Dominican Republic, entitled *Naboth's Vineyard* (New York, 1928).

5. Franklin D. Roosevelt, "Our Foreign Policy: A Democratic View," *Foreign Affairs*, Vol. VI (1928), pp. 573–586.

6. Benjamin Welles, *Sumner Welles*, p. 158.

7. Franklin Roosevelt Address before the Inter-American Conference for the Maintenance of Peace, Buenos Aires, Argentina, December 1, 1936, in Edgar B. Nixon (Ed.), *Franklin D. Roosevelt and Foreign Affairs*, First Series, Vol. III, September 1935–January 1937 (Cambridge, MA, 1969), pp. 516–521.

8. Sumner Welles, *Seven Decisions That Shaped History* (New York, 1950), p. 22.

9. Letter from Roosevelt to Chamberlain, 14 February 1940. President Franklin D. Roosevelt's Papers, Personal Secretary's Office Files (PSF) Departmental Correspondence, Reel 26, Roosevelt Study Center, Middelburg (hereafter FDR PSF RSC).

10. Christopher O'Sullivan, *Sumner Welles, Postwar Planning, and the Quest for a New World Order, 1937–1943* (Columbia, SC, 2003), p. 1.

11. Thus when Roosevelt hinted at the prospect of an international conference in his famous interview with the *New York Times'* Arthur Krock in August 1937, it raised little furore in the State Department. Berle also makes mention of the plan not being particularly novel. On 26 October 1937, he stated the proposal was "along the line of a suggestion . . . discussed with me in Washington a few weeks ago." Memorandum by Berle, 26 October 1937, ABP, Box 210.

12. C.A. Macdonald, *The United States, Britain and Appeasement, 1936–39* (London, 1981), p. 41.

13. Franklin D. Roosevelt Fireside Chat, 12 October 1937, www.presidency. ucsb.edu.

14. The diary entries of Adolf Berle show that the matter was discussed on various occasions during October and early November: 13, 26, 28, 29 October and 1, 8 November 1937. For example, Memorandum by Berle, 26 October 1937, ABP, Box 210.

15. Letter from Welles to Roosevelt, 26 October 1937. The Franklin D. Roosevelt Papers: The President's Secretary's File (hereafter FDR PSF), State Department, Box 70, Franklin D. Roosevelt Presidential Library, Hyde Park, NY.

16. Memorandum by Berle, 26 October 1937, ABP, Box 210.

17. Kenneth S. Davis, *FDR into the Storm—A History* (New York, 1993), p. 186.

18. First Draft undated accompanied by letter from Welles to Roosevelt, 26 October 1937, FDR PSF, Box 70.

19. Franklin D. Roosevelt Fireside Chat, 12 October 1937, http://www.presidency. ucsb.edu/docs/fireside/101237.php.

20. Memorandum by Berle, 8 November 1937, ABP, Box 210.

21. Robert Dallek, *Franklin D. Roosevelt and American Foreign Policy, 1932–1945* (Oxford and New York, 1995), p. 153.

22. Sumner Welles, *Seven Decisions*, p. 23.
23. Benjamin Welles, *Sumner Welles*, p. 199.
24. Memorandum from Roosevelt to Welles, 28 May 1937, FDR PSF, Box 32.
25. Welles had always worked hard on subjects that interested him and did not concern himself with those that did not. As far back as his school days, Welles' "mind, when stimulated, was quick, wide-ranging and retentive," skills that were vital in his diplomatic career; "when bored, his grades plummeted." Benjamin Welles, *Sumner Welles*, p. 11.
26. Irwin F. Gellman, *Secret Affairs: Franklin Roosevelt, Cordell Hull and Sumner Welles* (Baltimore, MD, and London, 1995), p. 68.
27. Benjamin Welles, *Sumner Welles*, p. 199.
28. Mathilde Townsend was an exceedingly wealthy lady, but her marriage to Welles had caused some scandal in Washington as she was ten years older than Welles and had herself divorced a Senator to marry Welles.
29. Memorandum by Berle, 20 April 1939, ABP, Box 210.
30. Handwritten notes by Drew Pearson. Container G-236, undated Drew Pearson's Personal Papers, Lyndon B. Johnson Library, Austin, TX. Quoted in Benjamin Welles, *Sumner Welles*, p. 398. Drew Pearson was an old friend of Welles who would become a well renowned radio and print journalist for his columns and radio show entitled *The Washington Merry-Go-Round* (Pearson and Robert S. Allen, Washington Bureau Chief for *The Christian Science Monitor*, had anonymously published a book entitled *Washington Merry-Go-Round* in 1931 New York, H. Liverlight). Through his column in the *Baltimore Sun* in the 1930s and 1940s Pearson would often praise Welles while criticizing other members of the administration and aspects of the New Deal.
31. Memorandum from Welles to Roosevelt, 12 January 1940, FDR PSF, Box 76.
32. President Roosevelt's plan MOST SECRET, 21 March 1938, A 2127/64/45 Foreign Office (hereafter FO) FO 371 21526, National Archives, Kew, London (hereafter NA).
33. Notice of Roosevelt's plan to Chamberlain left by Welles at the Embassy in Washington, 11 January 1938. Embassy and Consular Archives, United States of America Correspondence, FO 115 3416, NA.
34. The accounts of Welles and Hull differ on the decisive factor in redeployment. See Sumner Welles, *Seven Decisions*, Chapter 1; and Cordell Hull, *The Memoirs of Cordell Hull*, Vol. 1 (New York, 1948).
35. The *Panay* incident involved the Japanese strafing of the USS *Panay* and the British Ship, the HMS *Bee*, at the beginning of December 1937. This will be examined in reference to the Ingersoll mission later in this chapter.
36. Lindsay was evidently aware of the wider implications of Welles' proposal. In writing to London he added were the British to "kill the scheme before it is propounded by withholding their support . . . [it] . . . would annul all progress . . . made in the last two years." Telegram No. 42 from Lindsay to Foreign Office, 12 January 1938, A 2127/64/45 FO 371 21526, NA.
37. Telegram No. 35 from Chamberlain to Lindsay for the President, 13 January 1938, A 2127/64/45 FO 371 21526, NA.
38. Sumner Welles, *The Time for Decision* (Washington, DC, 1994), p. 56.

39. The repercussions were felt at the time of the Munich crisis, which will be discussed later in this chapter. Before Chamberlain's objections had permanently
mothballed the Welles plan Roosevelt suggested in late January that
Washington and London share information on certain aspects of foreign
policy. At the time Roosevelt was keen to see how Chamberlain's appeasement
policies would affect his own foreign policy. Given Chamberlain's response to
Roosevelt's plan it might be supposed that the President's request would have
received little support. Instead, he wrote to Lindsay, "[W]e shall gladly give
him the fullest information on these matters in which we are both so much
interested." Telegram No. 60 from Chamberlain to Lindsay for the attention
of Roosevelt, 21 January 1938, A 2127/64/45 FO 371 21526, NA. This
reflected Chamberlain's view that as long as it did not interfere with his own
plans he did not object to cooperation with Washington. Guidelines and subject matter were quickly established by Welles and Lindsay, and the two governments agreed to open a line of communication that kept them informed
during the summer of 1938. Exchange of Information between U.S. and
British Governments, 26 January 1938, A 651/64/45 FO 371 21525, NA.
Initially, matters such as the British Ambassador in Berlin's attempt to sound
out Hitler on the colonial question and central Europe were the subjects of
this dialogue. Later in the summer, reports of the Runciman mission were
passed to Washington. In this sense historian William Wallace was correct
when he wrote of the legacy of the January 1938 approach that "crucial
Anglo-American exchanges continued to flow from it." William V. Wallace,
"Roosevelt and British Appeasement in 1938," *Bulletin—British Association
of American Studies* (December 1962), pp. 4–30.

40. Greg Kennedy, "Neville Chamberlain and Strategic Relations with the US
during his Chancellorship," *Diplomacy & Statecraft*, Vol. 13, No. 1
(March 2002), pp. 95–120. Kennedy sees 1933 as "the pivotal year in the formulation of Chamberlain's view of the US," when two key elements with
implications for Anglo-American relations were being considered, namely,
Britain's economic position and the condition of the Royal Navy especially in
the Far East.

41. Letter from Chamberlain to Mrs. Morton Prince, Boston, MA, 16 January
1938. The Papers of Neville Chamberlain, Special Collections, University of
Birmingham, UK (hereafter NC). Sir Alexander Cadogan, who would
become his Permanent Under Secretary at the Foreign Office at the beginning
of 1938, went further, as he summed up Chamberlain's attitude to Americans
as one of an "almost instinctive contempt." David Dilks (Ed.), *The Diaries of
Sir Alexander Cadogan OM 1938–45* (London, 1971), p. 54.

42. Entry for 19 February 1938, Chamberlain's Diary, The Papers of Neville
Chamberlain, NC 2/24A, Diaries 1937–1940, NC.

43. Memorandum of Chamberlain's views on the Baruch Conversation,
September 8 1937, FO 371 20663, NA.

44. Viscount Templewood, *Nine Troubled Years* (London, 1954), p. 262.

45. The literature on appeasement comprises a vast body of historical study.
Much of it is intimately connected with the characters involved, most notably

Neville Chamberlain. Other important volumes include *The Appeasers* by Martin Gilbert and Richard Gott, which has been republished in 2000 with a new foreword. There is the classic repudiation of appeasement in Cato's (Cato Cato is a pseudonym for a collective of individuals who were critical of the Chamberlain government: Michael Foot [future leader of the Labour Party], Frank Owen [a former Liberal MP], and Peter Howard [a cross bencher MP]. *Guilty Men* (London, 1940).

46. Sir Samuel Hoare, Chamberlain's Home Secretary, wrote in his memoirs: "Appeasement was not his personal policy. Not only was it supported by his colleagues; it expressed the general desire of the British people." Templewood, *Nine Troubled Years*, p. 262. Sir Nevile Henderson, the British Ambassador to Berlin, declared appeasement to be "the search for just solutions by negotiations in the light of higher reason instead of resort to force." Sir Nevile Henderson, *Failure of a Mission* (London, 1940), p. 49.

47. David Dutton, *Neville Chamberlain* (London, 2001), p. 200.

48. Message from Roosevelt to Chamberlain composed by Welles, 17 January 1938, 740.00/264b, in *The Foreign Relations of the United States*, 1938, Vol. 1 (USGPO, 1955), p. 121 (hereafter *FRUS*).

49. Telegram No. 78 from Lindsay to Foreign Office, 23 January 1938, A 2127/64/45 FO 371 21526, NA.

50. Eden later recognized Welles' efforts in this direction: "I have known no man in the United States who had a clearer perception than he of the course of international diplomacy in the last years before the Second World War." Anthony Eden, Earl of Avon, *The Eden Memoirs—Facing the Dictators* (London, 1962), p. 568.

51. Letter from Eden to Chamberlain, 17 January 1938. The Papers of Anthony Eden as Foreign Secretary (Lord Avon) (hereafter AEP), US/38/3 FO 954/29A.

52. Letter from Eden to Chamberlain, 18 January 1938. The Papers of the Earl of Avon, Special Collections, University of Birmingham, in Eden, *The Eden Memoirs*, p. 558.

53. Halifax, austere and well organized, was not going to challenge the Prime Minister's views and in fact has been described as "a quintessential, if not an altogether extreme," appeaser. John Lukacs, *Five Days in London May 1940* (New Haven, CT, and London, 1999), p. 62.

54. Eden, *The Eden Memoirs*, p. 552.

55. Sumner Welles, *The Time for Decision*, p. 56. Welles was joined in agreement in this belief by Anthony Eden when the pair met after the war. "We agreed that a comparable opportunity had never occurred, nor been created, after this date to avert that catastrophe." Eden, *The Eden Memoirs*, p. 568.

56. Arthur Schatz, "The Anglo-American Trade Agreement and Cordell Hull's Search for Peace, 1936–38," *Journal of American History*, Vol. 57 (1970–1971), pp. 85–103.

57. Letter from Lindsay to Eden, 7 February 1938, AEP, US/38/11 FO 954/29A, NA. Lindsay also enlightened Eden as to the risks Roosevelt was taking as he alluded to the President's domestic problems. "I do wish the President would

be less temperamental in his treatment of the domestic economic situation. He has got every business man in the country, great and small, into a state of nervous exasperation in which they are hardly fit to consider any question of public policy in a sensible manner."

58. Eden, *The Eden Memoirs*, p. 552.

59. Eden, *The Eden Memoirs*, p. 568.

60. Many in Washington and London accepted breaches of the Treaty of Versailles as a fait accompli. Although never admitted in public, Cadogan's sentiment in February appropriately conveyed this. Explaining that he had been summoned to the Foreign Office "as there was a flap about Austria," he recorded, "I almost wish Germany would swallow Austria and get it over." This was followed by the admission, "She is probably going to do so anyway—anyway we can't stop her." Dilks, *Cadogan*, p. 47. Hitler succeeding in joining his homeland into the German Reich by insisting that the Austrian Chancellor Kurt von Schuschnigg incorporate the Austrian Nazi Party into his government at a meeting at Berchtesgaden in February 1938. When Schuschnigg tried to stall Hitler, an ultimatum was submitted that forced his resignation, and the new regime simply invited a German occupation on 13 March 1938.

61. Entry for 22 March 1938, in Nancy Harvison Hooker (Ed.), *The Moffat Papers—Selections from the Diplomatic Journals of Jay Pierrepont Moffat 1919–1943* (Cambridge, MA, 1956), p. 291.

62. There is a vast array of material on the Munich crisis. Some suggested sources are John W. Wheeler-Bennett, *Munich—Prologue to Tragedy* (London, 1948); Maya Latynski (Ed.), *Re-Appraising the Munich Pact—Continental Perspectives* (Washington, DC, 1992); Dwight E. Lee (Ed.), *Munich—Blunder, Plot or Tragic Necessity?* (Cambridge, MA, 1970); Barbara Farnham, *Roosevelt and the Munich Crisis—A Study of Political Decision Making* (Princeton, NJ, 2000); Keith Feiling, *The Life of Neville Chamberlain* (London, 1946); Duff Cooper, *Old Men Forget—The Autobiography of Duff Cooper* (London, 1953); Wolfgang Mommsen and Lothar Kettenacker (Eds.), *The Fascist Challenge and the Policy of Appeasement* (London, 1983); Edward L. Henson, Jr., "Britain, America and the Month of Munich," *International Relations*, Vol. 2 (1962), pp. 291–301; and Igor Lukes and Erik Goldstein, "The Munich Crisis," *Diplomacy & Statecraft* (Special Issue), Vol. 10, Nos. 2 and 3 (July/November 1999).

63. Wheeler-Bennett, *Munich*, pp. 157–158.

64. Berle wrote of Welles' draft that it was "infinitely better" than his own attempt at an appeal for peace. Memorandum by Berle, 26 December 1939, ABP, Box 211.

65. Memorandum by Berle, 28 December 1939, ABP, Box 211.

66. Farnham, *Roosevelt and the Munich Crisis*.

67. Historian Nicholas Cull suggests that Chamberlain actually was considering public opinion, and American opinion particularly, in securing the supplementary declaration to the Munich Agreement (this declaration pledged the two countries to abide by the Munich Agreement and "never to go to war

with one another again"). Cull points to the prominence given to American newsreel crews at Heston at the behest of Downing Street. However, the "image of the 'piece of paper' contrived to woo American opinion [became] an enduring icon of political folly" and thus did nothing to improve British standing across the Atlantic. This author is unconvinced by Cull's assertion that at the time of Munich "Chamberlain finally attempted to fuse his European appeasement policies with a concern for American public opinion." If the cameras were positioned to the benefit of American newsreels, then this reveals Chamberlain's lack of understanding of the manner in which to influence of American opinion. A single image was not going to overcome what looked like a deal to carve up Czechoslovakia. Nicholas Cull, "The Munich Crisis and British Propaganda Policy in the United States," *Diplomacy & Statecraft* (Special Edition), Vol. 10, Nos. 2 and 3 (July/ November 1999), pp. 216–235.

68. Dutton, *Neville Chamberlain*, p. 23.
69. Hooker, *The Moffat Papers*, p. 226; and Frank Warren Graff, *The Strategy of Involvement: A Diplomatic Biography of Sumner Welles—1933–43* (New York, 1988), p. 248.
70. Hooker, *Moffat Papers*, p. 226.
71. That is not to say Welles was blind to the implications of Britain's new foreign policy. He told Kennedy that Chamberlain's speech in Birmingham was a "very far-reaching step." Kennedy, who still had the ear of the British Cabinet, stated "that the fat is now on the fire," because "if Poland's independence is threatened England will go in there with all their resources." Memorandum of telephone conversation between Welles and Kennedy, 31 March 1939, The Sumner Welles Papers Franklin D. Roosevelt Presidential Library, Hyde Park, NY (hereafter SWP), SWP, Box 162.
72. "Message for the Personal and Confidential Information of the President" from British Embassy, Washington, DC, 29 March 1939. Reel 11, Great Britain, January–December 1939, Part 2, Diplomatic Correspondence File, President Franklin D. Roosevelt's Office Files, 1933–1945, Roosevelt Study Center, Middelburg, Holland (hereafter FDR OF RSC).
73. Hooker, *The Moffat Papers*, p. 231.
74. Telegram from Roosevelt to Hitler, 14 April 1939, 7400.00/817a: Telegram, in *FRUS*, 1939, Vol. 1, pp. 130–131. Simultaneously sent to Mussolini. "It was a personal appeal, first for a guarantee of the status quo and, secondly for co-operation in dealing peacefully with the problems that were facing the world." Arnold J. Toynbee, *Survey of International Affairs 1939 Volume 1* (London, 1941), p. 629.
75. Letter from Roosevelt to Hitler, 14 April 1939, SWP, Box 150.
76. Arnold Offner states that the proposals made were "evidently to be organised along the lines of Welles' scheme" for an international conference, first mooted in the aftermath of the "Quarantine" speech of October 1937 and later adapted by Roosevelt in his proposal to Chamberlain in the following January. Offner, *Journal of American History*, Vol. 64, pp. 375–376.

77. Hooker, *The Moffat Papers*, p. 234. Yet Hitler's words resonated with at least one of the Administration's opponents, Senator Borah, who stated that if war broke out "a more sordid, imperialistic war could hardly be imagined." Borah, quoted in Telegram No. 432 from Lindsay to Foreign Office, 14 April 1939, A 2982/98/45 FO 371 22813, NA. The Idaho Senator's views as "a strong Isolationist" were known in London. "He has been the *enfant terrible* of American politics; at all times concerned jealously to assert the rights of the legislature to control the action of the Executive" (italics in the original). Report No. 17 on personalities in the United States from Lindsay, 6 January 1939, A 471/471/45 FO 371 21541, NA.

78. Phone conversation between Roosevelt and Morgenthau, 15 April 1939, 31 January–27 June 1939, Card 2, The Diaries and Presidential Diaries of Henry Morgenthau, Franklin D. Roosevelt Presidential Library, Hyde Park, NY (hereafter MPD). In undertaking these appeals Roosevelt was not without criticism. Leading isolationist Senator Hiram Johnson wrote in late April that of the "critical or fair-minded" with whom he had talked agreed with his analysis that it was Hitler who had "all the better" of the exchanges, yet despite that everybody is bound "to denounce Hitler and praise Roosevelt." Letter from Hiram Johnson to Hiram Johnson, Jr., 29 April 1939. The Hiram W. Johnson Papers, The Bancroft Library, University of California, Berkeley, CA (hereafter HJP).

79. Comments by Sargent (17/11/38) on comments made by Ex-President Herbert Hoover attached to Telegram No. 964 from Lindsay to Foreign Office, 3 November 1938, A 8441/64/45 FO 371 21527, NA.

80. Hull, *The Memoirs*, Vol. 1, p. 62. Although not named, when Roosevelt spoke to Morgenthau about the possibility of sending a message he mentioned he would have to get around the influence of someone in the State Department. Given Hull's caution the inference is clear. Memorandum by Morgenthau, 11 April 1939, MPD, Card 2.

81. Hooker, *The Moffat Papers*, p. 231.

82. Memorandum by Berle, 15 April 1939, ABP, Box 210.

83. Hooker, *The Moffat Papers*, p. 231.

84. Memorandum by Berle, 20 April 1939, ABP, Box 210.

85. Hull recorded that Lindsay "expressed his great satisfaction with the President's communication to Hitler and Mussolini." Memorandum of conversation between Hull and Lothian, 17 April 1939. The Papers of Cordell Hull, The Library of Congress, Manuscripts Division, Washington, DC (hereafter CHP).

86. Memorandum by Berle, 13 April 1939, ABP, Box 210.

87. Memorandum by Berle, 17 August 1939, ABP, Box 210.

88. Telegram from Welles to Roosevelt, 17 August 1939, SWP, Box 150.

89. Hooker, *The Moffat Papers*, p. 248.

90. Hooker, *The Moffat Papers*, p. 253.

91. Memorandum by Berle, 22 August 1939, ABP, Box 210.

92. Hooker, *The Moffat Papers*, p. 245.

93. Hooker, *The Moffat Papers*, pp. 257–258.

94. Roosevelt's return came after the announcement of the Nazi-Soviet Pact on 23 August 1939. "The announcement of the German-Russian understanding," Berle recorded, "is not surprising, since it has been perfectly obvious that the Russians were double-dealing right along; but the timing is unpleasant, for it can only be regarded as an indication by the Russians that the Germans can have a free hand so far as they are concerned. This is as cynical a piece of international business as has happened in a long time." Memorandum by Berle, 22 August 1939, ABP, Box 210.

95. Memorandum by Berle, 16 August 1939, ABP, Box 210.

96. This principle had been inaugurated in the Ottawa agreements of 1932 essentially as the British Empire's answer to the Great Depression. It was at odds with Cordell Hull's view of international trade because he saw it as protectionist. The "closed market" was modified in the agreement that came into force on 1 January 1939.

97. Letter from Balfour to Stirling, 24 January 1938, FO 371 21490, NA.

98. Feiling, *The Life of Neville Chamberlain*, p. 308.

99. Annual Report on United States for 1938 from Lindsay, 17 February 1939, A 1882/1882/45 FO 371 22832, NA.

100. Commercial Policy of Great Britain, Telegram No. 69E from Mallet, 19 January 1939, A 780/26/45 FO 371 22796, NA.

101. McCulloch states that the Trade Agreement was important to the Anglo-American relationship: "A trade agreement was signed in 1938, by which time Anglo-American relations were closer than for many years." Tony McCulloch, "Anglo-American Economic Diplomacy and the European Crisis, 1933–1939," September 1978, DPhil, Oxford, p. 1.

102. McCulloch, "Anglo-American Economic Diplomacy," p. 1.

103. Record of conversation between Hull and Lindsay, 3 September 1938, CHP, Roll 29.

104. For an example of this assessment of Hull's views, see Hans-Jurgen Schroder, "The Ambiguities of Appeasement: Great Britain, the United States and Germany, 1937–39," in Wolfgang J. Mommsen and Lothar Kettenacker (Eds.), *The Fascist Challenge and the Policy of Appeasement* (London, 1983), pp. 390–399. For a detailed examination of the facets of wider economic diplomacy in the early 1930s one should examine the work of Patricia Clavin, *The Failure of Economic Diplomacy; Britain, Germany, France and the United States, 1931–36* (London, 1996).

105. Moffat Memorandum, 31 January 1938, NA, RG 59, 611.6231/1002½ from Schroder, in Mommsen and Kettenacker (Eds.), *The Fascist Challenge and the Policy of Appeasement*, p. 392.

106. Telegram No. 218 from Lindsay to Foreign Office, 17 May 1939, A 3554/26/45 FO 371 22797, NA.

107. Comments by Beith (15/5/39) attached to "Proposal for Exchange of Raw Materials," FO Minute by Beith, 26 April 1939, A 3055/26/45 FO 371 22797, NA.

108. Letter from Hiram Johnson to Hiram Johnson, Jr., 29 April 1939, HJP.
109. Letter from Hiram Johnson to Hiram Johnson, Jr., 3 June 1939, HJP; and Letter from Hiram Johnson to Hiram Johnson, Jr., 2 July 1939, HJP.
110. Phone conversation between Roosevelt and Morgenthau, 30 June 1939, MPD, Card 3.
111. Letter No. 772 from Lothian to Halifax, 3 September 1940. Political Review of the Year 1939 by Lord Lothian, A 429/1631/45, in David K. Adams (Ed.), *British Documents on Foreign Affairs: Reports and Papers from the Foreign Office Confidential Print*. Part II from the First to the Second World War Series C North American 1919–1939, Vol. 25 (Frederick, MD: University Publications of America, 1995).
112. Roosevelt had utilized this tactic earlier in his Administration. Richard Harrison's explores a number of occasions when Roosevelt endeavored to use discussions on "technical" matters to further Anglo-American relations. See both Richard Harrison, "Testing the Water: A Secret Probe towards Anglo-American Military Cooperation in 1936," *International History Review*, Vol. VII (2 May 1985), pp. 214–234; and Richard Harrison, "A Presidential Demarché—Franklin D. Roosevelt's Personal Diplomacy and Great Britain 1936–1937," *Diplomatic History*, Vol. 5, No. 3 (Summer 1981), p. 246. See Richard Harrison, "The Runciman Visit to Washington in January 1937," *Canadian Journal of History*, Vol. XIX (August 1984), pp. 217–239. This visit is also examined by Tony McCulloch, who asserts that the Runciman mission was largely arranged by Roosevelt's good friend Arthur Murray although initiated by the President himself. Tony McCulloch, "Franklin Roosevelt and the Runciman Mission of August in 1938: A Sidelight on Anglo-American Relations in the Era of Appeasement," *Journal of Transatlantic Studies*, Vol. 1, No. 2 (2003).
113. At the time Chamberlain's focus was on Continental Europe, not to mention the limited capacity of the Royal Navy. Anthony Eden explained, "The despatch of an adequate fleet to the Far East would expose us to the risk of complications nearer home." He was of course referring to the potential of Germany and Italy threaten to British interests. Report of final two months by Anthony Eden (undated), AEP, US/38/6 FO 954/29A, NA. Ian Cowman states that "by deliberately delaying their response to the Japanese attack, the Roosevelt Administration allowed time for a peaceful solution to emerge." Ian Cowman, *Dominion or Decline—Anglo-American Naval Relations in the Pacific, 1937–41* (Oxford and Washington, DC, 1996), p. 135.
114. Roosevelt had already been thinking along these lines, by instructing Admiral Leahy, Chief of Naval Operations, to hold talks with the British Naval Attaché in Washington. Alan Bullock, *Hitler: A Study in Tyranny* (London, 1962), pp. 361–362.
115. Records of conversation on Anglo-American Cooperation in the Far East between Herschel Johnson, Captain Ingersoll, Eden, and Cadogan, 1 January 1938, F 95/84/10 FO 371 22106, NA.
116. Telegram No. 19 from Eden to Lindsay, 4 January 1938, AEP, US/38/1 FO 954/29A, NA.

117. Memo of meeting with Captain Ingersoll, Lord Chatfield, Admiral Sir W.M. James, and Captain Wilson (U.S. Naval Attaché), 3 January 1938, F 95/84/10 FO 371 22106, NA.

118. Macdonald, *The United States, Britain and Appeasement*, p. 61. Cadogan put this slightly differently; noting the talks "resulted in an agreed record but no commitments." Dilks, *Cadogan*, p. 32.

119. Telegram No. 74 from Foreign Office to Lindsay, 28 January 1938, A 2127/64/45 FO 371 21526, NA. Also referenced under F 1179/80/10 F0 371 22107, NA. Eden had already written to Lindsay as to how British conduct was being perceived in Washington. Eden wrote, "It would be interesting to know [the] reaction of US Government," and if the Ambassador could glean any "indication of intentions of US Government." Telegram No. 19 from Eden to Lindsay, 4 January 1938, AEP, US/38/1 FO 954/29A, NA.

120. Accompanying comments by Eden from Markham (Admiralty) to Harvey, 17 January 1938, F 716/84/10 FO 371 22106, NA.

121. Regarding the Far East, Cowman suggests that the period until 1941 was characterized as one where the military considerations were paramount over diplomatic relations; "Yet in the period 1937 to 1941 strategic considerations underpinned diplomatic relations; the origins of the alliance were always essentially military." Cowman, *Dominion or Decline*, p. 1. This view is confirmed by Christopher Thorne, *Allies of a Kind: The United States, Britain and the War against Japan, 1941–1945* (London, 1978).

122. Letter from Roosevelt to King George VI, 25 August 1938. Reel 16 Great Britain King and Queen, June 1938–June 1939, Part 2, Diplomatic Correspondence File, FDR OF RSC.

123. The King added, "Before I end this letter, I feel that I must say how greatly I welcomed your interventions in the recent crisis. I have little doubt that they contributed largely to the preservation of peace." Letter from King to Roosevelt, 8 October 1938, FDR OF RSC.

124. Letter from Lindsay to Halifax, 25 October 1938, FO 794/17, NA.

125. As it transpired, when details of the trip were announced in early November 1938, the itinerary allowed only four days in the United States and so the practical possibility of a trip to Chicago was dropped. However, the Chicago issue remained under consideration. The following March questions were raised in parliament as to the dangers of visiting only the Eastern states. The Foreign Office responded, "We have consistently advocated the extension of the Royal visit to the United States as far as Chicago at least, but this has proved impossible owing to the shortness of the visit." The brevity of the Royal visit was explained by Beith. "It must be remembered that the United States visit was essentially an afterthought to the Canadian visit." Comments by Beith (9/3/39) attached to FO Minute Loxley, 2 March 1939, A 1698/27/45 FO 371 22800, NA.

126. The couple's travels through Canada provided an appetizer for the American people's interest in the King and Queen. It was estimated that of 11 million Canadians, 6 million of them personally saw the King and Queen. Rhodes,

"The Royal Visit of 1939 and the 'Psychological Approach' to the United States," *Diplomatic History*, Vol. 2, No. 2 (Spring 1978), p. 207.

127. Hooker, *The Moffat Papers*, p. 242.

128. This was a line Roosevelt had taken when meeting with the future Ambassador to Washington, Lord Lothian (Philip Kerr) in January 1939. Lothian was given a "strong rebuff" by the President, and the episode is recorded by David Reynolds in "FDR on the British: A Postscript," *Massachusetts Historical Society Proceedings*, Vol. 90, 1978.

129. David Reynolds, "FDR's Foreign Policy and the British Royal Visit to the USA 1939," *Historian*, Vol. 45 (August 1983), p. 468.

130. Dispatch No. 211 from Haggard (British Counsel General in New York) to Lindsay, 14 June 1939, A 4435/27/45 FO 371 22801, NA.

131. No. 679 from Lindsay to Foreign Office, 20 June 1939, A 4443/27/45 FO 371 22801, NA.

132. Dispatch No. 67 from Lindsay to the Foreign Office, "US Press Reaction to the Visit of Their Majesties," 27 June 1939, A 4441/27/45 FO 371 22801, NA.

133. No. 679 from Lindsay to Foreign Office, 20 June 1939, A 4443/27/45 FO 371 22801, NA. Lindsay believed that to further the cause of the British position one had to appeal to the emotion of American opinion. Lindsay had first pushed this thesis in a telegram he sent to Eden in March 1937. The implications of this telegram and its longer-term impact upon the thinking of those in London are discussed by Thomas E. Hachey in "Winning Friends and Influencing Policy—British Strategy to Woo America in 1937," *Wisconsin Magazine of History*, Vol. 55 (1972), pp. 120–129.

134. Memorandum by Berle, 12 June 1939, ABP, Box 210.

135. Letter from Borah to L.T. Gaddis (Rhode Island), 13 June 1939. Box 514, The Papers of William E. Borah (hereafter PWB), The Library of Congress, Manuscripts Division, Washington, DC.

136. Eden, *The Eden Memoirs*, p. 568.

137. Memorandum by Berle, 18 August 1939, ABP, Box 210.

138. Warren Kimball, *The Juggler—Franklin Roosevelt as Wartime Statesman* (Princeton, NJ, 1991), p. 4.

139. Comments by Scott (4/4/39) and Vansittart (9/4/39) attached to Telegram No. 339 from Lindsay to Foreign Office, 23 March 1939, A 2439/1292/45 FO 371 22829, NA.

140. Hull, *The Memoirs*, Vol. 1, p. 563.

2   WAR AND PEACE—ROOSEVELTIAN FOREIGN POLICY AND THE "PHONY WAR": "LIKE SPECTATORS AT A FOOTBALL MATCH"

1. 141 Dispatch No. 119 from Lothian to Halifax, 1 February 1940, Secret Re: Public Opinion. The Papers of Viscount Halifax as Foreign Secretary, Miscellaneous Correspondence, folio 324 FO 800 324 (hereafter HFS), NA.

2. Welles began his address to those assembled in Panama by reminding the delegates of their previous agreements: "In accordance with the principles of

the Convention for the Maintenance, Preservation, and Reestablishment of Peace, the Declaration of Inter-American Solidarity of Buenos Aires, and the Declaration of Lima, the Ministers of Foreign Relations of the American republics or their representatives are meeting here in Panama for the purpose of consultation. Under the terms of the agreements I have cited, this coming together to consult is not an undertaking into which we have entered lightly. We have, on the contrary, agreed and clearly stipulated that the consultation provided for in these agreements shall be undertaken when there exists in the belief of our respective governments a menace to the peace of the continent." U.S. Department of State, *Bulletin—United States 1939 Vol. 1* (Washington, 1939), p. 299.

3. Benjamin Welles, *Sumner Welles—FDR's Global Strategist* (London, 1997), pp. 216–217.

4. Robert W. Love, Jr., *The History of the US Navy 1775–1941* (Harrisburg, PA, 1992), p. 619.

5. Cordell Hull, *The Memoirs of Cordell Hull*, Vol. 1 (New York, 1948), p. 599.

6. Roosevelt had broached the subject of a security zone in his conversations with King George VI during the visit of the monarch in June 1939. An important feature of the effectiveness of this neutral zone and the reason that Roosevelt mentioned it to the British at an early date was that he knew in order to make it effective he would need bases in the British Caribbean. Indeed Roosevelt discussed the prospect with Henry Morgenthau in the middle of September. The Treasury Secretary recorded, "He told me in strictest confidence, that he is leasing hangars and bases for sea planes in Bermuda and two other places in the West Indies; that nobody knew this." Conversation between Morgenthau and Roosevelt, 18 September 1939, MPD. The secrecy was important as the implication is that of military and political cooperation with the British. After some British reservations, and with the hope from some quarters that these bases would increase the chances of the United States entering the war, the British agreed to the leases by December. The significance of this was limited during the winter of 1939–1940 as the United States lacked the ships to patrol the zone effectively but, as Reynolds states, "the episode constituted a precedent for the 1940 destroyers-bases deal." David Reynolds, *The Creation of the Anglo-American Alliance 1937–1941: A Study in Competitive Co-operation* (London, 1981), p. 65. See also Charlie Whitham, "On Dealing with Gangsters: The Limits of British 'Generosity' in the Leasing of Bases to the United States, 1940–41," *Diplomacy & Statecraft*, Vol. 7, No. 3 (November 1996).

7. London, 13 March 1940, account by Ambassador Kennedy in Draft Chapter 40 "Welles' Visit to London," p. 578. Parts of Joseph Kennedy's unpublished biography can be found in the Papers of his writing partner James M. Landis in the Library of Congress. They were drafted between 1948 and 1950. The Papers of James M. Landis, Box 51, 1948–1950, Kennedy Joseph P. Memoirs, The Library of Congress, Manuscripts Division, Washington, DC (hereafter Kennedy Memoirs PJL).

8. U.S. Department of State, *Bulletin*, p. 299.

9. Irwin F. Gellman, *Secret Affairs—Franklin Roosevelt, Cordell Hull and Sumner Welles* (Baltimore, MD, and London), p. 167.

10. Samuel L. Rosenman, *The Public Papers and Addresses of Franklin D. Roosevelt, 1939 Vol., War and Neutrality* (London, 1941), pp. 512–522.

11. Letter from Borah to Nye, 24 October 1939, PWB. Borah's view is succinctly expressed in a letter he wrote in early September: "I am satisfied that to repeal the neutrality law at this time and to henceforth furnish arms and munitions and the implements of war to one side, would send us far down the road to actual conflict with European powers." Letter from Borah to Marcus J. Ware (an Idaho attorney), 12 September 1939, PWB.

12. Robert Dallek, *Franklin D. Roosevelt and American Foreign Policy, 1932–1945* (Oxford and New York, 1995), p. 202.

13. 97 Letter from Lothian to Halifax, 3 November 1939, HFS. In an earlier letter at the outset of the war Lothian had stated, "The general impression is that provided the situation is well handled the embargo on the export of arms will be abandoned and the cash and carry system restored. Nobody, however, under this constitution and in view of the personal resentments and party politics which now divide the White House and Capitol Hill can prophecy with certainty." 48 Letter from Lothian to Halifax, 5 September 1939, HFS.

14. Letter from Hiram Johnson to Hiram Johnson, Jr., 5 November 1939, HJP.

15. Memorandum of conversation between Hull and Lothian, 4 September 1939, CHP.

16. Robert W. Matson, "The British Naval Blockade and US Trade 1939–40," *Historian*, Vol. 53 (Summer 1991), p. 750.

17. David Dilks (Ed.), *The Diaries of Sir Alexander Cadogan OM, 1938–45* (London, 1971), p. 210.

18. Matson, *Historian*, Vol. 53, p. 751. See also Robert W. Matson, *Neutrality and Navicerts—Britain, The United States, and Economic Warfare, 1939–1940* (New York and London), 1994; and W. Medlicott, *The Economic Blockade* (London, 1952). According to Moffat, only one man held a strongly contrary opinion in the State Department and that was Herbert Feis: "Nearly everyone was in agreement along these lines—except Herbert Feis who as usual spoke up in opposition to any action on our part which would in any ways embarrass England. His attitude is so extreme that Walter Hines Page would have seemed a sturdy American by comparison." Nancy Harvison Hooker, *The Moffat Papers—Selections from the Diplomatic Journals of Jay Pierrepont Moffat 1919–1943* (Cambridge, MA, 1956), p. 287. Walter Hines Page was Woodrow Wilson's Ambassador to London between 1913 and 1918 and was perceived to have been taken in wholly by British propaganda during the First World War.

19. 5 September 1939, Breckinridge Long Papers, Box 5. The Library of Congress, Manuscripts Division, Washington, DC (hereafter BLP).

20. Hooker, *The Moffat Papers*, p. 275.

21. Matson, *Historian*, Vol. 53, p. 750.

22. Hooker, *The Moffat Papers*, pp. 275–276.

23. Hooker, *The Moffat Papers*, p. 291. This opinion was shared subsequently by Langer and Gleason: "It was, in fact, British interference with American mails which produced the angriest public reaction in this country." Draft of Chapter 10 "The Phony Peace," by William L. Langer and Everett S. Gleason, *The Challenge to Isolation 1937–40* (New York, 1952), p. 27. This draft can be found in SWP, Box 207, at the Franklin D. Roosevelt Presidential Library, Hyde Park, NY. Welles had been asked to proofread this chapter and returned it with to the authors and they wrote on it: "Apparently no changes were suggested by Welles."

24. Both the Americans and the British were aware of the danger of a major incident caused by the loss of American lives in the war zone. The memory was strong among many of the sinking of the *Lusitania* by a German submarine off the Irish coast on 7 May 1915 with the loss of 1,153 passengers, including 128 Americans. The uproar this aroused in America, which included a call for war to be declared, caused the Secretary of State William Jennings Bryan to resign. The Germans had claimed the ship was carrying war materials, and when the wreck was examined in the early 1990s small quantities of materials were found.

25. 128 Memo prepared by Lothian for Halifax, 8 January 1940, HFS. To alleviate the danger in early 1940, of an American ship being the victim of a German U-boat in warring seas, Churchill wrote to Roosevelt that "no American ships should in any circumstances be diverted into the combat zone around the British Isles declared by you." Telegram No. 265 from Churchill to Roosevelt, 29 January 1940, 740.00111A, Combat Areas/140: Telegram, in *FRUS*, 1940, Vol. II (USGPO, 1957), p. 10.

26. Memorandum of conversation between Hull and Lothian, 22 January 1940, CHP.

27. Letter from Roosevelt to Churchill, 1 February 1940, in Elliot Roosevelt (Ed.), *F.D.R: His Personal Letters, 1928–1945*, Vol. 3 (New York, 1952), p. 350. Roosevelt was writing in response to Churchill's account of the Battle of the River Plate. The battle, which took place deep within the Administration's neutrality zone, saw three British warships trap the German pocket battleship *Graf Spee* in Montevideo harbor in December 1939. With no chance of escape, the German captain, under orders from Berlin, put the crew ashore, scuttled the ship, and committed suicide. Account of the Battle of River Plate sent by Churchill to Roosevelt, 7 January 1940, Roosevelt-Churchill File, FDR PPF. Churchill knew Roosevelt's interest in naval matters, and this was confirmed in the President's response to Churchill. "Ever so much thanks for that tremendously interesting account," Roosevelt wrote, "of the extraordinarily well fought action of your three cruisers." Letter from Franklin Roosevelt to Winston Churchill, 1 February 1940, in Roosevelt (Ed.), *F.D.R: His Per Letters*, p. 350. The correspondence over this battle reflected their common interest in naval matters, which Joseph P. Lash discusses in chapter two of his book *Roosevelt and Churchill 1939–41—The Partnership That Saved the West* (London, 1977).

28. Memorandum of conversation between Hull and Lothian, 14 February 1940, CHP.

29. Fred L. Israel, *The War Diary of Breckinridge Long—Selections from the Years 1939–44* (Lincoln, NE, 1966), p. 59.

30. Hull, *The Memoirs*, Vol. 1, p. 735.

31. 132 Letter from Lothian to Halifax, 27 January 1940, HFS. Lothian had evidently picked this up from a meeting that he had with Moffat the day before. Moffat suggested the following criterion that should be used by the British: "Is a given course of action which is irritating to the United States absolutely necessary to win the war? If so, American public opinion cannot prevail; if it is merely a convenience and not a necessity, the British Government should definitely bear American reaction in mind." Hooker, *The Moffat Papers*, p. 290.

32. 141 Dispatch No. 119 Lothian to Halifax, 1 February 1940, HFS. To summarize the rest of the dispatch, Lothian continued by recounting the movement within American public opinion since the outbreak of the war, the reaction to the Russo-Finnish conflict, and role the United States sought to play in the Far East.

33. 141 Dispatch No. 119 Lothian to Halifax, 1 February 1940, HFS.

34. Lothian prefaced his telegram with a letter explaining that he had sent the dispatch to the Foreign Office so that Halifax would not "miss it in the tide of papers which must flow through your boxes." This individual touch characterized Lothian's style as Ambassador and reinforced his belief in the Anglo-American relationship. 140 Letter from Lothian to Halifax, 3 February 1940, HFS.

35. Telegram No. 142 from Lothian to Halifax, 1 February 1940 (sent 1:37 a.m., 2 February; received 10:35 a.m., 2 February [all times are local]), HFS.

36. Matson, *Historian*, Vol. 53, p. 752. The mission was conducted by Frank Ashton-Gwatkin of the Ministry of Economic Warfare and Charles Rist of the French Ministry of Blockade. The aim was to negotiate a resolution to the navicert question whilst giving "particular emphasis [to] the possibility of meeting the various protests and complaints which have recently been received from the State Department." Foreign Office Minute, 9 February 1940, W 2390/79/49 FO 371 25137, NA.

37. Memorandum by Balfour, 19 February 1940, A 1285/434/45 FO 371 24248, NA.

38. Telegram No. 1578 from Kennedy to Hull (seen by the President), 11 September 1939, 740.0011 European War, 1939/258: M 982, European War 740, Roll 9, Confidential U.S. State Department Central Files, Archive II, College Park, MD (hereafter SDCF).

39. Telegram No. 905 from Hull to Kennedy, 11 September 1939, 740.0011 European War, 1939/258: M 982, European War 740, Roll 9, SDCF.

40. Joseph Kennedy's Ambassadorship is the subject of two notable works: Ralph F. De Bedts, *Ambassador Joseph Kennedy 1938–40—An Anatomy of Appeasement* (New York, 1985); and Michael R. Beschloss, *Kennedy and Roosevelt—The Uneasy Alliance* (New York and London, 1980). Throughout the autumn of 1939 Kennedy continued to voice his opinion that the war would spell ruination for Europe and the rise of Bolshevism on the Continent. Elliot Roosevelt

shared this same assessment: "Ambassador Kennedy, during this period, wanted FDR to initiate a peace move. Kennedy was pessimistic over the results of a continuation of the war, and believed that either England and France would be defeated, or, if Germany lost, that communism would follow in Central Europe." Roosevelt (Ed.), *F.D.R.: His Personal Letters, 1928–1945*, Vol. 4 (New York, 1950), p. 950.

41. Lunch meeting between Morgenthau and Roosevelt, 3 October 1939, MPD, Card 4.

42. Kennedy's health began to fail in the autumn of 1939, possibly as a result of his worrying over the course of the war. He cabled the State Department "for permission to come home, pointing out to them that I was ready to fly back at a moment's notice. Welles agreed but stated that it would be best for me to be officially recalled for consultation so as to avoid the impression that our diplomats at this stage of the war could have the customary type of leave." This last sentence shows the concern of the State Department over its image both in Europe and at home. Kennedy Memoirs PJL, p. 488.

43. Hooker, *The Moffat Papers*, p. 5.

44. Telegram No. 142 from Lothian to Halifax, 1 February 1940 (sent 1:37 a.m. 2 February; received 10:35 a.m., 2 February [all times are local]), HFS.

45. *Documents on German Foreign Policy* 1918–1945 Vol. VIII, *The War Years* 4 September 1939–18 March 1940 (London, 1954), p. 229 (hereafter *DGFP*).

46. Hull, *The Memoirs*, Vol. 1, p. 711; and Hooker, *The Moffat Papers*, p. 272.

47. Hooker, *The Moffat Papers*, p. 272; and 11 October 1939, BLP.

48. Hooker, *The Moffat Papers*, p. 272.

49. Hooker, *The Moffat Papers*, p. 272.

50. 11 October 1939, BLP.

51. Memorandum by Berle, 10 October 1939, Box 211, ABP.

52. Other individuals included a Swedish businessman, M. Dahlerus, who approached the British government through Alexander Cadogan. Cadogan's colleague, Frank Roberts, wrote of the Swede; he "had a hero worship of Göring who, in his eyes, could do no wrong." Roberts surmised Dahlerus's efforts as those of "an honest man who sincerely wished to avoid war and bring about better Anglo-German relations. I think he acted perfectly uprightly throughout." Letter from Frank K. Roberts to Sir Llewellyn Woodward, 27 November 1942. The activities of Mr. Dahlerus, A 4. 410.3.10 (i), The Papers of Lord Halifax, The Borthwick Institute, York (hereafter HP).

53. Memorandum by Berle, 10 October 1939, Box 211, ABP.

54. Memorandums by Berle, 12 and 13 October 1939, Box 211, ABP.

55. This telegram was signed in Hull's own hand. Telegram from Hull to Kirk 13 (crossed out and 16 written over in pencil), October 1939, 740.00119 European War, 1939/78, State Department Decimal Files, RG 59 1930–1939, Archive II, College Park, MD (hereafter SDDF).

56. Telegram No. 125 from Harrison (Consul at Berne) to Hull, 12 October 1939, 740.00119 European War, 1939/78, in *FRUS* 1939, Vol. 1 (USGPO, 1956), p. 512.

57. Telegram No. 126 from Harrison (Consul at Berne) to Hull, 12 October 1939, 740.00119 European War, 1939/79: M 982 European War 740, SDCF.

58. The Russo-Finnish War provided another surreal aspect to the "phony war," although it ended with victory for the Russians on 12 March 1940. Conflict had begun on 30 November 1939, when Soviet troops crossed the border and Soviet planes began bombing Helsinki. For further information on the war see Carl Van Dyke, *The Soviet Invasion of Finland 1939–40* (London, 1997). The fate of Finland was of particular interest to the U.S. people, as the Finns had made strenuous and ultimately successful efforts to repay their war debts. That this was still a source of contention in American relations with the Allies is clear in comments made by Moffat when in Paris in March 1940. He recorded in his previously undiscovered account of the trip that the only "offensive remark" he heard in the entire trip was when a Frenchmen said that American "reluctance to advance money to Finland" has at least convinced the French that they had done the right thing in not making a greater effort to repay their war debts. "Diary of Trip to Europe with Sumner Welles," by Moffat, p. 24, SWP, Box 211.

59. Memorandum by Berle, 11 December 1939, Box 211, ABP.

60. Foreign Office Minute entitled "American Peace Moves" by Roberts, 9 February 1940, C 2759/89/18 FO 371 24405, NA.

61. Memorandum by Berle, 28 November 1939, Box 211, ABP. Berle continued to lament the next day. He confessed to his diary that Geist "knowing Göring well; . . . has seen the effect of the Russian alliance; . . . that one cannot make peace; . . . that there is a distinct possibility that that British and French may be worn out, that in that case we shall have to enter the war." This was something Berle, and the rest of the Administration, knew they could not countenance at this stage. Memorandum by Adolf A. Berle, 29 November 1939. Beatrice B. Berle and Travis B. Jacobs (Eds.), *Navigating the Rapids 1918–1971: From the Papers of Adolf A. Berle* (New York, 1973).

62. Box 6448, FDR PPF.

63. Louis P. Lochner, *Always the Unexpected—A Book of Reminisces* (New York, 1956), p. 263; and Benjamin Welles, *Sumner Welles*, p. 242.

64. Lochner, *Always the Unexpected*, pp. 262–265.

65. Foreign Office Minute entitled "American Peace Moves" by Roberts, 9 February 1940, C 2759/89/18 FO 371 24405, NA.

66. Telegram No. 1308 from Hull to Bullitt, 25 October 1939, 740.00119 European War, 1939/34, in *FRUS* 1939, Vol. 1 (USGPO, 1956), p. 520.

67. Dilks, *Cadogan*, p. 220.

68. Foreign Office Minute entitled "American Peace Moves" by Roberts, 9 February 1940, C 2759/89/18 FO 371 24405, NA.

69. Lochner, *Always the Unexpected*, p. 267.

70. Telegram No. 489 from Davies to Hull, 10 October 1939, 740.00119 European War, 1939/113, SDDF.

71. Roosevelt, *F.D.R.: His Personal Letters, 1928–1945*, p. 938.

72. Telegram No. 258 from Gordon (The Hague) to Hull, 7 November 1939, 740.00119 European War, 1939/126, in *FRUS* 1939, Vol. 1 (USGPO, 1956), p. 524.

73. Telegram No. 170 from Davies to Hull, 7 November 1939, 740.00119 European War, 1939/128, SDDF.
74. 8 November 1939, BLP; and Telegram No. 2309 from Kennedy to Hull, 8 November 1939, 740.00119 European War, 1939/133, in *FRUS* 1939, Vol. 1 (USGPO, 1956), p. 527.
75. Telegram No. 173 from Davies to Hull, 8 November 1939, 740.00119 European War, 1939/134, in *FRUS* 1939, Vol. 1 (USGPO, 1956), p. 524.
76. Morgenthau had learned at the beginning of October that Adam Von Trott, an associate of Schacht, was in America arguing that if the United States "were going to back the English in a policy to exterminate the Germans," then it would only force the German people to back Hitler. However, "if the English would be reasonable, there would be chance for peace." Lunch meeting between Morgenthau and Roosevelt, 9 October 1939, MPD.
77. Telegram No. 1954 from Kirk to Hull, 5 November 1939, 740.00119 European War, 1939/122, in *FRUS* 1939, Vol. 1 (USGPO, 1956), p. 522.
78. Memorandum by Messersmith to Moffat, 9 November 1939, attached to Telegram No. 1954 from Kirk to Hull, 5 November 1939, 740.00119 European War 1939/122, in *FRUS* 1939, Vol. 1 (USGPO, 1956), p. 523.
79. Letter from Welles to Roosevelt, 1 December 1939, FDR PSF, Box 76.
80. Van Zeeland's proposals in 1937 included the following: "A meeting in the immediate future of representatives of the Governments of the United States, Great Britain, France, Belgium, Holland, and Switzerland—in other words, the nations now supporting the principles embodied in the tripartite agreement—for the purpose of considering and agreeing upon certain steps which they might jointly or simultaneously take in order to advance disarmament, monetary stabilisation, and the furtherance of the United States liberal trade policy." Memorandum from Welles to Roosevelt re: Conversation Welles had with Belgian Prime Minister and Mr. Van Zeeland, 25 June 1937, SWP, Box 149.
81. Letter from Roosevelt to Welles, 4 December 1939, FDR PSF, Box 76.
82. Orville H. Bullitt, *For the President Personal and Secret—Correspondence between Franklin D. Roosevelt and William C. Bullitt* (Boston, MA, 1972), p. 389.
83. Memorandum by Berle, 5 December 1939, Box 211, ABP.
84. 103 Letter from Lothian to Halifax, 14 December 1939, HFS.
85. The more immediate history of relations with the Vatican began at the end of July 1939. Hull and Welles both argued to open relations with the Vatican as the Secretary reasoned "that the Vatican had many sources of information, particularly with regard to what was occurring in Germany, Italy, and Spain, which we did not possess." Hull, *The Memoirs*, Vol. 1, p. 713. Langer and Gleason suggest that "the President was moved by the laudable if rather tenuous hope of pooling his influence and coordinating his efforts with those of the Pope in preventing the spread of the war and providing a just peace." Draft of Chapter 10 "The Phony Peace" by Langer and Gleason, *The Challenge to Isolation 1937–40*, p. 8, SWP, Box 207. The choice of Taylor was a unanimous one. Hull agreed, "A more suitable selection than Mr Taylor could not have been made. He possessed wide intelligence and unusual common sense. In addition to his work at the Vatican he became one of the moving

spirits in our work of initiating and developing the outlines of a proposed world peace organisation." Hull, *The Memoirs*, Vol. 1, p. 715.

86. 103 Letter from Lothian to Halifax, 14 December 1939, HFS.
87. Rosenman, *The Public Papers and Addresses of Franklin D. Roosevelt*. 1940 Vol., *War and Aid to Democracies* (London, 1941), pp. 1–6.
88. Memorandum by Berle, 4 January 1940, Box 211, ABP.
89. Memorandum by Berle, 11 January 1940, Box 211, ABP.
90. 13 January 1940, BLP.
91. Memorandum by Berle, 11 January 1940, Box 211, ABP.
92. Draft of Chapter 10 "The Phony Peace" by Langer and Gleason, *The Challenge to Isolation 1937–40*, p. 6.
93. Sumner Welles, *The Time for Decision* (Washington, DC, 1944), p. 74.
94. 141 Dispatch No. 119 from Lothian to Halifax, 1 February 1940, HFS.
95. Margin notes by Chamberlain attached to 103 Letter from Lothian to Halifax, 14 December 1939, HFS.
96. Memorandum by Berle, 15 September 1939, Box 211, ABP.
97. 119 Memorandum by Vansittart on letter from Lothian to Halifax, 14 December 1939, HFS.
98. Memorandum by Berle, 29 December 1939, Box 211, ABP.

3 "WISHING WELLES": THE IMMEDIATE ORIGINS OF THE WELLES MISSION, JANUARY AND FEBRUARY 1940

1. Please see appendix 1. The press release can be found in PSF, Box 76 at The Franklin D. Presidential Roosevelt Library, Hyde Park, NY.
2. Samuel L. Rosenman, *The Public Papers and Addresses of Franklin D. Roosevelt*, 1940 Vol., *War and Aid to Democracies* (London, 1941), pp. 79–80.
3. *New York Times*, 10 February 1940.
4. Rosenman, *The Public Papers and Addresses of Franklin D. Roosevelt*, 1940 Vol., *War and Aid to Democracies*, p. 77.
5. President's Secretary File, Box 76, Franklin D. Roosevelt Papers. The Franklin D. Roosevelt Library, Hyde Park, NY.
6. Kennedy Memoirs PJL, p. 538.
7. Although no definite date exists, Benjamin Welles suggests that two meetings that the pair had on 5 and 10 January 1940 were the occasions when a mission was agreed upon. SWP Box 262.
8. Memorandum by Berle, 15 September 1939, ABP, Box 211.
9. Memorandum by Berle, 3 April 1940, ABP, Box 211.
10. Memorandum by Berle, 19 April 1940, ABP, Box 211.
11. Benjamin Welles, *Sumner Welles—FDR's Global Strategist* (London, 1997), p. 245.
12. David Dilks (Ed.), *The Diaries of Sir Alexander Cadogan OM, 1938–45* (London, 1971), pp. 209–210.
13. Mallet suggests that "it was generally believed within official circles that Italy would almost certainly join the conflict at some point in the future, an

eventuality for which London was far from prepared militarily." Robert Mallet, "The Anglo-Italian War Trade Negotiations, Contraband Control and the Failure to Appease Mussolini 1939–40," *Diplomacy & Statecraft*, Vol. 8, No. 1 (March 1997).

14. Harold L. Ickes, *The Secret Diary of Harold L. Ickes—Volume II, The Inside Struggle 1936–1939* (New York, 1954), p. 351.

15. Irwin F. Gellman, *Secret Affairs—Franklin Roosevelt, Cordell Hull and Sumner Welles* (Baltimore, MD, and London, 1995), p. 173.

16. Harold L. Ickes, *The Secret Diary of Harold L. Ickes—Volume III, The Lowering Cloud 1939–1941* (New York, 1954), p. 138.

17. Cordell Hull, *The Memoirs of Cordell Hull*, Vol. 1 (New York, 1948), p. 737.

18. Arnold Offner, "The United States and National Socialist Germany," in Wolfgang J. Mommsen and Lothar Kettenacker (Eds.), *The Fascist Challenge and the Policy of Appeasement* (London, 1983), p. 421.

19. Benjamin Welles writes that when Sumner Welles' "doctor ordered two weeks' convalescence, FDR agreed to wait." Benjamin Welles, *Sumner Welles*, p. 243. This is agreed to in Sumner Welles' own account. Sumner Welles, *The Time for Decision* (Washington, DC, 1944), p. 73. Welles failed to remain in bed for the full two weeks as despite his illness he was intimately involved at the mission's conception. He personally informed the embassies of his prospective destinations of the mission. This task was made harder by the fact that the French representative was ill, and the German Chargé d'Affaires not at his embassy either; nevertheless, Welles saw both personally. Gellman, *Secret Affairs*, p. 174. Welles suffered a brief relapse before embarking for Europe. He wrote to a colleague on 15 February that he had "been laid up during the past two days." Letter from Welles to Duggan, 15 February 1940, SWP, Box 65.

20. Telegram No. 147 from Lothian to Halifax, 2 February 1940, HFS.

21. Memorandum by Berle, 18 March 1940, ABP, Box 211.

22. This opinion of *The Time for Decision* is shared by Gellman, *Secret Affairs*, p. 352.

23. Hull, *The Memoirs*, Vol. 1, pp. 737–738.

24. Gellman argues that "Hull had no inkling of the mission." Gellman, *Secret Affairs*, p. 174; and Telegram No. 160 from Lothian to Chamberlain, 6 February 1940, HFS.

25. Hull, *The Memoirs*, Vol. 1, pp. 737–738.

26. Dictated after conversation between Stimson and Feis, 8 May 1940. Diaries of Henry Lewis Stimson, Vol. 29, January 1939–25 June 1940, Microfilm from the Yale University Library, Roosevelt Study Center, Middelburg, Holland.

27. Hull, *The Memoirs*, Vol. 1, pp. 737–738.

28. Telegram No. 142 from Lothian to Halifax, 1 February 1940 (sent 1:37 a.m., 2 February; received 10:35 a.m., 2 February [all times are local]), HFS.

29. Telegram No. 142 from Lothian to Halifax, 1 February 1940 (sent 1:37 a.m., 2 February; received 10:35 a.m., 2 February [all times are local]), HFS.

30. Dilks (Ed.), *Cadogan*, p. 253.

31. This document comes on the first page of volume 1 of the 1940 *Foreign Relations of the United States* with the footnote that its text is taken from a "[p]hotostatic copy of [an] undated telegram obtained from the Franklin D. Roosevelt Library, Hyde Park, N.Y." Footnote 1 to Telegram from Neville Chamberlain to Lord Lothian, 121.840 Welles, Sumner/69½, in *FRUS* 1940, Vol. 1 (USGPO, 1959), p. 1.

32. This telegram was written on 3 February 1940, and dispatched in the early hours of the next day, 4 February 1940: Telegram No. 172 from Chamberlain to Lothian, 3 February 1940, HFS. The telegram began, "You may certainly take the earliest opportunity of informing the President that I am most interested in his proposal and appreciate fully the motives that have inspired it." This sentence is footnoted in the *FRUS* with the following statement: "Evidently the proposed mission to Europe of the Under Secretary of State had been discussed by President Roosevelt with the British Ambassador previously. No earlier record of these discussions has been found in Department Files." The document they were unable to trace when the volume was published is Telegram No. 142 from Lothian to Halifax, 1 February 1940, HFS, Footnote 2 to Telegram from Chamberlain to Lothian 121.840 Welles, Sumner/69½, in *FRUS* 1940, Vol. 1 (USGPO, 1959), p. 1.

33. Telegram No. 160 from Lothian to Chamberlain, 6 February 1940, HFS.

34. The final point of Telegram No. 173 explained its purpose and what Lothian should do with it: "This telegram is intended to supply you with the background against which we see the President's new move. It is not intended for communication to him as it stands, but you may draw on it so far as you think fit in the course of conversation." Telegram No. 173 from Chamberlain to Lothian, 3 February 1940 (dispatched 1:45 a.m., 4 February [all times are local]), HFS.

35. Telegram No. 173 from Chamberlain to Lothian, 3 February 1940 (dispatched 1:45 a.m., 4 February [all times are local]), HFS.

36. Telegram No. 160 from Lothian to Chamberlain, 6 February 1940, HFS.

37. Reynolds, *The Creation of the Anglo-American Alliance 1937–1941: A Study in Competitive Co-operation* (London, 1981), p. 81.

38. Letter No. 135 from Lothian to Halifax, 7 February 1940, HFS.

39. Telegram Unnumbered from Chamberlain to Lothian, 7 February 1940, HFS.

40. Comments by Cadogan, 7 February 1940, attached to conversation between Hutton and Butterworth, 5 February 1940, A 1309/131/45 FO 371 24238, NA (originally entered in C 2695/G).

41. Telegram unnumbered from Chamberlain to Lothian, 7 February 1940, HFS.

42. Comments by Scott, Cadogan, and Vansittart, 7 February 1940, attached to conversation between Hutton and Butterworth, 5 February 1940, A 1309/131/45 FO 371 24238, NA.

43. Telegram No. 173 from Lothian to Chamberlain, 8 February 1940, HFS.

44. Dilks (Ed.), *Cadogan*, p. 254.

45. Letter from Roosevelt to Chamberlain, 14 February 1940, FDR PSF RSC, Reel 26.

46. Telegram No. 173 from Lothian to Chamberlain, 8 February 1940, HFS.

47. Historian Alan Dobson has said that the Destroyers-Bases Deal signaled that the United States "no longer even had the formal appearance of being neutral." Alan Dobson, *U.S. War Time Aid to Britain 1940–1946* (London and Sydney, 1986), p. 24.

48. Cordell Hull's press release. *New York Times*, 10 February 1940.

49. Lothian's response illustrated further his concern to prevent any recurrence of the "minor crisis" in Anglo-American relations. He thought the conversations a good idea as long as the discussions were "concerned with mobilising neutral opinion about fundamentals of world peace and did not degenerate into proposals for whittling away [the] Allied blockade or belligerent rights in [the] name of neutral rights." Discussion of this matter ended when Roosevelt said that he "entirely shared" Lothian's concerns. Telegram No. 142 from Lothian to Halifax, 1 February 1940, HFS.

50. Robert Dallek, *Franklin D. Roosevelt and American Foreign Policy, 1932–1945* (Oxford and New York, 1995), p. 216.

51. Cordell Hull's press release. *New York Times*, 10 February 1940.

52. Memorandum from Welles to Roosevelt, 12 January 1940, PSF, Box 76.

53. Memo from Welles to Wilson, 5 February 1940, Folder 15, Office Correspondence 1920–1943, Hugh Wilson 1940, SWP, Box 65.

54. *Daily Telegraph*, 10 February 1940.

55. *New York Times*, 10 February 1940.

56. Harold B. Hinton, *Cordell Hull—A Biography* (London, New York, and Melbourne, 1941), p. 231.

57. Draft of Chapter 10 "The Phony Peace" by William L. Langer and Everett S. Gleason, *The Challenge to Isolation 1937–40* (New York, 1952), p. 19, SWP, Box 207.

58. Memorandum by Berle, 9 February 1940, ABP, Box 211.

59. Nancy Harrison Hooker (Ed.), *The Moffat Papers—Selections from the Diplomatic Journals of Jay Pierrepont Moffat 1919–1943*, foreword by Sumner Welles (Cambridge, MA, 1956), p. 291.

60. 9 February 1940, BLP, Box 5.

61. Ickes, *The Secret Diary*, Vol. III, p. 138.

62. Robert Murphy, the Chargé in Paris, stated later that Bullitt "was furious that Welles was about to make a swing around Europe for Roosevelt—even going to Paris." This was because "Bullitt considered himself FDR's viceroy for Europe": he thought "he had an understanding with President Roosevelt which made him the principal White House adviser on European affairs." Conversation between Murphy and Benjamin Welles in New York, 1974, in Benjamin Welles, *Sumner Welles*, p. 246; Robert Murphy, *Diplomat among Warriors* (New York, 1964), p. 35.

63. *Chicago Tribune* article by Arthur Sears Henning, 14 February 1940.

64. Bullitt's anger at being usurped would lead to the most vigorous campaign against the Under Secretary, which would eventually "destroy Welles." For a full account of Bullitt's ongoing campaign, see Benjamin Welles, *Sumner Welles*. An alternative account is supplied by Orville H. Bullitt, William C.'s brother, who explains Welles' resignation purely in terms of a disagreement

between Hull and Welles in which Roosevelt was forced to decide between them. Orville H. Bullitt (Ed.), *For the President Personal and Secret— Correspondence between Franklin D. Roosevelt and William C Bullitt* (Boston, MA, 1972), p. 517.

65. 17 February 1940, BLP, Box 5.
66. Michael R. Beschloss, *Kennedy and Roosevelt—The Uneasy Alliance* (New York and London, 1980), p. 204.
67. Letter from Davies to Roosevelt, 10 February 1940, FDR PSF RSC, Reel 23.
68. Lunch meeting between Morgenthau and Roosevelt, 3 October 1939, MPD, Card 4.
69. Rosenman, *The Public Papers and Addresses of Franklin D. Roosevelt*, 1940 Vol., *War and Neutrality*, p. 78.
70. Letter from Davies to Roosevelt, 10 February 1940, FDR PSF RSC, Reel 23.
71. *New York Times* article by Felix Belair, Jr., in Washington, 10 February 1940.
72. Telegram No. 194 from Murphy to Hull, 10 February 1940, 121.840 Welles, Sumner/11: Telegram, in *FRUS* 1940, Vol. 1 (USGPO, 1959), p. 6.
73. Conversation between Strang and Cambon, 10 February 1940, C 2488/89/18 FO 371 24405, NA.
74. Telegram No. 196 from Murphy to Hull, 10 February 1940, including a copy of Havas press release, Paris, 2 p.m., 10 February 1940, 121.840 Welles Sumner/8: Telegram, in *FRUS* 1940, Vol. 1 (USGPO, 1959), p. 5.
75. *Le Temps* was typical: "Mr Sumner Welles will have no mandate to undertake any negotiations whatever or to act as an intermediary between the various European Governments, and there can be no question of an indirect attempt to set in motion a mediation or intervention of any kind in the present war." Nevertheless the paper added something of a counter in case these thoughts were in Roosevelt's mind: "Any attempt of this nature would be particularly inopportune at the present time." *Le Temps*, 10 February 1940.
76. Telegram from Campbell to the Foreign Office, 11 February 1940, C 2188/ 89/18 FO 371 24405, NA.
77. Telegram No. 388 from Kirk to Hull, 14 February 1940, 121.840 Welles, Sumner/32: Telegram, in *FRUS* 1940, Vol. 1 (USGPO, 1959), p. 8.
78. Von Ribbentrop to Thomsen, 14 February 1940, Document No. 613 33/25221. The Germans were informed of the Welles mission on 8 February when Thomsen dispatched a copy of the press release to Berlin. Thomsen to von Ribbentrop, 8 February 1940, Document No. 598 33/25205, in *DGFP*, p. 750.
79. Thomsen to von Ribbentrop, 8 February 1940, Document No. 598 33/ 25205, in *DGFP*, p. 750.
80. Thomsen to von Ribbentrop, 9 February 1940, Document No. 603 33/25209-10, in *DGFP*, p. 757.
81. Nevertheless, Berle saw some hope in this. He wrote in his diary that the "German papers are not using it for propaganda, but are reporting it straight. This augers a certain degree of hope." Memorandum by Berle, 10 February 1940, ABP, Box 211. This is important, as the British in particular as well as some in the Administration, had feared that the German government might

claim that the Allies had approached the United States to facilitate a peace settlement and so turn the announcement of the Welles mission into a propaganda coup.

82. Telegram No. 94 from Phillips to Hull, 10 February 1940, 121.840 Welles, Sumner/2: Telegram, in *FRUS* 1940, Vol. 1 (USGPO, 1959), p. 5.

83. *New York Times*, 10 February 1940.

84. Comments by Scott, Sargent, and Cadogan, 7 February 1940 on the record of a conversation between Mr. Graham Hutton and Mr. Walton Butterworth of the U.S. Embassy at the country house of Ronald Tree, 5 February 1940 (originally entered in C 2695/G), A 1309/131/45 FO 371 24238, NA.

85. Comment by Vansittart (18/3/40) attached to the accounts of conversations with Welles by Prime Minister, Churchill, the Chancellor, and Sir Kingsley Wood, 13 March 1940, C 3949/89/18 FO 371 24406, NA.

86. *Times*, 10 February 1940.

87. Telegram from Lothian, 13 February 1940, C 2400/89/18 FO 371 24405, NA.

88. Thomsen to von Ribbentrop, 9 February 1940, Document No. 603 33/25209-10, in *DGFP*, p. 757.

89. Ickes, *The Secret Diary*, Vol. III, p. 146.

90. The prospect of the third term was picked up on by Thomsen in Washington. He wrote that the chances of Roosevelt running for a third-term had "greatly increased" since the war began. The Chargé concluded that if Roosevelt were reelected "a continuation of his policies must be reckoned with." Letter from Thomsen to von Ribbentrop, 7 February 1940, Document No. 597 2997/587589-92, in *DGFP*, p. 748.

91. In typically mischievous mode Roosevelt told Morgenthau, "I definitely know what I want to do," before continuing, "it has gotten so far that it is a game with me. They ask me a lot of questions, and I really enjoy trying to avoid them." Conversation between Morgenthau and Roosevelt, 24 January 1940, MPD, Card 5.

92. Letter from Hiram Johnson to Hiram Johnson, Jr., 10 February 1940. Johnson later wrote that Roosevelt wanted "to knock down two dictators in Europe, so that one may be firmly implanted in America." Letter from Hiram Johnson to Hiram Johnson, Jr., 29 April 1939, HJP.

93. *Chicago Tribune*, 10 February 1940.

94. Conversation between Morgenthau and Roosevelt, 24 January 1940, MPD, Card 5.

95. Telegram No. 388 from Kirk to Hull, 14 February 1940, 121.840 Welles, Sumner/32: Telegram. *FRUS* 1940 Vol. 1. (USGPO, 1959), p. 8.

96. Stanley Hilton, "The Welles Mission to Europe, February–March 1940: Illusion or Realism," *Journal of American History*, Vol. 58 (1971–1972), p. 105; and Elizabeth Wiskemann, *The Rome-Berlin Axis—A History of the Relations between Hitler and Mussolini* (London, 1949), p. 193.

97. Hilton, *Journal of American History*, Vol. 58, p. 99.

98. Hugh Brogan, *The Penguin History of the United States* (London, 1990), p. 487.

99. Telegram No. 142 from Lothian to Halifax, 1 February 1940, HFS.

100. 9 February 1940, BLP 5.
101. *Chicago Tribune*, 10, 11, 13 1940, in Hilton, *Journal of American History*, Vol. 58, p. 58.
102. Telegram from Campbell to the Foreign Office, 11 February 1940, C 2188/89/18 FO 371 24405, NA.
103. Hooker, *The Moffat Papers*, p. 293.
104. Telegram No. 388 from Kirk to Hull, 14 February 1940, 121.840 Welles, Sumner/32: Telegram, in *FRUS* 1940, Vol. 1 (USGPO, 1959), p. 8.
105. Hilton, *Journal of American History*, Vol. 58, p. 103.
106. Record of conversation with Roosevelt, 12 March 1940, BLP, Box 5.
107. Memorandum Re: Conversation with the President, Warm Springs, Georgia, April 23–24, 1940. The Diaries of William Lyon Mackenzie King, National Archives of Canada, Ottawa.
108. Benjamin Welles, *Sumner Welles*, p. 241.
109. Comments from the American Department attached to telegram from Lothian, 13 February 1940, C 2400/89/18 FO 371 24405, NA.
110. Circular to the Governments of Canada, Commonwealth of Australia, New Zealand, and Union of South Africa and Brief, 15 February 1940, C 2546/89/18 FO 371 24405, NA.

4 HOPE, DESPAIR, FRIENDS—WELLES IN ROME, BERLIN, AND PARIS, 17 FEBRUARY–12 MARCH 1940

1. Welles was accompanied on his mission by Jay Pierrepont Moffat, the Chief of the Department's European division, and Hartwell Johnson, a junior aide, as well as by his wife, Mathilde, her cousin, their maids, Welles' English butler, Reeks, and even his Scottish terrier, Toby. Benjamin Welles, *Sumner Welles—FDR's Global Strategist* (London, 1997), p. 246.
2. Record of conversation between Welles and Ciano (Phillips also present), 26 February 1940, Report by Welles on His Special Mission to Europe, 121.840 Welles, Sumner/132½, in *FRUS* 1940, Vol. 1 (USGPO, 1959), pp. 21–27. (Welles' report can also be found in the following sources: The President's Secretary's File, Container 6, The Welles Report, The Franklin D. Roosevelt Library, Hyde Park, NY; The Cordell Hull Papers Subject File, Container No. 95, Reel No. 55, Welles Sumner—European Trip 1940, Folder No. 406, in both the Library of Congress, Washington, DC, and at the Roosevelt Study Center, Middelburg, Holland, the Netherlands; The Sumner Welles Papers, Box 206, Europe 1940 Report, The Franklin D. Roosevelt Library, Hyde Park, NY.).
3. Record of conversation between Welles and Ciano (Phillips also present), 26 February 1940, Report by Welles on His Special Mission to Europe, 121.840 Welles, Sumner/132½, in *FRUS* 1940, Vol. 1 (USGPO, 1959), pp. 21–27. (Welles' report can also be found in the following sources: The President's Secretary's File, Container 6, The Welles Report, The Franklin D. Roosevelt

Library, Hyde Park, NY; The Cordell Hull Papers Subject File, Container No. 95, Reel No. 55, Welles Sumner—European Trip 1940, Folder No. 406, in both the Library of Congress, Washington, DC, and at the Roosevelt Study Center, Middelburg, Holland, the Netherlands; The Sumner Welles Papers, Box 206, Europe 1940 Report, The Franklin D. Roosevelt Library, Hyde Park, NY.).

4. Draft of Ciano's Diary, 26 March 1940, SWP, Box 210.

5. Malcolm Muggeridge (Ed.), *Ciano's Diary 1939–1943*, foreword by Sumner Welles (London and Toronto, 1947), pp. vii–xii.

6. Record of conversation between Welles and Mussolini (Ciano and Phillips also present), 26 February 1940, Report by the Under Secretary of State (Welles) on His Special Mission to Europe, 121.840 Welles, Sumner/132½, in *FRUS* 1940, Vol. 1 (USGPO, 1959), pp. 27–33.

7. Ray Moseley, *Mussolini's Shadow—The Double Life of Count Galeazzo Ciano* (New Haven, CT, 1999), p. 92.

8. Mussolini had made a speech to the Italian Grand Council on 4 February 1939, in which he said that "Italy has in fact no free access to the oceans. She is really a prisoner in the Mediterranean, and the more populous and powerful she becomes, the more she will suffer from her imprisonment." F.W. Deakin, *The Brutal Friendship—Mussolini, Hitler and the Fall of Italian Fascism* (London, 1962), p. 6.

9. Record of conversation between Welles and Mussolini (Ciano and Phillips also present), 26 February 1940, Report by the Under Secretary of State (Welles) on His Special Mission to Europe, 121.840 Welles, Sumner/132½, in *FRUS* 1940, Vol. 1 (USGPO, 1959), p. 33.

10. Entry for 26 February 1940, in Muggeridge (Ed.), *Ciano's Diary*, p. 213.

11. Richard Bosworth, *Mussolini* (London, 2002), p. 365.

12. This is in line with Bosworth's view that Mussolini was "always, anxious to govern, and to be seen to govern." Bosworth, *Mussolini*, pp. 1–2.

13. William Phillips, *Ventures in Diplomacy* (London, 1952), p. 151.

14. Telegram No. 127 from Welles to Roosevelt and Hull, 27 February 1940, FDR PSF RSC, Reel 3.

15. "Diary of Trip to Europe with Sumner Welles" by Moffat, p. 1, SWP, Box 211.

16. Memorandum by Berle, 16 February 1940, ABP, Box 211.

17. Telegram from Loraine to Halifax, 26 February 1940, C 2997/89/18 FO 371 24405, NA.

18. Telegram No. 32 from Welles to Phillips, 12 February 1940, 121.840 Welles, Sumner/2: Telegram, in *FRUS* 1940, Vol. 1 (USGPO, 1959), p. 7.

19. Telegram from Loraine to Halifax, 27 February 1940, C 3117/89/18 FO 371 24405, NA. "Diary of Trip to Europe with Sumner Welles" by Moffat, p. 7, SWP, Box 211.

20. "Diary of Trip to Europe with Sumner Welles" by Moffat, p. 7, SWP, Box 211.

21. Telegram from Loraine to Halifax, 27 February 1940, C 3117/89/18 FO 371 24405, NA.

22. Memorandum by the Führer "Directive for Conversation with Mr Sumner Welles," February 29 1940, Document No. 637 66/46595-98, in *DGFP*, pp. 817–819.

23. Record of conversation between Welles and Ribbentrop (Kirk [United States Chargé]), von Dornberg [Chief of Protocol], and Schmidt [the official interpreter] were also present), 1 March 1940, Report by the Under Secretary of State (Welles) on His Special Mission to Europe, 121.840 Welles, Sumner/132½, in *FRUS* 1940, Vol. 1 (USGPO, 1959), pp. 34–41. The German account of the meeting can be found in the following location: Memorandum by an official of the Foreign Minister's Secretariat "Conversation between the Reich Foreign Minister and Mr Welles in the Presence of American Chargé d'Affaires, Kirk and Minister von Dornberg," 1 March 1940, Document No. 640 F14/353-79, in *DGFP*, pp. 821–830.

24. Record of conversation between Welles and von Ribbentrop (Kirk, von Dornberg, and Schmidt were also present), 1 March 1940, Report by the Under Secretary of State (Welles) on His Special Mission to Europe, 121.840 Welles, Sumner/132½, in *FRUS* 1940, Vol. 1 (USGPO, 1959), pp. 34–41.

25. Record of conversation between Sumner Welles and Ernst von Weizäcker, 1 March 1940, Report by the Under Secretary of State (Welles) on His Special Mission to Europe, 121.840 Welles, Sumner/132½, in *FRUS* 1940, Vol. 1 (USGPO, 1959), pp. 42–43.

26. Memorandum by Staatsekretar Ernst Von Weizäcker on his conversation with Welles, 1 March 1940, Document No. 642 33/25243-44, in *DGFP*, p. 830.

27. Record of conversation between Welles and von Weizäcker, 1 March 1940, Report by the Under Secretary of State (Welles) on His Special Mission to Europe, 121.840 Welles, Sumner/132½, in *FRUS* 1940, Vol. 1 (USGPO, 1959), p. 43.

28. Record of conversation between Welles and Hitler (Kirk von Ribbentrop, Reichsminister Meissner [Head of Hitler's Chancery], and Schmidt were also present), 2 March 1940, Report by the Under Secretary of State (Welles) on His Special Mission to Europe, 121.840 Welles, Sumner/132½, in *FRUS* 1940, Vol. 1 (USGPO, 1959), p. 46.

29. Record of conversation between Welles and Hitler (Kirk, von Ribbentrop, Meissner, and Schmidt also present), 2 March 1940, Report by the Under Secretary of State (Welles) on His Special Mission to Europe, 121.840 Welles, Sumner/132½, in *FRUS* 1940, Vol. 1 (USGPO, 1959), p. 49.

30. Draft of Chapter 10 "The Phony Peace" by William L. Langer and Everett S. Gleason, *The Challenge to Isolation, 1937–40* (New York, 1952), pp. 34–45, SWP, Box 207.

31. Record of conversation between Welles and Hitler (Kirk, von Ribbentrop, Meissner, and Schmidt were also present), 2 March 1940, Report by the Under Secretary of State (Welles) on His Special Mission to Europe, 121.840 Welles, Sumner/132½, in *FRUS* 1940, Vol. 1 (USGPO, 1959), p. 46.

32. Record of conversation between Welles and Hess (Kirk and Schmidt were also present), 3 March 1940, Report by the Under Secretary of State (Welles) on

His Special Mission to Europe, 121.840 Welles, Sumner/132½, in *FRUS* 1940, Vol. 1 (USGPO, 1959), p. 51.

33. Memorandum by an official of the Foreign Minister's Secretariat on the conversation between Field Marshal Göring and Under Secretary of State Sumner Welles in Karinhall (Kirk and Schmidt were also present), 3 March 1940, recorded 4 March 1940, Document No. 653 66/46573-94, in *DGFP*, p. 851.

34. Record of conversation between Welles and Göring (Kirk and Schmidt were also present), 3 March 1940, Report by the Under Secretary of State (Welles) on His Special Mission to Europe, 121.840 Welles, Sumner/132½, in *FRUS* 1940, Vol. 1 (USGPO, 1959), p. 52.

35. Memorandum by an official of the Foreign Minister's Secretariat on the conversation between Göring and Welles in Karinhall (Kirk and Schmidt were also present), 3 March 1940, recorded 4 March 1940, Document No. 653 66/46573-94, in *DGFP*, p. 851.

36. Record of conversation between Welles and Göring (Kirk and Schmidt were also present), 3 March 1940, Report by the Under Secretary of State (Welles) on His Special Mission to Europe, 121.840 Welles, Sumner/132½, in *FRUS* 1940, Vol. 1 (USGPO, 1959), p. 56.

37. Record of conversation between Welles and Schacht (Kirk was also present), 3 March 1940, Report by the Under Secretary of State (Welles) on His Special Mission to Europe, 121.840 Welles, Sumner/132½, in *FRUS* 1940, Vol. 1 (USGPO, 1959), p. 57.

38. Memorandum of a conversation between Hull, Welles, Dunn, Moffat, and Feis by Messersmith, 14 January 1939, T1253 1930–1939, Germany 711.62/175, Roll 1, SDCF.

39. Record of conversation between Welles and Schacht (Kirk was also present), 3 March 1940, Report by the Under Secretary of State (Welles) on His Special Mission to Europe, 121.840 Welles, Sumner/132½, in *FRUS* 1940, Vol. 1 (USGPO, 1959), p. 58.

40. Memorandum by Dieckhoff, 4 March 1940, Document No. 655 33/25282, in *DGFP*, p. 864.

41. Record of conversation between Dieckhoff and Kirk, 4 March 1940, Document No. 655 33/25282, in *DGFP*, p. 864.

42. Memorandum No. 656 by Dieckhoff on his conversation with Mooney, 5 March 1940, B 21/B 005423, in *DGFP*, p. 865.

43. Ralph F. de Bedts, *Ambassador Joseph Kennedy 1938–40—An Anatomy of Appeasement* (New York, 1985), p. 188.

44. "Diary of Trip to Europe with Sumner Welles" by Moffat, p. 15, SWP, Box 211.

45. Kennedy Memoirs PJL, p. 538.

46. Ribbentrop arrived in Rome on 10 March for separate talks with Mussolini, and the Pope. Elizabeth Wiskemann, *The Rome-Berlin Axis—A History of the Relations between Hitler and Mussolini* (London, 1949).

47. Kennedy Memoirs PJL, pp. 541–542.

48. Record of conversation between Welles and Lebrun (Murphy [United States Chargé] was also present), 7 March 1940, Report by the Under Secretary of

State (Welles) on His Special Mission to Europe, 121.840 Welles, Sumner/132½, in *FRUS* 1940, Vol. 1 (USGPO, 1959), p. 59.

49. Record of conversation between Welles and Daladier (Murphy was also present), 7 March 1940, Report by the Under Secretary of State (Welles) on His Special Mission to Europe, 121.840 Welles, Sumner/132½, in *FRUS* 1940, Vol. 1 (USGPO, 1959), pp. 59–67.

50. Telegram from Campbell to the Foreign Office, 8 March 1940, C 3654/89/18 FO 371 24406, NA.

51. Record of conversations by Sumner Welles with, in turn, Senator Jeanneney, M. Herriot, M. Chautemps, and M. Bonnet (Murphy was also present), 8 March 1940, Report by the Under Secretary of State (Welles) on His Special Mission to Europe, 121.840 Welles, Sumner/132½, in *FRUS* 1940, Vol. 1 (USGPO, 1959), pp. 68–69.

52. Quoted in a telegram from Campbell to the Foreign Office, 8 March 1940, C 3606/89/18 FO 371 24406, NA.

53. Telegram No. 309 from Murphy to Hull, 8 March 1940, 121.840 Welles, Sumner/101: General Records of the Department of State 1940–1944, Central Decimal File, Box 296, Archive II, College Park, MD.

54. "Diary of Trip to Europe with Sumner Welles" by Moffat, p. 24, SWP, Box 211.

55. Record of conversation between Welles and Reynaud (Murphy was also present), 8 March 1940, Report by the Under Secretary of State (Welles) on His Special Mission to Europe, 121.840 Welles, Sumner/132½, in *FRUS* 1940, Vol. 1 (USGPO, 1959), p. 70.

56. Text of memorandum handed by Welles to Reynaud, in a Telegram from Campbell to the Foreign Office, 10 March 1940, C 3689/89/18 FO 371 24406, NA. (See also Telegram No. 105 from Welles to Hull, 9 March 1940, 121.840 Welles, Sumner/105: Telegram, in *FRUS* 1940, Vol. 1 [USGPO, 1959], p. 16.)

57. Record of conversation between Welles and Reynaud (Murphy was also present), 8 March 1940, Report by the Under Secretary of State (Welles) on His Special Mission to Europe, 121.840 Welles, Sumner/132½, in *FRUS* 1940, Vol. 1 (USGPO, 1959), p. 71.

58. Record of conversation between Welles and General Sikorski (Prime Minister in exile of Poland) and M. Zaleski (Foreign Minister in exile of Poland), 9 March 1940, Report by the Under Secretary of State (Welles) on His Special Mission to Europe, 121.840 Welles, Sumner/132½, in *FRUS* 1940, Vol. 1 (USGPO, 1959), p. 72.

59. Stanley Hilton, "The Welles Mission to Europe, February–March 1940: Illusion or Realism," *Journal of American History*, Vol. 58 (1971–1972), p. 103.

60. Telegram from Campbell to the Foreign Office, 8 March 1940, C 3654/89/18 FO 371 24406, NA.

61. Telegram from Campbell to the Foreign Office on conversation at the French Foreign Ministry, 8 March 1940, C 3654/89/18 FO 371 24406, NA.

62. Muggeridge (Ed.), *Ciano's Diary*, pp. vii–xii.

63. Kennedy Memoirs PJL, p. 553.
64. Kennedy Memoirs PJL, p. 554.

5 "THE GRASS SNAKE" ARRIVES: WELLES IN LONDON, 10 MARCH–13 MARCH 1940

1. Record of conversation between Welles, Chamberlain, and Halifax in dispatch from the Foreign Office to Lothian, 11 March 1940, No. 256, C 3815/89/18 FO 371 24406, NA.
2. Telegram No. 605 from Kennedy to Hull, 9 March 1940, 121.840 Welles, Sumner/108: Telegram, in *FRUS* 1940, Vol. 1 (USGPO, 1959), pp. 14–15.
3. Kennedy Memoirs PJL, pp. 548–549.
4. Kennedy Memoirs PJL, pp. 553–558.
5. This notwithstanding Welles did answer one question in more depth, but that only served to illustrate his dry sense of humor. When asked to comment on whether his face looked "gloomier than usual" when he left his meeting with Hitler, Welles rejoined, "No Sir. Like you, one of my greatest defects is that I cannot see my own face." Report on press conference by Mr. Sumner Welles at the U.S. Embassy in London, *New York Times*, 11 March 1940.
6. Kennedy Memoirs PJL, pp. 558–559.
7. Record of conversation between Sumner Welles and King George VI, 11 March 1940, FDR PSF, Container 6. Also in the FDR PSF RSC, Reel 5. Kennedy accompanied Welles on all of his meetings in London.
8. Letter from R.C. Skrine Stevenson (Foreign Office) to the Right Honorable Sir Alexander Hardinge (King's Private Secretary), 11 March 1940, HFS.
9. Andrew Roberts, *The Holy Fox—A Biography of Lord Halifax* (London, 1991), p. 191.
10. Record of conversation between Sumner Welles and King George VI, 11 March 1940, FDR PSF, Container 6.
11. Record of conversation between Welles and Halifax in dispatch from the Foreign Office to Lord Lothian, 11 March 1940, C 3814/89/18 FO 371 24406, NA. This document is also referenced C 3814/5 No. 253 and 3241/G27 SECRET FO 115 Embassy and Consular Archives, United States of America Correspondence, NA.
12. Record of conversation between Welles and Halifax, 11 March 1940, Report by the Under Secretary of State (Welles) on His Special Mission to Europe, 121.840 Welles, Sumner/132½, in *FRUS* 1940, Vol. 1 (USGPO, 1959), p. 73.
13. Kennedy Memoirs PJL, p. 558.
14. Notes by Vansittart attached to record of conversation between Welles and Halifax in dispatch from the Foreign Office to Lothian, 11 March 1940, C 3814/89/18 FO 371 24406, NA.
15. Record of conversation between Welles and Halifax, 11 March 1940, Report by the Under Secretary of State (Welles) on His Special Mission to Europe, 121.840 Welles, Sumner/132½, in *FRUS* 1940, Vol. 1 (USGPO, 1959), p. 73.

16. Letter from Roosevelt to Chamberlain, 14 February 1940, FDR PSF RSC, Reel 26.

17. Record of conversation between Welles, Chamberlain, and Halifax, 11 March 1940, Report by the Under Secretary of State (Welles) on His Special Mission to Europe, 121.840 Welles, Sumner/132½, in *FRUS* 1940, Vol. 1 (USGPO, 1959), p. 75.

18. "Diary of Trip to Europe with Sumner Welles" by Moffat, p. 25, SWP, Box 211.

19. Record of conversation between Welles, Chamberlain, and Halifax, 11 March 1940, Report by the Under Secretary of State (Welles) on His Special Mission to Europe, 121.840 Welles, Sumner/132½, in *FRUS* 1940, Vol. 1 (USGPO, 1959), pp. 76–77.

20. Record of conversation between Welles, Chamberlain, and Halifax in dispatch from the Foreign Office to Lothian, 11 March 1940, No. 256, C 3815/89/18 FO 371 24406, NA.

21. Record of conversation between Welles, Chamberlain, and Halifax, 11 March 1940, Kennedy Memoirs PJL, p. 565.

22. PM's account of his impressions of Welles War Cabinet Conclusions 67 (40) extract 7 of meeting held 13 March 1940, C 3949/89/18 FO 371 24406, NA. This document is also referenced Vol. VI, 1 March–30 April, CAB 65, NA.

23. Record of conversation between Welles, Chamberlain, and Halifax, 11 March 1940, Kennedy Memoirs PJL, p. 565.

24. Record of conversation between Welles, Chamberlain, and Halifax in dispatch from the Foreign Office to Lothian, 11 March 1940, No. 256, C 3815/89/18 FO 371 24406, NA.

25. PM's account of his impressions of Welles War Cabinet Conclusions 67 (40) extract 7 of meeting held 13 March 1940, C 3949/89/18 FO 371 24406, NA.

26. Record of conversation between Welles, Chamberlain, and Halifax in dispatch from the Foreign Office to Lothian, 11 March 1940, No. 256, C 3815/89/18 FO 371 24406, NA.

27. Record of conversation between Welles, Chamberlain, and Halifax, 11 March 1940, Report by the Under Secretary of State (Welles) on His Special Mission to Europe, 121.840 Welles, Sumner/132½, in *FRUS* 1940, Vol. 1 (USGPO, 1959), p. 77.

28. Benjamin Welles, *Sumner Welles—FDR's Global Strategist* (London, 1997), p. 251.

29. PM's account of his impressions of Welles War Cabinet Conclusions 67 (40) extract 7 of meeting held 13 March 1940, C 3949/89/18 FO 371 24406, NA.

30. Record of conversation between Welles and Halifax, 11 March 1940, Report by the Under Secretary of State (Welles) on His Special Mission to Europe, 121.840 Welles, Sumner/132½, in *FRUS* 1940, Vol. 1 (USGPO, 1959), p. 74.

31. Notes by Vansittart attached to Record of conversation between Welles, Chamberlain, and Halifax in dispatch from the Foreign Office to Lothian, 11 March 1940, No. 256, C 3815/89/18 FO 371 24406, NA.

32. In a cabinet meeting on 12 May 1940, Ickes recorded of Welles' opinion of Churchill that he "was the best man that England had, even if he was drunk

half of the time." Harold L. Ickes, *The Secret Diary of Harold L. Ickes—Volume III, The Lowering Cloud 1939–1941* (New York, 1954), p. 176.

33. Record of conversation between Welles, Attlee, and Greenwood, 12 March 1940, Report by the Under Secretary of State (Welles) on His Special Mission to Europe, 121.840 Welles, Sumner/132½, in *FRUS* 1940, Vol. 1 (USGPO, 1959), p. 81.

34. Record of conversation between Welles and Sinclair, 12 March 1940, Report by the Under Secretary of State (Welles) on His Special Mission to Europe, 121.840 Welles, Sumner/132½, in *FRUS* 1940, Vol. 1 (USGPO, 1959), p. 81.

35. Memorandum handed to Welles by Bruce, 12 March 1940, FDR PSF, Box 23.

36. Record of conversation between Welles and Bruce, 12 March 1940, Report by the Under Secretary of State (Welles) on His Special Mission to Europe, 121.840 Welles, Sumner/132½, in *FRUS* 1940, Vol. 1 (USGPO, 1959), p. 82.

37. Record of lunch meeting with Welles, 12 March 1940, Report by the Under Secretary of State (Welles) on His Special Mission to Europe, 121.840 Welles, Sumner/132½, in *FRUS* 1940, Vol. 1 (USGPO, 1959), pp. 82–83; Chancellor's Luncheon, No. 11 Downing Street, Tuesday, 12 March, 1:30 p.m.: Sir John Simon (Chancellor of the Exchequer), Lord Hankey (Minister without Portfolio), Lord Chatfield (Minister of Defence Coordination), Sir Kingsley Wood (Secretary of State for Air), Sir Andrew Duncan (President of the board of trade), Sir Horace Wilson (Permanent Secretary, Treasury), and Vansittart (Chief Diplomatic Adviser to the Foreign Office). Sir Ronald Lindsay (the former Ambassador to Washington) was invited but was unable to attend.

38. Sir John Simon's account of his impressions of Mr. Welles War Cabinet Conclusions 67 (40) extract 7 of meeting held 13 March 1940, C 3949/89/18 FO 371 24406, NA.

39. 194 Letter from Chatfield to Lothian, 14 March 1940, CHT/6/2 Papers relating to Anglo-American Relations 1939–1940, Correspondence with the Marquis of Lothian. Lord Chatfield Papers, National Maritime Museum, Greenwich.

40. 116 Letter from Lothian to Chatfield, 15 September 1939. CHT/6/2 Papers relating to Anglo-American Relations 1939–1940, Correspondence with the Marquis of Lothian, Lord Chatfield Papers, National Maritime Museum, Greenwich.

41. Record of conversation between Welles and Eden, Kennedy Memoirs PJL, p. 571.

42. Record of conversation between Welles and Eden, 12 March 1940, a memorandum from Mr. Bourdillon (Dominions Office) to Mr. Lawford (Central Department of the Foreign Office), 14 March 1940, C 4010/89/18 FO 371 24406, NA. The record of conversation is also referenced as PREM 86–90 4–25–2 194 Foreign 47 (USA), NA.

43. Record of conversation between Welles and Eden, 12 March 1940, Report by the Under Secretary of State (Welles) on His Special Mission to Europe, 121.840 Welles, Sumner/132½, in *FRUS* 1940, Vol. 1 (USGPO, 1959), p. 83.

44. Record of conversation between Welles and Eden, 12 March 1940, a memorandum from Bourdillon to Lawford, 14 March 1940, C 4010/89/18 FO 371 24406, NA.

45. Record of conversation between Welles and Eden, 12 March 1940, Report by the Under Secretary of State (Welles) on His Special Mission to Europe, 121.840 Welles, Sumner/132½, in *FRUS* 1940, Vol. 1 (USGPO, 1959), p. 83.

46. Record of conversation between Welles and Churchill, 12 March 1940, Report by the Under Secretary of State (Welles) on His Special Mission to Europe, 121.840 Welles, Sumner/132½, in *FRUS* 1940, Vol. 1 (USGPO, 1959), pp. 83–85.

47. Foreign Office Minute by Gage after conversation with Lothian, 28 March 1940, C 4618/89/18 FO 371 24407, NA.

48. Record of conversation between Welles and Churchill, 12 March 1940, Report by the Under Secretary of State (Welles) on His Special Mission to Europe, 121.840 Welles, Sumner/132½, in *FRUS* 1940, Vol. 1 (USGPO, 1959), pp. 83–85.

49. Record of conversation between Welles and Lloyd George, 13 March 1940, Report by the Under Secretary of State (Welles) on His Special Mission to Europe, 121.840 Welles, Sumner/132½, in *FRUS* 1940, Vol. 1 (USGPO, 1959), pp. 85–86.

50. Record of conversation between Welles and Lloyd George, Kennedy Memoirs PJL, pp. 570–571.

51. Another marginal figure with whom Welles met on 13 March was James Maxton, a dissident labor MP and notable socialist. He was keen to press Welles to implore Roosevelt to make a move for peace—"He saw no other possibility of averting a disastrous and fatal war of complete devastation." Record of conversation between Welles and Maxton, 13 March 1940, Report by the Under Secretary of State (Welles) on His Special Mission to Europe, 121.840 Welles, Sumner/132½, in *FRUS* 1940, Vol. 1 (USGPO, 1959), p. 87.

52. Comments by Perowne attached to Telegram No. 280 from Lothian to Foreign Office, 29 February 1940, A 1544/431/45 FO 371 24248, NA.

53. Record of conversation between Welles and Wilson, 13 March 1940, A 2300/431/45 FO 371 24248, NA.

54. This conversation was followed up when Sir George Schuster, the Chairman of the British Committee, wrote to Welles on 9 April, with Welles responding on 6 May 1940 (A 2880/431/45 FO 371 24248 PRO). Welles was especially interested to learn that the aim of Schuster's committee was "the finding of a practical form for the embodiment of the general idea of organised international economic cooperation for the sake of creating material welfare as a foundation for a regime of peace and advancing civilisation."

55. Record of conversation between Welles, Chamberlain, and Halifax, 13 March 1940, Report by the Under Secretary of State (Welles) on His Special Mission to Europe, 121.840 Welles, Sumner/132½, in *FRUS* 1940, Vol. 1 (USGPO,

1959), pp. 87–90. The full text of Chamberlain's letter of 13 March 1940, reads as follows:

> My Dear Roosevelt: Your very kind letter of the 14th Feb was duly handed to me by Sumner Welles, whom it was a great pleasure to me to meet. We have had two frank and intimate talks and he knows exactly how the situation appears to me. I sincerely hope that his mission may have fruitful results, if not immediately, yet in time to avert the worst catastrophe. Meanwhile may I say how deeply I admire the courage and humanity with which you are striving to grapple with this last and culminating effort to establish the rule of force. Yours sincerely, Neville Chamberlain.

56. Record of conversation between Welles, Chamberlain, and Halifax in dispatch from the Foreign Office to Lothian, 13 March 1940, No. 274, C 3999/89/18 FO 371 24406, NA.

57. Record of conversation between Welles, Chamberlain, and Halifax, 13 March 1940, Report by the Under Secretary of State (Welles) on His Special Mission to Europe, 121.840 Welles, Sumner/132½, in *FRUS* 1940, Vol. 1 (USGPO, 1959), pp. 87–90.

58. Record of conversation between Welles, Chamberlain, and Halifax in dispatch from the Foreign Office to Lothian, 13 March 1940, No. 274, C 3999/89/18 FO 371 24406, NA.

59. Record of conversation between Welles, Chamberlain, and Halifax, 13 March 1940, Report by the Under Secretary of State (Welles) on His Special Mission to Europe, 121.840 Welles, Sumner/132½, in *FRUS* 1940, Vol. 1 (USGPO, 1959), pp. 87–90.

60. Record of conversation between Welles, Chamberlain, and Halifax in dispatch from the Foreign Office to Lothian, 13 March 1940, No. 274, C 3999/89/18 FO 371 24406, NA.

61. Record of conversation between Welles, Chamberlain, and Halifax, 13 March 1940, Report by the Under Secretary of State (Welles) on His Special Mission to Europe, 121.840 Welles, Sumner/132½, in *FRUS* 1940, Vol. 1 (USGPO, 1959), pp. 87–90.

62. Record of conversation between Welles, Chamberlain, and Halifax in dispatch from the Foreign Office to Lothian, 13 March 1940, No. 274, C 3999/89/18 FO 371 24406, NA.

63. Record of conversation between Welles, Chamberlain, and Halifax, 13 March 1940, Report by the Under Secretary of State (Welles) on His Special Mission to Europe, 121.840 Welles, Sumner/132½, in *FRUS* 1940, Vol. 1 (USGPO, 1959), pp. 87–90.

64. Chamberlain's consideration in the last instance—a miracle—of a settlement with the Nazi regime reflected the last vestiges of appeasement in London and some consistency in his opinion. After Hitler's October offer of "peace," Cadogan recorded that Chamberlain was reluctant to entirely dismiss the speech and say absolutely definitively, "we won't make peace with Hitler." David Dilks (Ed.), *The Diaries of Sir Alexander Cadogan OM, 1938–45*

(London, 1971), p. 221. Such sentiment helps explains the dilemmas facing the British government in late May 1940 when a settlement with Hitler's regime was being considered, as explored in John Lukacs, *Five Days in London May 1940* (New Haven, CT, and London, 1999). In March of 1940 such a prospect was not, as Chamberlain tried to put forward, British resolve.

65. Record of conversation between Welles, Chamberlain, and Halifax, Kennedy Memoirs PJL, p. 577.

66. Record of conversation between Welles, Chamberlain, and Halifax in dispatch from the Foreign Office to Lothian, 13 March 1940, No. 274, C 3999/89/18 FO 371 24406 PRO.

67. Record of conversation between Welles, Chamberlain, and Halifax, 13 March 1940, Report by the Under Secretary of State (Welles) on His Special Mission to Europe, 121.840 Welles, Sumner/132½, *FRUS* 1940, Vol. 1 (USGPO, 1959), pp. 87–90.

68. Record of conversation between Welles, Chamberlain, and Halifax, Kennedy Memoirs PJL, p. 576.

69. Record of conversation between Welles, Chamberlain, and Halifax in dispatch from the Foreign Office to Lothian, 13 March 1940, No. 274, C 3999/89/18 FO 371 24406, NA.

70. Stanley Hilton, "The Welles Mission to Europe, February–March 1940: Illusion or Realism," *Journal of American History*, Vol. 58 (1971–1972), p. 105.

71. Record of conversation between Welles, Chamberlain, and Halifax in dispatch from the Foreign Office to Lothian, 13 March 1940, No. 274, C 3999/89/18 FO 371 24406, NA.

72. Record of conversation between Welles, Chamberlain, and Halifax in dispatch from the Foreign Office to Lothian, 13 March 1940, No. 274, C 3999/89/18 FO 371 24406, NA.

73. Record of conversation between Welles and King Emmanuel III, 16 March 1940, Report by the Under Secretary of State (Welles) on His Special Mission to Europe, 121.840 Welles, Sumner/132½, in *FRUS* 1940, Vol. 1 (USGPO, 1959), p. 93.

74. Prime Minister's Dinner, No. 10 Downing Street, Wednesday, 13 March, 8:30 p.m.: Chamberlain, Welles, Churchill, Kennedy, Sinclair, Attlee, Moffat, R.A. Butler (Parliamentary Undersecretary of the Foreign Office), Sir Samuel Hoare (Home Secretary), and Sir Cyril Newall (Chief of the Air Staff of the Royal Air Force and Air Chief Marshal).

75. Nancy Harrison Hooker (Ed.), *The Moffat Papers—Selections from the Diplomatic Journals of Jay Pierrepont Moffat 1919–1943*, foreword by Sumner Welles (Cambridge, MA, 1956), p. 303.

76. Record of dinner conversation London, 13 March 1940, Report by the Under Secretary of State (Welles) on His Special Mission to Europe, 121.840 Welles, Sumner/132½, in *FRUS* 1940, Vol. 1 (USGPO, 1959), pp. 90–91.

77. 137 Telegram No. 142 from Lothian to Halifax, 1 February 1940, HFS.

78. 190 Telegram from Lothian to Scott (Head of the American Desk), 29 February 1940, HFS.

79. Memorandum to Halifax, 9 March 1940, 101 PREM 4-25-2 194 Foreign 47 (USA), NA.

80. Hooker (Ed.), *The Moffat Papers*, pp. 298–9. Welles knew also of Butler's ambition as the Under Secretary recorded in his report that Butler was "understood to be Mr Chamberlain's particular protege." Record of dinner conversation, 13 March 1940, Report by the Under Secretary of State (Welles) on His Special Mission to Europe, 121.840 Welles, Sumner/132½, in *FRUS* 1940, Vol. 1 (USGPO, 1959), pp. 90–91.

81. "Diary of Trip to Europe with Sumner Welles" by Moffat, pp. 32–35, SWP, Box 211.

82. Hooker (Ed.), *The Moffat Papers*, pp. 300–301.

83. Robert W. Matson, *Neutrality and Navicerts—Britain, the United States and Economic Warfare, 1939–1940* (New York and London, 1994), p. 46.

84. Moffat's role in London allowed him to meet with a number of the members of the Foreign Office. At lunch on 11 March, Moffat had the opportunity to meet with Scott, Strang, Balfour, Makins, and others at the Foreign Office who dealt with the United States. Moffat noted that the British were well informed of the "minor crisis" as Lothian had reported the American position "fairly and in detail." "Diary of Trip to Europe with Sumner Welles" by Moffat, p. 26, SWP, Box 211.

85. Comments by Vansittart (18/3/40) attached to War Cabinet Conclusions 67 (40) extract 7 of meeting held 13 March 1940, C 3949/89/18 FO 371 24406, NA.

86. Telegram from Campbell to Halifax, 14 March 1940, C 3977/89/18 FO 371 24406, NA.

87. Samuel L. Rosenman, *The Public Papers and Addresses of Franklin D. Roosevelt*, 1940 Vol., *War and Aid to Democracies* (London, 1941), pp. 102–104. The text can also be found in Telegram No. 376 from Lothian to Halifax, 17 March 1940, C 4031/89/18 FO 371 24406, NA.

88. Draft telegram from Halifax to Lothian, 21 March 1940, C 4031/89/18 FO 371 24406, NA.

89. Memorandum of conversation with Lothian by Hull, 22 March 1940, 740.00119 European War, 1939/301, in *FRUS* 1940, Vol. 1 (USGPO, 1959), pp. 19–20.

90. Foreign Office "Impressions of Welles" Minute, 27 March 1940, C 4564/89/18 FO 371 24407, NA.

91. Kennedy Memoirs PJL, p. 578.

6 INCREASINGLY FORLORN: WELLES HEADS HOME VIA ROME

1. "Diary of Trip to Europe with Sumner Welles" by Moffat, p. 46, SWP, Box 211.

2. Telegram No. 191 from Welles to State Department, 17 March 1940, 121.840 Welles, Sumner/143: General Records of the Department of State 1940–1944, Box 296, Archive II, College Park, MD.

3. Samuel L. Rosenman, *The Public Papers and Addresses of Franklin D. Roosevelt*, 1940 Vol., *War and Aid to Democracies* (London, 1941), pp. 102–104. The text can also be found in Telegram No. 376 from Lothian to Halifax, 17 March 1940, C 4031/89/18 FO 371 24406, NA.

4. Record of conversation between Welles and Ciano, 16 March 1940, Report by the Under Secretary of State (Welles) on His Special Mission to Europe, 121.840 Welles, Sumner/132½, in *FRUS* 1940, Vol. 1 (USGPO, 1959), pp. 96–97.

5. Malcolm Muggeridge (Ed.), *Ciano's Diary 1939–1943*, foreword by Sumner Welles (London and Toronto, 1947), pp. vii–ix.

6. "Diary of Trip to Europe with Sumner Welles" by Moffat, p. 37, SWP, Box 211.

7. Record of conversation between Welles and Ciano, 16 March 1940, Report by the Under Secretary of State (Welles) on His Special Mission to Europe, 121.840 Welles, Sumner/132½, in *FRUS* 1940, Vol. 1 (USGPO, 1959), p. 97.

8. Record of conversation between Welles and Mussolini (Ciano and Phillips also present), Rome, 26 February 1940, Report by the Under Secretary of State (Welles) on His Special Mission to Europe, 121.840 Welles, Sumner/132½, in *FRUS* 1940, Vol. 1 (USGPO, 1959), pp. 27–33.

9. "Diary of Trip to Europe with Sumner Welles" by Moffat, pp. 45–51, SWP, Box 211.

10. Record of conversation between Welles and Mussolini (Ciano also present), 16 March 1940, Report by the Under Secretary of State (Welles) on His Special Mission to Europe, 121.840 Welles, Sumner/132½, in *FRUS* 1940, Vol. 1 (USGPO, 1959), pp. 100–106.

11. Record of conversation between Welles and Mussolini (Ciano also present), 16 March 1940, Telegram No. 191 from Welles (Rome) to State Department, 17 March 1940, 121.840 Welles, Sumner/143: General Records of the Department of State 1940–1944, Box 296, Archive II, College Park, MD.

12. Record of conversation between Welles and Mussolini (Ciano also present), 16 March 1940, Report by the Under Secretary of State (Welles) on His Special Mission to Europe, 121.840 Welles, Sumner/132½, in *FRUS* 1940, Vol. 1 (USGPO, 1959), pp. 100–106.

13. Record of conversation between Welles and Mussolini (Ciano also present), 16 March 1940, Telegram No. 191 from Welles (Rome) to State Department, 17 March 1940, 121.840 Welles, Sumner/143: General Records of the Department of State 1940–1944, Box 296, Archive II, College Park, MD.

14. Record of conversation between Welles and Mussolini (Ciano also present), 16 March 1940, Report by the Under Secretary of State (Welles) on His Special Mission to Europe, 121.840 Welles, Sumner/132½, in *FRUS* 1940, Vol. 1 (USGPO, 1959), pp. 100–106.

15. Record of conversation between Welles and Mussolini (Ciano also present), 16 March 1940, Report by the Under Secretary of State (Welles) on His Special Mission to Europe, 121.840 Welles, Sumner/132½, in *FRUS* 1940, Vol. 1 (USGPO, 1959), pp. 100–106.

16. "Diary of Trip to Europe with Sumner Welles" by Moffat, p. 46, SWP, Box 211.

17. Record of telephone conversation between Welles and Roosevelt, 16 March 1940, Report by the Under Secretary of State (Welles) on His Special Mission to Europe, 121.840 Welles, Sumner/132½, in *FRUS* 1940, Vol. 1 (USGPO, 1959), pp. 100–106.

18. "Diary of Trip to Europe with Sumner Welles" by Moffat, p. 46, SWP, Box 211.

19. Record of conversation between Ribbentrop and Mussolini (Ciano also present), 10 March 1940—XVIII, in Malcolm Muggeridge (Ed.), *Ciano's Diplomatic Papers* (London, 1948), p. 342.

20. Record of conversation between Welles and Mussolini (Ciano also present), 16 March 1940, Report by the Under Secretary of State (Welles) on His Special Mission to Europe, 121.840 Welles, Sumner/132½, in *FRUS* 1940, Vol. 1 (USGPO, 1959), pp. 100–106.

21. Lecture by Denis Mack Smith, 21 October 1998, University of Wales, Swansea.

22. Record of conversation between Welles and Mussolini (Ciano also present), 16 March 1940, Report by the Under Secretary of State (Welles) on His Special Mission to Europe, 121.840 Welles, Sumner/132½, in *FRUS* 1940, Vol. 1 (USGPO, 1959), pp. 100–106.

23. Record of conversation between Welles and Ciano, 16 March 1940, Report by the Under Secretary of State (Welles) on His Special Mission to Europe, 121.840 Welles, Sumner/132½, in *FRUS* 1940, Vol. 1 (USGPO, 1959), pp. 96–100.

24. Entry for 16 March, in Muggeridge (Ed.), *Ciano's Diary*, p. 222.

25. Record of conversation between Welles and Ciano, 16 March 1940, Report by the Under Secretary of State (Welles) on His Special Mission to Europe, 121.840 Welles, Sumner/132½, in *FRUS* 1940, Vol. 1 (USGPO, 1959), pp. 96–100.

26. Ray Moseley, *Mussolini's Shadow—The Double Life of Count Galeazzo Ciano* (New Haven, CT, 1999), p. 114.

27. Entry for 16 March, in Muggeridge (Ed.), *Ciano's Diary*, p. 222.

28. The likelihood of this occurring helps explain why Roosevelt and Welles did not use the telephone to communicate but a specially encrypted diplomatic code. Welles' awareness of the risks that his conversations would be bugged is shown by comments he made when he arrived in London. Welles' party was moved to the Dorchester after it was originally intended they would stay at Claridges. The reason was that the manager at Claridges was thought to be a member of the Italian Fascist Party. Kennedy recorded of Moffat "that perhaps the British wanted to move the mission to a hotel where they instead of the Italians had the microphone privileges." To which Welles responded, "saying that he suspected something like this wherever he stayed and so he had dutifully refrained from saying anything." Kennedy Memoirs PJL, p. 551.

29. Entry for 17 March, in Muggeridge (Ed.), *Ciano's Diary*, p. 223.

30. Telegram No. 191 from Welles (Rome) to State Department, 17 March 1940, 121.840 Welles, Sumner/143: General Records of the Department of State 1940–1944, Box 296, Archive II, College Park, MD.

31. Telegram No. 399 from Lothian to Halifax, 22 March 1940, C 4490/89/18 FO 371 24407, NA.

32. Memorandum of conversation with Lothian by the Secretary of State, 22 March 1940, 740.00119 European War, 1939/301, in *FRUS* 1940, Vol. 1 (USGPO, 1959), pp. 19–20.

33. Memorandum by Berle, 18 January 1940, Box 211, ABP.

34. "Diary of Trip to Europe with Sumner Welles" by Moffat, p. 45, SWP, Box 211.

35. Telegram from Osborne (the Vatican) to the Foreign Office, 19 March 1940, C 4215/89/18 FO 371 24406, NA.

36. Record of conversation between Welles and Pope Pius XII, 18 March 1940, Report by the Under Secretary of State (Welles) on His Special Mission to Europe, 121.840 Welles, Sumner/132½, in *FRUS* 1940, Vol. 1 (USGPO, 1959), pp. 106–108.

37. "Diary of Trip to Europe with Sumner Welles" by Moffat, p. 45, SWP, Box 211.

38. Record of conversation between Welles and Cardinal Maglione, 18 March 1940, Report by the Under Secretary of State (Welles) on His Special Mission to Europe, 121.840 Welles, Sumner/132½, in *FRUS* 1940, Vol. 1 (USGPO, 1959), pp. 108–110.

39. Entry for 19 March, in Muggeridge (Ed.), *Ciano's Diary*, p. 224.

40. Record of conversation between Welles and Ciano, 19 March 1940, Report by the Under Secretary of State (Welles) on His Special Mission to Europe, 121.840 Welles, Sumner/132½, in *FRUS* 1940, Vol. 1 (USGPO, 1959), pp. 110–113.

41. Memorandum Re: Conversation with the President, Warm Springs, GA, 23–24 April 1940. The Diaries of William Lyon Mackenzie, National Archives of Canada, Ottawa.

42. Record of conversation between Welles and Ciano, 19 March 1940, Report by the Under Secretary of State (Welles) on His Special Mission to Europe, 121.840 Welles, Sumner/132½, in *FRUS* 1940, Vol. 1 (USGPO, 1959), pp. 110–113.

43. Record of conversation between Welles and Ciano, 19 March 1940, Report by the Under Secretary of State (Welles) on His Special Mission to Europe, 121.840 Welles, Sumner/132½, in *FRUS* 1940, Vol. 1 (USGPO, 1959), pp. 110–113.

44. The reference to Welles being "carp-like" was made by "Rab" Butler in conversation with Miasky (Soviet Ambassador), 18 March 1940, C 4325/89/18 FO 371 24407, PRO, Kew, London.

45. Memorandum from Hull to Roosevelt, 18 March 1940, 121.840 Welles, Sumner/132a: General Records of the Department of State 1940–1944, Box 296, Archive II, College Park, MD.

46. "Diary of Trip to Europe with Sumner Welles" by Moffat, p. 52, SWP, Box 211.

47. Quoted in Telegram No. 66 from Hull to Welles, 19 March 1940, 121.840 Welles, Sumner/142b, in *FRUS* 1940, Vol. 1 (USGPO, 1959), p. 18.

48. Telegram No. 198 from Welles to Hull, 19 March 1940, 121.840 Welles, Sumner/135, in *FRUS* 1940, Vol. 1 (USGPO, 1959), p. 19.

49. "Diary of Trip to Europe with Sumner Welles" by Moffat, p. 52, SWP, Box 211.

50. "Italy and Peace in Europe," Report by the Under Secretary of State (Welles) on His Special Mission to Europe, 121.840 Welles, Sumner/132½, in *FRUS* 1940, Vol. 1 (USGPO, 1959), pp. 113–116.

51. Report by the Under Secretary of State (Welles) on His Special Mission to Europe, 121.840 Welles, Sumner/132½, in *FRUS* 1940, Vol. 1 (USGPO, 1959), pp. 116–117.

52. Statement by the President Issued to the Press, 29 March 1940, in *FRUS* 1940, Vol. 1 (USGPO, 1959), p. 20. Rosenman, *The Public Papers and Addresses of Franklin D. Roosevelt*, 1940 Vol., *War and Aid to Democracies*, pp. 111–112. Quoted in full on page 5 of *New York Times*, 30 March 1940.

53. Telegram No. 191 from Welles (Rome) to State Department, 17 March 1940, 121.840 Welles, Sumner/143: General Records of the Department of State 1940–1944, Box 296, Archive II, College Park, MD.

54. Foreword by Sumner Welles, in Muggeridge (Ed.), *Ciano's Diary*, pp. vii–ix.

55. Felix Belair, Jr., in *New York Times*, 30 March 1940.

7 THE WELLES MISSION: A SHORT-TERM LEGACY TO THE ANGLO-AMERICAN RELATIONSHIP AND ROOSEVELTIAN FOREIGN POLICY

1. Lothian had already telephoned the Department with his concerns. Moffat recorded on 28 April that Lothian had called and asked "if there was anything that the President could do to restrain Mussolini, or any message that he could send, the Allies would be enormously grateful." Nancy Harrison Hooker (Ed.), *The Moffat Papers—Selections from the Diplomatic Journals of Jay Pierrepont Moffat 1919–1943*, foreword by Sumner Welles (Cambridge, MA, 1956), p. 305.

2. Memorandum of conversation between Hull and Lothian, 29 April 1940, CHP.

3. Cordell Hull, *The Memoirs of Cordell Hull*, Vol. 1 (New York, 1948), p. 778.

4. Telegram No. 45 from Roosevelt to Mussolini, 29 April 1940, Department of State Publications, in *Peace and War: United States Foreign Policy, 1931–1941* (Washington, DC, 1943), pp. 518–19.

5. Malcolm Muggeridge (Ed.), *Ciano's Diary 1939–1943*, foreword by Sumner Welles (London and Toronto, 1947), pp. 241–242.

6. Hooker (Ed.), *The Moffat Papers*, p. 305.

7. Telegram No. 47 Roosevelt to Mussolini, 14 May 1940, Department of State Publications, in *Peace and War*, pp. 524–525.

8. William Phillips, *Ventures in Diplomacy* (London, 1952), p. 160.

9. Telegram No. 47 from Roosevelt to Mussolini, 14 May 1940, Department of State Publications, in *Peace and War*, pp. 524–525.

10. Telegram No. 348 from Phillips to Washington, 15 May 1940, FDR PSF, Box 3.

11. Telegram No. 49 Roosevelt to Mussolini, 26 May 1940, Department of State Publications, in *Peace and War*, p. 536.

12. Frank Warren Graff, *The Strategy of Involvement: A Diplomatic Biography of Sumner Welles—1933–43* (New York, 1988), p. 313. Clive Ponting agrees that Churchill, and Reynaud asked Roosevelt to ascertain from Mussolini "what price he wanted for a settlement." Clive Ponting, *Churchill* (London, 1995), p. 450.

13. John Lukacs, *Five Days in London May 1940* (New Haven, CT, and London, 1999), p. 119.

14. Guy Nicholas Esnouf, "British Government War Aims and Attitudes towards a Negotiated Peace, September 1939 to July 1940," PhD dissertation, University of Cambridge, 1988, p. 223.

   There is considerable debate as to how far members of the British Cabinet were prepared to negotiate with Mussolini at this stage. In the tense cabinet meetings of 26–28 May, Churchill's will to fight on eventually prevailed over Halifax's desire to consider negotiation. This is well covered in Lukacs, *Five Days in London*.

15. Lukacs, *Five Days in London*, p. 118.

16. Phillips, *Ventures in Diplomacy*, p. 161.

17. Muggeridge (Ed.), *Ciano's Diary*, p. 255.

18. Phillips, *Ventures in Diplomacy*, p. 160.

19. Graff, *The Strategy of Involvement*, p. 313.

20. Telegram from Hull to Phillips, 30 May 1940, Department of State Publications, in *Peace and War*, pp. 538–539.

21. Muggeridge (Ed.), *Ciano's Diary*, pp. 257–258.

22. Muggeridge (Ed.), *Ciano's Diary*, p. 257.

23. Samuel L. Rosenman (Ed.), *The Public Papers and Addresses of Franklin D. Roosevelt*, 1940 Vol., *War and Aid to Democracies* (London, 1941), pp. 259–264.

24. Telegram No. 843 from Washington to Kirk, 5 April 1940, 121.840 Welles, Sumner/165b: General Records of the Department of State 1940–1944, Central Decimal File, Box 297, Archive II, College Park, MD.

25. Telegram No. 459 from Lothian to Foreign Office, 3 April 1940, C 5073/89/18 FO 371 24407, NA.

26. Record of conversation between Welles, Chamberlain, and Halifax in dispatch from the Foreign Office to Lothian, 13 March 1940, No. 274, C 3999/89/18 FO 371 24406, NA.

27. Comments by Makins (8/4/40) attached to Telegram No. 459 from Lothian to Foreign Office, 3 April 1940, C 5073/89/18 FO 371 24407, NA.

28. Comments by Vansittart (8/4/40) attached to Telegram No. 459 from Lothian to Foreign Office, 3 April 1940, C 5073/89/18 FO 371 24407, NA.

29. Comments by Makins (17/4/40) attached to Telegram No. 459 from Lothian to Foreign Office, 3 April 1940, C 5073/89/18 FO 371 24407, NA.

30. Telegram No. 621 from Halifax to Lothian, 20 April 1940, C 5073/89/18 FO 371 24407, NA.

31. David Reynolds, *The Creation of the Anglo-American Alliance 1937–1941: A Study in Competitive Co-operation* (London, 1981), p. 116.

32. Warren F. Kimball, *The Most Unsordid Act—Lend-Lease, 1939–1941* (Baltimore, MD, 1969), p. 9.

33. John Lamberton Harper, *American Visions of Europe: Franklin D. Roosevelt, George F. Kennan, and Dean G. Acheson* (New York and Cambridge, 1994), p. 178.

34. Warren F. Kimball, *The Juggler—Franklin Roosevelt as Wartime Statesman* (Princeton, NJ, 1991), p. 4.

35. Kimball, *The Most Unsordid Act*, p. 34.

36. Memorandum Re: Conversation with the President, Warm Springs, GA, April 23–24, 1940, The Diaries of William Lyon Mackenzie, National Archives of Canada, Ottawa.

37. Jonathon Daniels, *The Complete Presidential Press Conferences of Franklin D. Roosevelt*, Vol. XV (New York, 1972), p. 242.

38. Letter No. 362 from Lothian to Halifax, 23 April 1940, 3241/182/9 FO 115, NA.

39. Letter No. 362 from Lothian to Halifax, 23 April 1940, 3241/182/9 FO 115, NA.

40. David Dilks (Ed.), *The Diaries of Sir Alexander Cadogan OM, 1938–45* (London, 1971), p. 285.

41. Edward R. Stettinius, *Lend-Lease—A Weapon for Victory* (London and New York, 1944), p. 24.

42. Muggeridge (Ed.), *Ciano's Diary*, pp. viii–ix.

43. Letter No. 362 from Lothian to Halifax, 23 April 1940, 3241/182/9 FO 115, NA.

44. Letter from Lothian to Halifax, 29 April 1940, HFS.

45. Record of conversation with Roosevelt, 12 March 1940, BLP, Box 5.

46. Record of conversation between Kennan and Graff, 16 February 1971, in footnote 39, Graff, *The Strategy of Involvement*, p. 283.

BIBLIOGRAPHY

ARCHIVAL SOURCES

AT THE NATIONAL ARCHIVES, KEW, LONDON

Foreign Office (FO) files. FO 371: 20659, 20663, 21490, 21505, 21517, 21524, 21526, 21527, 21528, 21544, 21547, 21700, 21745, 21757, 21776, 22106, 22107, 22158, 22190, 22301, 22796, 22797, 22798, 22799, 22800, 22801, 22813, 22823, 22827, 22829, 22830, 22832, 22839, 24238, 24248, 24254, 24405, 24406, 24407.

FO 115: Embassy and Consular Archives, United States of America Correspondence. FO 115 3416, FO 115 3421.

FO 794/17 Letter from Lindsay to Halifax, 25 October 1938.

FO 800: 324 The Papers of Viscount Halifax as Foreign Secretary (HFS).

279 The Private Papers of Sir Orme Sargent.

293–294 The Private Papers of Sir A. Cadogan.

424 The Papers of Sir Neville Butler.

433 The Papers of Sir John Balfour.

FO 954 29A The Papers of Anthony Eden as Foreign Secretary (Lord Avon) (AEP).

Cabinet Files (CAB). CAB 65 Vols. V and VI.

Admiralty Papers (ADM). ADM 199.

AT THE FRANKLIN D. ROOSEVELT PRESIDENTIAL LIBRARY, HYDE PARK, NY

The Adolf A. Berle Papers (ABP).

The Diaries and the Presidential Diaries of Henry Morgenthau (MPD).

The Franklin D. Roosevelt Papers: The President's Official File (FDR OF).

The Franklin D. Roosevelt Papers: The President's Personal File (FDR PPF).

The Franklin D. Roosevelt Papers: The President's Secretary's File (FDR PSF).

The Papers of Charles W. Taussig.

The Papers of Harry L. Hopkins.

The Samuel I. Rosenman Papers (SRP).

The Sumner Welles Papers (SWP).

The Vertical File.

AT THE NATIONAL ARCHIVES (II), COLLEGE PARK, MD

State Department Files—Confidential U.S. State Department Central Files (SDCF) and State Department Decimal Files (SDDF). University Publications of America, Bethesda, MD.

AT THE LIBRARY OF CONGRESS—MANUSCRIPTS DIVISION, WASHINGTON, DC

The Breckinridge Long Papers (BLP).
The Norman H. Davis Papers.
The Papers of Cordell Hull (CHP).
The Papers of James M. Landis.
The Papers of William D. Leahy.
The Papers of William E. Borah (PWB).

AT THE ROOSEVELT STUDY CENTER, MIDDELBURG, HOLLAND, THE NETHERLANDS

The Diaries of Henry Lewis Stimson.
The Diaries of William Lyon Mackenzie King. Online version: http://king. collectionscanada.ca/EN/default.asp. Original copy held at the National Archives of Canada, Ottawa.
The Diplomatic Diaries of Jay Pierrepont Moffat. Houghton Library, Harvard, MA.
The Hiram W. Johnson Papers (HJP). The Bancroft Library University of California, Berkeley, CA.
The Papers of Lord Chatfield. National Maritime Museum, Greenwich.
The Papers of Lord Halifax (HP). The Borthwick Institute, York.
The Papers of Neville Chamberlain. University of Birmingham, Special Collections.
The Papers of Winston Churchill. Churchill Archive Centre, Churchill College, Cambridge.
President Franklin D. Roosevelt's Office Files, 1933–1945 (FDR PSF RSC).

PRINTED SOURCES

Adams, David K. (Ed). *British Documents of Foreign Affairs: Reports and Papers from the Foreign Office Confidential Print.* Kenneth Bowen and D. Cameron Watt (Gen. Eds.), Vols. 1–16 and Michael Partridge (Gen. Ed.), Vols. 16–24. Part II from the First to the Second World War Series C North America 1919–39. University Publications of America, 1986–1995, Vols. 1–24.
Daniels, Jonathon. *The Complete Presidential Press Conference of Franklin D. Roosevelt.* 1937, Vols. 9–10; 1938, Vols. 11–12; 1939, Vols. 13–14; 1940, Vols. 15–16. New York: Da Capo Press, 1972.
Documents on German Foreign Policy 1918–1945. Series D (1937–1945). 9 August–3 September, 1939, Vol. VII, *The Last Days of Peace*; 4 September 1939–18 March 1940, Vol. VIII, *The War Years*. London: Her Majesty's Stationary Office, 1956.

Foreign Relations of the United States. 1937, Vol. 1, General (USGPO, 1954), Vol. 2, The British Commonwealth Europe, Near East and Africa (USGPO 1954); 1938, Vol. 1, General (USGPO, 1955), Vol. 2, The British Commonwealth, Europe, Near East and Africa (USGPO, 1955); 1939, Vol. 1, General (USGPO, 1956), Vol. 2, General, The British Commonwealth and Europe (USGPO, 1956); 1940, Vol. 1, General (USGPO, 1959), Vol. 2, General and Europe (USGPO, 1957), Vol. 3, The British Commonwealth, the Soviet Union, the Near East and Africa (USGPO, 1958); 1937–1940, Department of State Publications 1727. Washington, DC: U.S. Government Printing Office.

Gilbert, Martin. *The Churchill War Papers—Volume 1 at the Admiralty September 1939–May 1940.* London: Heinemann, 1993.

Kimball, Warren F. (Ed.). *Churchill & Roosevelt—The Complete Correspondence I Alliance Emerging October 1933–November 1942.* Vols. 1–3. Princeton, NJ: Princeton University Press, 1984–1988.

Loewenheim, Francis L., Harold D. Langley, and Manfred Jonas (Eds.). *Roosevelt and Churchill—Their Secret Wartime Correspondence.* London: Barrie & Jenkins, 1975.

Medlicott, W.N. *Documents on British Foreign Policy 1919–1939.* London: His Majesty's Stationary Office, 1947.

———. *The Economic Blockade—Volume 1.* London: His Majesty's Stationary Office, 1952. *New York Times.* 1937–1941.

Nixon, Edgar B. (Ed.). *Franklin D. Roosevelt and Foreign Affairs.* First Series, January 1933–1937. 3 Vols. FDR Library, Hyde Park, NY. Cambridge, MA: Belknap Press of Harvard University Press, 1969.

Roosevelt, Elliot (Ed.). *F.D.R.: His Personal Letters, 1928–1945.* Vol. 4. New York: Duell, Sloan and Pearce, 1950.

Rosenman, Samuel L. *The Public Papers and Addresses of Franklin D. Roosevelt.* 1937 Vol., *The Constitution Prevails*; 1938 Vol., *The Continuing Struggle for Liberalism;* 1939 Vol., *War and Neutrality*; 1940 Vol., *War and Aid to Democracies.* London: Macmillan & Co. Ltd., 1941.

Scheure, Donald B. (Ed). *FDR and Foreign Affairs Second Series January 1937— August 1939.* April–June 1937, Vol. 5; July–September 1937, Vol. 6; October–December 1937, Vol. 7; January–February 1938, Vol. 8; March–April 1938, Vol. 9; May–July 1938, Vol. 10; August–October 1938, Vol. 11; November–December 1938, Vol. 12; January–February 1939, Vol. 13; March–April 1939, Vol. 14; May–June 1939, Vol. 15. FDR Library, Hyde Park, NY. New York and Toronto: Clearwater Publishing, 1979–1995.

Times. 1937–1941.

Woodward, Sir Llewellyn. *British Foreign Policy during the Second World War.* Vol. 1. London: Her Majesty's Stationary Office, 1970.

MEMOIRS

Berle, Beatrice B., and Travis B. Jacobs (Eds.). *Navigating the Rapids 1918–1971: From the Papers of Adolf A. Berle.* New York: Harcourt Brace Jovanovich, 1973.

Blum, John Morton. *From the Morgenthau Diaries—Years of Crisis 1928–1938.* Boston, MA: Houghton Mifflin, 1959.

Blum, John Morton. *From the Morgenthau Diaries—Years of Urgency 1938–1941.* Boston, MA: Houghton Mifflin, 1965.

——— (Ed.). *The Prince of Vision—The Diary of Henry A. Wallace 1942–46.* Boston, MA: Houghton Mifflin, 1973.

———. *Roosevelt and Morgenthau—A Revision and Condensation of "From the Morgenthau Diaries."* Boston, MA: Houghton Mifflin, 1970.

Bullitt, Orville H. (Ed.). *For the President Personal and Secret—Correspondence between Franklin D. Roosevelt and William C. Bullitt.* Boston, MA: Houghton Mifflin, 1972.

Burke, Robert E. *The Diary Letters of Hiram Warren Johnson 1917–1945.* Vols. 1–7. New York and London: Garland, 1983.

Butler, J.R.M. *Lord Lothian (Philip Kerr) 1882–1940.* London: Macmillan & Co. Ltd., 1960.

Churchill, Winston S. *The Second World War.* Vol. 1, *The Gathering Storm;* Vol. 2, *Their Finest Hour.* London, Toronto, Melbourne, and Sydney: Cassell, 1948.

Cooper, Duff. *Old Men Forget—The Autobiography of Duff Cooper (Viscount Norwich).* London: Rupert Hart-Davis, 1953.

Dilks, David (Ed.). *The Diaries of Sir Alexander Cadogan OM, 1938–45.* London: Cassell, 1971.

———. *Neville Chamberlain Vol. 1.* Cambridge: Cambridge University Press, 1984.

Eden, Anthony, Earl of Avon. *The Eden Memoirs—Facing the Dictators.* London: Cassell, 1962.

———. *Foreign Affairs.* London: Faber and Faber, 1939.

Feiling, Keith. *The Life of Neville Chamberlain.* London: Macmillan & Co. Ltd., 1946.

Feis, Herbert. *Seen from EA.* New York: Alfred A. Knopf, 1947.

Harvey, John (Ed.). *The Diplomatic Diaries of Oliver Harvey 1937–1940.* London: Collins, 1970.

Hooker, Nancy Harrison (Ed.). *The Moffat Papers—Selections from the Diplomatic Journals of Jay Pierrepont Moffat 1919–1943.* Foreword by Sumner Welles. Cambridge, MA: Harvard University Press, 1956.

Hull, Cordell. *The Memoirs of Cordell Hull.* 2 Vols. New York: Macmillan, 1948.

Ickes, Harold L. *The Secret Diary of Harold L. Ickes—Volume II, The Inside Struggle 1936–1939.* New York: Simon & Schuster, 1954.

———. *The Secret Diary of Harold L. Ickes—Volume III, The Lowering Cloud 1939–1941.* New York: Simon & Schuster, 1954.

Israel, Fred L. *The War Diary of Breckinridge Long—Selections from the Years 1939–44.* Lincoln, NE: University of Nebraska Press, 1966.

Jenkins, Roy. *Churchill.* London: Pan Macmillan, 2001.

Lochner, Loius P. *Always the Unexpected—A Book of Reminisces.* New York: Macmillan Company, 1956.

Muggeridge, Malcolm (Ed.). *Ciano's Diary 1939–43.* Foreword by Sumner Welles. London and Toronto: William Heinemann, 1947.

———. *Ciano's Diplomatic Papers.* London: Odhams Press, 1948.

Murphy, Robert. *Diplomat among Warriors.* New York: Doubleday, 1964.

Murray, C. Arthur. *At Close Quarters—A Sidelight on Anglo-American Diplomatic Relations*. London: John Murray, 1946.

Phillips, William. *Ventures in Diplomacy*. London: John Murray, 1952.

Roberts, Andrew. *The Holy Fox—A Biography of Lord Halifax*. London: Weidenfeld and Nicolson, 1991.

Roosevelt, Elliot. *As He Saw It*. New York: Duell, Sloan and Pearce, 1946.

Skidelsky, Robert. *John Maynard Keynes—Fighting for Britain 1937–1946*. London: Macmillan Publishers, 2000.

Stead, Wickham. *Words on the Air 1938–1945 Volume 1 1938–1940*. London: Christopher Johnson, 1946.

Strang, Lord. *Home and Abroad*. London: Andre Deutsch, 1956.

Templewood, Viscount. *Nine Troubled Years*. London: Collins, 1954.

Welles, Benjamin. *Sumner Welles—FDR's Global Strategist*. London: Macmillan Press, 1997.

Welles, Sumner. *Seven Decisions That Shaped History*. New York: Harper & Brothers, 1950.

———. *The Time for Decision*. Washington, DC: Morrison & Gibb, 1944.

Vansittart, Sir Robert. *The Mist Procession*. London: Collins, 1958.

EDITED COLLECTIONS

Baylis, John (Ed.). *Anglo-American Relations since 1939—The Enduring Alliance*. Manchester and New York: Manchester University Press, 1997.

Boyce, Robert, and Joseph A. Maiolo. *The Origins of World War Two—The Debate Continues*. London: Palgrave Macmillan, 2003.

Dilks, David (Ed.). *Retreat from Power—Studies in Britain's Foreign Policy of the Twentieth Century*. 1906–1939, Vol. 1; after 1939, Vol. 2. London: Macmillan Press, 1981.

Garson, Robert A., and Stuart S. Kidd (Eds.). *The Roosevelt Years—New Perspectives on American History, 1933–1945*. Edinburgh: Edinburgh University Press, 1999.

Latynski, Maya (Ed.). *Re-Appraising the Munich Pact—Continental Perspectives*. Washington, DC: Woodrow Wilson Center Press, 1992.

Lee, Dwight E. (Ed.). *Munich—Blunder, Plot, or Tragic Necessity?* Boston, MA: D.C. Heath, 1970.

Louis, W.M. Roger, and Hedley Bull (Eds.). *The Special Relationship—Anglo-American Relations since 1945*. Oxford: Clarendon, 1986.

Lukes, Igor, and Erik Goldstein (Eds.). "The Munich Crisis—Special Issue." *Diplomacy & Statecraft* Vol. 10 (July/November 1999).

McCormick, Thomas J., and Walter Lafeber (Eds.). *Behind the Throne—Servants of Power to Imperial Presidents, 1898–1968*. Madison, WI: University of Wisconsin Press, 1993.

McKercher, Brian, and Michael Dockrill (Eds.). *Diplomacy and World Power: Studies in British Foreign Policy, 1890–1950*. Cambridge: Cambridge University Press, 1996.

Mommsen, Wolfgang J., and Lothar Kettenacker (Eds.). *The Fascist Challenge and the Policy of Appeasement*. London: George Allen & Unwin, 1983.

Pugh, Martin (Ed.). *A Companion to Modern European History 1871–1945.* Oxford: Blackwell, 1997.

Toynbee, Arnold J., and Veronica M. Toynbee (Eds.). *The Initial Triumph of the Axis-Survey of International Affairs 1939–46.* Royal Institute of International Affairs. London: Oxford University Press, 1958.

SECONDARY WORKS

Ambrose, Stephen E. *Rise to Globalism—American Foreign Policy since 1938.* Fourth revised edition. London: Penguin Books, 1987.

Ashton-Gwatkin, Frank T. *The British Foreign Service—A Discussion of the Development and Function of the British Foreign Service.* New York: Syracuse University Press, 1946.

de Bedts Ralph F. *Ambassador Joseph Kennedy 1938–40—An Anatomy of Appeasement.* New York: Peter Lang, 1985.

Bell, Christopher M. *The Royal Navy, Seapower and Strategy between the Wars.* London: Macmillan Press, 2000.

Beschloss, Michael R. *Kennedy and Roosevelt—The Uneasy Alliance.* New York and London: W.W. Norton, 1980.

Borg, Dorothy. *The United States and the Far Eastern Crisis of 1933–1938.* Cambridge, MA: Harvard University Press, 1964.

Brewer, Thomas L. *American Foreign Policy—A Contemporary Introduction.* Englewood Cliffs, NJ: Prentice-Hall, 1992.

Brogan, Hugh. *The Penguin History of the United States of America.* London: Penguin Books, 1990.

Bullock, Alan. *Hitler and Stalin—Parallel Lives.* London: Fontana Press, 1993.

Burns, James MacGregor. *Roosevelt: The Lion and the Fox.* New York: Harcourt, Brace and World, Inc., 1956.

Carr, E.H. *The Twenty Years Crisis 1919–1939.* London: Macmillan Press, 1939.

Clavin, Patricia. *The Failure of Economic Diplomacy—Britain, Germany, France and the United States, 1931–36.* London: Macmillan Press, 1996.

Colvin, Ian. *The Chamberlain Cabinet—How the Meetings in 10 Downing Street, 1937–39 Led to the Second World War.* London: Victor Gollancz, 1971.

———. *Vansittart in Office.* London: Victor Gollancz, 1965.

Cowman, Ian. *Dominion or Decline—Anglo-American Naval Relations in the Pacific, 1937–41.* Oxford and Washington, DC: Berg, 1996.

Dallek, Robert. *Franklin D. Roosevelt and American Foreign Policy, 1932–1945.* Oxford and New York: Oxford University Press, 1995.

Davis, Kenneth S. *FDR into the Storm—A History.* New York: Random House, 1993.

Deakin, F.W. *The Brutal Friendship—Mussolini, Hitler and the Fall of Italian Fascism.* London: Weidenfeld and Nicolson, 1962.

Divine, Robert A. *The Illusion of Neutrality.* Chicago, IL: University of Chicago Press, 1962.

Dobson, Alan P. *Anglo-American Relations in the Twentieth Century.* London and New York: Routledge, 1995.

———. *U.S. Wartime Aid to Britain 1940–1946.* London and Sydney: Croom Helm, 1986.

Douglas, Roy. *The Advent of War 1939–40.* London: Macmillan Press, 1978.

Drummond, Ian M. *British Economic Policy and the Empire 1919–1932.* London: George Allen & Unwin, 1972.

Dutton, David. *Anthony Eden—A Life and Reputation.* London: Arnold, 1997.

———. *Neville Chamberlain.* London: Arnold, 2001.

Farnham, Barbara. *Roosevelt and the Munich Crisis—A Study of Political Decision Making.* Princeton, NJ: Princeton University Press, 2000.

Gallup, George H. *The Gallup International Public Opinion Polls—Great Britain 1937–1975.* Vol. 1. New York: Random House, 1977.

Gelderman, Carol. *Chapter One All the President's Words—The Bully Pulpit and the Creation of the Virtual Presidency.* New York: Walker and Company, 1997.

Gellman, Irwin F. *Good Neighbour Policy: United States Policies in Latin America, 1933–1945.* Baltimore and London, MD: John Hopkins University Press, 1979.

———. *Secret Affairs—Franklin Roosevelt, Cordell Hull and Sumner Welles.* Baltimore, MD and London: John Hopkins University Press, 1995.

Gilbert, Martin. *Second World War.* London: Weidenfeld and Nicolson, 1989.

Gilbert, Martin, with Richard Gott. *The Appeasers.* London: Phoenix Press, 2000.

Graff, Frank Warren. *The Strategy of Involvement: A Diplomatic Biography of Sumner Welles—1933–43.* New York: Garland, 1988.

Greenstein, Fred L. *The Presidential Difference—Leadership Style from FDR to George W. Bush.* Second edition. Princeton, NJ and Oxford: Princeton University Press, 2004.

Haigh, R.H., and P.W. Turner. *British Politics and Society 1919–1938: The Effect on Appeasement.* Sheffield: Sheffield City Polytechnic, 1979.

———. *The Path to Re-Armament in Britain 1919–1939.* Sheffield: Sheffield City Polytechnic, 1978.

Harper, John Lamberton. *American Visions of Europe: Franklin D. Roosevelt, George F. Kennan and Dean G Acheson.* Cambridge: Cambridge University Press, 1996.

Heale, M.J. *Franklin D. Roosevelt—The New Deal and War.* London and New York: Routledge, 1999.

Hinton, Harold B. *Cordell Hull—A Biography.* London, New York, and Melbourne: Hurst & Blackett, 1941.

Hoopes, Townsend, and Douglas Brinkley. *FDR and the Creation of the U.N.* New Haven, CT: Yale University Press, 1997.

Jonas, Manfred. *The United States and Germany—A Diplomatic History.* Ithaca, NY, and London: Cornell University Press, 1984.

Kaldor, Mary. *Old and New Wars—Organised Violence in a Global Era.* Cambridge, UK and Oxford: Blackwell, 2001.

Kimball, Warren F. *Franklin D. Roosevelt and the World Crisis, 1937–1945.* Lexington, MA, and London: D.C. Heath, 1973.

———. *The Juggler—Franklin Roosevelt as Wartime Statesman.* Princeton, NJ: Princeton University Press, 1991.

———. *The Most Unsordid Act, Lend-Lease, 1939–45.* Baltimore, MD: John Hopkins University Press, 1969.

Kissinger, Henry. *Diplomacy.* New York: Simon & Schuster, 1994.

Lafeber, Walter. *The American Age.* New York and London: W.W. Norton, 1994.

Langer, William L., and S. Everett Gleason. *The Challenge to Isolation, 1937–40.* New York: Harper & Brothers, 1952.

———. *The Undeclared War.* New York: Harper & Brothers, 1953.

Lash, Joseph P. *Roosevelt and Churchill 1939–1941—The Partnership That Saved the West.* London: Andre Deutsch, 1977.

Lippmann, Walter. *US War Aims.* Boston, MA: Little, Brown, 1944.

Love, Robert W. Jr. *The History of the U.S. Navy 1775–1941.* Harrisburg, PA: Stackpole Books, 1992.

Leutz, James R. *Bargaining for Supremacy—Anglo-American Naval Collaboration 1937–41.* Chapel Hill, NC: University of North Carolina Press, 1977.

Lukacs, John. *The Duel—The Eighty Day Struggle between Churchill and Hitler.* New Haven, CT, and London: Yale University Press, 1990.

———. *Five Days in London May 1940.* New Haven, CT, and London: Yale University Press, 1999.

Macdonald, C.A. *The United States, Britain and Appeasement, 1936–39.* London: Macmillan Press, 1981.

Macleod, Iain. *Neville Chamberlain.* London: Frederick Muller, 1961.

Matson, Robert W. *Neutrality and Navicerts—Britain, the United States, and Economic Warfare, 1939–1940.* New York and London: Garland, 1994.

McJimsey, George. *The Presidency of Franklin Delano Roosevelt.* Lawrence, KS: University Press of Kansas, 2000.

McKercher, B.J.C. *Anglo-American Relations in the 1920's—The Struggle for Supremacy.* London: Macmillan Press, 1991.

———. *The Second Baldwin Government and the United States 1924–1929.* Cambridge: Cambridge University Press, 1987.

———. *Transition of Power—Britain's Loss of Global Pre-Eminence to the United States, 1930–1945.* Cambridge: Cambridge University Press, 1999.

Miller, James Edward. *The United States and Italy 1940–50.* Chapel Hill, NC: University of North Carolina Press, 1986.

Moseley, Ray. *Mussolini's Shadow—The Double Life of Count Galeazzo Ciano.* New Haven, CT: Yale University Press, 1999.

Neustadt, Richard E. *Presidential Power.* New York: John Wiley & Sons, 1960.

Neville, Peter. *Neville Chamberlain: A Study in Failure?* London: Hodder and Stoughton, 1993.

Notter, Harley. *Postwar Foreign Policy Preparation, 1939–1945.* Washington, DC: U.S. State Department, 1949.

O'Sullivan, Christopher. *Sumner Welles, Postwar Planning, and the Quest for a New World Order, 1937–1943.* New York: Gutenberg-e Press and Columbia University Press, 2003.

Ovendale, Ritchie. *"Appeasement" and the English Speaking World: Britain, the United States the Dominions and the Policy of Appeasement.* Cardiff: University of Wales Press, 1975.

Parmar, Inderjeet. *Special Interests, the State and the Anglo-American Alliance 1939–1945.* London: Frank Cass, 1995.

Perry, Hamilton Darby. *The Panay Incident—Prelude to Pearl Harbour.* Toronto: Macmillan Company, 1969.

Pickles, Dorothy. *The Uneasy Alliance French Foreign Policy and Franco-British Misunderstandings.* London and New York: Oxford University, Press Chatham House Essays, 1966.

Ponting, Clive. *Churchill*. London: Sinclair-Stevenson, 1995.

Rauch, Basil. *Roosevelt—From Munich to Pearl Harbor: A Study in the Creation of a Foreign Policy*. New York: Creative Age Press, 1950.

Reynolds, David. *The Creation of the Anglo-American Alliance 1937–1941: A Study in Competitive Co-operation*. London: Europa Publications, 1981.

———. *From Munich to Pearl Harbor—Roosevelt's American and the Origins of the Second World War*. Chicago, IL: Ivan R. Dee, 2001.

Reynolds, Paul A. *British Foreign Policy in the Inter-War Years*. London, New York, and Toronto: Longmans, Green & Co., 1954.

Robbins, Keith. *Appeasement*. Oxford: Basil Blackwell, 1988.

———. *Munich 1938*. London: Cassell, 1968.

Rooth, Tim. *British Protectionism and the International Economy: Overseas Commercial Policy in the 1930s*. Cambridge: Cambridge University Press, 1993.

Shogun, Robert. *Hard Bargain—How Franklin D Roosevelt Twisted Churchill's Arm, Evaded the Law, and Changed the Role of the American Presidency*. New York: Schriber, 1995.

Smart, Nick. *British Strategy and Politics during the Phony War—Before the Balloon Went Up*. London: Praeger, 2003.

Stettinius, Edward R. *Lend-Lease—A Weapon for Victory*. London and New York: Penguin Books, 1944.

Thorne, Christopher. *Allies of a Kind: The United States, Britain and the War against Japan, 1941–1945*. London: Hamish Hamilton, 1978.

Toynbee, Arnold J. *Survey of International Affairs 1938*. Vol. 1. London, New York, and Toronto: Oxford University Press, 1941.

Trefousse, H.L. *Germany and American Neutrality 1939–1941*. New York: Bookman Associates, 1951.

Watt, D.C. *Personalities and Policies*. London: Longmans, 1965.

———. *Succeeding John Bull: American in Britain's Place, 1900–1975*. New York: Cambridge University Press, 1984.

Williams, Andrew. *Failed Imagination? New World Orders of the Twentieth Century*. Manchester, NH, and New York: Manchester University Press, 1998.

Wheeler-Bennett, John W. *Munich—Prologue to Tragedy*. London: Macmillan & Co. Ltd., 1948.

Wiskemann, Elizabeth. *The Rome-Berlin Axis—A History of the Relations between Hitler and Mussolini*. London, New York, and Toronto: Oxford University Press, 1949.

Van Dyke, Carl. *The Soviet Invasion of Finland 1939–40*. London: Frank Cass, 1997.

Young, Robert J. *In Command of France—French Foreign Policy and Military Planning, 1933–40*. Cambridge, MA, and London: Harvard University Press, 1978.

ARTICLES

Agbi, S.O. "The British Foreign Office and the Roosevelt-Hugessen Bid to Stabilise Asia and the Pacific in 1937." *Australian Journal of Politics and History* Vol. 26, No. 2 (1980).

Alexander, Martin S. "Safes and Houses: William C. Bullitt, Embassy Security and the Shortcomings of the U.S. Foreign Service in Europe before the Second World War." *Diplomacy & Statecraft* Vol. 2, No. 2 (July 1991).

Boyle, Peter. "Reversion to Isolationism? The British Foreign Office View of American Attitudes to Isolationism and Internationalism during World War II." *Diplomacy & Statecraft* Vol. 8, No. 1 (March 1997).

Clifford, J. Garry. Review Essay: "Both Ends of the Telescope: New Perspectives on FDR and American Entry into the World War II." *Diplomatic History* Vol. 13 (Spring 1989), pp. 213–230.

Clifford, Nicholas R. "Britain, America, and the Far East, 1937–40: A Failure in Co-Operation." *Journal of British Studies* Vol. III (1963–1964), pp. 137–154.

Costigliola, Frank. "Anglo-American Financial Rivalry in the 1920's." *Journal of Economic History* Vol. 37, No. 4 (1977).

———. "The Other Side of Isolationism: The Establishment of the First World Bank, 1929–30." *Journal of American History* Vol. 59, No. 3 (1972–1973).

———. "The United States and the Reconstruction of Germany in the 1920's." *Business History Review* Vol. 50, No.4 (1976).

Cull, Nicholas J. "The Munich Crisis & British Propaganda in the United States." *Diplomacy & Statecraft* Vol. 10, Nos. 2 and 3 (July/November 1999), pp. 216–235.

———. "Selling Peace: The Origins, Promotion and Fate of the Anglo-American New Order during the Second World War." *Diplomacy & Statecraft* Vol. 7, No. 1 (March 1996), pp. 1–29.

Doencke, Justus, D. "Historiography U.S. Policy and the European War, 1939–41." *Diplomatic History* Vol. 19, No. 4 (Fall 1995).

Douglas, Roy. "Chamberlain and Appeasement," in Wolfgang J. Mommsen and Lothar Kettenacker (Eds.), *The Fascist Challenge and the Policy of Appeasement* (pp. 79–88). London: George Allen & Unwin, 1983.

Gilbert, Martin. "Munich and the New Appeasement," in Dwight E. Lee (Ed.), *Munich—Blunder, Plot, or Tragic Necessity?* (pp. 35–39) Lexington, MA: D.C. Heath, 1970.

Goldstein, Erik. "The British Official Mind and Europe." *Diplomacy & Statecraft* Vol. 8, No. 3 (November 1997).

Hachey, Thomas E. "Winning Friends and Influencing Policy—British Strategy to Woo America in 1937." *Wisconsin Magazine of History* Vol. 55 (1972), pp. 120–129.

Haight, John McV. "Roosevelt and the Aftermath of the Quarantine Speech." *Review of Politics* Vol. 24 (April 1962).

Harrison, Richard A. "A Presidential *Demarche*: Franklin D Roosevelt's Personal Diplomacy and Great Britain, 1936–7." *Diplomatic History* Vol. 5, No. 3 (Summer 1981), pp. 245–271.

———. "The Runciman Visit to Washington in January 1937." *Canadian Journal of History* Vol. XIX (August 1984), pp. 217–239.

———. "Testing the Water: A Secret Probe towards Anglo-American Military Cooperation in 1936." *International History Review* Vol. VII (2 May 1985), pp. 214–234.

Henson, Edward L. Jr. "Britain, America, and the Month of Munich." *International Relations* Vol. 2 (1962), pp. 291–301.

Hilton, Stanley. "The Welles Mission to Europe, February–March 1940: Illusion or Realism." *Journal of American History* Vol. 58 (1971–1972), pp. 93–120.

Jeffrey-Jones, Rhodri. Review Article: "The Inestimable Advantage of Not Being English: Lord Lothian's American Ambassadorship 1939–40." *Scottish Historical Review* Vol. LXIII, No. 175 (April 1984).

Kennedy, Paul M. "Appeasement and British Defence Policy in the Inter-War Years." *British Journal of International Studies* No. 4 (1978), pp. 161–177.

Leutze, James. "The Secret of the Churchill-Roosevelt Correspondence: September 1939—May 1940." *Journal of Contemporary History* Vol. 10 (1975).

Lowenthal, Mark M. "Roosevelt and the Coming of the War: The Search for United States Policy 1937–42." *Journal of Contemporary History* Vol. 16 (1981), pp. 413–439.

Macdonald, C.A. "The United States, Appeasement and the Open Door," in Wolfgang J. Mommsen and Lothar Kettenacker (Eds.), *The Fascist Challenge and the Policy of Appeasement* (pp. 400–412). London: George Allen & Unwin, 1983.

Macleod, Ian. "Neville Chamberlain Defended," in Dwight E. Lee (Ed.), *Munich—Blunder, Plot, or Tragic Necessity?* Lexington, MA: D.C. Heath, 1970.

Mallet, Robert. "The Anglo-Italian War Trade Negotiations, Contraband Control and the Failure to Appease Mussolini 1939–40." *Diplomacy & Statecraft* Vol. 8, No. 1 (March 1997).

Matson, Robert W. "The British Naval Blockade and US Trade 1939–40." *Historian* Vol. 53 (Summer 1991).

McKercher, Brian. "A British View of American Foreign Policy: The Settlement of Blockade Claims, 1924–27." *International History Review* Vol. III, No. 1 (1981).

Offner, Arnold A. "Appeasement Revisited: The United States, Great Britain, and Germany, 1933–40." *Journal of American History* Vol. 64 (1978), pp. 373–393.

———. "The United States and National Socialist Germany," in Wolfgang J. Mommsen and Lothar Kettenacker (Eds.), *The Fascist Challenge and the Policy of Appeasement* (pp. 413–427). London: George Allen & Unwin, 1983.

Parker, R.A.C. "The Failure of Collective Security in British Appeasement," in Wolfgang J. Mommsen and Lothar Kettenacker (Eds.), *The Fascist Challenge and the Policy of Appeasement* (pp. 23–29). London: George Allen & Unwin, 1983.

———. "The Pound Sterling, the American Treasury and British Preparations for War, 1938–39." *English Historical Review* Vol. 108, No. 387 (April 1983), pp. 261–279.

Pratt, Lawrence. "The Anglo-American Naval Conversations on the Far East of January 1938." *International Affairs* Vol. 48 (October 1971), pp. 745–763.

Reynolds, David. "FDR on the British: A Postscript." *Massachusetts Historical Society Proceedings* Vol. 90 (1978).

———. "FDR's Foreign Policy and the British Royal Visit to the USA 1939." *Historian* Vol. 45 (August 1983).

———. "Lord Lothian and Anglo-American Relations 1939–1940." *Transactions of the American Philosophical Society* Vol. 73, Part 2 (1983).

Rhodes, Benjamin D. "The Royal Visit of 1939 and the 'Psychological Approach' to the United States." *Diplomatic History* Vol. 2, No. 2 (Spring 1978).

Salamon, Patrick. "Reluctant Engagement: Britain and Continental Europe 1890–1939." *Diplomacy & Statecraft* Vol. 8, No. 3 (November 1997).

Schatz, Arthur W. "The Anglo-American Trade Agreement and Cordell Hull's Search for Peace 1936–38." *Journal of American History* Vol. 57 (1970–1971), pp. 85–103.

Schmidt, Gustav. "The Domestic Background to British Appeasement Policy," in Wolfgang J. Mommsen and Lothar Kettenacker (Eds.), *The Fascist Challenge and the Policy of Appeasement* (pp. 101–124). London: George Allen & Unwin, 1983.

Schroder, Hans-Jurgen. "The Ambiguities of Appeasement: Great Britain, the United States and Germany, 1937–39," in Wolfgang J. Mommsen and Lothar Kettenacker (Eds.), *The Fascist Challenge and the Policy of Appeasement* (pp. 390–399). London: George Allen & Unwin, 1983.

Toynbee, Arnold J. "Chamberlain and Hitler—Britain and France," in Dwight E. Lee (Ed.), *Munich—Blunder, Plot, or Tragic Necessity?* Lexington, MA: D.C. Heath, 1970.

———. *Survey of International Affairs 1938.* Vol. 1. London, New York, and Toronto: Oxford University Press, 1941.

Wallace, William V. "Roosevelt and British Appeasement in 1938." *Bulletin—British Association of American Studies* No. 5 (December 1962), pp. 4–30.

Watt, Donald. "The Commonwealth and Munich," in Dwight E. Lee (Ed.), *Munich—Blunder, Plot, or Tragic Necessity?* Lexington, MA: D.C. Heath, 1970.

———. "Roosevelt and Neville Chamberlain: Two Appeasers." *International Journal* Vol. 28 (1972–1973), pp. 185–204.

Wendt, Bernd-Jurgen. "Economic Appeasement," in Wolfgang J. Mommsen and Lothar Kettenacker (Eds.), *The Fascist Challenge and the Policy of Appeasement* (pp. 157–172). London: George Allen & Unwin, 1983.

Wheeler-Bennett, John W. "The Drama of Munich," in Dwight E. Lee (Ed.), *Munich—Blunder, Plot, or Tragic Necessity?* Lexington, MA: D.C. Heath, 1970, pp. 51–54.

Whitham, Charlie. "On Dealing with Gangsters: The Limits of British 'Generosity' in the Leasing of Bases to the United Sstates, 1940–41." *Diplomacy & Statecraft* Vol. 7, No. 3.

UNPUBLISHED THESES

Esnouf, Guy, Nicholas. "British Government War Aims and Attitudes towards Negotiated Peace, September 1939 to July 1940." PhD, University of Cambridge, Cambridge, 1988.

Gilman, Ernest. "Economic Aspects of Anglo-American Relations in the Era of Roosevelt and Chamberlain." PhD, University of London, London, 1976.

Harrison, Richard A. "Appeasement and Isolation—The Relationship of British and American Foreign Policies, 1935–1938." PhD, Princeton University, Princeton, NJ, 1974.

McCulloch, Tony. "Anglo-American Economic Diplomacy and the European Crisis, 1933–1939." DPhil, Oxford University, Oxford, 1978.

Murfett, Malcom H. "Anglo-American Relations in the Period of the Chamberlain Premiership May 1937–May 1940: The Relationship Between Naval Strategy and Foreign Policy." DPhil, Oxford, New College, 1980.

O'Sullivan, Christopher. "Sumner Welles, Postwar Planning, and the Quest for a New World Order, 1937–1943." PhD, University of London (LSE), 1999.

Rimmer, David John. "The Anglo-American Alliance 1939–47: The Myth of the 'Special Relationship.'" MA, Exeter University, 1984.

Rochau, Helmut. "Die europäische Mission des Unterstaatssekretärs Sumner Welles im Frühjahr 1940. Ein Beitag zu den amerikanischen Friedensbemühungen und zur Außenpolitik F.D. Roosevelts während der Periode des sogenannten Scheinkrieges." PhD, University of Tübingen, 1969.

Woolner, David B. "The Frustrated Idealists: Cordell Hull, Anthony Eden and the Search for Anglo-American Co-operation 1933–1938." PhD, McGill University, Montreal, 1996.

Index